Learning to Love God

Writers: Wendy McKain
Pam Whitaker
Cathy Allen Falk
Dorothy Brunson
Carrie Chesnut
Peggy DaHarb
Wanda Pelfrey
Sarah Lyons
Angela Smith
Jo Cluggish
Kristi Walter

STANDARD PUBLISHING
Cincinnati, Ohio

Cover design by Coleen Davis and Dale Meyers
Cover illustration by Gerry Oliveira
Inside illustrations by Kathleen Estes
Design and typography by Robert E. Korth
Project editor, Marian J. Bennett

The Standard Publishing Company, Cincinnati, Ohio.
A division of Standex International Corporation.

Printed in the United States of America.

03 02 01 00 99 98 97 96 5 4 3 2 1

ISBN 0-7847-0361-2

Table of Contents

Introduction

Welcome to the world of 2's and 3's. This is a world of adventure, fun, new experiences, wonder, and most of all, a world in which you will teach about God and His Son Jesus.

This program endeavors to teach 2's and 3's in the ways they like to be taught and the ways they learn best.

For example . . .

. . . 2's and 3's learn through doing.

Two's and 3's like hands-on activities and lots of action. This program is designed to meet these needs throughout the session—in the learning centers and during the Bible stories.

Two's and 3's are not going to want to sit and listen for any length of time. You will notice in the lesson plan that most of the time will be spent in the learning activities, whether in the centers, or as a group. The children will also be involved in the Bible story, as well as in worship. All this is designed to keep interest high. Remember, a tired and bored child is a problem child. When you involve the whole child, that child will learn!

. . . 2's and 3's learn through play.

They play all day, every day—and toys are their tools. So, much of your time will be spent at play with your 2's and 3's, but not just any play—play with a purpose. The children will play in the learning centers, between quiet times, any time they have an opportunity. And while they play, you will use guided conversation and the materials you have chosen to turn their playtime into learning experiences.

. . . 2's and 3's learn through the use of their five senses.

The more senses 2's and 3's use, the more they learn. This program employs many sensory experiences throughout the lessons—hands-on activities in the centers, worship songs as well as singing games to exercise large muscles, books and pictures to look at and talk about. All of these are fun and exciting for young children (and for teachers too)!

. . . 2's and 3's learn through repetition.

Repetition is very important for 2's and 3's. A child often says, "Read it again," or "Sing it again." A young child will sometimes work the same puzzle over and over until he masters it, or go back to the same activity when he has time. That's why the same theme or focus is used for an entire unit, with a review lesson at the end to make sure the children understand and remember what has been said and done during the unit.

The same simple Bible words are used during the unit, to ensure that the children remember them and can use them. While most 3's can learn much more difficult verses, memorized words without understanding are meaningless. You are encouraged to use these Bible words over and over throughout the lesson—in the learning centers, during worship and story time, in general conversation, as well as reading them directly from the Bible. Make sure that the children have a classroom Bible they can touch and hold. And when the Bible words are highlighted, the children can point to them, "read" them, and know that these words come from the Bible.

A Note on Repetition: These lessons follow the syllabus from Standard Publishing's Sunday school curriculum for 2's and 3's. This provides the repetition and reinforcement that is so important to 2's and 3's. One lesson well learned is worth far more than two or three unrelated lessons. Two's and 3's not only learn through repetition, they like it and feel comfortable with it. These lessons will reinforce the focus of the lessons, and also afford the children many opportunities to apply what they have learned in the morning. The Bible-story presentation, many of the songs and action rhymes, as well as the learning activities, visual aids, and crafts, are different from those used in the morning.

These lessons, however, do not depend upon the Sunday-school lessons. There is plenty of repetition and reinforcement within each lesson and throughout each unit.

How to Use This Course

This book has been designed to allow you as much flexibility as possible. The pages are perforated and reproducible. That means that the book is non-consumable—it can be used over and over if the materials are stored properly. You can use the book in one of two ways. Either pull out pages and give them to the teachers, or photocopy the necessary pages for the teachers and keep your book intact.

Set up a filing system in which to keep your materials. You will need twelve folders, one for each unit. Label these with the quarter title and unit title. Or, if you prefer, use one folder for each lesson. Label these folders with the quarter, unit, and lesson title. As you prepare lessons, store any reproduced material in the appropriate folder. When the lesson has been used, put all materials back in the folder, along with an evaluation of that lesson. This will be helpful for future use.

The book is divided into four quarters, with three related units in each quarter. Each unit is made up of four or five lessons with a common focus. The final lesson reviews and reinforces the previous lessons. This is important for 2's and 3's, as has already been mentioned. The children will be eager to tell you what they know of the past lessons. Make good use of their enthusiasm and interest. If teachers/teams work for short periods, change teachers/teams at the beginning of a new unit rather than at the beginning of a new month. This will give the children the continuity they need, as well as make it easier for the teachers.

Basic Supplies You Will Need

Construction paper
Manila or drawing paper
Shelf paper or butcher paper
Poster board
Tagboard and/or cardboard
Newspaper
Clear, self-adhesive plastic
Tempera paints; finger paints
Painting smocks or old shirts
Jumbo crayons
Play dough
Paper punch
Magazines, catalogs, calendars, old take-home papers (for pictures)
Paper fasteners
Large scissors (for teachers)
White glue; glue sticks
Yarn
Craft sticks
Masking tape
Transparent tape
Clean-up materials

NOTE: If you want an attendance chart to last the entire year, order *Classroom Chart* (#15-01660). This has space for 15 names; each of these books has 216 seals: *Autumn* Seals (#22-01777); *Winter* Seals (#22-01778); *Spring* Seals (#22-01775); *Summer* Seals (#22-01776).

Block Center—large wooden or cardboard blocks, such as Blockbusters; small plastic cars and trucks with wheels that cannot be removed
Family Living Center—dolls, doll clothes, small blankets, plastic dishes, small table and chairs, doll bed (optional), large unbreakable mirror, toy telephones, small cleaning equipment, dress-up clothes
Book/Picture Center—classroom Bible—one that looks like a Bible and has pictures (or add pictures from take-home papers), books and pictures suggested for each unit, small book rack and table and chairs (optional)
Music/Drama Center—cassette tape player/recorder, tapes suitable for children
Game Center—large soft balls (beach balls are good), beanbags
God's Wonders Center—small plants, watering cans, seasonal nature objects (non-poisonous)
Puzzles Center—wooden puzzles with 5 to 8 pieces, homemade ones as suggested in the lessons
Art Center—basic equipment (see above list), plus special needs in lessons

Step by Step Through the Book

Introduction to the Quarter

The introduction tells you what the quarter is about, how the units fit together, as well as goals for the quarter. There are also extra songs and action rhymes to use throughout the quarter as well as very simple party ideas. Each teacher working during this quarter should read these pages.

Introduction to the Unit

These pages give the teachers more specific information to help them understand and prepare for the unit.

Here are unit goals, a unit overview, the Bible words and ways to use them, a list of things to do to get ready, specific resources needed, as well as songs and action rhymes to use. Each teacher for that unit should read these pages along with the Lesson Outlines and Learning Center Cards.

Lesson Outlines

Each lesson consists of two pages that can be folded into a compact four-page outline when pulled out of the book. The lesson will include the lesson value and a list of behavioral goals for the children.

Here is the way the lesson is set up:

Let's Get Ready

This includes specific items needed for the Bible story, plus a listing of the learning centers to use. If you have a very large class, have two of the more popular centers set up at opposite ends of the room, or in smaller rooms. Even though a book center is not suggested in a lesson, this is a good one to add if you have appropriate books and/or pictures. Remember, you will need to have a teacher in each learning center.

Learning Activities

Let's Get Started

This section includes ways to greet the children, what to do when they come, how to get them interested in an activity, and so forth. The class mascot, Zach, will be a helpful friend to use here. Thirty minutes has been allotted for these activities. This includes approximately 10 minutes before the scheduled time for the class to begin—the presession. Getting the children actively involved the minute they enter the classroom is essential.

Three learning activities are suggested here. Materials and teachers should be ready before the first child arrives. The activities will lead up to the worship and story time. A specific learning activity is suggested if there is only one teacher in the classroom. More than one activity can be used, however, by the teacher by using one after the other.

All materials needed, how to prepare them, how to proceed in class, and suggestions for guided conversation are spelled out on the Learning Center Cards that follow the Lesson Outlines. These cards can be pulled out and cut apart if you wish, or you may prefer to photocopy them. You will find the cards much more usable if you copy them, mount them front and back on cardboard, and cover them with clear, self-adhesive plastic. The cards can be placed in the learning centers for the benefit of the teachers, then filed with the lesson materials or placed in a separate file box or drawer.

Worship and Bible Story

Let's Worship God

This may be the only together time the children have. The worship/story area can be a circle of small chairs or just a large rug or individual rugs for the children. The worship suggestions have been kept to a minimum. That's all 2's and 3's can handle at one time. There will be other times of spontaneous worship with the group or with individuals, perhaps as you hold and smell a flower God made. A simple, *"Thank You, God, for this pretty flower,"* is far more meaningful to a young child than is a long prayer given by an adult. A child is also more apt to repeat that short prayer and be encouraged to word his or her own later on.

Let's Learn From the Bible

If your group is small, the Bible story may be told as the children sit in their circle. However, if your group is fairly large or spread apart in age, divide the group into older and younger children or into groups of children who get along well together. You will need a teacher for each group.

Make the Bible story real, exciting, and fun for the children. No one should ever be bored with the Bible! How do you do this?

- Be enthusiastic as you tell the story. If you are excited by the Bible story, the children will be too.
- Keep the Bible story short. Two's and 3's have very short attention spans, especially when it comes to sitting and listening.
- Involve the children. Each lesson has suggestions for doing this. The more the children are involved, the more they will get out of the story.
- Use visual aids. Each story has some type of visual aid to get and hold the children's attention. Some of these are to be made using the patterns on the pages that follow the Learning Center Cards. Others may be pictures or objects that you will find ahead of time.
- Don't sermonize! End the Bible story, then go right into the follow up that is given.

Let's Apply the Lesson

Here is where the lesson is specifically applied to the lives of the children. Zach, the puppet, can be used here to help the children retell the story, ask questions, and so on.

Learning Activities

Let's Play Awhile

By now, the children will be ready to stand up and move around. An action rhyme or song may be suggested here, but if there is none mentioned and your children are unusually restless, use a familiar rhyme, song, or exercise now. Have the suggested learning activity ready to do before going home. If you have a large group and multiple teachers, however, you will want to use several of the centers used previously.

Let's Go Home

Because the children will be tired by now, it is important to keep them occupied in some meaningful activity until parents arrive. Continue with the activity as long as possible, as each child leaves with his or her parent. Make sure the children take home any artwork they have made. Small paper bags are helpful for this purpose. Also, see that parents get their letters at the beginning of each unit.

Extra Helps

Parents' Letters: At the end of each unit is a letter to parents. A copy of this should be given to parents at the end of the first lesson, or better yet, at the end of the previous unit. The letters will help parents repeat and reinforce the lessons.

Unit Planning Sheet: A copy of this 2-page sheet, found on pages 319 and 320, will help you prepare for the entire unit.

A Partnership With Parents

Somewhere along the line things got mixed up. In Deuteronomy 6, God commands parents to tell their children and grandchildren about the Lord. In Proverbs He commands them to train up their children in the Lord. Unfortunately, in the church age something has gone askew and the church now seems to have taken responsibility for the spiritual rearing of children. Where did the parents' role go?

In an effort to help parents resume their right and responsibility to bring up their children in the Lord, we need to do our best to bring parents into the teaching situation. How can we help parents in their role, and in turn, allow them to help us in ours?

Communication

How often do we communicate with parents about what we're doing in the church to encourage their reinforcement of it in the home? Not often enough. Here are some ways to remedy this situation.

- **Parents' Letters.** Send home a weekly or monthly letter telling parents what the Bible lessons and Bible words will be for their children (our unit Parents' Letters!). Suggest that parents use the information in daily devotions.
- **Newsletter.** Put together a simple newsletter each quarter to keep parents informed of upcoming events as well as articles that will help them become better Christian parents.
- **Progress Reports.** At the end of each month have teachers send home "progress reports" regarding the children's activities at church. Encourage parents to build on these achievements. "Sarah prayed along with me for the first time last week. She said a hearty 'amen' when we finished!" . . . "Jeremy is really learning to share. His favorite Bible story was the one about David and Jonathan."
- **Telephone Calls.** Make it a point to call all the parents once or twice a year to get to know them better. Ask questions such as, "What is Brett's favorite part of Sunday school?" . . . "Does Amy ask as many questions at home as she does in class? She seems so eager to learn!"
- **Parents' Input.** Solicit input from parents. Send home a note asking, "What can we as your child's teachers do to help you better communicate God's love with your child?"

Our communication will help set the stage for parents to take the reigns of their children's spiritual development. We'll just be along as navigators.

Involvement

Although we want to instill in parents the desire to teach their children at home, teachers still have wonderful opportunities to teach children at church too! And in order to do our best, we need the involvement of the parents. (For one thing, it's great for children to see their parents involved. It shows the children how important church is!) So, how do we get parents involved? By providing as many, and as varied opportunities as possible.

Too many people think teaching a class is all that needs to be done. And if they don't have the skills or temperament to do that, then they don't have a place. Not so! Let's look at a few supplementary positions that will not only help your parents become involved, but will also enhance your preschool teaching program.

- **Greeters.** Having someone with a smiling face in the classroom is a good thing. It's even better to have someone with a smiling face meet people, especially visitors, in the hallway—someone to show them to the right class, answer questions, and make them feel at home! Prerequisite: A smile!
- **Hall Runners.** This term is self-explanatory—people who run through the halls of your department helping teachers. These people can do "potty patrol," get extra materials for crafts,

assist when a teacher needs a break or there is an emergency, and much more. When teachers have outside assistance, they are better teachers.

- **Room Parents.** This concept has worked for years in the school system. Let's move it into the church. Assign room parents to each class to provide special events, assist teachers in preparation, and lead in teacher appreciation.
- **Preparation.** Some people want to teach, but don't have time to do a lot of preparation. Some people have time to prepare, but don't want to teach. Let's team up these people. Recruit parents and/or grandparents who have extra time to help punch out and assemble visuals; look for pictures in magazines, catalogs, etc.; cover teaching pictures with clear laminate; cut out crafts, and much more. Encourage these people to come into the classroom periodically to see the fruits of their labors.
- **Bulletin Boards.** Do you have some gifted artists who aren't gifted teachers? Encourage them to make bulletin boards and hallway displays to enhance the unit's theme.
- **Supply Coordinators.** There's nothing more frustrating than trying to teach without proper supplies. Encourage a non-teacher to come by the church building weekly or monthly to check and replenish all classroom supplies. What a surprise to the classroom teacher!
- **Follow Up.** Is there a mom in your department who loves to write notes or make phone calls? Give her the assignment of following up on sick children and absentees with postcards or phone calls.
- **Teaching.** Never forget this task, nor let parents believe they must hold a teaching degree in order to teach. Nothing will help a parent learn how to teach his or her child at home better than to teach at church. An elder's wife once said to me, "I always knew I should be doing more with my children at home. It's my responsibility. But until I began teaching in the preschool department, I just didn't know what to teach or how to go about it!" Now she knows. Now she does it!

Parents + Church = Partnership. One is not complete without the other. Let's join hands so that both parents and teachers can be successful as we all strive to instill the love of Jesus into the hearts of little ones.

—Rebecca J. Bennett

Autumn Quarter

Learning About God's Gifts

Two's and 3's are full of questions! Some of these can be answered simply, while others require more in-depth answers. Some not-so-easy-to-answer questions concern God—Who is He? What does He look like? Where is He? How can we talk to Him? Can He hear us?" and so on.

We can tell preschoolers that God is the creator, the giver of every good and perfect gift, our heavenly Father, and so much more. But these are not answers 2's and 3's can understand. They are concrete thinkers. Because of this we talk about specific things God does for us or gives us.

Unit 1, "God Makes the World," allows the 2's and 3's to explore with their senses the wonderful world God made for us. Through the lives of Bible people, the 2's and 3's will discover that God gives wonderful things to see, taste, feel, and hear.

In Unit 2, "God Makes People," the 2's and 3's will learn that God gives them families, friends, and helpers to love, care for, and protect them.

The emphasis in Unit 3, "God Cares for Me," is that God's care is all-encompassing. He cares for us night and day, wherever we live, and wherever we go. Through the Bible stories as well as the learning activities, 2's and 3's will know that God does care—playtime and bedtime, at nursery school, day care, or home, and on trips to the store or to grandparents' homes.

As a result of these lessons, 2's and 3's will

KNOW

Know that God gives us wonderful things; God made people we know; and God takes care of us all the time.

FEEL

Feel happy because of what and who God made and because of His care.

DO

Thank God for His wonderful gifts.

Use these songs and action rhymes throughout the quarter, in addition to those specifically mentioned in the units.

Let's Be Very Quiet

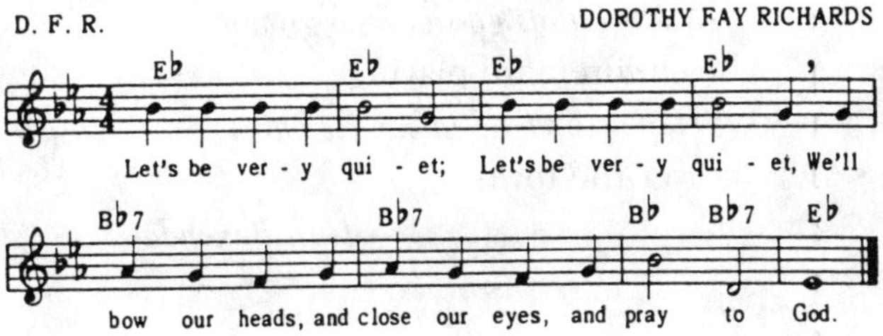
D. F. R.
DOROTHY FAY RICHARDS
Eb Eb Eb Eb
Let's be ver - y qui - et; Let's be ver - y qui - et, We'll
Bb7 Bb7 Bb Bb7 Eb
bow our heads, and close our eyes, and pray to God.

Thank You, God, for All the World

(Tune: "Jesus Loves the Little Children")

Thank You, God, for all the world.
You made everything there is.
Things I see, and things I taste.
Things I feel, and things I hear.
Thank You, God, for making everything there is.

Unit 2:
Thank You, God, for making people.
You made everyone I know.
Family, friends, and helpers too.
Everyone was made by You.
Thank You, God, for making everyone I know.

Unit 3:
Thank You, God, You care for me.
You care for me all the time.
Day and night, and at my home.
In my car, or anywhere.
Thank You, God, for caring for me all the time.

My Bible

This is my Bible; *(Palms held together.)*
I'll open it wide *(Open hands; keep them touching.)*
And see (or say) what is written on the inside!
(Say Bible verse together.)

—*Jean Baxendale*

Autumn

The wind is blowing.
(Blow with mouth or wave arms in air.)
The leaves come down.
(Make hands go slowly to ground.)
The children are playing
(Hop or pretend to bounce ball.)
All over the town.

—*Jean Baxendale*

I Can

I can stand up straight and tall, *(Do so.)*
I can curl up like a ball,
(Squat with arms around knees.)
I can spread out like a tree,
(Arms high, spread out.)
I can sit down quietly.
(Place finger to lips and then sit down.)

—*Dorothy Fay Richards*

Listening Rhyme

First our feet go tap-tap-tap, *(Tap feet on floor.)*
Then our hands go clap-clap-clap. *(Clap hands.)*
We look with both our eyes,
(Make glasses by circling fingers around eyes.)
We hear with both our ears, *(Cup hands behind ears.)*
And then our hands fall in our laps.
(Fold hands in lap.)

—*Dorothy Fay Richards*

Autumn Party Suggestions

September—Preschool Picnic

Purpose: A family event in which parents, teachers, and kids interact
When: A Saturday or Sunday afternoon
Games: Father/Son and Mother /Daughter relays
Food: Sack lunches
Bible Story: Jesus Feeds the 5,000

October—Noah's Ark Extravaganza

Purpose: A fun "alternative" to Halloween parties
When: During class time
Costumes: Children dress in animal costumes, bring stuffed animals, or make animal masks from paper plates during your party.
Games: Run animal relay races; guess animal sounds; or play "Pin the Tail on *Anything!*"
Craft: Make a group collage of all the animal pictures you can find in magazines/calendars, etc.
Food: Animal crackers
Bible Story: Noah's Ark

November—Thanksgiving Celebration

Purpose: To help the children be thankful and focus on others
When: During class time
Preparation: Ask parents to send goodies for a basket for shut-ins (cookies, hand lotion, cards, etc.).
Craft: Children make goody baskets for shut-ins from strawberry baskets. Use ribbon to decorate. Fill with items sent in by parents. Children can add homemade cards and pictures.
Game: "I see something I'm thankful for . . ."
Food: Pumpkin shaped cookies or cupcakes decorated with pumpkin candies
Devotion: Instead of a Bible story, let the children thank God for Jesus, for families, for special people in their lives, and so forth.

Unit 1: God Makes the World

Lessons 1–5

By the end of the unit, the children will

Know that God gives us wonderful things to see, taste, feel, and hear.

Feel happy to use senses to explore what God has given us.

Thank God for wonderful things to see, taste, feel, and hear.

Unit Bible Words

"God . . . made the world" (Acts 17:24, *NIV*).

Books

from Standard Publishing

The Story of Creation (24-03103)

All Creatures Great and Small (24-03145)

God Made Me Special (24-04205)

God Is Great (24-03704)

God Feeds the Animals (24-03118)

This Unit at a Glance

1 God Makes Things to See — **Genesis 1:1-27**
God has created the world with many wonderful things in it for us to see and enjoy.

2 God Makes Things to Taste — **Exodus 16:2-18, 31**
God gave the Israelites manna to eat, and He gives us good food to eat.

3 God Makes Things to Feel — **1 Samuel 16:11, 18; 17:40**
David experienced God's world through the sense of touch; God gives us many textures to feel.

4 God Makes Things to Hear — **1 Samuel 16:11, 18-23**
David could enjoy the wonderful sounds in God's world; we too have wonderful things from God to hear.

5 Thank God for His World — **Review of Lessons 1–4**
God gave us so many wonderful things for which we can be thankful.

Why Teach This Unit?

Children love to receive gifts. How important it is, therefore, to teach children about the gifts God has given—the wonderful things we can see, taste, feel, and hear. This unit's Bible stories do just that. This unit's study of God's creation of the world takes on a new approach by emphasizing the use of the senses of sight, taste, hearing, and touch.

Two's and 3's have a natural curiosity about the world around them. Use this curiosity to teach them about God's creation. Make God evident in everything you experience in nature with your children. Use the Bible words to help with this. Say, **When "God made the world," He made kittens. He made the kitty you are petting. Isn't God wonderful! Thank You, God, for making kittens.**

The common tie that joins these lessons into a unit is the fact that God made all things. Repeat this fact to your children as they play, sing, listen to the Bible stories, and pray. Through guided conversation and hands-on activities, 2's and 3's will learn that God made the world and all the wonderful things therein!

Teaching 2's and 3's Bible words is important. The words for this unit are simple enough for the children to understand. Highlight these words in your classroom Bible and keep a bookmark in the Bible so the children can locate the words easily. Have the children repeat the words after you have said them.

Use the Bible words over and over throughout each lesson. For example, say, **When "God made the world," He made kittens. . . . "God made the world." That means He made you too. . . "God made the world" so we could have wonderful things to see. Thank You, God, for making the world.**

Teaching Tip: Have the children say the memory verse before you allow them to move to another activity. This gives you a specific time to review the Bible words with the children.

Things to Do for This Unit

- Make photocopies of the Parents' Letter (page 38) and the Unit Planning Sheet (pages 319 and 320).
- Make visual aids from pages 33-37. Color these ahead of time.
- Photocopy the Learning Center Cards (pages 25-30); cut pages on solid lines. To make each card, glue side 1 on cardboard and side 2 on opposite side of cardboard; laminate for durability (optional).
- Gather materials listed on Learning Center Cards.
- Find the following pictures from magazines, catalogs, calendars, or children's coloring books: animals, flowers, trees, food (in natural forms), people, and any other of God's creations.

Use These Songs and Action Rhyme During Unit 1

Thank You, God, for All the World

(Tune: "Jesus Loves the Little Children")

Thank You, God, for all the world.
You made everything there is.
Things I see, and things I taste.
Things I feel, and things I hear.
Thank You, God, for making everything there is.

Thank You, God

(Tune: "Old MacDonald Had a Farm")

Thank You, God, for eyes that see. I can see the sky. *(Repeat.)*
With a star here, and a star there.
Here a star, there a star, everywhere a star, star.
Thank You, God, for eyes that see. I can see the sky.

2. Thank You, God, for mouths that taste. I can taste an apple, etc.
3. . . . hands that feel . . . rock, etc.
4. . . . ears that hear . . . bird, etc.

God's World

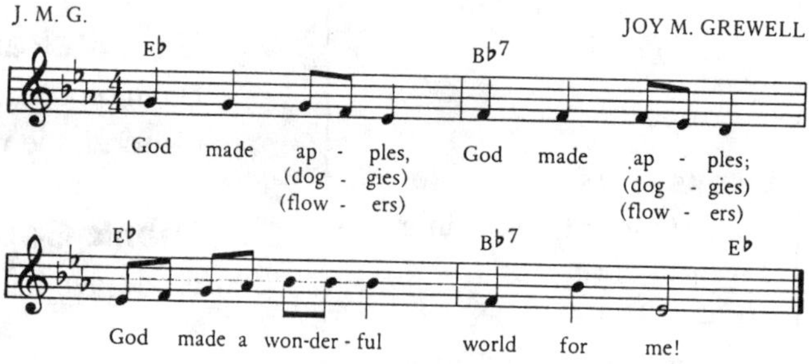

1. God made everything . . . for us. God made flowers . . . to see. 2. God made manna . . . food to eat. 3. God made soft things . . . to feel. 4. God made birds to sing . . . things to hear.

God Made Me

God made the sun. *(Join hands in a circle above head.)*
God made the tree. *(Spread arms to indicate branches.)*
God made you. *(Point to another person.)*
And God made me! *(Point to self.)* —*Joy Grewell*

He made YOU! *(Let children see themselves in the mirror, or point to each child.)*

(Show the teaching picture made from page 33.) God was very happy when He looked at all He had made! Now we can look at the wonderful things God has made!

Let's Apply the Lesson

Show pictures from the Book and Picture Center. **Jeremy, what do you see that God made? Good! Point to the dog. Who made the dog? That's right, God did. Thank You, God, for making dogs. Thank You for all the wonderful things You made for us to see.** Continue with this until all children have had turns to name or point to things God made for us to see.

Learning Activities

(20 minutes)

Let's Play Awhile

Have Zach say, "OK, let's stand up. We're going to sing a song." Sing "Thank You, God." Sing several stanzas until children begin to lose interest. Have pictures of items that can be mentioned in the song for the children to hold during the song.

Have materials ready in the Art Center and direct the children there when you finish singing. Talk about the things God made that you see on the spinner. If your class is large and you have several teachers, use the other centers also.

Let's Go Home

If there is time, let the children use the puzzles from the Puzzle Center. Help the children put the puzzles together until their parents come. Talk with them about the wonderful things God made for us to see. **What do you see, Abby? A tree? That's right. God made the tree. Can you say the Bible words with me? "God made the world." Very good!**

Send the Parents' Letter home along with art the children have made.

God Makes Things to See

Genesis 1:1-27

Bible Words: "God . . . made the world" (Acts 17:24, *NIV*).

Lesson Value: This lesson introduces God's creation of the world, with a special emphasis on wonderful things to see. Two's and 3's will be able to relate to this easily as they use their sense of sight throughout the lesson.

You will be offering your children a variety of experiences to learn about the wonderful things that God has created for them to see. As the children are encouraged to look at God's creations, they will be led to thank Him for His wonderful things to see.

Know: Know that God gives us wonderful things to see.
Feel: Feel happy to use the sense of sight to explore what God has given.
Do: Thank God for wonderful things to see.

Children will accomplish the goals when they:

1. Say the Bible words, "God made the world."
2. Explore something God has made for them to see.
3. Name things God has made for them to see.
4. Pray, "Thank You, God, for wonderful things to see."

Let's Get Ready

Prepare Zach the puppet or purchase a ready-made dog puppet or stuffed toy dog. See pages 315-317 for patterns and directions for various ways to make a puppet. Have the attendance charts ready with children's names on them. Stickers may be placed on the charts when the children arrive.

For the Bible story, you will need a Bible, an enlarged copy of the picture on page 33, a dog puppet, either a pair of children's sunglasses or a telescope made from a paper-towel tube, and an unbreakable hand mirror.

Prepare materials for the God's Wonders Center, the Book/Picture Center, and the Puzzle Center. If you are the only teacher, use just the God's Wonders Center. The Art Center will be used after the Bible story. Page 14 has instructions for making the cards. Instructions for preparing the learning centers are on pages 25-30. Set the Learning Center Cards in the centers for the benefit of the teachers.

Learning Activities

(30 minutes, including 10 minutes presession)

Let's Get Started

As the children come into the room, help them hang up any clothes, purses, or put away any toys they brought. Use Zach to guide the children to place stickers on the attendance chart. Guide each child to a learning center and help him become involved.

Hannah, what pictures do you see? Can you point to the sunshine? Good! Do you know God made the sun? He made everything. The Bible tells us, "God made the world." See, here are the words in our Bible. Use the words *see, look,* and *eyes* often throughout this lesson.

Worship and Bible Story

(15 minutes)

Let's Worship God

Have Zach tell the children it's time to pick up toys and come to the worship/story area. Begin to sing when the first child sits down. Others will quickly follow. Introduce the song, "Thank You, God, for All the World." Use the rhyme, "God Made Me" (page 14). Then sing "God's World," inserting items the children suggest. When you have finished singing, pray, **Thank You, God, for the wonderful things You have given us to see.**

Let's Learn From the Bible

Introduction: Put the sunglasses on Zach (or hold up the paper-towel tube in front of his eye). Have Zach say, "Hi! I have special glasses that let me see wonderful things that God has made. I see flowers, sunshine, and YOU. God made so many wonderful things for us to see. What do you see?" Allow the children to respond. Then put Zach away.

Hold up the Bible and point to the highlighted words. **The Bible says, "God made the world." Can you say those words with me?** Say the Bible words and have the children repeat them with you. **Good! Now let's talk about some of the wonderful things God made.**

The Bible Story: (*Keep the Bible opened in your lap or beside you. Explain to the children that they will be helping you tell the story by doing some actions or sounds with you.*) Let's all cover our eyes. It's dark, isn't it! This is how it was in the beginning. *(Uncover eyes.)* What did you see? *(Nothing.)* A long, long time ago, everything was dark. There was no sky. There was no sun and no moon. There was no land. There were no people and no animals. Then, God made the world.

God made wonderful things for us to see. *(Make pretend binoculars by holding hands in front of eyes.)* He made the dark *(cover eyes)* and He made the light *(uncover eyes)*. He made the sky *(point up)*. He made the sun *(make a large circle with arms)* and the moon *(make small circle with hands)*. He made dogs *(bark)* and fish *(hold hands together and wiggle them forward or make a "fish face")*. He made trees *(stand with arms spread out over head)*, flowers *(fan out hands on either side of face)*, and food to eat *(pretend to eat)*. And best of all,

world," He made good food. Let children take turns holding the Bible and "reading" the highlighted words.

Learning Activities

(20 minutes)

Let's Play Awhile

Make one enlarged copy of each fruit on page 32. Tape these in various places throughout the room, where they can be seen easily by the children. As you call out a fruit, the children are to find that fruit and stand by it until you call another one. Two's may need some help with this. As the children stand by a fruit, say, **Thank You, God, for grapes,** naming the appropriate fruit.

After you have done all four fruits, direct the children to the Game Center for the matching game described on the Learning Center Card. If your class is large and you have multiple teachers, have the centers used earlier available.

Let's Go Home

Have the children put away all their materials except the food pictures from the Game Center. Sit in a circle with the pictures spread out in the middle of the circle. Allow the children to take turns holding up a picture as the class sings "God's World," inserting the name of the pictured food.

Have Zach tell each child good-bye as she leaves. Make sure children take home their artwork. Try to have something positive to say about the children as parents arrive. Positive reinforcement works!

God Makes Things to Taste

Exodus 16:2-18, 31

Bible Words: "God . . . made the world" (Acts 17:24, *NIV*).

Lesson Value: God has always provided for His children. The account of the Israelites receiving the manna in the wilderness is a good example of God's provision of food. It is also a good lesson in trust. God met the needs of the Israelites for forty years in the wilderness.

God meets our needs at just the right times as well. How thankful we should be! God has so much for us to taste and see that He is good (Psalm 34:8). We can trust Him to provide—and enjoy the variety He has given us! Two's and 3's will love using their sense of taste to learn this lesson!

Know: Know that God gives wonderful things to taste.
Feel: Feel happy to use the sense of taste to explore what God has given.
Do: Thank God for wonderful things to taste.

Children will accomplish the goals when they:

1. Say the Bible words, "God made the world."
2. Explore things God has made for them to taste.
3. Name things God has made for them to taste.
4. Pray, "Thank You, God, for wonderful things to taste."

Let's Get Ready

For the Bible story, you will need a Bible with the Bible words highlighted, Zach, a large clean sheet, and puffed rice cereal.

Set up the God's Wonders Center, the Art Center, and the Music Center before class. The materials are listed on the Learning Center Cards. If you are the only teacher, use just the God's Wonders Center. Have materials for the Game Center ready to use after the Bible story. You will also need a large copy of each piece of fruit on page 32 to use at the beginning of the second Learning Activities time.

Learning Activities

(30 minutes, including 10 minutes presession)

Let's Get Started

Have Zach greet each child by name. Zach can also help children place stickers on the attendance chart.

Use Zach to lead each child to the God's Wonders Center first. **Hi, Jeremy! Today we're going to talk about the good food God gives us. When "God made the world," He made lots of good things to eat. Look at all these foods. Which one do you want to try first?** Make sure each child tries one or two foods before going to another learning center. Encourage each child to thank God for at least one of the foods.

Worship and Bible Story

(15 minutes)

Let's Worship God

Have Zach say, "It's time to put our things away!" Have Zach pick up a toy or two to set a good example for the children. As the children join you, begin singing "God's World." Then sing "Thank You, God, for All the World" and "Thank You, God," using "manna" and foods the children suggest.

When you have finished singing, pray, **Thank You, God, for giving us mouths to taste. Thank You for wonderful things to taste.**

Let's Learn From the Bible

Introduction: Have a sheet spread out on the floor where you tell the story. You will be putting the puffed rice on this later. Zach says, "I'm hungry. My tummy is empty *(rub tummy)*. Have you ever been hungry? Let's all rub our tummies and pretend to be hungry. Today your teacher is going to tell you about some people who were very hungry, and how God gave them food to eat." Put Zach away and hold your Bible on your lap. Have the puffed rice hidden behind you.

The Bible Story: God's people were on a long trip. They had run out of food, and now they were very hungry. Their tummies made rumble, rumble sounds. *(Rub your tummy.)* They were hungry and tired. There was no food anywhere.

(Yawn.) The people went to bed hungry. Let's close our eyes and go to sleep too. *(Pretend to sleep; encourage the children to imitate. Toss the puffed rice out on the sheet.)*

When the people woke up, do you know what they saw? There was food on the ground! Look! Here it is. The food was called manna and it looked something like this. The people tasted the manna. It tasted good. Soon their tummies were full. *(Pick up the cereal and begin to eat it. The children will follow your example.)* Where did the manna come from? Yes, God gave the people manna. God gave them wonderful things to eat.

Let's Apply the Lesson

Hold up some "manna." **What is this?** *(Manna.)* **Who gave this food to the people? Yes, God did. He gave the people wonderful things to eat. Can you tell me some foods God gives us to eat?** Encourage the children to name foods they tasted earlier. Also ask their favorites. **When "God made the**

Let's Apply the Lesson

Have the items you used in the Bible story spread out in front of the children. Ask them to point to something soft (wool), something rough (rock), and so forth. Or, if you prefer, hold up an enlarged copy of the coloring page and ask the children to point to something soft, something rough, and so forth. **What was the name of the shepherd boy in our Bible story? David, that's right. Who made all these things to feel? God did! When "God made the world," He made wonderful things for us to feel. What kinds of things do you like to feel?** Allow the children time to suggest things—their blankets, their mothers' arms around them, and so forth.

Let's say our Bible words together, "God made the world." Very good! Thank You, God, for all the wonderful things You have given for us to touch.

Learning Activities

(20 minutes)

Let's Play Awhile

Play the game from the Game Center at this time. Have each child take a turn to reach in the bag and pick up an object. Remind the children to show the items to the class. Guide them to say, "Thank You, God, for this soft teddy bear," naming the item and texture.

If you have a large class and several teachers, also have the centers used earlier.

Let's Go Home

In the time that is left, let the children sing the songs used earlier. Have rhythm instruments and allow the children to march as they sing. Also do the action rhyme, "God Made Me." As parents come, lead each child to the door while the others continue to sing and march. Make sure the child takes home his picture of the Bible story.

God Makes Things to Feel

1 Samuel 16:11, 18; 17:40

Bible Words: "God . . . made the world" (Acts 17:24, *NIV*).

Lesson Value: The world contains a variety of textures from soft to rough. The story of David the shepherd introduces many of these textures to the world of 2's and 3's. The feel of the sheep's wool, the breeze blowing, the cool water, and the rough rocks are all a part of David's world that can bring the sense of feeling to life for the 2- and 3-year old. Your children will enjoy experiencing the many textures in their world, and will learn to appreciate the wonderful sense of touch God has given us.

Know: Know that God gives wonderful things to feel.
Feel: Feel happy to use the sense of touch to explore what God has given.
Do: Thank God for wonderful things to feel.

Children will accomplish the goals when they:

1. Say the Bible words, "God . . . made the world."
2. Name things God has made for them to feel.
3. Explore something God has made for them to feel.
4. Pray, "Thank You, God, for wonderful things to feel."

Let's Get Ready

For the Bible story, you will need your classroom Bible, Zach, a rough rock and a smooth one, a stuffed lamb (or picture of one), and wool (or material with a similar texture).

Have materials ready in the Art Center, the Book/Picture Center, and the God's Wonders Center. If you are the only teacher, use just the God's Wonders Center. Have the Game Center ready to use after the Bible story. Instructions for the centers are on the Learning Center Cards.

Learning Activities

(30 minutes, including 10 minutes presession)

Let's Get Started

As each child arrives, have Zach greet him by name, then feel something the child is wearing and make a comment, such as, "That sweater feels soft. I like that! I'm glad God has given us so many things to feel." Help the children hang up any coats and purses, and lead them to place stickers on the attendance chart.

Direct each child to a learning center and make sure she gets involved. A child who wanders from place to place not only does not learn, but can cause problems for others. **Jacob, come here and look at this. There is some wool from a lamb. How does it feel to you? Thank You, God, for soft wool. When "God made the world," He made many wonderful things for us to feel. We are going to talk about some of them in our Bible story.**

Worship and Bible Story

(15 minutes)

Let's Worship God

Have Zach tell the children to pick up their toys and come to the worship/story area. Let him begin singing "Thank You, God, for All the World." Then sing "God's World," using words that describe things to feel.

When you have finished, get ready to pray. If you take time to tell the children ahead of time just what you are going to say in your prayer, they will learn to say the words with you. Begin by saying, **Now we are going to tell God, "Thank You, God, for giving us hands to feel. Thank You for the wonderful things You have given us to feel."** Then bow your head, close your eyes, fold your hands, and pray those same words. The example you set in attitude and words will teach the children more about prayer than all the instructions you can give them.

Let's Learn From the Bible

Introduction: Have Zach play with the lamb or look at the picture. "This is my friend Lambie. He is a baby sheep. The Bible tells of a young man named David who took care of his father's sheep. Listen to your teacher as she tells you about him."

If the weather is good, walk outside with the children and sit under a tree to tell the story. If not, gather grass and wool before the lesson begins.

The Bible Story: Our Bible story is about David the shepherd boy. As Zach told you, he took care of his father's sheep. All day, David worked outside watching the sheep. Perhaps he would sit under a tree to keep cool. David liked to take care of the sheep. He liked to feel their soft wool. It felt good on his hands. *(Pass around the lamb or piece of woolly cloth if you have either one.)*

Sometimes when David rested, he sat on the grass. How do you think the grass felt? This grass is nice and cool, isn't it? Other times, David probably sat on a rock. Maybe the rock felt rough like this one. *(Pass around the rough rock.)* Sometimes he used smooth rocks in his slingshot. *(Let the children feel the smooth rock.)*

David loved the world God made because there were so many wonderful things to feel. God made a wonderful world.

Let's Apply the Lesson

Have Zach by the autoharp. "That was a good story. God gave David many sounds to hear. Do you remember some of them?" *(Sheep baa-a-ing, wind blowing, sheep drinking, music.)* "I'm so glad God gave us animals and music to hear. Let's make our own music right now. We can pretend we are shepherds and play our harps." If children made these earlier, use them now, or have the children pretend to strum harps. Sing "Thank You, God, for All the World." **What are some sounds God has created for us to hear? That's right, Amanda. God made music. Thank You, God, for music.** Continue in this way as children name other sounds.

If you have time, allow each child to have a turn to play the autoharp. Have Zach show the children how to use a comb or pick to strum the strings gently. Praise children for their efforts! **Jonah, you are doing a great job! I like the way you make music to God!**

Learning Activities

(20 minutes)

Let's Play Awhile

God made our ears so we can hear the wonderful things He has made for us. Can you all touch your ears? Very good! Let's listen to Zach. He is going to tell us something to do. But we have to listen very carefully with our ears. Let Zach give instructions for the game, "Zach Says," from the Game Center.

Let's Go Home

When the children tire of the game, let them play the instruments they made in the Art Center. Walk in a circle as you sing "God's World." When you finish the song say, **Thank You, God, for music to hear.** Continue until parents arrive. Make sure children take their instruments as they leave.

God Makes Things to Hear

1 Samuel 16:11, 18-23

Bible Words: "God . . . made the world" (Acts 17:24, *NIV*).

Lesson Value: The sense of hearing is perhaps one of the finest of God's creations. Two's and 3's will enjoy learning through hearing, and it is so easy to teach this way! Every sound you make helps reinforce the fact that God made wonderful things to hear.

This lesson on wonderful things to hear is based on the sounds David would have heard as he cared for his father's sheep. As you describe David's world of sounds to the children, focus on God the Creator and the various sounds He has given us to experience in His world.

Know: Know that God gives wonderful things to hear.
Feel: Feel happy to use the sense of hearing to explore what God has given.
Do: Thank God for wonderful things to hear.

Children will accomplish the goals when they:

1. Say the Bible words, "God made the world."
2. Explore something God has made for them to hear.
3. Name things God has made for them to hear.
4. Pray, "Thank You, God, for wonderful things to hear."

Let's Get Ready

For the Bible story, you will need your classroom Bible, an enlarged copy of the coloring picture (page 36), and an autoharp. (If you do not have an autoharp, record music on a cassette or find a tape of instrumental music.) Provide "shepherd" or "sheep" clothes for the children to wear during the Bible story—pieces of cloth to drape around the shoulders of the shepherds, and fuzzy towels for the sheep. Have a piece of cloth to put around Zach. He will also need a staff—a small branch with a curved end. Have the lamb or picture of one from last week.

Prepare the Art Center, the Puzzle Center, and the Music Center. If you are the only teacher, use just the Art Center. You will be playing the game from the Game Center after the Bible story.

Learning Activities

(30 minutes, including 10 minutes presession)

Let's Get Started

Have Zach invite the children in the room. "Hello Hannah! It's good to see you! I'm glad you are here!"

After the children remove and hang up their wraps, guide them to put their stickers on the attendance chart. Direct them to a learning center. **Emily, we are going to make musical instruments. When "God made the world," He created music for us to enjoy. He created many wonderful things for us to hear! We are going to be talking about them.**

Worship and Bible Story

(15 minutes)

Let's Worship God

As children finish picking up and join the circle, have Zach be playing the autoharp, if you have one. **Let's sing some songs. I love to sing and listen to the music God has for me to hear. God has so many wonderful things for us to hear!** Sing "Thank You, God, for All the World," "God's World," and "Thank You, God," all from page 14. Let the children suggest things to hear.

When you have finished singing, pray, **Thank You, God, for giving us ears to hear. Thank You for wonderful things to hear.**

Let's Learn From the Bible

Have Zach dressed in shepherd's clothing, including a staff. Have him explain to the children that they can pretend to be shepherds or sheep. Help the "shepherds" put cloths around their shoulders and the "sheep" put the towels over them.

Introduction: "Hi, boys and girls! Today I am a shepherd, just like David was. We are going to learn more about David. He had wonderful things to hear as he took care of the sheep. You can be my sheep today! Let's practice, Baa! Baa! Baa! Good job. You'll be saying that and making other sounds in our Bible story. The teacher will tell you when, but you'll have to listen carefully. Now, let's learn about David and the wonderful things he heard as he watched his father's sheep."

The Bible Story: Every day, David took care of his father's sheep. *(Cue children to say, "Baa, baa.")* David was a shepherd. He worked outside. He could hear many sounds as he did this. David could hear the sheep. *(Children say, "Baa, baa.")* He could hear the wind blowing. *(Have children make blowing sounds.)* When the sheep drank water from a stream, David could hear the soft noises they made. *(Show children how to make lapping noises with your mouth.)* Perhaps he could hear a bird singing somewhere. *(Whistle like a bird.)*

David could also make some special sounds. He could play music on his harp and sing to God. The harp made sounds something like this. *(Play the autoharp or cassette.)* David loved the sounds that he heard. He loved to play pretty music to the Lord. David was thankful for wonderful sounds to hear.

made pretty sounds. David loved the sounds that he heard. He was thankful for wonderful things to hear.

Let's Apply the Lesson

Take this time to help the children think about the many wonderful things God has given them to see, taste, feel, and hear. If children don't respond well, have pictures from previous lessons to help them. Use the song, "Thank You, God," and allow the children to suggest things to see, etc. End by praying, **Thank You, God, for wonderful things to see, taste, feel, and hear.**

Learning Activities

(20 minutes)

Let's Play Awhile

If your class is large and you have multiple teachers, play all three games from the Game Center. If you are the only teacher, however, play the game your children liked best, or play the following game that will involve all the senses.

Have the children seated in a circle on the floor; place pictures and objects from previous lessons in front of you. As you hold up an object or picture of something, the children must point to their ears if it can be heard, to their eyes if they can see it, to their mouths if it is something to eat, or hold out their hands if they can feel it. Some objects or pictures may involve more than one sense. To vary the game, allow one child at a time to pick up a picture or object and show it to the other children.

Let's Go Home

When the children tire of the game(s), sit in a circle and sing songs from the unit. As you finish a song, say the Bible words together before going on to the next song. Take one child at a time to the door as her parents arrive.

Thank God for His World

Review of Lessons 1–4

Bible Words: "God . . . made the world" (Acts 17:24, *NIV*).

Lesson Value: Repetition is very important for 2's and 3's. It helps them recall the facts of the stories they have heard, and to reinforce the concepts to which they have already been exposed. This lesson will emphasize the fact that "God made the world" with wonderful things to see, taste, feel, and hear in it. Focus on helping your children feel thankful for their senses, and for all the wonderful things God has provided for them to see, taste, feel, and hear.

Know: Know that God gives wonderful things to see, taste, feel, and hear.

Feel: Feel happy to use their senses to explore what God has given.

Do: Thank God for wonderful things to see, taste, feel, and hear.

Children will accomplish the goals when they:

1. Say the Bible words, "God made the world."
2. Explore things God has made for them to see, taste, feel and hear.
3. Name one thing God has made for us to see, taste, feel, or hear.
4. Pray, "Thank You, God, for wonderful things to see, taste, feel, and hear."

Let's Get Ready

For the Bible story, have your classroom Bible as well as enlarged copies of the coloring pictures from the first four lessons, plus any other visuals/resources you used during those lessons. Also have a large sheet and puffed rice cereal if you plan to use "manna."

Prepare items for the Art Center, the Book/Picture Center, and the God's Wonders Center. If you are the only teacher, use the God's Wonders Center now. Use the Game Center after the Bible story.

Learning Activities

(30 minutes, including 10 minutes presession)

Let's Get Started

Let Zach greet each child and guide him to the attendance chart. **God made the world and all the wonderful things in it. He made wonderful things to see, taste, feel, and hear. Let's learn about some of them.** Guide each child to a learning center and see that he gets involved in the activity.

Worship and Bible Story

(15 minutes)

Let's Worship God

Sing "Thank You, God, for All the World," and "God's World." Allow each child to suggest something God made. If there is a song that the children enjoy singing more than another, sing that. Then pray, **Thank You, God, for the wonderful world You have made. Thank You for wonderful things to see, taste, feel, and hear.**

Let's Learn From the Bible

Introduction: Have Zach say, "Hi, kids! We've learned so many wonderful things about God. Let's say the Bible words. 'God made the world.' Now let's listen as the teacher reminds us of the many things God has made for us to see, taste, feel, and hear." Put Zach away. Have items from the first four lessons to pass around or use the enlarged pictures and let the children point to or tell you what God made to see, taste, feel, and hear. Spread the sheet in the middle of your circle if you plan to have the "manna."

The Bible Story: *(As you tell the story, both you and the children use the actions indicated.)* God made wonderful things for us to see *(make binoculars with hands)*. He made the dark *(cover eyes)* and the light *(remove hands)*. He made the sky *(point up)*. He made the sun and moon *(make large circle with arms, then small circle with hands)*. He made the dog and fish *(bark, then hold hands together and wiggle them forward or make a "fish face")*. He made trees *(stand with arms spread out over head)*, and flowers *(fan out hands on either side of face)*.

God's people were on a long trip. They had no food anywhere *(yawn)*. They went to bed *(pretend to sleep; encourage children to imitate; toss "manna" on sheet)* and when they woke up, guess what they saw! There was food on the ground. It tasted good. Their tummies were full. God gave them the good food to eat!

When David watched his father's sheep, he could feel many things. The sheep were soft and fluffy. *(Pass around the toy lamb or piece of wool.)* When David rested, he sat on the soft grass, or perhaps on a rock. The rock might have felt rough like this one. *(Pass around the rough rock.)* He could have felt the cool wind as it blew around him. God gave David many things to feel.

David could hear many sounds as he took care of the sheep. He could hear the sheep baa-ing. *(Children baa.)* He could hear the wind blowing. *(Everyone blows.)* And sometimes David would make his own sounds by playing his harp and singing. The harp

God's Wonders Center

Unit 1—God Makes the World

Items to Include:

Lesson 1
Masking tape
Walking rope
Paper punch
Scissors (optional)
Clear, self-adhesive plastic (optional)
Yarn (optional)

Lesson 2
Fruits
Vegetables

Purpose: The child will use the senses to explore various things God has made.

Things to Do and Say

Lesson 1

Go on a nature walk. Use a walking rope (a rope tied in knots at intervals; each child holds a knot). If you are the only teacher, or the weather is bad, gather leaves and flowers before class.

Turn pieces of masking tape inside out and put around the children's wrists. **Can you point to a tree leaf? Who made this flower? That's right, God did! He made everything. "God made the world."** Help the children collect items and attach them to the bracelets. Create bookmarks by putting the leaves and flowers between the self-adhesive plastic. Punch a hole in the top of each and add yarn.

Lesson 2

Have a variety of fruits and vegetables cut into bite-size pieces for the children to taste. Encourage each child to try something new. You may want to include something sour and something salty along with the fruits and vegetables.

God has made wonderful things for us to taste. This is a piece of melon. It tastes sweet. Look at the pretty grapes. They are sweet too. Who gives us good things to eat? Yes, God does. Tell me something else God gives us to eat.

Music Center

Unit 1—God Makes the World

Items to Include:

Lesson 2
Pictures of natural foods mounted on construction paper

Lesson 4
Cassette tape of sounds
Tape player
Tape of children's music (optional)

Purpose: The child will sing about the things God has made.

Things to Do and Say

Lesson 2

Have the food pictures spread out on a table or on the floor. Lead the children in singing "God's World," from page 14. Let a child pick out a food and then sing about that food as the child holds up the picture. "God made apples, etc."

Rachel has chosen a picture of a banana. Let's sing our song using bananas. *(Do so.)* **Thank You, God, for making bananas. . . . What food would you like to sing about, Kyle?**

If the children want to continue, sing "Thank You, God," using the words, "Thank You, God, for mouths that taste. I can taste an apple, etc." Point to your mouth at that word.

Lesson 4

Find a tape of various sounds. If you do not have a tape, make your own. Include any sounds a 2- or 3-year-old would recognize. For example, barking dog, bell, notes played on a musical instrument, hammering, people talking, a car starting, someone laughing, etc. Play the tape and have the children guess what the sound is.

Camille, can you tell me what that sound is? Yes, it's a dog. What do we use to hear sounds? That's right, our ears. God made our ears to hear wonderful things. Thank

God's Wonders Center, continued

Lesson 3
Wool cloth
Rocks
Sandpaper
Grass
Other textured items

Lesson 5
Things to see, taste, feel, and hear

Lesson 3

Gather the items and place them on a tray or table. Have the children touch and feel the textures. Talk with them about the things God has created.

God has given us so many wonderful things to feel. What is this? What does it feel like? David had many things to feel when he watched the sheep. . . . Thank You, God, for wonderful things to feel.

Lesson 5

Have as many examples of things to see, taste, feel, and hear as possible. Things to see—a flower, pinecone, seashell, pretty rocks, pictures of mountains, ocean, etc. Have raisins or other fruits to eat. Use textured items from Lesson 3 to feel. Items to hear could include a variety of bells, a play musical instrument, or an autoharp, as well as the tape of sounds from Lesson 4 Music Center.

When "God made the world," He made wonderful things to see. Thank You, God, for wonderful things to see. Thank You for eyes with which to see. Repeat with the other items and senses.

Music Center, continued

You, God, for our ears. And thank You for wonderful things to hear.

If the children tire of listening to sounds, play a tape of children's music or sing some songs from this unit.

Art Center

Unit 1—God Makes the World

Items to Include:

Lesson 1
Copies of page 31
Drinking straws
Tape
Crayons

Lesson 2
Copies of page 34
Crayons
Glue
Puffed rice

Purpose: The child will make visual representations of some of God's creation.

Things to Do and Say

Lesson 1

Gather items listed above. Before class, follow the instructions on page 31 to prepare the spinners. Let children color their pages.

What do you see in the picture, Josh? You see the eyes. God has given us eyes to see His wonderful world. . . . What do you see, Kori? The flower? Thank You, God, for giving us pretty flowers to see. When "God made the world," He gave us so many wonderful things to see!

Lesson 2

Have puffed rice cereal in small bowls, along with bottles of glue. Let children color their pages. Then put a drop of glue on each child's page and show how to stick one piece of cereal in the glue. Add more as children finish.

When "God made the world," He made good food to eat. The people in this picture are picking up food. What was it called? Yes, manna. Thank You, God, for giving us good food.

Book/Picture Center

Unit 1—God Makes the World

Items to Include:

Lesson 1
Books on creation (see list on page 13)

Purpose: The child will learn about the world God made.

Things to Do and Say

Lesson 1

Gather books suggested on the unit page as well as other appropriate ones on the subject of creation. Allow time for the children to look at the pictures as you read a book. If a book has too much story, "picture read" the book by looking at the pictures, asking questions, having the children point to specific things, and so forth. If you have mature children, you may wish to tape record a book before class begins so the children can listen and look independently. At the beginning of the tape, give the children instructions for turning the pages ("When you hear this sound"—bell, tap on a drinking glass, etc.), and perhaps things to look for in the book.

Kylie, let's look at this book. It is a book about things God has made. What do you see in this picture? . . . "God made the world." He made you and me and everything we see.

Book/Picture Center, continued

Lesson 3
Touch-and-feel book

Lesson 3

To prepare a touch-and-feel book, gather items with varying textures. For example, include sandpaper, cotton, silk ribbon, sand/salt, and anything else that will lie flat in a book form. Mount these on stiff cardboard, punch holes, and place in a loose-leaf notebook, or hold pages together with twisters or ribbon.

Richie, can you tell me what this is? How does it feel? It looks like it would feel soft, doesn't it? Who made all these wonderful things to feel? Yes, God did.

Lesson 5
Books from this unit

Lesson 5

Provide books used this unit. Allow the children to view these as they wish. Be available to read to them or simply to talk about the pictures. Let the children tell you the story if they can.

Lakeisha, can you tell me about this book? Yes, it's about things God made. Very good! . . . Show me a picture of something God made, Eric. Let's say the Bible words, "God made the world." Very good!

Art Center, continued

Lesson 3
Copies of page 35
Crayons
Glue
Touch-and-feel items

Lesson 3

Have copies of the picture from page 35 ready for the children to color. Also have a variety of touch-and-feel items to add to give the children a sensory experience. For example, cotton balls on a sheep, a piece of rough fabric on David's clothing or sandpaper on a rock, torn pieces of green construction paper on the grass and/or tree, etc.

You've done a good job of coloring your picture, Amy. Now you are ready to put some of this soft cotton on your sheep. Doesn't that feel good! Thank You, God, for wonderful things to feel!

Lesson 4
Shoe boxes
Rubber bands
Waxed paper
Paper towel tubes
Crayons

Lesson 4

Have items ready to make musical instruments. Allow children to scribble-color the paper-towel tubes and shoe boxes. For the pretend horn, attach a small piece of waxed paper to the end of the paper-towel tube with a rubber band. Blow into the other end to make a sound. To make a pretend harp, cut slits into the shoe box and attach rubber bands.

Jared, you are doing a good job on your horn. God made wonderful things for us to hear! Let's play our instruments and sing to God.

Lesson 5
Copies of page 37
Glue
Crayons
9" squares of black construction paper

Lesson 5

Copy and cut out the squares. Glue these to the 9" black squares. See instructions on page 37. Allow the children to scribble-color their pictures. Talk with them about all the wonderful things God has made for us to see, taste, feel, and hear.

When the children have finished coloring, show them how to fold and open the picture. **Look at the world before God made everything. Now look at it. God has made so many wonderful things for us to see!** Point these out; then the things to hear, etc.

Puzzle Center

Unit 1—God Makes the World

Items to Include:

Lesson 1
Wooden puzzles of things God made
Pictures of sky, sea, sun, moon, people, animals, anything that God made
Cardboard and glue

Lesson 4
Wooden puzzles of animals (4 or 5 pieces)

Purpose: The child will explore something God has created.

Things to Do and Say

Lesson 1

Have pictures listed in the lefthand column. Glue these to cardboard and cut apart into 3 to 5 large puzzle pieces. (Do not cut across faces.) Spread these and any appropriate wooden puzzles you have on a large table. Teach the children good "puzzle" behavior. Children should be seated at the table to work puzzles. Puzzles should be taken apart (not dumped) and a child must finish a puzzle before doing another one or leaving the table. Give assistance if needed, but allow the children to work independently. Talk with them about the wonderful things God made for us to see. Use the words *see, eyes,* and *look* often as you talk to the children.

What do you see Abby? An elephant? That's right. When "God made the world," He made big elephants. You are doing a good job of putting the puzzle together. Can you say the Bible words with me? "God made the world." Very good!

Lesson 4

If you do not have puzzles of animals, make your own as suggested above. To make puzzles last longer, cover them with clear, self-adhesive plastic before cutting them. You will be talking about the sounds the animals and birds make, so choose pictures of those that make familiar sounds. Use the words *sound, ears,* and *hear* often in your conversation.

Game Center

Unit 1—God Makes the World

Items to Include:

Lesson 2
Pictures of food (2 of each)

Lesson 3
Bag
Items from Bible story
Touch-and-feel items

Purpose: The child will learn, through play, about the world God made.

Things to Do and Say

Lesson 2

Gather two identical sets of different types of food. You may want to use the fruits on page 32. Lay one set out on the table or floor. Give each child a piece of the other set Allow the children to find the matching pictures on the floor and lay their pictures on top of them. When a match has been made, have the children say the Bible words.

Marco, what picture do you have? Can you find the picture on the floor that looks just like it? Very good. When "God made the world," He made food for us to eat. Thank You, God, for good food.

Lesson 3

Have a bag with the items from the Bible story in it. Also include additional touch-and-feel items the children will recognize. Let each child have a turn to reach in the bag and pick up an item. Let him guess what the item is, if possible, before pulling it out and showing it to the class. Then say, **Thank You, God, for** (name of item) **to feel.**

Stephan, what do you think you are holding? Can you guess? Very good! Show it to the class. Let's say, "Thank You, God, for smooth rocks to feel."

Puzzle Center, continued

Pictures of animals
Cardboard
Glue

What is this animal, Sarah? How does the kitten sound? That's very good! Thank You, God, for making kittens that say, "Meow." . . . Yes, Doug, the lion roars! God gave him a big voice so he could be heard by all the other animals. . . . Do you like to hear birds sing, Matthew? I'm glad God gave birds pretty voices to sing, and I'm glad I can hear them.

Game Center, continued

Lesson 4
Zach (puppet)

Lesson 4

Play "Simon Says," using Zach in place of Simon. Seat everyone in a circle, facing Zach. Make sure you use, **Zach says, "Say the Bible words, 'God . . . made the world,'"** as one of the instructions. Do not remove a child from the game if she makes a mistake. This must be fun for everyone!

Let's play a game. God gave us ears to hear. Use your ears to listen to my instructions. If I say, "Zach says, 'Jump up and down,'" you jump up and down. You have to use your ears to listen closely. Ready, let's start!

Lesson 5

If your class is large and you have multiple teachers, use all the games described on this card. If you teach alone, use the game your children like the best, or use the game described at the end of Lesson 5.

Creation Spinner—Autumn, Unit 1

This creation spinner will remind 2's and 3's about the wonderful things God has made for us to see. Let them take the spinners home to show their parents what they are learning.

Instructions

1. Make a copy of this page for each child and one for your sample.
2. Let the children scribble-color the pictures.
3. Cut out the pictures and fold in half.
4. Poke a hole in each spinner on the fold line.
5. Insert a drinking straw in each.
6. Show children how to make their pictures spin.
7. Talk about the things God has made for us to see.

Patterns—Autumn, Unit 1

Instructions

1. Make one copy of each fruit; enlarge if possible.
2. Color fruit or use colored construction paper for copying.
3. Cut out fruit.
4. Mount on cardboard for durability.

When God made the world, He made wonderful things for us to see.
Thank You, God, for wonderful things to see.

Teaching/Coloring Picture 1—Autumn, Unit 1

When God's people had no food, He gave them manna to eat. He gives us good food too. Thank You, God, for making wonderful things to taste.

Teaching/Coloring Picture 2—Autumn, Unit 1

When God made the world, He made wonderful things for us to feel. David had many wonderful things to feel as he cared for his father's sheep. Can you point to some of them?
Thank You, God, for wonderful things to feel.

Teaching/Coloring Picture 3—Autumn, Unit 1

When David took care of his father's sheep, he could hear many wonderful sounds. What could he hear? The bird singing, the sheep baa-a-a-ing, the wind blowing through a tree, and the music he made on his harp. Point to each one of these. Thank You, God, for wonderful things to hear.

Creation Action Picture—Autumn, Unit 1

Instructions

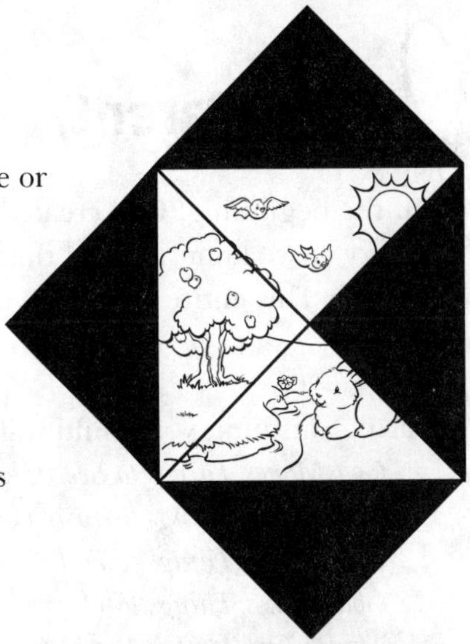

1. Enlarge this picture to fit on a 9" x 12" piece of construction paper (white or light color) or manila paper. Make a copy for each child and one for you sample. This will be your visual for lesson 5. The children will make theirs in the Art Center.
2. Color the picture.
3. Cut off excess paper.
4. Glue the square to a 9" square of black construction paper.
5. Fold the corners in where indicated so that only the black shows.
6. Show the children how to open one corner at a time to see what God has made to see, taste, feel, and hear.

Dear Parent,

"In the beginning, God created the heavens and the earth" (Genesis 1:1, *NIV*). This is the start of history as we know it—and the best place to start teaching your child about the world God has created. This entire unit is devoted to the world around us and the things God has created for us to enjoy.

During this unit, your child will be learning that . . .
. . . *God Makes Things to See* (Genesis 1:1-27);
. . . *God Makes Things to Taste* (Exodus 16:2-18, 31);
. . . *God Makes Things to Feel* (1 Samuel 16:11, 18; 17:40);
. . . *God Makes Things to Hear* (1 Samuel 16:11, 18-23); and your child will
. . . *Thank God for His World* (review of Lessons 1–4).

Below are some ways to reinforce the lessons your child will learn in class. Spend time with your child focusing on God's creation. It will be a wonderful bonding experience!

- Go on a nature walk. Touch leaves, tree trunks, and grass. Smell the flowers. Look at the blue sky. Hear the birds chirping. Taste the sweetness of an apple. Say, "Thank You, God," for these things.
- Visit a petting zoo and pet the animals. Notice the sounds the animals make.
- Listen to cassettes of familiar sounds (animals, nature, sea, wind, etc.).
- Bake cookies with your child. Talk about the feel of the dough, the smell of the cookies as they bake, and how good they taste! Thank God for good cookies.
- Taste new and different foods.
- Look at books and pictures of the wonderful things God has made for us.
- Say the Bible words with your child. "God . . . made the world" (Acts 17:24). Highlight or underline these words in a Bible so your child can see them, point to them, and "read" them with your help. Seeing the same Bible words at home that your child sees at church tells your child that those words are important to you and your family.
- Sing this song and do the action rhyme below with your child.

Thank You, God, for All the World

(Tune: "Jesus Loves the Little Children")

Thank You, God, for all the world.
You made everything there is.
Things I see, and things I taste;
Things I feel, and things I hear.
Thank You, God, for making everything there is.

God Made Me

God made the sun. *(Join hands in a circle above head.)*
God made the tree. *(Spread arms out wide to indicate branches.)*
God made you. *(Point to your child.)*
And God made me. *(Point to self.)*

—*Joy M. Grewell*

Experience the wonderful things God has created for us to see, taste, feel, and hear. Then thank Him for His wonderful world.

Your child's teacher,

Unit 2: God Makes People

Lessons 6–9

By the end of the unit, the children will

Know that God gives us families, friends, and helpers.

Feel happy because God gives us families, friends, and helpers.

Thank God for families, friends, and helpers.

Unit Bible Words

"God is good" (Psalm 73:1, *NIV*).

Books

from Standard Publishing

My Family and Me (24-03701)

My Family and Friends (24-03114)

Sharing Makes Me Happy (24-04214)

All About Hands (24-04248)

Busy Feet (24-04249)

This Unit at a Glance

6 God Makes Families — **Genesis 2:18-22; 4:1, 2**

God creates the first family—Adam, Eve, Cain, and Abel.

7 God Makes Friends — **Genesis 13:1-12**

When conditions become crowded, Abram shows he is a true friend to Lot by allowing him first choice of the land.

8 God Makes Helpers — **Exodus 3; 4:1-18**

When the Egyptian king begins to work the Hebrews too hard, God sends Moses to lead them out of Egypt.

9 Thank God for the People I Know — **Review of Lessons 6–8**

Why Teach This Unit?

God created all people in His own image. Young children need to know that they, and all people, are the unique creation of a loving God who cares and provides for them. The security of two- and three-year-olds comes from the people who are part of their world. God knows we need others, so He provides people, particularly families, friends, and helpers, to help us all feel secure. By hearing Bible stories, singing songs, and participating in activities about people, the children will learn about people and God's provision and will be led to thank God for families, friends, and helpers.

The Bible words should be used in conversation, at learning centers, in the Bible stories, in prayer, and as often as possible. For example, **The Bible tells us that "God is good." . . . "God is good" to give us friends and family.**

Have your classroom Bible in a learning center or in a place where it can be seen easily. Also have it on your lap or nearby as you teach. Have the Bible words highlighted or underlined so the children can see the words, point to them, and "read" them with your help.

Things to Do for This Unit

- Make copies of the Parents' Letter (page 62) and the Unit Planning Sheet (pages 319 and 320).
- Photocopy Learning Center Cards (pages 49-54). Cut pages apart on heavy lines. Mount side 1 on cardboard, then side 2 on back. Cover with clear, self-adhesive plastic to make cards more durable (optional).
- See Learning Center Cards for materials to prepare for each week.
- Find magazine pictures of various family members, community helpers (firefighters, police officers, doctors, etc.), and friends. Mount pictures on construction paper and cover with clear, self-adhesive plastic (optional).
- For Lesson 6, make stand-up figures of first family (page 56).
- For Lesson 7 visual aid, enlarge and photocopy pages 59 and 60 back-to-back (or glue separate pages back-to-back). Add color and stick-on animals. Page 60 will be the children's artwork page.
- For Lesson 8, make a burning bush (see Let's Get Ready, Lesson 8).
- For Lesson 9, make copies of review page (61) and prepare stickers.

Use These Songs and Action Rhymes During Unit 2

God Is Good

(Tune: "God Is So Good")

God is good; God is good.
God is good; He is good to me.

God Gives Us Families

(Tune: "Mary Had a Little Lamb")

God gives us families, families, families.
God gives us families. Thank You, God, for them.
(In place of "families" use mommies, daddies, sisters, grandmas, etc.; for Lesson 7, all our friends.)

Adam and Eve

(Tune: "Are You Sleeping?")

Adam and Eve, Adam and Eve,
Had two sons, had two sons.
They were very special. They were very special.
'Cause God made them; God made them.

Helpers Song

(Tune: "Have You Ever Seen a Lassie?")

The mailman is a helper, a helper, a helper.
The mailman is a helper. We thank God for him.
(In place of "mailman" use preacher, doctor, nurse, etc.)

God Made Families

God made daddies big and strong. *(Flex muscles.)*
God made mommies to hug us long. *(Hug yourself.)*
God made people like you and me. *(Point to another, then to yourself.)*
I'm glad God made fam-i-lies. *(Clap 3 times on fam-i-lies.)*

When I Pray

When I pray, I fold my hands *(Fold hands.)*
And close my eyes; *(Close eyes.)*
I think about God, and He hears me.
—*Jean Katt*

mommy and daddy, Adam and Eve. Who does God give us to take care of us? Our mommies and daddies (grandparents, etc.). Are we special to God? Yes we are! Let's say thank-you to God for our families. If you are familiar with each home situation, say, "Thank You, God, for Hannah's mommy and daddy. Thank You for Drew's grandma and grandpa," etc. If you don't know all the families, let the children name those who care for them; then thank God for these people.

Learning Activities

(20 minutes)

Let's Play Awhile

Let's stand up and learn a new rhyme. It's a lot of fun. I want you to watch me first, and then you can try it. Use the rhyme, "God Made Families," from page 40. Do one line at a time, have the children repeat it, and then put it all together. **Great job! Now let's sing a song about the very first family God made. Do you remember their names?** Wait for responses. Then sing "Adam and Eve," from page 40. Hold up the Bible and have the children repeat the Bible words.

Have the Family Living Center set up. If you have more than one teacher, use one or more of the learning activities used previously.

Let's Go Home

Boys and girls, Zach says it is time to go. Let's make sure we pick up all the toys. If a child is reluctant to help, give her a specific job. **Please put this doll in the suitcase, Amy. Now we can teach Zach our new action rhyme about families.** When everything has been picked up, do the action rhyme again. Make sure art work and letters to parents are ready to go home.

God Makes Families

Genesis 2:18-22; 4:1, 2

Bible Words: "God is good" (Psalm 73:1, *NIV*).

Lesson Value: In this lesson, the children will learn about the first family God created. The security of family and friends is very important to two- and three-year-olds. They can learn that God is a good God who provides families for us because He loves us.

Know: Know that God gives us families.
Feel: Feel happy because we have families.
Do: Thank God for families.

Children will accomplish the goals when they:

1. Say the Bible words, "God is good."
2. Pray, "Thank You, God, for my mommy, daddy, etc."
3. Point to or name the people in the first family.
4. Pretend to be people in the first family.
5. Pretend to be people in their own families.

Let's Get Ready

For the Bible story, you will need your classroom Bible with the new words highlighted and the stand-up figures of the first family made from the patterns on page 56. Have copies of the Parents' Letter ready for the children to take home.

Prepare the Art Center, the Book/Picture Center, and the

Block Center. Also have materials for the Family Living Center ready to use after the Bible story. If you are teaching alone, use just the books and pictures now.

Learning Activities

(30 minutes, including 10 minutes presession)

Let's Get Started

Have Zach greet each child by name as he enters. Make some remark about each child's family if possible. **I see that you came to church with your family, Beth. "God is good." He gives us families.**

Let Zach help each child with an attendance sticker. Tell the children, **We are going to be learning about the first family God made. Would you like to look at books or play with the blocks, Corey?** Allow each child to choose an activity and then see that she gets involved. Zach should tell the children when it is time to stop playing and get ready for worship.

Worship and Bible Story

(15 minutes)

Let's Worship God

Let Zach say, "Boys and girls, let's sit in a circle so we can sing." **This song tells us that "God is good." Those are our Bible words.** Show the children the Bible with these words underlined or highlighted. Teach children "God Is Good" by singing it several times. Sing "Jesus Loves Me," or another quiet song. Then pray, **Thank You, God, for all the boys and girls. Thank You for being a good God who gives us families.**

Let's Learn From the Bible

Introduction: Have Zach say, "Boys and girls, can you count to four with me? Let's try." Count slowly several times. "Good! Raise your hand if you have a family. You're right, we *all* have families! Our Bible story is about the very first family God made. And there were four people in it!" Put Zach down. Have the Bible on your lap or beside you.

The Bible Story: *(Use the stand-up figures, starting with Adam.)* This is the very first person God made; his name was Adam. What was his name? That's right, Adam. He was the daddy in the family. *(Stand up Eve figure).* This is the second person God made; her name was Eve and she was the mommy of the family. What was the mommy's name?

(Stand up Cain and Abel.) These are Cain and Abel. They were children like you, and they were the sons of Adam and Eve. *(Hold up just Cain figure.)* Who is this? Yes, Cain. And what is this boy's name? *(Hold up Abel.)* Now, help me count the people in this family. *(Count to four, pointing to each figure.)* Good job!

God gave this family a special place to live. It was a garden full of plants and trees. Do we have special places to live? *(Answer with the children.)* Yes we do! Did God provide our special places to live? Yes He did! Where are our special places? *(Some live in houses, some in apartments, and some in mobile homes, etc.)*

God gave Cain and Abel a mommy and a daddy to take care of them. Do we have people to take care of us? Yes, we do! Our mommies and daddies and grandparents take care of us! *(Name any other caregivers of which you are aware.)* Who gives us these special people to take care of us? God does! God does this because He loves us. *(Sing "God Gives Us Families.")*

Let's Apply the Lesson

Help me count the number of people in the first family. Count slowly to four. **Who made the first family?** Let children answer. **God did! That's right! Point to the daddy in the family. That's right. What was his name? Who was the mommy? Yes, that's Eve, the mommy. Are there children in this family like you? Very good! Cain and Abel are the children. Who did God give Cain and Abel to take care of them? That's right, their**

Let's Apply the Lesson

Hold up the large picture of Abram and Lot. **This is Abram; this is Lot. Abram was a friend to Lot. Abram let Lot have first choice.** Turn over the picture. **Now look. The land isn't crowded any more. Who was a good friend? Abram was! Who was God happy with for being a good friend? Abram! Who gives us friends? God does! How can we be good friends?** Let the children suggest ways. *(Let others go first, share with others, help someone, etc.)* Mention any "friendly" actions you observed in the classroom earlier.

Learning Activities

(20 minutes)

Let's Play Awhile

Stand in a circle and sing "God Gives Us Families," using "all our friends." Let Zach go around the circle, naming each friend. Then sing "God Is Good," using the words, "God gives us friends, etc.; He is good to us."

Have the Art Center ready so children can make a reminder of the Bible story. Talk about ways children are being friends as they work. **Thank you, Jennifer, for sharing the crayons with your friend Josh. . . . I like the way Eric let his friend Michael use the glue first.** Use the other centers also if yours is a large class with multiple teachers.

Let's Go Home

Have Zach tell the children that it is time to get ready to go home. Remind them that they can be good friends to Zach and you by helping to clean up items they were using.

God Makes Friends

Genesis 13:1-12

Bible Words: "God is good" (Psalm 73:1, *NIV*).

Lesson Value: Through the story of Abram and Lot, the children will learn about friends and how we act like good friends. When the herdsmen of Abram and Lot began to argue over whose animals should graze where, Abram settled the dispute by allowing Lot first pick of the land. By allowing Lot the choice, he showed he was Lot's friend. As you teach, emphasize that our positive actions show others that we are their friends.

Know: Know that God gives us friends.
Feel: Feel happy because we have friends.
Do: Thank God for friends.

The children will accomplish the goals when they:

1. Say the Bible words, "God is good."
2. Pray, "Thank You, God, for my friends" (by name).
3. Point to or name the people in the picture who are friends.
4. Point to or name the person who gave the choice.
5. Pretend to be Lot and Abram.

Let's Get Ready

For the Bible story, have a large table draped with a blanket or sheet like a tent. Pin one side open. If your class is large, set up several "tents." They need to seem crowded. Make an enlarged copy of the picture of Abram and Lot (page 59) and another of page 60. Glue these back-to-back, or photocopy on both sides.

Set up the Block Center, the Music/Drama Center, and the Family Living Center. If you are teaching alone, use the Music Center. Have the Art Center ready to use after the story.

Learning Activities

(30 minutes, including 10 minutes presession)

Let's Get Started

As the children come in, have Zach greet each one by name. "Hello, I'm glad to see my friend Benjamin." Make sure you use the word *friend* often, and point out when someone is being a friend. **Lucy, you were a good friend when you shared the blocks with Becky.**

Worship and Bible Story

(15 minutes)

Let's Worship God

Who remembers our song, "God Is Good"? Great! You all do. Let's sing it now. Do so. **"God is good." He gives us friends.** Sing the version of "God Gives Us Families" for Lesson 7. Use the action rhyme, "When I Pray"; then pray, **Thank You, God, for being so good and for giving us so many friends.**

Let's Learn From the Bible

Introduction: Hold up Zach. **Zach, who are your friends?** Zach looks around, and then responds, "I see my friend Joey, my friend Beth, etc." Have Zach name all of the children. "All the boys and girls here are my friends!" **I'm glad God gives us so many friends, aren't you, Zach?** Zach nods his head. Put Zach away. Hold your Bible or place it beside you.

The Bible Story: Our Bible story is about two friends, Abram and Lot. Let's say those names together. *(Do so.)* Abram and Lot lived in tents a little like the one we have. They slept and ate in their tents. During the day they lived outside so they could take care of the sheep and cows they owned. Let's all go inside the tent to pretend that we are Abram and Lot. *(If possible, let everyone get inside. The story will seem more real if it is crowded.)*

Let's pretend it is nighttime and we are sleeping. *(Pretend to sleep.)* Who slept in a tent like this? Abram and Lot! Can you hear the cows and the sheep outside the tent? *(Put hand to your ear.)* What sounds do cows and sheep make? *(Wait for responses.)* Now I hear the cows and the sheep! Who owned cows and sheep? Abram and Lot!

Abram and Lot were good friends, but they had a problem. Do you know what that was? *(Let children answer.)* Yes, they were very crowded! There wasn't enough land for all their animals and their families. They needed more room! Do we need more room inside our tent? Yes, we do! Abram and Lot needed to find more space for their sheep and cattle. How did they do this? Abram was a good friend. He told Lot that he could pick whatever land he wanted so they wouldn't be crowded. Lot looked around and picked a green field with lots of grass for his animals. Lot told Abram, "I will go here." So Abram moved his family and animals somewhere else. Now everyone had plenty of room.

Abram was a good friend because he let Lot choose first. Do you think Lot was glad for his friend Abram? Yes! Was God happy with Abram for being a good friend? Yes, He was! The Bible tells us that "God is good." *(Show these words in the Bible. Have the children take turns holding the Bible and "reading" the words.)* How was God good to Lot? Yes, He gave him a good friend named Abram.

by the king. I want you to go to Egypt and lead my people to a new place."

Moses wanted to be God's helper so he listened while God told him what to do. Then he went to be God's helper in Egypt. God used the bush that wasn't burning up to get Moses to listen to him. Moses became a great helper for God.

Let's Apply the Lesson

Bring Zach out. **Zach wants to know the name of the man who saw the burning bush. Moses! That's right!** Zach asks, "Was Moses a helper for God? Who sent Moses to be a helper?" *(God did!)* "Does God give us helpers?" *(Yes, He does!)* Let children name the helpers in their lives.

Learning Activities

(20 minutes)

Let's Play Awhile

Use the Music Center activity now. Have the helpers' equipment ready to use as you sing the "Helpers Song," from page 40. Allow the children to go to centers used earlier if there is time, or if you have a large class and multiple teachers. Encourage each child to be a helper.

Let's Go Home

Have Zach tell the children that it is time to be helpers by picking up and getting ready to go home. **I see Emmy being a good helper by picking up the blocks. . . . Thank you, Angie, for putting away the books.**

Tell the parents about any ways their children were helpers. Remind the children to be helpers during the week and to thank God for their helpers.

God Makes Helpers

Exodus 3; 4:1-18

Bible Words: "God is good" (Psalm 73:1, *NIV*).

Lesson Value: In this lesson the children will learn how God provides us with helpers when we need them most. After the Hebrews had been in Egypt for over four hundred years, they had increased in numbers so greatly that Pharaoh feared for the control of his kingdom. He made the Hebrews' work more strenuous for them in an effort to decrease their growth. God sent an unlikely helper in Moses to lead His people out of Egypt.

Know: Know that God gives us helpers.
Feel: Feel happy because we have helpers.
Do: Thank God for helpers.

The children will accomplish the goals when they:

1. Say the Bible words, "God is good."
2. Sing about people who are their helpers.
3. Point to or name some helpers and what they do.
4. Pray, "Thank You, God, for my helpers."

Let's Get Ready

For the Bible story you will need a small potted plant or bush and red tissue paper, crumpled up and placed in the bush to look like a flame. Attach tissue with a rubber band or tape.

Set up the Book/Picture Center, the Art Center, and the Block Center. If you are teaching alone, use either the Book and Picture Center or the Block Center. Use the Music/Drama Center after the lesson.

Learning Activities

(30 minutes, including 10 minutes presession)

Let's Get Started

Have the "burning bush" on display where the children will see it when they arrive. Have Zach say, "Look at this bush, Hannah. It looks like it's on fire. We're going to hear a story about a man named Moses and a burning bush. I can't wait to hear the story!" Make sure each child becomes involved in one of the activities.

Worship and Bible Story

(15 minutes)

Let's Worship God

Have Zach tell the children it's time to sit in the circle. Then begin to sing "God Is Good." **Those are our Bible words.** Let children take turns holding the Bible and "reading" the words.

God is so good to us! He gives us families and friends to love us and help us. He also gives us helpers. Today let's thank God for helpers. Use the action rhyme, "When I Pray." Then pray, **Thank You, God, for all the helpers You give us.** Sing this helpers song to the tune, "Mary Had a Little Lamb."

God made all my helpers, helpers, helpers.
God made all my helpers.
Thank You, God, for helpers.

Then sing the song inserting helpers the children name, making up actions for each. For example: firefighter (holding a hose and spraying it), a teacher (holding an open book), a mail carrier (putting a letter in a mailbox), a preacher (bowing head and folding hands to pray), and so forth.

Let's Learn From the Bible

Introduction: Zach, have you ever seen a fire? Zach responds, "Yes, I saw one in the fireplace once." **Boys and girls, have you ever seen a fire? What did it look like? Were the logs burning up and changing? Our Bible story is about a person named Moses who saw a special kind of fire.**

Boys and girls, you will need to listen and watch me very carefully. I want you to help me tell this story. When I say the name *Moses,* I want you to repeat it. Do so. **When I say "fire," you say, "Hot!" When I say "shoes," point to your feet. When you hear the word *sheep,* you baa-a-a like a sheep. Can you do all this? Let's practice.** Demonstrate all the words/actions for the children. Let them practice. Do this several times if necessary. Put Zach away; have your Bible nearby.

The Bible Story: Moses was a shepherd who took care of his family's sheep. One day when he was out in the field, he saw *(put hand up as though shading your eyes)* a bush like this one. *(Put bush out so the children can see it.)* But there was something different about the bush. It was on fire, but it wasn't burning up! *(Pull hands away from "heat.")* Do you see the pretend fire in this bush? Is this bush burning up? No!

As Moses got closer to the bush, he heard a voice *(cup hand behind ear)*. It was God calling him. God told Moses to take off his shoes and listen to Him. God said, "Moses, I want you to be my helper. My people who live in the land of Egypt are being hurt

Learning Activities

(20 minutes)

Let's Play Awhile

At the Art Center, show a copy of the review activity page. **Look at this page. On one side we have pictures and on the other side we have spaces where we are going to put our stickers. In this first picture I see a tree and flowers. It must be a garden. Who lived in a garden like this? Adam and Eve! Find the sticker with the first family on it and put it across from the garden.**

What do you see in this next picture? Lots of sheep and tents. They look very crowded. What are the names of the men who were crowded? Abram and Lot! Was Abram a good friend? What did he do? Yes, he let Lot take first pick of the land. Let's find the sticker of Abram letting Lot choose his land.

What is in this last picture? A burning bush. Who spoke to Moses out of a burning bush? God did! What did Moses do? Yes, he became a good helper. Let's find the sticker of Moses listening to God.

As children finish, let them go to one of the centers used earlier. If your class is large and you have several teachers, have these centers open while a small group of children uses the Art Center, then let children trade places when the first group finishes the art project.

Let's Go Home

Zach says, "It is almost time to go. Let's be good helpers and pick up our toys." After the children have picked up, gather them in a circle. Choose one child to stand in the middle while the others march around him. Sing the song from the Lesson 7 Music Center, inserting the name of the child in the middle. "Billy is our friend; yes, Billy is our friend. Thank You, God, for all our friends, etc." Repeat, allowing each child to have a turn standing in the middle of the circle.

Send the review activity page home with each child.

Thank God for the People I Know

Review of Lessons 6–8

Bible Words: "God is good" (Psalm 73:1, *NIV*).

Lesson Value: To review the lessons learned the past three weeks, and to reinforce the concept that God created all people.

Know: Know that God gives us families, friends, and helpers.
Feel: Feel happy because we have families, friends, and helpers.
Do: Thank God for families, friends, and helpers.

The children will accomplish the goals when they:

1. Say the Bible words, "God is good."
2. Pray for families, friends, and helpers.
3. Sing about people who are their families, friends, and helpers.
4. Name family members, friends, and helpers.
5. Point to or name Bible people or tell what they did.

Let's Get Ready

For the review lesson, gather the following aids: the stand-up Bible figures from Lesson 6; the "tent" used in Lesson 7 (or use the activity sheet visual aid from Lesson 7); the helpers' equipment and the "burning bush" from Lesson 8.

Prepare the Family Living Center, the Block Center, and the Book/Picture Center. If you are the only teacher, use just the Book/Picture Center. Have copies of the review activity page (61) and the stickers ready in the Art Center to be used after the Bible story.

Learning Activities

(30 minutes, including 10 minutes presession)

Let's Get Started

Have Zach greet each child personally. "Here's my friend David, etc." Make sure each child gets involved in an activity. As you talk to the children, remind them of the past Bible stories. **Joey, I see you are in the tent like Abram and Lot lived in. Is it crowded in there? . . . Katie, you are playing with the first family. Do you remember the mommy's name?**

Worship and Bible Story

(15 minutes)

Let's Worship God

Let's all sit in our circle and sing. Who remembers the song with our Bible words in it? Sing "God Is Good." Sing several stanzas of "God Gives Us Families," using various family members, friends, and helpers. Then do the rhyme, "When I Pray," and pray, **Thank You, God, for giving us families who care for us, friends to love us, and people to help us.**

Let's Learn From the Bible

Introduction: Hold up Zach. **Well, hello Zach!** Zach responds, "Hello!" **We've learned that "God is good," and that He gives us families, friends, and helpers. Let's tell Zach our Bible words together** Do so. Put Zach away after the children say the Bible words. Have your Bible and visual aids ready.

The Bible-story Review: *(Hold up the stand-up figures of the first family.)* Which one is the daddy? What was his name? *(Let a child hold each figure as it is named.)* Who made this family? God did! He gives us families too.

Who lived in a crowded tent like this one? *(Point to "tent" or the picture from Lesson 7.)* Yes, Abram and Lot did! Who showed he was a good friend by allowing Lot to choose first? Yes, Abram. God gives us friends too.

(Point to the "burning bush.") Who saw a burning bush? *(Children answer.)* Who spoke to Moses out of a burning bush? God did! What did He want Moses to do? Be His helper! Who are some of the helpers God gives us? *(If the children have trouble responding, give them hints such as, "I can think of one helper who makes sure we are well. What helper is that?")*

Let's Apply the Lesson

Who can point to the first family God made? Has God given us families? Yes He has! Let children name their family members. Sing "Adam and Eve," and then do the rhyme, "God Made Families."

Who can tell me the name of the Bible person who was a good friend? Abram. Very good! Does God gives us friends? Yes, He does! Children name some friends. Sing "God Gives Us Families," using "all our friends" in place of "families."

Who became a helper for God? Yes, Moses. Does God give us helpers? Yes, He does! Children name helpers. Sing the "Helpers Song."

Family Living Center

Unit 2—God Makes People

Items to Include:

Loose dress-up clothes, such as aprons, large shirts, skirts, hats, shoes
Dolls
Blankets
Doll clothes
Play dishes
If your area is small or you are the only teacher, have all these materials packed in a large suitcase, ready to open and use.

Purpose: The child will learn through dramatic play that God gives us families, friends, and helpers.

Things to Do and Say

Lesson 6

As children dress up, encourage them to pretend to be a family. **When God made the first family, He made a mommy, a daddy, and two little boys, brothers. I'm glad God made families. . . . God gives us families to take care of us. Sara, I see you are taking care of your baby like a good mommy does. Adam, are you pretending to be the daddy just like the Adam who was the daddy in the first family? . . . "God is good." He gives us families who love us. Thank You, God, for families.**

Lesson 7

Have a small folding table covered with a blanket to use as a tent. Inside this, have small blankets and pillows, and stuffed animals such as sheep and cows.

Encourage children to play like they are Abram and Lot. **My, it's crowded in this tent! Listen to the animal noises outside. There are so many sheep and cows out there. I don't think there is enough grass for all of them. What are we going to do?** Let children make suggestions. **In our Bible story we will learn how Abram was a good friend to Lot. . . . "God is good." He gives us friends to play with, friends to help us do things, and friends we can share with. I'm glad God has given us so many friends!**

Block Center

Unit 2—God Makes People

Items to Include:

Large wooden or cardboard blocks of various shapes and sizes
Toy airplanes, trucks, cars, etc.
Multiple sets of family figures using the patterns and directions on pages 57 and 58.

Purpose: The child will know that God gives us families, friends, and helpers.

Things to Do and Say

Lesson 6

Encourage the children to build houses for the "families." As the children build say, **Our Bible tells us "God is good." He gives us families to love us. I'm glad He made our families. . . . That's a good house you have built, Andy. Who lives in your house? The mommy and two children? That's just like your family. Thank You, God, for Andy's family.**

Lesson 7

Spread out the blocks, vehicles, and family figures, ready for some creative block play. Allow the children to use the toys any way they please. As they build and play, talk about friends and point out any acts of friendship you observe among the children.

It's fun to play with our friends. I'm glad God has given us so many friends. "God is good." Those are our Bible words, aren't they. Thank you for sharing some blocks with me, Christina. You are a friend! . . . Daniel and Stephen are building a house together. They are being good friends! Our Bible story is about two friends, Abram and Lot. I'll tell you about them later.

Family Living Center, continued

Lesson 9

Use dolls and equipment for creative play. Talk about families, friends, and helpers as children play. Have stand-up figures from Lesson 6 here.

Block Center, continued

Lesson 8

Help the children build any kind of structures they want. **In our Bible story, a king was making the Hebrew people work hard to build very tall buildings. God sent a helper named Moses to help His people. . . . Can you build a tall building? Can you build a wide building? Can you build a place where we see helpers today? Is that the grocery store? There are lots of helpers there. I see a road that could lead to the post office! Post office people help us get letters.**

Lesson 9

Let the children play with the materials used previously. Use conversation about families, friends, and helpers.

Book/Picture Center

Unit 2—God Makes People

Items to Include:

- The classroom Bible
- Appropriate books (see page 39)
- Pictures of families /friends/helpers cut from magazines, catalogs, and newspapers
- Also display small framed pictures of your family members, friends, helpers, etc.

Purpose: The child will know that God made all people and will feel glad about this.

Things to Do and Say

Lesson 6

Show the children family pictures and/or books and say something like this: **When God made the first family, He made a daddy, a mommy, and two boys. I'm glad God made families. . . . The Bible tells us, "God is good." I'm glad He has given us families. Who do you think is the mommy in this picture? What other family member do you see? . . . Who is in your family, Ashley? Thank You, God, for Ashley's mommy, daddy, and big brother.**

Lesson 8

Enlarge the page of "helper" equipment (pages 53-55). Let the children tell you what helper uses the hose, the stethoscope, and so forth. If you want, put each piece of equipment on a separate page. Use these like flash cards and play a game with the children. When a child guesses correctly, he holds the card until all have been guessed. Then play again.

"God is good." He gives us helpers who take care of us. Thank You, God, for the policeman who keeps us safe. Say something like this for each helper.

Music/Drama Center

Unit 2—God Makes People

Items to Include:

Lesson 7
- Large soft ball, large space to spread out, and lots of enthusiasm!

Lesson 8
- Helper equipment
- Bible

Purpose: The child will express happy feelings about the people God made.

Things to Do and Say

Lesson 7

Instruct the children to sit on the floor in a large circle. Roll the ball to a child while singing these words to the tune of "Farmer in the Dell."

Michael is our friend; yes, Michael is our friend.
Thank You, God, for all our friends; yes, Michael is our friend.

Ask Michael to roll the ball back to you. Repeat this process until you have rolled the ball to each child in the group. Encourage the children to sing with you.

Lesson 8

Have an addressed envelope with a stamp on it, and a mailbag with a sign on it that says "Mail" (an old purse with a long strap, a grocery bag with a rope handle, a shopping bag, or a canvas bag). Also have a large Bible, a toy stethoscope or thermometer, and any other "helper" items.

There are many kinds of helpers. Let's sing a song about them. Teach the children the "Helpers Song," from page 40. After singing the song once, add the props by asking children to identify each and who uses it. Let the children take turns holding up an item

Book/Picture Center, continued

Lesson 9

Have books from previous lessons. Include pictures of families, friends, and helpers. Look at pictures and books and have children point out helpers and tell how they help, etc. You might want to have the books and pictures inside the tent from Lesson 7.

Music/Drama Center, continued

when the helper is mentioned. Then repeat the song and add marching. Switch the props so that every child has a turn to hold one during the song.

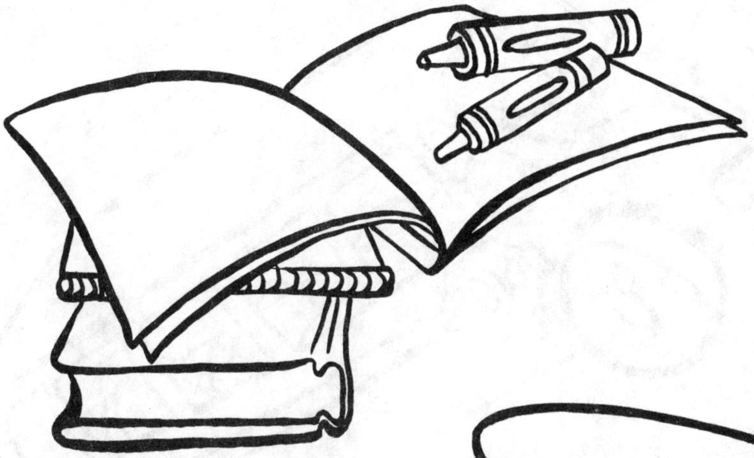

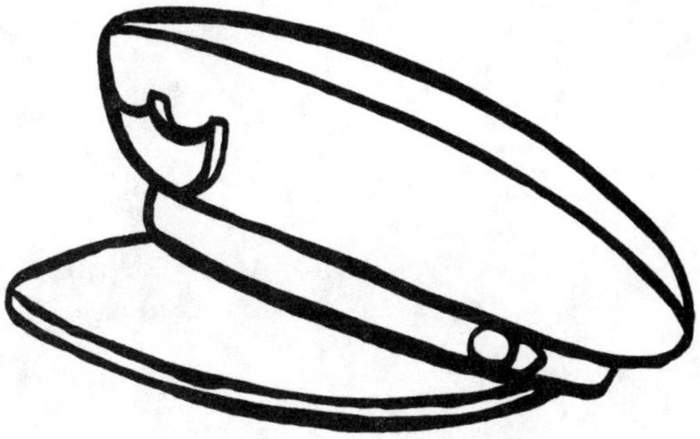

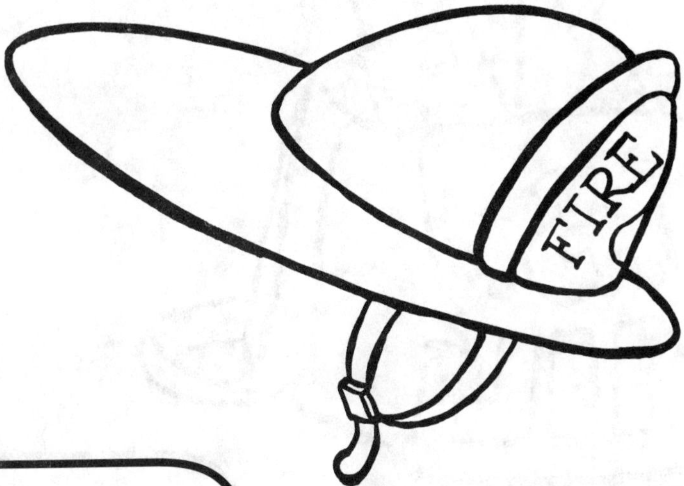

Art Center

Unit 2—God Makes People

Items to Include:

Lesson 6
Foam sponges
Family patterns (pages 57 and 58)
Tempera paint
Thick paper for painting
Shallow dishes for paint

Lesson 7
Copies of page 60
Sheep stickers
Cotton, cloth, and glue (optional)

Purpose: The child will learn that God made all people.

Things to Do and Say

Lesson 6

Trace family shapes onto enough sponges for each child to have at least one to work with. Pour in just enough paint to cover the bottoms of the dishes. Show the children how to paint with the sponges.

Talk about families. **I'm glad God made families. I see a daddy and a mommy in your picture, Eric. Where is the child like you?** Move paintings to a place where they can dry undisturbed.

If you will not have time for this activity in class, photocopy the family figures from pages 57 or 58 arranged on a sheet of 8 1/2" x 11" paper and send one home with each child to be colored during the week.

Lesson 7

Have a copy of page 60 for each child. Make multiple copies of the sheep. Prepare them to be stickers. Also have cloth, cotton balls, and glue available (optional).

Let the children color the backgrounds if there is time. Give each child one sheep at a time. After the sheep are in place, children may add small amounts of cotton to the sheep and pieces of cloth to the tents.

Look at how much room Lot's sheep have. How did that happen? Yes, Abram let

Lot choose a good place for his sheep and tent. Abram was a good friend, wasn't he? "God is good." He gave Lot a good friend—Abram. And he gives us friends too.

Lesson 8
Construction paper
Stickers (pages 53-55)

Lesson 8

Cut 9" x 12" construction paper in half, then fold each piece to make a four-page booklet, 4 1/2" x 6". On the front of each, print "God gives us helpers." Make multiple copies of helping equipment on pages 53-55 and prepare them for stickers. The children will add these inside and on the backs of their "books." Talk about the helpers as the children add their stickers, then thank God for each helper when the booklets are complete.

Lesson 9
Copies of page 61
Stickers

Lesson 9

Use this activity as a review of the previous lessons. Give each child a copy of the review stickers. Let the children color the stickers. While a teacher cuts out the stickers, the children can color page 61. Help the children decide where each sticker goes. Use the conversation from the lesson plan.

For all lessons
Paper towels or wet cloth
Newspaper to cover tables
Wet sponges for stickers
Paint smocks for painting

Stickers for page 61—Autumn, Unit 2

Stickers for page 60—Autumn, Unit 2

How to Make Stickers

Brush a thin coat of the following mixture onto the backs of the stickers and let dry. To adhere, simply lick!

Mixture:
- one part vinegar
- two parts white glue
- a few drops of peppermint extract (or any other flavor)

Helper Equipment—Autumn, Unit 2

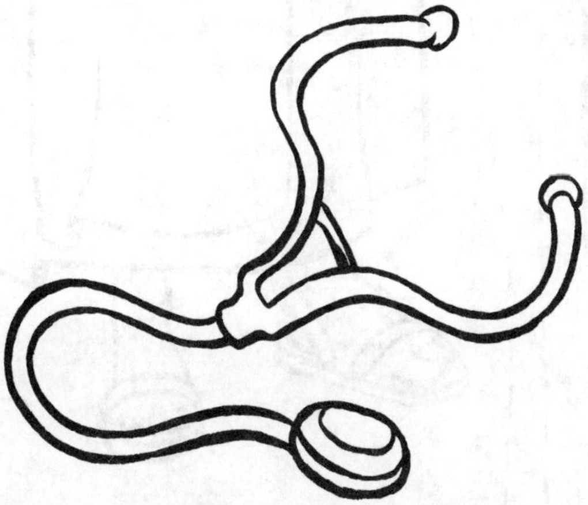

Patterns—Autumn, Unit 2

Use patterns after the Bible story.

Instructions

1. Photocopy figures onto heavy paper. Enlarge if you want larger visuals.
2. Color figures with crayons or markers.
3. Cut out figures and mount on cardboard.
4. Cover figures with clear, self-adhesive plastic for durability (optional).
5. Make cardboard stands as shown; glue one on the back of each figure.

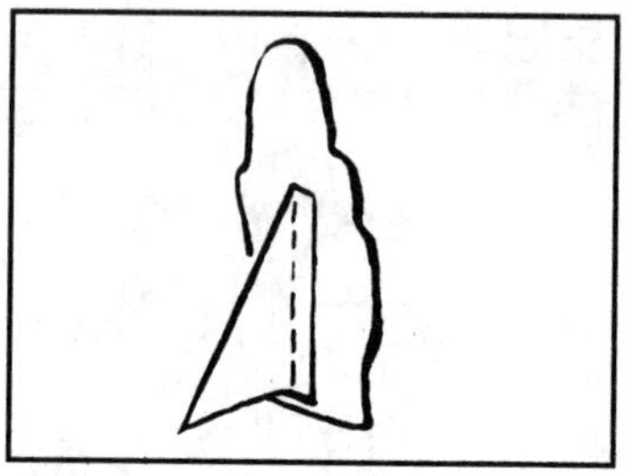

Figures—Autumn, Unit 2

Instructions

1. To use in the Block Center, photocopy family figures from this page or page 58, as many as you need. Add color, cut around figures, and mount on cardboard. Make cardboard stands as shown on page 56.
2. To use in the Art Center for lesson 6, trace outlines of figures and use to cut sponges in "family" shapes. See the Art Center card for how to use.

Teaching/Coloring Picture—Autumn, Unit 2

Instructions for pages 59 and 60

1. Photocopy pages 59 and 60. Copy back-to-back if possible. If not, copy each and glue pages together, back-to-back.
2. Color both pictures.

Abram and his friend, Lot, had many sheep and cattle. They were very crowded. Abram let Lot have first choice of the land. Abram was a good friend to Lot. Thank You, God, for friends.

Review Activity—Autumn, Unit 2

When God made the world, He made families, friends, and helpers.

Thank You, God, for families.

Thank You, God, for friends.

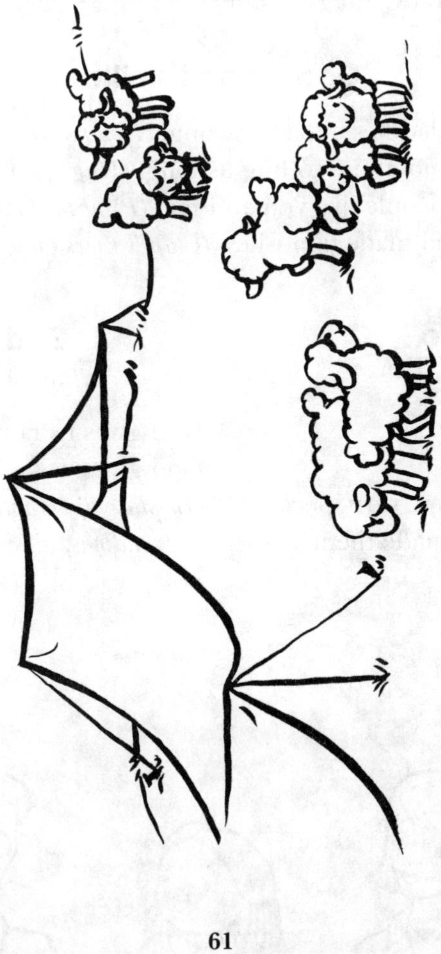

Thank You, God, for helpers.

Dear Parent,

I am excited to have your child as a part of our class! We will be having the following lessons:
God Makes Families (Genesis 2:18-22; 4:1, 2)
God Makes Friends (Genesis 13:1-12)
God Makes Helpers (Exodus 3; 4:1-18)
Thank God for the People I Know (Review of Lessons 6–8)

In these lessons, your child will be learning that God gives families, friends, and helpers, and that all are special to Him. Your child will feel glad that God gives families, friends, and helpers, and will thank God for those family members, friends, and helpers he or she knows.

Here are some ways to reinforce these lessons at home.

- Practice saying the Bible words, "God is good," with your child.
- Look at and read books about families.
- As you read or color with your child, ask her to identify the family members in the story/picture.
- Show your child pictures of family members/friends the child knows and remind her that God made all people.
- Encourage your child to draw pictures of family, friends, and helpers, and remind her that these people are special to God, just as they are special to your child.
- Away from home, take time to point out helpers to the child and talk about ways they help us. (For example: police officers, postal workers, grocery store staff, etc.)
- Help your child word prayers thanking God for family members the first week, friends the second week, and helpers the third week. Thank God for all these people the last week.
- Use this action rhyme and these songs at home.

God Made Families

God made daddies big and strong. *(Flex muscles.)*
God made mommies to hug us long. *(Hug yourself.)*
God made people like you and me. *(Point to child, then to self.)*
I'm glad God made fam-i-lies. *(Clap 3 times on fam-i-lies.)*

Adam and Eve

(Tune: "Are You Sleeping?")

Adam and Eve, Adam and Eve,
Had two sons, had two sons.
They were very special. They were very special.
'Cause God made them; God made them.

God Gives Us Families

(Tune: "Mary Had a Little Lamb")

God gives us families, families, families.
God gives us families. Thank You, God, for them.
(In place of "families," use mommies, daddies, sisters, grandmas, all our friends, etc.)

Your child's teacher,

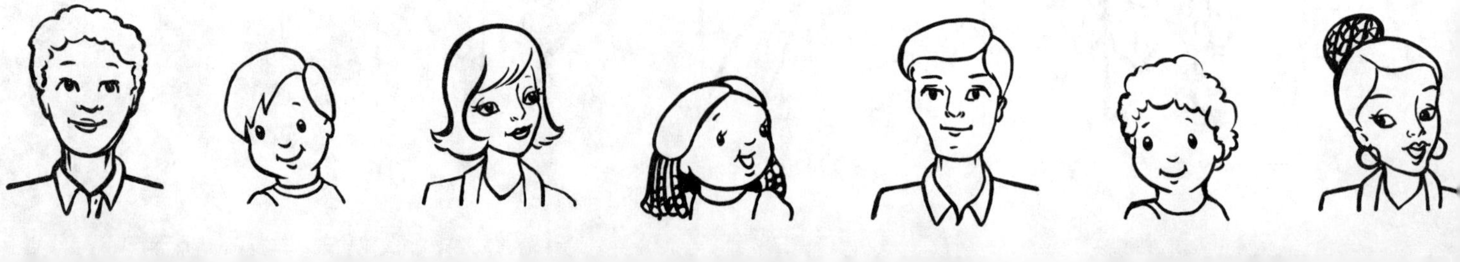

Unit 3: God Cares for Me

Lessons 10–13

By the end of the unit, the children will

Know that God takes care of me all the time.
Feel happy for God's care.
Thank God for His care.

Unit Bible Words:

"He cares for you" (1 Peter 5:7, *NIV*).

Books

from Standard Publishing
God Cares for Me (24-03112)
Now the Day Is Over (24-03146)
God Is With Me (24-04229)

This Unit at a Glance

10 God Cares All the Time — **Exodus 6:2-8; 12:31-38; 13:17-22**

God guides the Israelites through the wilderness with a pillar of cloud by day and a pillar of fire by night, illustrating God's constant care.

11 God Cares Wherever We Live — **Genesis 6:8-10, 14-22; 7; 8:1-20**

Noah spends a year living on the ark. This story will help your children understand that God cares for us wherever we live.

12 God Cares Wherever We Go — **Genesis 28:10-17**

Jacob encounters God in a dream while traveling. God cares for us, as He did Jacob, no matter where we go.

13 Thank God for His Care — **Review of Lessons 10–12**

Reviewing the first three stories in this unit about God's loving care will provide the opportunity to reinforce the idea that we should be grateful to God for His constant care.

Why Teach This Unit?

Each Bible story in Unit 3 illustrates an aspect of God's care. Day or night, at home or away—the circumstances do not matter—God cares for us. You can share this reassuring fact with the young children in your class. We teach young children about God's care by showing them tangible examples. Through song, movement, art, and play, children will see the many ways God cares for us.

God's care is closely tied to His love for us. His love and care do not, however, prevent trials and troubles in our lives. Be careful not to give the children the impression that knowing God means life will always be easy. God promises to sustain us through difficult times, not to prevent them. It is important that we begin to teach biblical truths to these young children and not create stumbling blocks in their continuing faith development.

Use every opportunity to try to explain the depth of God's love to the children. After completing this unit, children should know there is nothing that can separate them from God's loving care.

Repeat the Bible words at every opportunity. Incorporate them into your conversation with the children, during the Bible story, while they are playing at the learning centers, and in prayers. Make sure the children understand that the word *He* refers to God. For example, **I like to work in the garden. Picking these tomatoes reminds me that God cares for us. The Bible says, "He cares for you." God cares for you, Eric. He cares for you, Renee, and He cares for me.**

Things to Do for This Unit

- Make copies of the Parents' Letter (page 86) and the Unit Planning Sheet (pages 319 and 320).
- Photocopy Learning Center Cards from pages 73-78. Cut pages apart on heavy lines. Mount side 1 on cardboard, then side 2 on the back of the cardboard. Cover with clear, self-adhesive plastic to make cards more durable. Place these in the learning centers during class.
- Prepare materials listed on the Learning Center Cards.
- For Lesson 10, make a visual using page 79. Find a basket for each child or use paper grocery bags.
- For Lesson 11, locate several toy and model houses or pictures of various living accommodations. Learn the song, "Noah." Find a simple picture book of animals.
- For Lesson 12, purchase a mini gift-wrap bag. Put the following items in a paper grocery bag: sandal, large rock, angel Christmas ornament or picture of an angel. Learn the new words for "God Is Good."

Use These Songs and Action Rhymes During Unit 3

God Cares for Me

(Tune: "He's Got the Whole World in His Hands")

God cares for me* all the time**.
God cares for me all the time.
God cares for me all the time.
Thank You, God. You care for me.
**Insert names of children.*
***Wherever I live, wherever I go, etc.*

God Is Near

God is near when the sun shines bright.
(Raise arms above head to form sun.)
God takes care of me all through the night.
(Rest cheek against hands.)
God is with me when I play.
(Pretend to push toy truck or rock doll.)
God is with me every day! *(Clap hands.)*
—Mildred Merkel

Noah

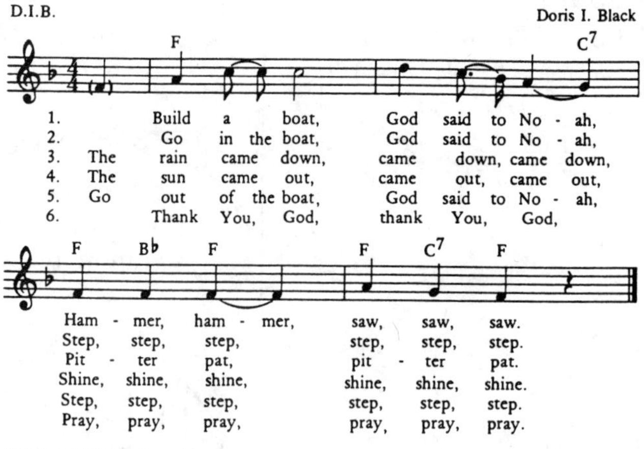

God Is Good

(Tune: "God Is So Good")

God is good. God is good.
God is good. God is good to me.

He cares for you (us, me) . . .
God is good to you (us, me).

good care of His people all day and all night. God will take care of you too.

Let's Apply the Lesson

This story was about a special time God took care of His people. The Bible says, "He cares for you." Let the children take turns "reading" the words from the Bible. **God cared for His people by sending something to show them which way they should go. What did God send?** *(A pillar of cloud and fire.)* **God cared for His people day and night.** Encourage the children to share ways God cares for them. Ask, **How does God care for you in the daytime, Jeremy?** *(He gives me food, home, parents, etc.)* **Amy, how does God care for you at night?** *(He keeps me safe, helps me not to be afraid, etc.)*

Learning Activities

(20 minutes)

Let's Play Awhile

Sing "God Is Good." Make up additional verses and add actions to the words. For example, "God sends us rain. . . . God is good to us." Flutter fingers to represent falling rain. Introduce the action rhyme, "God Is Near," from page 64.

Have the art supplies ready to make the day-and-night pictures. Talk about the way God cares for each child, day and night. If there is more than one teacher you can invite children to go to the learning centers of their choice. Make sure that each child has an opportunity to make a picture.

Let's Go Home

If there is time, play the Bible-words game from the Game Center. Or, have Zach lead the children in saying the Bible words. Suggest that the children say the verse for their parents as they arrive. Make sure that each child has his day-and-night picture and a copy of this month's Parents' Letter.

Lesson 10
Date: ____________

God Cares All the Time

Exodus 6:2-8; 12:31-38; 13:17-22

Bible Words: "He cares for you" (1 Peter 5:7, *NIV*).

Lesson Value: Children will begin to understand that it doesn't matter what time it is, day or night, we are in God's care. The story of God's guiding the Israelites away from Egypt with a pillar of cloud and a pillar of fire is used as an example of God's constant care, day and night.

Know: Know that God takes care of us day and night.
Feel: Feel happy for God's care.
Do: Thank God for His care.

Children will accomplish the goals when they:

1. Answer the question, "Who cares for you?"
2. Say the Bible words, "He cares for you."
3. Name ways God cares for us.
4. Act out ways God cares for us.
5. Pray, "Thank You, God, for caring for us day and night."

Let's Get Ready

For the Bible story, you will need your classroom Bible with the new Bible words highlighted, the pillar of cloud/fire visual, dolls, and the baskets/bags from the Music/Drama Center.

Set up the Family Living Center, the Music/Drama Center, and the Game Center. If only one teacher is available today, use just the Music/Drama Center. The Art Center will be used after the Bible story.

Learning Activities

(30 minutes, including 10 minutes presession)

Let's Get Started

Let Zach greet each child, help with wraps and the attendance sticker, and offer each child a choice of activities. "Ryan, would you like to play house in the Family Living Center or play a game in the Music/Drama Center?" Direct an indecisive child to the activity that has the smallest number of children. **Rachel, I think you'd like to play a game.**

Worship and Bible Story

(15 minutes)

Let's Worship God

Have Zach invite children to join you for some singing. Begin by singing "God Cares for Me" as soon as the first child arrives. Let another adult help stragglers finish picking up and find their way to the group. Repeat the song, using each child's name in place of the word *me.*

Let's talk to God. Explain and demonstrate the posture you'd like the children to take. Two's may not do this readily. **Thank You, God, for caring for us day and night.**

Zach asks, "When you prayed, did you say God cares for us?" **Yes, Zach, we did. What a good listener you are!** Zach asks, "How do you know God cares for you?" **The Bible tells us that, and everything in the Bible is true.** Show the Bible words. Whisper to the boys and girls, **Let's tell Zach these words from the Bible. "He cares for you."** Encourage all the children to repeat the words. **Zach, can you say those words?** Zach responds, "I'll try. He, uhm, He . . . what's the next word?" Have the children help Zach learn the words.

Have Zach say, "The Bible words say, 'He cares for you,' but who is *He?*" Let the children tell Zach that "He" means "God." **God cares for you.** Put Zach away.

Let's Learn From the Bible

Introduction: Hold up the pillar of cloud and fire. **What does this look like?** Accept all responses. **This side is a cloud.** Turn over the visual. **This side is a fire. Let me tell you how God used these two things to show His people where to go.**

The Bible Story: There was a time when God's people were in Egypt. The king of Egypt made the people work very, very hard. They could not leave Egypt. Perhaps they prayed, "Help us, God, help us!"

God heard His people. He sent a man named Moses to help. Moses talked to the king and asked him to let God's people go. At first, the king said, "No!" But finally, he changed his mind.

All of God's people hurried to pack their belongings. When the people left Egypt, God led them in the daytime with a big cloud. All day the cloud moved and the people followed. They didn't have cars or vans. They didn't even have wagons. So they had to carry their belongings as they walked. *(Hand out the bags and baskets used earlier. Also, use dolls so that everyone has something to carry. Lead the children around the room with the cloud facing them.)*

When it got dark, God sent fire to light the night and show the people which way to walk. *(Lead the children around the room with the fire facing them. Dim the lights, but do not risk frightening a young child by making the room dark.)* When the pillar stopped, the people stopped to eat and to sleep. *(Pretend to do so.)* God took

Encourage the children to tell you where they live. **Sarah, where do you live? . . . What color is your house? . . . Is it a big apartment building?** It really doesn't matter whether or not the children's responses are accurate. **Does God care for those who live in apartment buildings? Yes! Does He care for those who live in mobile homes? Yes! What about those who live in tents? Yes! No matter where you live, "God cares for you."**

Learning Activities

(20 minutes)

Let's Play Awhile

Sing "Noah" again, using appropriate movements. Ask the children, **Did God care for Noah when he was on the ark-boat? Did God care for Noah when he had a house? Does it matter to God where you live?** *(Wait for children's replies.)* **It doesn't matter to God what kind of house you have or where you live, He cares for you!**

Let Zach direct the children to the God's Wonders Center. If you prefer not to use water, use blocks to build the outline of a boat. Have various stuffed animals for the children to bring in the ark-boat. Pretend to listen to the rain; talk about God's care as you sit in the ark-boat. Then announce that the water is all gone and it's time to leave the ark-boat. Thank God for His care.

Let's Go Home

While waiting for parents, look at a picture book of animals. Ask the children what sound each animal makes and how the animal moves. Pretend to be some of the animals Noah took on board the ark-boat. **Noah brought cows on the ark-boat. Let's pretend to be cows and climb into the big boat.** Use chairs or blocks to make the outline of a boat. Pretend to be various animals and move onto the ark-boat as those animals would—hop like a bunny, plod like an elephant, fly like a bird, and so forth.

Make sure the children have their paper bags with their ark-boats and animal crackers inside to take home.

God Cares Wherever We Live

Genesis 6:8-10, 14-22; 7; 8:1-20

Bible Words: "He cares for you" (1 Peter 5:7, *NIV*).

Lesson Value: The story of Noah is often used to teach the concept of obeying God. Noah was indeed a righteous man who followed God's instructions. For this unit, the familiar story will be used to illustrate one aspect of God's care. It makes no difference to God where we live, He still cares for us. Noah certainly had unusual living arrangements while aboard the ark, but where he lived made no impact on God's love and concern. Last week the children learned that God cares for us both night and day; now they will learn that where we live is irrelevant to Him.

Know: Know that God takes care of us wherever we live.
Feel: Feel happy for God's care.
Do: Thank God for His care.

Children will accomplish the goals when they:

1. Answer the question, "Who cares for you?"
2. Say the Bible words, "He cares for you."
3. Sing about God's care.
4. Pray, "Thank You, God, for caring for us wherever we live."

Let's Get Ready

For the Bible story, locate several toy and/or model houses or pictures of various living accommodations.

Set up the Game Center, the Art Center, and the Family Living Center. If there is only one teacher, use the Family Living Center. Have the God's Wonders Center materials ready to use after the Bible story.

Learning Activities

(30 minutes, including 10 minutes presession)

Let's Get Started

Greet each child by name. Have Zach tell which centers are available. "Hi, Megan. I'm glad to see you. Come in and see what we're going to do. You can work in a garden or you can march animal crackers onto an ark. Or, if you liked the ball-rolling game from last week, you can go to the Game Center."

Worship and Bible Story

(15 minutes)

Let's Worship God

Have Zach say, "Teacher, I remember the Bible words from last week." **Zach, that's great! Whisper them to me.** Hold the puppet to your ear and move its mouth. **That's right, Zach! Tell the boys and girls the Bible words.** "The Bible says, 'He cares for you.'" **Everyone say the Bible words with Zach.** Repeat the verse several times for the benefit of newcomers.

Introduce the song, "Noah," found on page 64. Sing it several times. Sing "God Cares for Me" and "God Is Good." Then pray, **Thank You, God, for caring for us wherever we live.** Let the children stand and do the action rhyme, "God Is Near."

Let's Learn From the Bible

Before you begin the story, have Zach demonstrate the actions/sounds you want the children to do as you tell the story. "Boys and girls, you are going to help with the story. Let's practice what you have to do. First, chop down a tree." *(Show chopping motion.)* "Now, pretend to drag something heavy." *(Do so.)* "Let's saw wood; now hammer." *(Do these.)* "Now, load the food." *(Move object from left to right.)* "Get on board!" *(Move feet in place.)* "Shut the door." *(One loud clap.)* "Rain." *(Pat thighs slowly and lightly, increasing speed and volume to indicate heavy rain.)* "Pray." *(Fold hands; look up.)* "Very good! Now you are ready. Listen and watch carefully!"

Introduction: People live in all kinds of houses. Show models or pictures of various houses. **Our Bible story is about a family who lived on a very big boat for a long time. This boat was called an ark. We'll call it an ark-boat.**

The Bible Story: Noah was a good man. One day, God told Noah to build a very big ark-boat for his family and for two of every kind of animal in the world!

First, Noah cut down trees. *(Chop.)* Then he hauled the trees to the place he was building the ark. *(Drag something heavy.)* Next, the trees were cut into boards *(saw)* and hammered into place *(hammer)*.

After Noah finished the ark-boat, he loaded it with food *(load)*. Then he and his family and all the animals climbed on board. *(Pretend to walk.)* The door was shut *(clap)* and it began to rain *(pat thighs)*. It rained until the whole earth was covered with water, but Noah and his family were safe inside the ark-boat. For a year they lived on the ark-boat.

When the water went away, Noah came out of the ark-boat. Noah and his family said, "Thank You, God, for taking care of us on the ark-boat."*(Pray.)* It didn't matter where Noah and his family lived, whether it was on the ark-boat or on dry ground, God cared for them.

Let's Apply the Lesson

Ask, **Where did Noah live for a year?** *(On the ark-boat.)* **Who cared for Noah?** *(God.)* **Who cares for you?** *(God.)* **Does it matter where you live?** *(No.)* **God cares for you no matter where you live.**

Zach should ask, "Will God care for me on my trip?" **Yes, Zach, God will care for you wherever you go. Boys and girls, tell Zach our Bible words.** Encourage the children to say, "He cares for you."

Learning Activities

(20 minutes)

Let's Play Awhile

Let's act out the story of Jacob. Everyone stand. First, Jacob went on a long trip. Walk in place. **At night, Jacob was tired from walking so he sat on the ground.** Sit on the floor. **He stretched and yawned** (stretch and yawn) **and looked for something to use as a pillow.** Hold one hand over your eyebrows and look about. **Jacob found a smooth stone and used that for his pillow.** Lift an imaginary rock into place. **Jacob lay down and fell asleep.** Pretend to sleep. **In his dream Jacob saw angels climbing stairs. Jacob heard God say, "I will care for you wherever you go." Wherever we go, God is with us because He cares for us. Who cares for you wherever you go? Yes, God does.**

Direct children to the Art Center. Give each child the stickers to color first. Use conversation suggestions from the Learning Center Card. If yours is a large class with multiple teachers, also use the learning centers from earlier in the lesson.

Let's Go Home

Have Zach talk with the children about the Bible words for this unit. Ask Zach, **Do you think you can say the Bible words all by yourself?** "I'll try." Have Zach correctly repeat the Bible words. Ask the children if Zach's attempt is correct; then have them say the words with him. Lead the children in singing the words, "He cares for you," to the tune of "God Is So Good."

God Cares Wherever We Go

Genesis 28:10-17

Bible Words: "He cares for you" (1 Peter 5:7, *NIV*).

Lesson Value: In this lesson, children will be introduced to a third aspect of God's care. It doesn't matter where you go, God's care is constant. The focus of this lesson is not Jacob's dream but rather his travels. The dream demonstrates that even when Jacob left his home and traveled to a new land, God cared for him. Help children to understand that wherever they go, God goes with them. He is always with them and He cares for them.

Know: Know that God takes care of us wherever we go.
Feel: Feel happy for God's care.
Do: Thank God for His care.

Children will accomplish the goals when they:

1. Answer the question, "Who cares for you wherever you go?"
2. Say the Bible words, "He cares for you."
3. Sing about God's care.
4. Act out ways God cares for us.
5. Pray, "Thank You, God, for caring for us wherever we go."

Let's Get Ready

For the Bible story, put the following items in a paper grocery bag: sandal, large rock, angel Christmas ornament or picture of an angel. Also have your classroom Bible.

Set up the Music/Drama Center, the God's Wonder Center, and the Family Living Center. If there is only one teacher, use the Music/Drama Center. The Art Center will be used after the Bible story.

Learning Activities

(30 minutes, including 10 minutes presession)

Let's Get Started

Purchase or find a mini gift-wrap bag with handles. Have Zach hold the bag. As children arrive, draw their attention to the bag. **Stephanie, why do you suppose Zach has this bag?** Ask Zach, **Why are you carrying this bag, Zach?** Zach says, "I'm going on a trip. Our Bible story is about a man named Jacob who went on a trip and I want to go on one too." Say to the child, **I'll tell you all about Jacob later. For now, what would you like to do?** Direct the child to one of the learning centers.

Worship and Bible Story

(15 minutes)

Let's Worship God

To the tune of "God Is So Good," sing these words: "He cares for you. . . . He's so good to you." **We've just sung our Bible words. God does care for us.** Sing "God Cares for Me," using the words, "wherever I go," in place of "all the time." **Let's thank God now for His care.** Encourage the children to fold their hands and bow their heads for prayer. **Dear God, thank You for caring for us wherever we go.**

Let's Learn From the Bible

Introduction: Have the grocery bag in front of you. Let Zach peek in, then name the items. "Those are strange things to bring to class. What are they for?" **These things remind me of today's Bible story. It's about a man named Jacob. Say that name with me.** Repeat the name until most of the children have said it. Put Zach away.

The Bible Story: Jacob lived a long time ago. When he took a trip he walked. *(Pull the sandal out of the bag.)* This sandal reminds me that Jacob walked a long way on his trip. He traveled for several days. At night there was nowhere to sleep so Jacob slept outside. He found a flat stone and used it for his pillow. *(Put the sandal in front of you and bring out the rock.)*

While Jacob slept he had a dream. He dreamed of stairs that reached from earth to Heaven. There were angels climbing the stairs. *(Place the rock by the bag and show children the angel.)* God was at the top of the stairs and He said, "I am with you and will care for you wherever you go." *(Put the items back in the bag.)*

The next morning when Jacob woke up he remembered his dream. He remembered God said, "I am with you and will care for you wherever you go." Perhaps Jacob said, "Thank You, God, for caring for me wherever I go."

Let's Apply the Lesson

Have Zach reappear with the mini-bag. Take the bag from him. **Hi, Zach. I see you still have your bag.** Zach says, "I'm ready to go." **But Zach, this bag is empty.** Have Zach peek into the grocery bag and say, "Teacher, I see you still have your bag packed." **Zach, these items remind us about Jacob.** Pick up the sandal and ask, **What does this sandal remind you of?** *(Jacob took a trip.)* Show the rock. **What did Jacob use a rock for?** *(A pillow.)* **While he was sleeping, Jacob had a dream. What did he see in his dream?** Hold up the angel as a prompt. *(He saw angels.)* **Then Jacob saw God in his dream. What did God say to Jacob?** *("I am with you and will care for you wherever you go.")*

Bible words with me. Repeat the verse until all the children can say the words.

Let's all say thank-you to God for His care. Encourage the children to say, "Thank You, God, for caring for me." **Let's say a quiet thank-you.** Everyone should whisper, "Thank You, God, for caring for me." **Now let's say a great big thank-you.** Use a strong voice to say, "Thank You, God, for caring for me."

Learning Activities

(20 minutes)

Let's Play Awhile

Sing "God Cares for Me," found on page 64. Include "wherever I live," and "wherever I go." You may wish to stand and walk in a circle while singing this song, reversing directions on each stanza.

Allow children to play with the boats at the water table. The story of Noah can be used to reinforce the theme of Lessons 10, 11, and 12. Remind the children of God's constant care—day and night, wherever we live, wherever we go.

Let's Go Home

Until parents arrive, let the children take turns helping Zach repeat the Bible words. While you hold the puppet, have the children pretend they have puppets on their hands and practice moving their fingers as they would to manipulate the puppets. Have the imaginary puppets sing the words, "God cares for us," to the tune of "God Is So Good."

Thank God for His Care

Review of Lessons 10–12

Bible Words: "He cares for you" (1 Peter 5:7, *NIV*).

Lesson Value: A review of the three previous stories in this unit will help the children realize that God's care never ends. No matter where we live, no matter where we go, day or night, we are always in God's care. With this realization, help the children express their gratitude to God.

Know: Know that God takes care of me all the time.
Feel: Feel happy for God's care.
Do: Thank God for His care.

Children will accomplish the goals when they:

1. Answer the question, "Who cares for you?"
2. Say the Bible words, "He cares for you."
3. Sing about God's care.
4. Act out ways God cares for us.
5. Pray, "Thank You, God, for taking care of me."

Let's Get Ready

For the Bible story, you will need the pillar of cloud and fire visual, pictures or toy models of various houses, and a sandal.

Set up the Family Living Center, the Games Center, and the Music/Drama Center. If you are the only teacher, use just the Family Living Center. Have materials for the God's Wonder Center ready to use after the Bible story.

Learning Activities

(30 minutes, including 10 minutes presession)

Let's Get Started

Have Zach greet each child. Zach is excited because he has learned the Bible words for this unit. "Hello, Meagan! Guess what! I've been practicing and I can say the Bible words. Listen. 'He cares for you.' Isn't that great? I'm so excited!" **Meagan, can you say the words with Zach?** Have the puppet say the words with each child as he enters. Tell each child, **I thank God for His loving care.**

Direct each child to a learning activity. **What would you like to do today? We have the Family Living Center, the Games Center, and the Music/Drama Center open.** Help each child get involved with an activity.

Worship and Story

(15 minutes)

Let's Worship God

Ask all the children to join you in the worship area. Begin by singing, "God Is Good." Ask, **Do you know why God is good? God is good because He cares for us. Who cares for us?** *(Let children answer.)* Sing the song again using the words, "God cares for us." **Now let's thank God for His care. Dear God, thank You for caring for us day and night, no matter where we live, no matter where we go.**

Let's Learn From the Bible

Introduction: Hold up the pillar of cloud and fire as you begin the review. Explain to the children that they are to fill in the word (in parentheses) when you hold up your hand.

The Bible-story Review: We've been talking about God's care. I told you a story about a time long ago when God led His people away from Egypt to a new land. During the day, God showed them the way by leading them with a (cloud). At night there was (fire) to show them where to go. Whenever the (cloud) or (fire) moved, God's people went that direction. Day and night, God cared for His people. God cares for us day and night.

(Show pictures or toy models of various houses.) The Bible tells about a man who lived on a big ark-boat for a year when there was a flood. His name was (Noah). On that ark-boat, Noah had his family and lots of (animals). A boat is an unusual place to live but it didn't change the fact that God cared for Noah. Wherever we live, God cares for us.

(Pick up the sandal.) Remember the story about a man who left his home and walked a long way to a strange land? His name was (Jacob). One night while he was traveling, Jacob had a (dream). He dreamed he saw God at the top of a flight of (stairs). Jacob heard God say, "I will be with you and care for you wherever you go." God cares for us wherever we go, just as He did for Jacob.

Let's Apply the Lesson

Hold up each item and ask, **What Bible story does this make you think of?** Allow children to respond. Ask as many leading questions as necessary to have the children retell the focus of each story. Conclude by saying, **The Bible has many stories that tell us about God's care. Remember, God not only cared for these Bible people, He also cares for you. Say the**

Family Living Center

Unit 3—God Cares for Me

Items to Include:

Lessons 10 and 13
Housekeeping items
Dolls and clothes
Blankets
Doll beds

Lesson 11
Hats
Empty baskets
Paper fruits and vegetables (pages 82 and 83)
Plastic gardening tools

Purpose: The child will act out ways God cares for us.

Things to Do and Say

Lessons 10 and 13

Encourage the children to assume nurturing roles. They may choose to be moms or dads, grandmas or grandpas, big sisters or brothers. Have children change the dolls' clothes and put them to bed (or just wrap blankets around them). Say, **Let's say a goodnight prayer with the baby. Thank You, God, for taking care of us at night. . . . God gives us moms and dads, grandmas and grandpas to help take care of the babies.**

Declare it to be morning. Ask the children to prepare breakfast for themselves and the babies. **Let's thank God before we eat. Thank You, God, for this food, and for taking care of us all night and all day. We're glad You care for us.**

Lesson 11

Make multiple copies of pages 82 and 83; enlarge if you want. Color the fruits and vegetables and cut them out. Have an area of the room represent a garden. Before class place the paper fruits and vegetables in the garden area.

Say, **One way God cares for us is by making food grow. We plant little seeds, then God sends the rain and sunshine and causes the plants to grow.** Point to the "garden area" you've prepared. **Today we are going to be gardeners. Our fruits and vegetables are ready to be picked. Here are baskets for the food. Noah gathered lots of food to**

Art Center

Unit 3—God Cares for Me

Items to Include:

Lesson 10
Blue construction paper
Black construction paper
Glue
White paper and markers
Cotton balls
Stickers (page 80)

Lesson 11
Animal crackers
Paper plates

Purpose: The child will see examples of God's care in daily life.

Things to Do and Say

Lesson 10

Glue sheets of black paper on top of the blue sheets, one per child. Make copies of page 80. Follow instructions for making stick-on glue and put this on the backs of the sheets. Give each child a piece of black and blue paper you have prepared. Also give each one a sheet of the stickers to color before they are cut out. Have someone ready to cut these as soon as a child is done. Let children glue cotton balls to the blue side of the paper to represent clouds. Then let children place their words and their suns and moons in place. A wet sponge is handy for this. Star stickers may also be added to the black side.

Say, **Let's add this sun to the blue paper. God gave us the sun to shine during the day because He cares for us. This black paper reminds me of night, when the sky is dark. Let's add our moons. Sometimes you can see stars in the black sky. Let's add stars to our nighttime picture. Even though it is dark, God can see us at night. God never stops caring for us. Remember our Bible words, "He cares for you." Who cares for you? Yes, God cares for you! Here are the Bible words to put on your pictures.**

Lesson 11

Using the pattern on page 81, cut paper plates into ark-boats. Print on each ark-boat, "He cares for you." Or, make stickers using the words on page 80.

Family Living Center, continued

take aboard the ark-boat. He had to feed his family and all the animals on the big boat. After children have collected all the food in the baskets, suggest they prepare the garden for the next crop. Show them how to rake and hoe. Help them redistribute the fruits and vegetables for others to collect.

Lesson 12
Child-sized chairs
Paper tickets (page 78)
Small pieces of luggage or bags with handles

Lesson 12

Set the chairs up in rows with a center aisle. Guide the children through an imaginary plane trip. Talk about where the children are going—to Grandma and Grandpa's, to see friends, etc. **Who will care for you on your trip? Yes, God will!** Take the tickets; pretend to be the pilot and direct them to take their seats and fasten their seat belts. Pretend to fly the plane and land. **Here we are in Washington D.C. Stay aboard if you want to go to New York.** Continue as long as the children are interested. Conclude with, **I'm glad God took care of us on our trip. No matter where we go, God cares for us.**

Art Center, continued

Scissors (for the teacher)
Crayons
Paper bags

Let children color their ark-boats. Give each child a few animal crackers. Let the children "march" their animals onto the ark-boats. Have extra crackers to eat during class. While the children snack remind them, **Animals like these lived on the ark-boat with Noah for a year. God took care of Noah and He will take care of us wherever we live.**

Put the ark-boats and animal crackers in the paper bags for the children to take home.

Lesson 12
Copies of page 84
Crayons
Stickers from page 83
Wet sponges
Scissors (for the teacher)

Lesson 12

Make copies of page 84 and the stickers of Jacob, the rock, and the moon from page 83. Prepare the stickers according to the directions on page 80.

Allow the children to scribble-color their stickers first, then give them their background pages to color while you or another teacher cut out the stickers. Help the children position their stickers but don't do this for them.

What was Jacob doing here? (*Sleeping.*) **What kind of pillow did he have?** (*A large rock.*) **Why was he sleeping outside?** (*He was taking a trip.*) **What happened while he slept?** (*He had a dream.*) **What did God say to Jacob in his dream?** (*I will be with you and care for you wherever you go.*) **Who cares for you, Beth? Yes, God does! Does He care for you when you go to your grandma's house? Yes, He cares for us wherever we go.**

Music/Drama Center

Unit 3—God Cares for Me

Items to Include:

Lesson 10
Baskets or grocery bags
Items to pack: toys, clothes, dishes, play food (or pictures), and so forth
Pillar of cloud/fire visual aid (page 79)

Purpose: The child will sing songs describing God's care.

Things to Do and Say

Lesson 10

Tell the children the following: **In our Bible story we'll hear about the time God's people were allowed to leave Egypt. The king said the people who had been slaves could all leave his country but they should leave quickly. All of God's people hurried to pack. They gathered baskets to put their things in.**

Give each child a basket or bag. **Let's pretend we're packing to leave Egypt. Let's put our clothes in the basket, and our dishes, our toys, and don't forget some food. Now pick up your basket and let's leave.** Lead the children around the room using the visual aid. Pretend to stop and eat, to sleep, and so forth. As you walk, sing "God Is Good." Keep the containers packed to use during the Bible story.

Game Center

Unit 3—God Cares for Me

Items to Include:

Large ball

Purpose: The child will learn the Bible words.

Things to Do and Say

This game can be used throughout the unit to help children learn and remember the Bible words. Play this game at the beginning of Lesson 10, and whenever you need a game to fill in time, help the children get out the "wiggles," or just for fun.

Ask the children to sit on the floor in a circle. Roll a large ball to one child and say the first word of the Bible verse, "He." The child rolls the ball to a second child while saying the word, "cares." Children continue rolling the ball to each other in random order and saying one word of the Bible verse each time. It may be hard for the youngest children to do two things at once (roll and talk). Make sure you say the words each time, encouraging the children to join in. During the course of the game ask, **Who cares for us? That's right, God cares for us. The Bible tells us, "He cares for you."**

By Lesson 12, the children should all know the words well enough to say the entire sentence at once. If a child has difficulty with this, help her get started. Praise children for their efforts as well as for being able to say the entire verse.

Lessons 12 and 13
Tape recorder and tape (optional)
Rhythm instruments (optional)

Lessons 12 and 13

If you like, make a recording of the song, "Skip to My Lou." Use the recording to accompany the children's singing.

Children join hands and sing the following words to the tune of "Skip to My Lou." Children walk in a circle to the first three lines, then stop and clap on the fourth. Tell the children, **The words we are going to sing are true. God is always with us; day or night He cares for us.**

God is always with me.
God is always with me.
God is always with me.
He's with me wherever I go*.

*(*Substitute "wherever I live," and "day and night.")*

God's Wonders Center

Unit 3—God Cares for Me

Items to Include:

Lessons 11 and 13
- Large basin or tub
- Water
- Boats
- Plastic animals
- Smocks or large shirts
- Towels for clean-up

Purpose: The child will know that God's care is constant.

Things to Do and Say

Lessons 11 and 13

Let the children reenact the time Noah and his family lived on the ark-boat. Have the children pretend to put animals on the boats and float them on the water. Make waves in the water and talk about what it might have been like to live in a house that rocked back and forth.

Do you know who built the big ark-boat? Yes, Noah built it for his family. Why did he do this? Because God told him there would be a big flood. What was on the ark-boat with Noah? Can you put some animals on our boats? Noah and his family slept on the ark-boat at night and spent all day caring for the animals. How busy they must have been!

Noah and his family and the animals lived on the ark-boat for a year. God took care of Noah and his family all the time they lived on the ark-boat. And God cares for us, no matter where we live. The Bible tells us, "He cares for you."

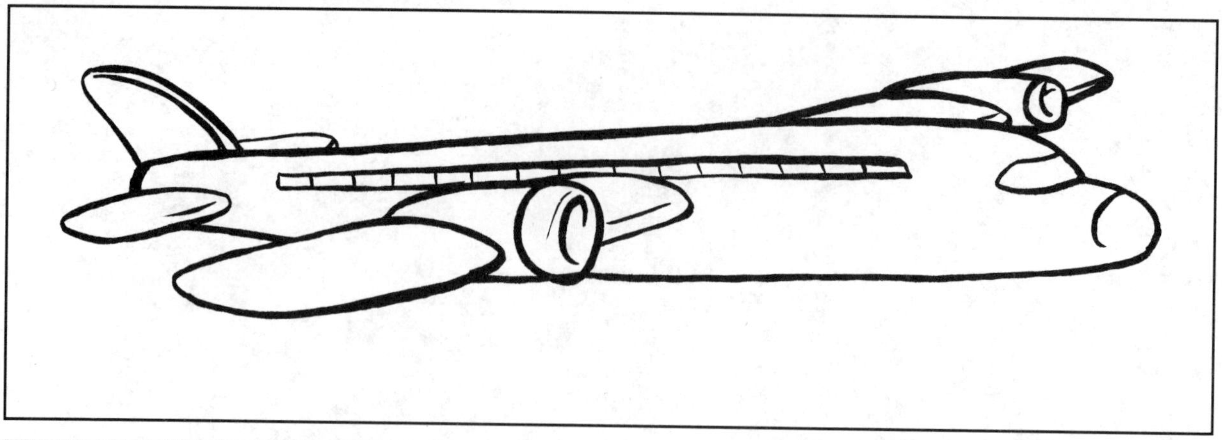

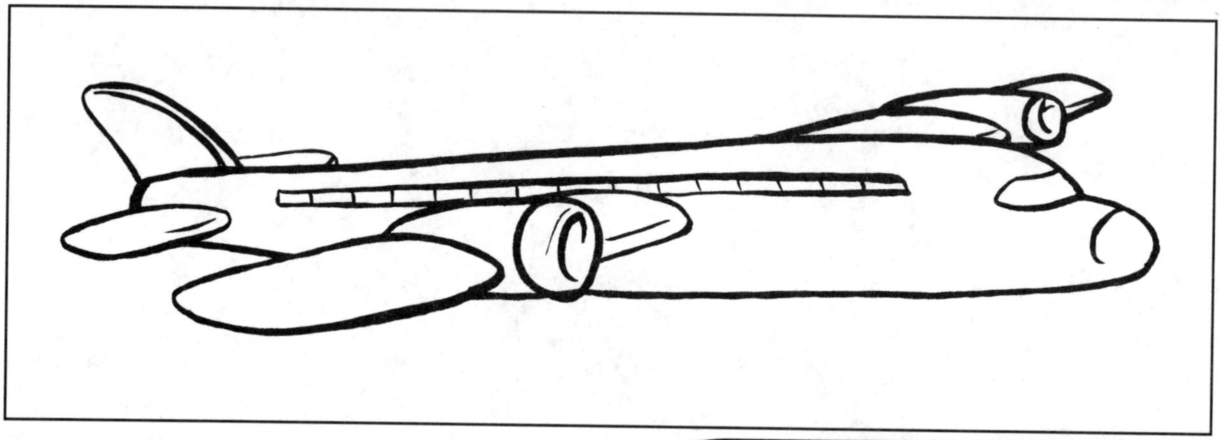

God's Wonders Center, continued

Lesson 12
Several nature objects to sort into hard or soft: rocks, shells, nuts, etc.; a hamster (or fur), flower, feather, etc.
Containers marked "Hard" and "Soft"

Lesson 12

Copy the signs from page 85. Tape these on shoe boxes or similar containers. Help the children sort the nature objects into two categories, hard and soft. Have the objects in a box or spread out on the table.

As the children pick up each object ask, **How does that feel? Is it hard or soft?** Direct placement of the object into the correct box. **Let's put the shell in the box marked "Hard." Let's put it with the rock. The Bible tells us that a man named Jacob took a long trip. At night, he used a hard rock for a pillow. When he traveled far from home, God still cared for him. No matter where we go, God cares for us. That's what our Bible words tell us. "He cares for you."**

Visual—Autumn, Unit 3

Instructions

1. Photocopy the page. For a larger visual, enlarge and copy each on a separate sheet of paper. If you want, use yellow paper for the flame and white or light gray for the cloud.
2. Use crayons or markers to add orange and red to make "fire."
3. Glue on cotton or polyester fiberfill to the cloud (optional).
4. Glue pillars back to back, inserting a craft stick between them for a handle.
5. Optional: Put cardboard between the fire and cloud to make them sturdier.

Stickers—Autumn, Unit 3

Instructions

1. Prepare background pages for children by gluing sheets of black paper to sheets of light blue paper.
2. Make copies of this page and prepare for stickers (see below).
3. Follow instructions on Art Center card.

"He cares for you" (1 Peter 5:7) . . . in the daytime.

"He cares for you" (1 Peter 5:7) . . . at night.

How to Make Stickers

Brush a thin coat of the following mixture onto backs of stickers and let dry. To adhere, simply lick!

Mixture:

- one part vinegar
- two parts white glue
- a few drops of peppermint extract (or any other flavor)

Paper-plate Ark-boat—Autumn, Unit 3

Instructions before class

1. Make a pattern from this page by tracing lines onto cardboard.
2. Fold each paper plate in half, then open the plate.
3. Lay the cardboard pattern on the fold of each plate and trace around the pattern.
4. Carefully cut on solid lines, using an X-Acto knife or something similar.
5. Fold down the "door."

In class

1. Let the children color their ark-boats.
2. Show them how to open their doors.
3. Give children animal crackers to "march" into their boats.
4. See Art Center card for conversation suggestions.

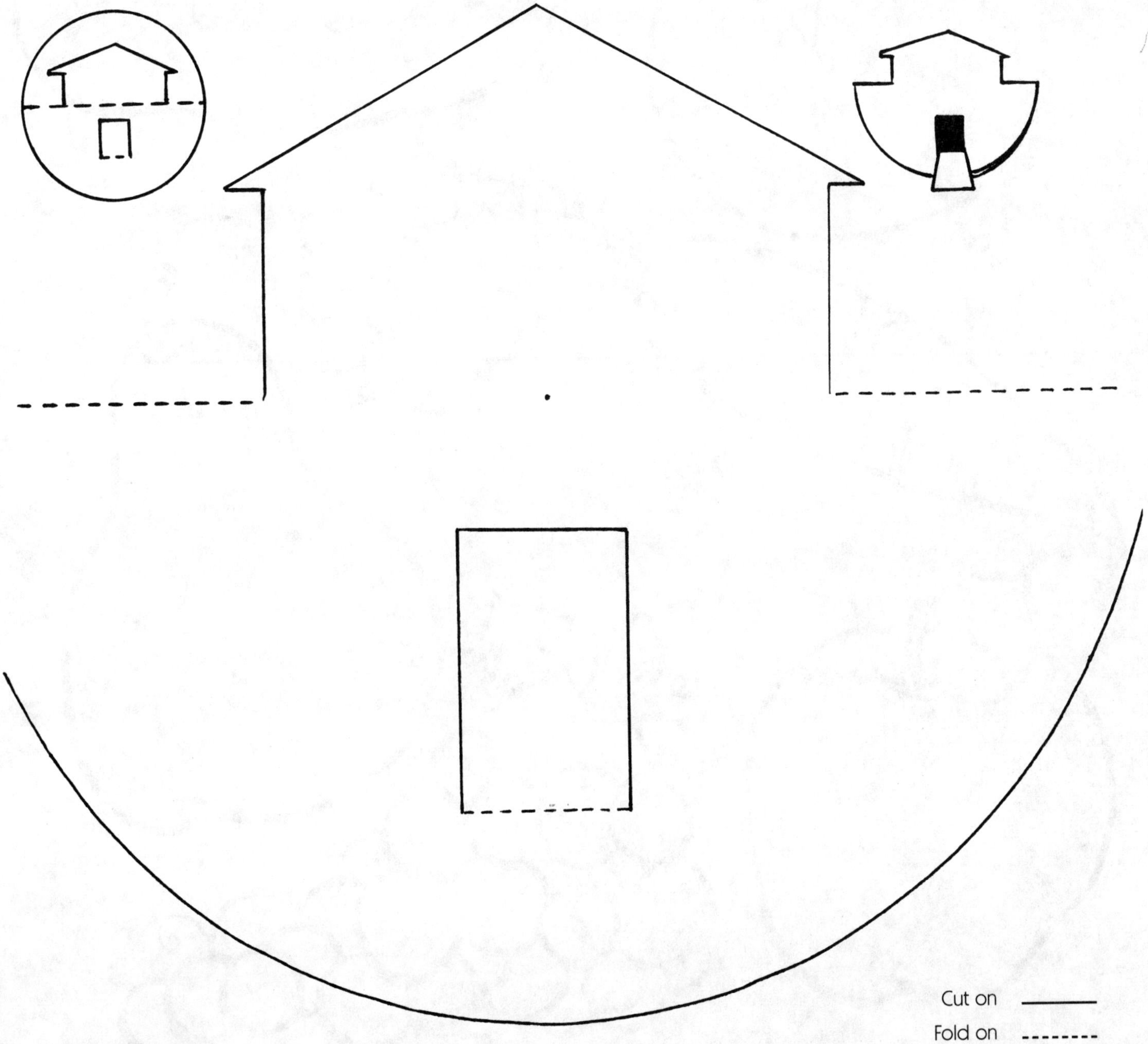

Cut on ———

Fold on - - - - - - -

Fruits and Vegetables—Autumn, Unit 3

Instructions

1. Make multiple copies of this page. Enlarge if you wish.
2. Color fruits and vegetables.
3. Mount on cardboard for durability.
4. Cut out and use in the Family Living Center.

Fruits and Vegetables—Autumn, Unit 3

Stickers—Autumn, Unit 3

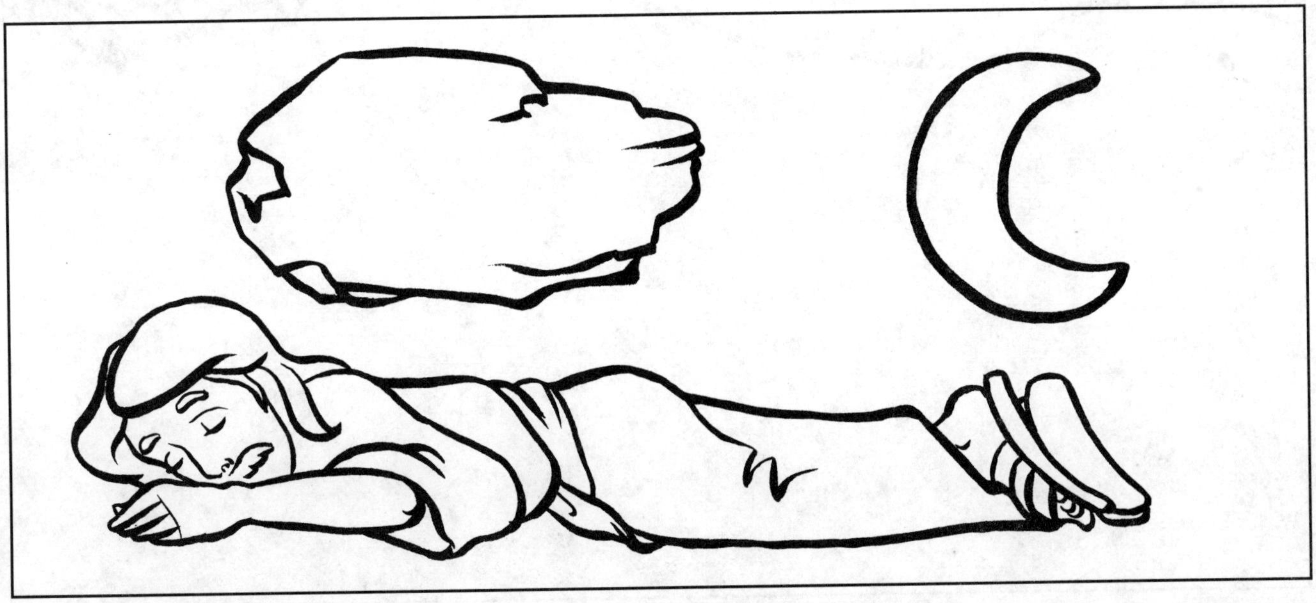

God took care of Jacob when he went on a long trip. God takes care of us wherever we go. Thank You, God, for taking care of us wherever we go.

Signs—Autumn, Unit 3

Instructions

1. Photocopy signs.
2. Color signs or copy them on colored paper.
3. Cut signs apart.
4. Glue each one to a shoe box, or similar box.
5. Use in the God's Wonders Center.

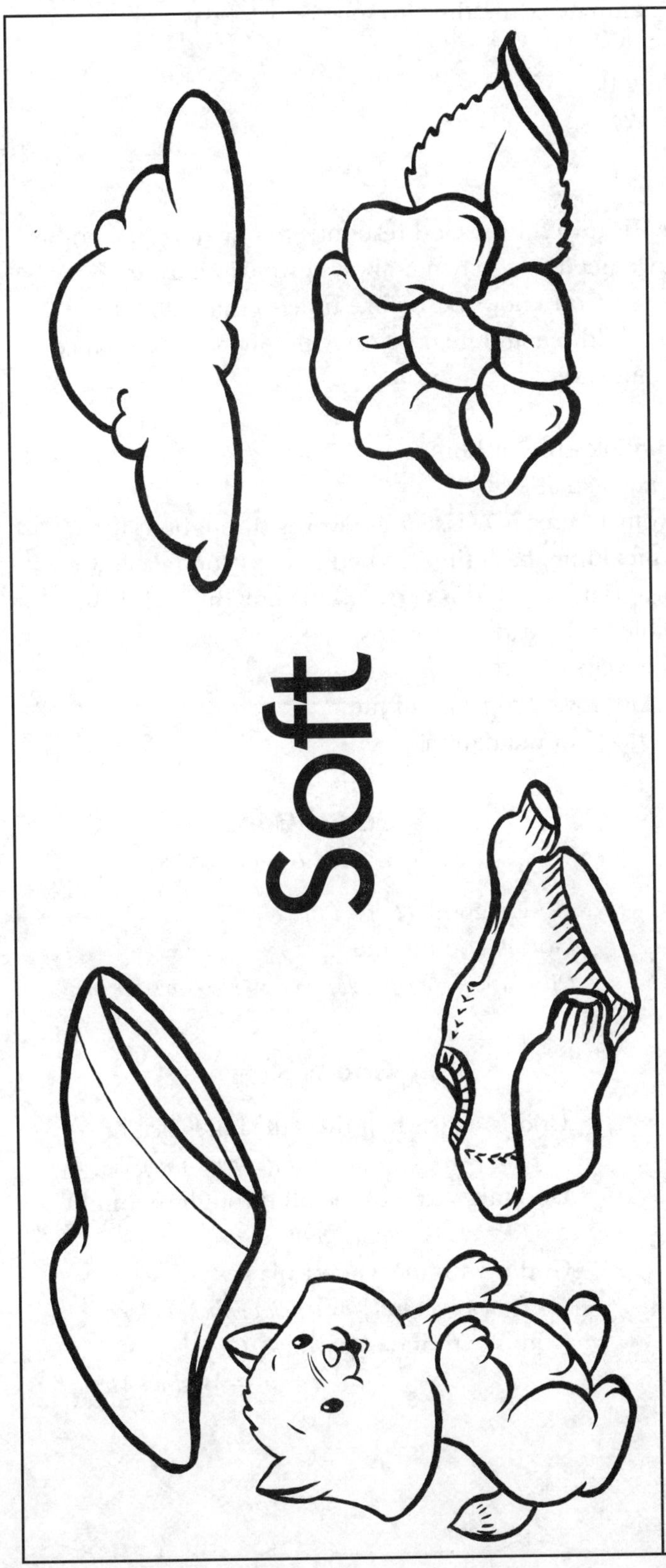

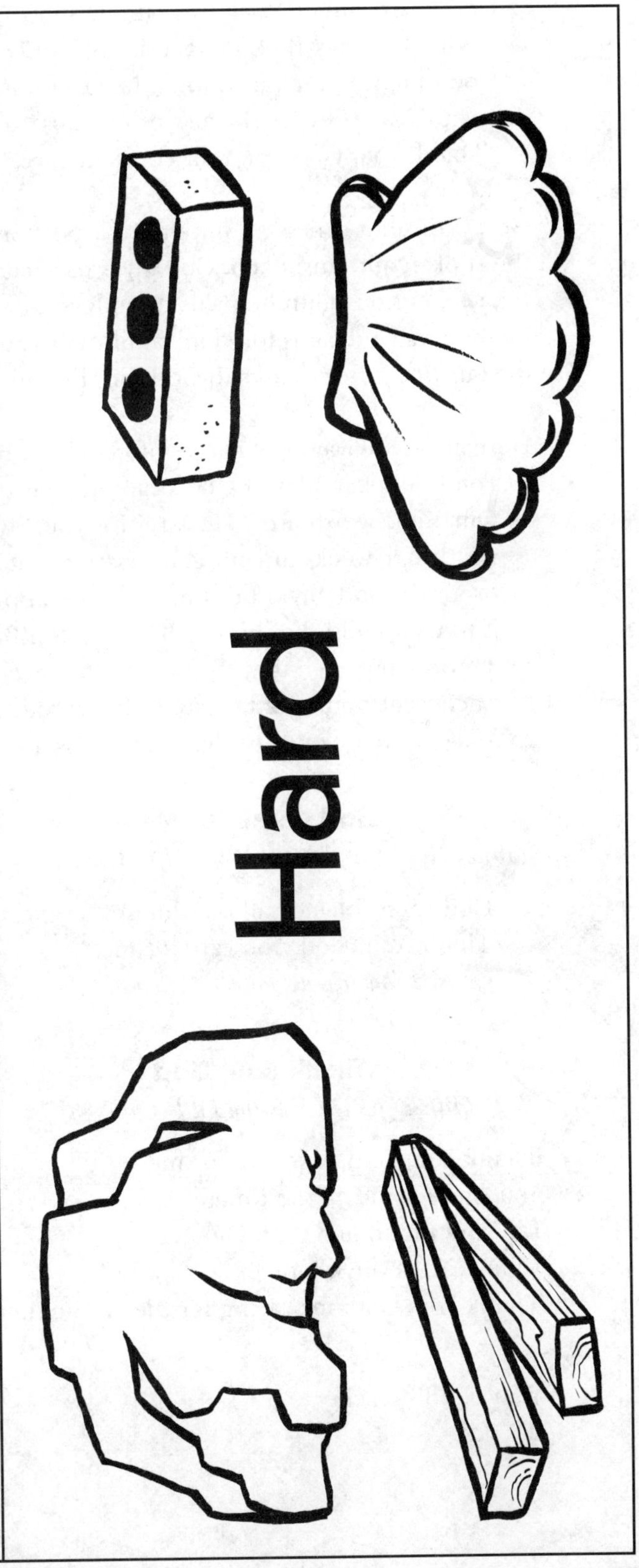

Dear Parent,

During this unit, your child will be learning the scope of God's care for His people. These three Bible stories are examples of specific instances when God's care was evident.

God Cares All the Time (Exodus 6:2-8; 12:31-38; 13:17-22)
God gives the pillars of cloud and fire to guide His people out of Egypt.

God Cares Wherever We Live (Genesis 6:8-10, 14-22; 7; 8:1-20)
God takes care of Noah, his family, and the animals while they live on the ark-boat.

God Cares Wherever We Go (Genesis 28:10-17)
God watches over Jacob when he takes a long trip.

Thank God for His Care (Review of Lessons 10–12)
"Thank You, God, for Your constant care."

God's constant care is an important aspect of His love for us. God responds to our requests, both the spoken and unspoken. God gives us what we need. He may not always give us what we request, but our faith helps us to understand that God knows best. Take time to think about the many ways God cares for your family. Let your child see and hear you relying on God's guidance in your life. Offer thanks to God for His constant care.

Here are some ways you can reinforce these Bible lessons at home.

- Point out examples of God's care in your daily activities.
- Our Bible words are, "He cares for you," from 1 Peter 5:7. Use these words throughout the next three weeks in your conversation—at mealtime, bath time, at bedtime, as you take a walk or a ride, and any other time they are appropriate. Look this verse up in your Bible and show it to your child. Let him or her hold the Bible and "read" the words.
- Throughout each day, thank God for specific ways He cares for you.
- Encourage your child to say, "Thank You, God, for taking care of me."
- Make up new words to the tunes below to reflect your situation.

God Cares for Me

(Tune: "He's Got the Whole World in His Hands")

God cares for me* all the time.**
Thank You, God. You care for me.*
*(*Insert your child's name. **Repeat twice.)*

God Is Good

(Tune: "God Is So Good")

God is good. *(Repeat twice.)*
God is good to me.
(Also use, "He cares for you"; "He cares for me.")

Thank You, God

(Tune: "Jesus Loves the Little Children")

Thank You, God, You care for me.
You care for me all the time.
Day and night, and at my home.
In my car, or anywhere.
Thank You, God, for caring for me all the time.

God Is Near

God is near when the sun shines bright.
(Raise arms above head to form sun.)
God takes care of me all through the night.
(Rest cheek against hands.)
God is with me when I play.
(Pretend to push toy truck or rock doll.)
God is with me every day! *(Clap hands.)*
—Mildred Merkel

Your child's teacher,

Winter Quarter

Learning About Jesus

As you study this quarter you will see that the 2's and 3's in your class will learn to think of Jesus as a real and special person, God's Son, who loves them very much. The realness of Jesus is very important to young children because they are subjected so much to TV and to secular books. They need to be able to distinguish between the imaginary characters in these and the reality of Jesus. Jesus will become very real to your children as you talk about Jesus' birth in Unit 1, "Jesus Is Born"; about how He grew and what He did in Unit 2, "Jesus Is God's Son"; and about His relationship with the people He came in contact with in Unit 3, "Jesus Loves Us."

Jesus will also become a very special person, not only through the lessons you teach, but most importantly, through your attitude toward Jesus and toward the Bible. The children may not understand the significance that Jesus is God's Son, but they will sense the specialness, the wonder of the things He does, by the way you talk about Jesus and the way you present the lessons.

As a result of these lessons, 2's and 3's will

KNOW

Know that Jesus is special.

FEEL

Feel happy because Jesus is special.

DO

Show love for Jesus and thank God for Jesus.

Use these songs and action rhymes throughout the quarter, in addition to those specifically mentioned in the units.

Let's Be Very Quiet

D. F. R. DOROTHY FAY RICHARDS

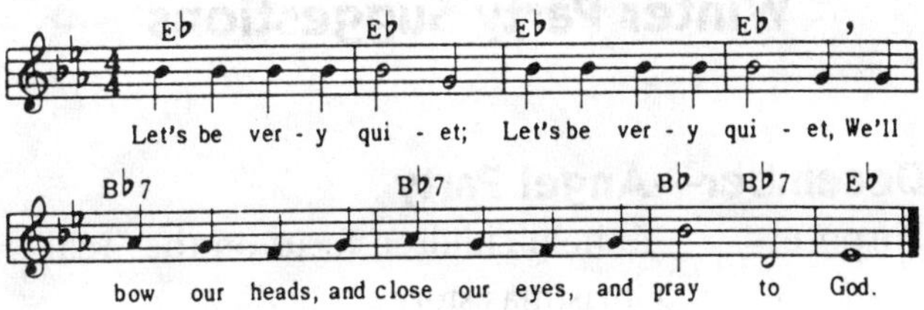
Eb Eb Eb Eb
Let's be ver - y qui - et; Let's be ver - y qui - et, We'll
Bb7 Bb7 Bb Bb7 Eb
bow our heads, and close our eyes, and pray to God.

It's Time to Put Our Toys Away

(Tune: "Mary Had a Little Lamb")

It's time to put our toys away, toys away, toys away.
It's time to put our toys away, so we know where to find them.*

**Friends come and help us.*

My Bible

This is my Bible; *(Palms held together.)*
I'll open it wide *(Open hands like a book.)*
And see (or say) what is written, on the inside!
(Say Bible words.)

—*Jean Baxendale*

If You're Happy and You Know It

If you're happy and you know it, clap your hands.*
(Repeat.)
If you're happy and you know it,
Then your face will surely show it.
If you're happy and you know it, clap your hands.

*(2) *Stomp your feet.*
(3) Say, "Amen."
(4) Do all three.

Winter Party Suggestions

December—Angel Party

Purpose:	To help children focus on the "real" Christmas story
When:	During class time
Preparation:	Ask parents to send large white T-shirts for their children.
Craft	Add wings (cut from cardboard, add glitter, pin to shirts) to the white T-shirts, and halos (circles of tinsel in each child's hair) to make "angels."
Decorate:	Put clouds (cut from large white paper) on the floor, ceiling, and walls.
Game:	Play "Pin the Wings on the Angel!" (Use circles of tape on backs of wings.)
Food:	Angel food cake
Bible Story:	Angels Tell the Shepherds Good News

January—Snowman Party

Purpose:	Fun!
When:	During class time
Preparation:	Everyone wears white.
Game:	Have a snowball fight with rolled up white socks.
Craft:	Make snowman pictures (Outline paper plate with cotton balls; take an instant picture of each child—with top hat and carrot nose—to put in the center of the plate.)
Food:	Vanilla ice cream
Bible Story:	God Made the Seasons or God Wants Us to Enjoy His Creation

February—Valentine's Party

Purpose:	To help children show their love for others
When:	During class time
Craft:	Make valentines for each other, family members, or shut-ins; or, make heart wreaths to give to your preschool leader, the minister, or a sick child. Each child decorates a heart to put on the paper wreath.
Food:	Lollipop cookies (Cut rolled-out dough into heart shapes, stick craft sticks in before baking.)
Game:	Holiday Hunt (Children hunt for paper hearts hidden around the room.)
Bible Story:	Jesus Loves the Children

Reminder: If you are using the year-round attendance chart, purchase the *Winter* seals (22-01778—216 seals) now.

Unit 1: Jesus Is Born

Lessons 1–5

By the end of the unit, the children will

Know that Jesus was a special baby.

Feel happy that Jesus was born.

Show they are happy Jesus was born (smile, sing, tell).

Unit Bible Words

"His name was . . . Jesus" (Luke 2:21).

Books

from Standard Publishing

One Tiny Baby (24-04219)

The First Christmas (24-03793)

Three Special Journeys (3 board books—24-03645)

Thank You, God, for Christmas (24-04221)

The Very Special Night (24-04222)

This Unit at a Glance

1 An Angel Brings Happy News Luke 1:26-38
An angel announces to Mary the miraculous virgin birth and she is happy to be the chosen mother.

2 Jesus Is Born Luke 2:1-7
Mary and Joseph find a stable in Bethlehem, where Jesus is born.

3 Shepherds Come to See Jesus Luke 2:8-20
The angels announce Jesus' birth to the shepherds, who immediately go to find the baby Son of God.

4 Wise Men Bring Gifts Matthew 2:1, 2, 9-11
The wise men travel for many, many miles to bring gifts to Jesus.

5 Thank You, God, for Jesus Review of Lessons 1–4

Why Teach This Unit?

When God sent His Son Jesus to earth as a baby, His birth was unique. It was foretold by prophets; predicted by an angel; He was born of a virgin; a multitude of angels announced it to shepherds; wise men brought expensive gifts to celebrate it. This unit's Bible stories tell about Jesus' birth and these unique surrounding events. The stories show how special Jesus was as a baby and how special we know Him to be today.

Two's and 3's are very interested in babies. They love to watch them, touch them, and "help" with them. They also like knowing they are no longer babies, but are growing bigger and learning to do more things. The children will learn about how special Jesus is by their interaction with baby dolls and a real baby, singing songs about Jesus' birth, and hearing the Bible stories. They will be happy that Jesus came to earth as a baby.

The Bible words should be used over and over in your conversation, in the Bible stories, at the learning centers, and in your prayers. For example, **Jesus came as a baby. "His name was Jesus." . . . The Bible tells us "His name was Jesus." Thank You, God, for Your Son.**

Have a classroom Bible available in a learning center, at the giving table, or wherever the children will see it. Also have it on your lap or at your side as you tell the Bible story. Have the Bible words highlighted or underlined so the children can see them, point to them, and "read" them.

Things to Do for This Unit

- Make copies of the Parents' Letter (page 112) and a copy of the Unit Planning Sheet (pages 319 and 320).
- Photocopy the Learning Center Cards (pages 101-106); cut apart on heavy lines. Mount side 1 on cardboard, then side 2 on back of cardboard. Cover with clear, self-adhesive plastic for durability (optional).
- Prepare materials listed on the Learning Center Cards.
- Find or purchase appropriate books on Jesus' birth (list on previous page).
- For Lesson 1, make visual aid by enlarging and coloring page 107. Cover with clear, self-adhesive plastic (optional).
- For Lesson 4, copy the star (page 111) onto yellow construction paper. Cut it out and add gold glitter. Glue a piece of outing flannel or sandpaper on the back for use on a flannelboard. Also, find a children's Christmas music tape.

Use These Songs and Action Rhymes During Unit 1

Jesus, You Are Special

(Tune: "Mulberry Bush")

Jesus was a special baby, special baby, special baby.
Jesus was a special baby. Jesus, You are special.

I Stand on Tiptoe

I stand on tiptoe, *(Stand on tiptoe.)*
And ring the bell, *(Pretend to ring doorbell.)*
Because I have something *(Point to self.)*
I want to tell. *(Cup hands to mouth.)*
Jesus is born. *(Make cradle with arms; rock cradle.)*

—Marjorie R. Miller

The Baby Jesus

A stable, *(Make house with hands.)*
A manger, *(Make box with hands.)*
A baby, *(Cradle baby.)*
With animals all around. *(Arms outstretched.)*
The baby is sleeping, *(Folded hands against cheek.)*
Let's tiptoe, *(Walk on tiptoe.)*
And not make even a sound. *(Sh-h-h!)*

—Dana Eynon

My Bible

This is my Bible; *(Palms held together.)*
I'll open it wide *(Open hands; keep them touching.)*
And see (or say) what is written
On the inside! *(Say Bible words: "His name was Jesus.")*

—Jean Baxendale

Jesus Is the Son of God

(Tune: "London Bridge")

Jesus is the Son of God, Son of God, Son of God.
Jesus is the Son of God. Jesus, You are special.

Smile, Mary, Smile

BARBARA EBERT
Arr. by MORINE BARNES

B. E.

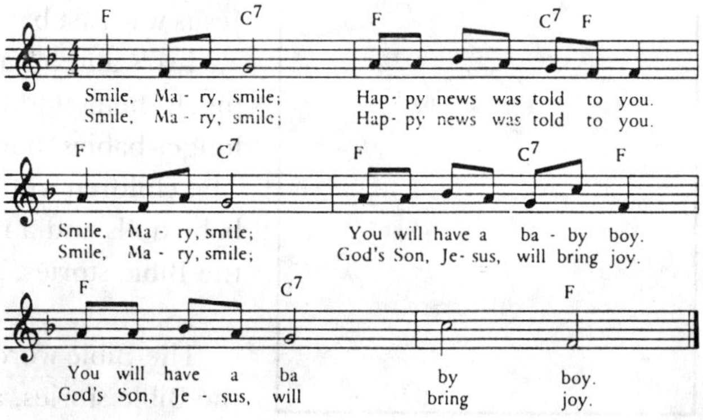

Who would like to dress up like the angel? like Mary? Let children take turns as you go over the story two or three more times. Older children say the words as they go along. Younger ones will need a shortened version of the story.

As groups of children dress up ask, **What did the angel tell Mary? Yes, that she would have a baby. What was special about this baby? Yes, He is God's Son. Was Mary happy? Yes! This was happy news.** Pray with the children, **Dear God, we are happy that Jesus was born.**

Learning Activities

(20 minutes)

Let's Play Awhile

While new children take turns role-playing the story, others can go to the Art Center to make their pictures. If your class is large, divide the children into small groups and let them repeat activities from before. Young children love repetition.

Let's Go Home

Have Zach tell the children it is time to pick up toys. Then have children make a circle and sit down. Play the game from the Game Center (Lesson 1). Most 2's and some 3's will need help with the Bible words today.

As parents arrive, take children to the door one by one. Make sure the children have their coloring pages, whether they did them in class or not. Also give each one a Parents' Letter since this is the first lesson of the unit.

An Angel Brings Happy News

Luke 1:26-38

Bible Words: "His name was . . . Jesus" (Luke 2:21).

Lesson Value: Babies are interesting to young children. They are very curious about babies and enjoy watching and touching them. They understand a baby is special. They also like the fact that they are bigger than a baby and are no longer considered babies. They like to hear happy news and happy voices. They are easily influenced by the tone of your voice. You can help them understand that the angel's announcement of the coming birth of baby Jesus was very happy news.

Know: Know that Jesus was a special baby.
Feel: Feel happy that Jesus was born.
Do: Show they are happy Jesus was born (smile, sing, tell).

Children will accomplish the goals when they:

1. Say the Bible words, "His name was Jesus."
2. Tell happy news to a friend.
3. Sing about Jesus' birth.
4. Pray, "We are happy that Jesus was born."

Let's Get Ready

For the Bible story, you will need your classroom Bible with the new Bible words highlighted, the puppet Zach, a toy telephone, costumes for Mary and the angel (small robes and/or towels, and cords or ties to tie head gear on, etc.), and an enlarged copy of the picture of Mary and the angel made from page 107.

Prepare the Family Living Center, the Book/Picture Center, and the Music/Drama Center. Have materials ready for the Art Center after the Bible story. If you are the only teacher, use just the Family Living Center now.

Learning Activities

(30 minutes, including 10 minutes presession)

Let's Get Started

Have Zach greet each child by name. Help children get coats hung up and name tags on. Let Zach help each child find a sticker to put on the attendance sheet. Then make sure the child gets involved in one of the learning activities. **Nathaniel, would you like to look at books or play with the babies? We are going to hear some happy news today.**

Worship and Bible Story

(15 minutes)

Let's Worship God

Have Zach say, "It's time to put away our things so we can sing and pray to God." Begin singing as soon as the first child sits in the circle with you. Sing songs from page 90. Make sure you include "Smile, Mary, Smile." Use "Let's Be Very Quiet" (page 88); then pray, **Thank You, God, for the happy news about Jesus. We are happy that Jesus was born.**

Let's Learn From the Bible

Introduction: Zach holds up a toy phone. **When you have some happy news, how can you tell your friends your happy news?** *(You can use a phone, go to your friend's house, or send your friend a letter.)* **Very good! There are lots of ways to tell people happy news. Happy news makes other people happy too. In our Bible story someone hears some happy news. Let's listen to find out that happy news.** Put Zach away. Have your Bible handy.

The Bible Story: The Bible tells about a young woman named Mary. *(Point to the open Bible.)* Mary loved God very much, and He loved her. God chose Mary for a very special job. He had some happy news for her. God didn't write Mary a letter or call her on the phone. He found a special way to tell her.

One day God sent an angel to tell Mary the happy news. Maybe the angel knocked on the door. Let's knock too. *(Do so.)* When the angel saw Mary, he said, "Hello, Mary. God loves you very much. He is with you." *(Show the teaching picture.)*

Mary was surprised. She had never met an angel before. Can you look surprised? *(Show the children what you want them to do.)* Mary wondered why the angel was there. Then he said, "Don't be afraid, Mary. You are going to have a baby. You will call His name Jesus. He will be God's Son."

Mary was happy to hear this good news. She smiled. Can you smile? *(Do this with the children.)* Mary told the angel, "I am happy to do this for God." *(Sing "Smile, Mary, Smile" several times with the children.)*

Let's Apply the Lesson

Having an angel come to see you is very special! What exciting news did the angel tell Mary? What was Mary to name her baby? In the Bible we can find the answer. Open your Bible and read "His name was . . . Jesus." **Jesus is the special baby. Can you say the Bible words with me? "His name was Jesus."**

born. They were especially happy because Jesus is God's Son. Why are we happy at Christmas? The children may give a variety of answers here. Accept them all, if possible, but make sure that the answer, "Because Jesus was born," is the final answer! Sing "Jesus, You Are Special."

Learning Activities

(20 minutes)

Let's Play Awhile

Have the children stand and do the action rhyme, "The Baby Jesus," then go to the Family Living Center. If your class is large and you have multiple teachers, use the other activities from the beginning of the lesson as well.

Let's Go Home

Let Zach sing "It's Time to Put Our Toys Away" (page 88). If some children are reluctant to pick up, give simple instructions such as, **Jason, put these two blocks in the box. Sarah, you put this baby in the bed.** As soon as most of the toys are picked up and there is one child with nothing to do, start the following activity. To the tune, "Row, Row, Row Your Boat," sing the following words:

Now, now, Jesus is born, Jesus is born today.
In a little stable, Jesus is born today.

After you sing this a couple of times and children become familiar with the song, let them take turns being Mary and Joseph. Have two chairs in the middle of your circle and a baby doll to be Jesus. "Joseph" should have a turn holding Jesus too.

Make sure the children take home their baby Jesus pictures they made in the Art Center.

Lesson 2
Date: ______

Jesus Is Born

Luke 2:1-7

Bible Words: "His name was . . . Jesus" (Luke 2:21).

Lesson Value: When a baby is born children know that the baby is special to his mother, father, and other family members as well. But the baby Jesus is the most special baby. He is God's Son. And yet He wasn't born in a palace or a nice hospital. There wasn't even a room in the inn for God's Son. God provided a quiet place, however, away from the noisy crowds, a place where the shepherds could come and see the baby the angel told about. Your children will feel the excitement and the wonder of the birth of God's Son, Jesus, as they participate in the activities and hear the story once more.

Know: Know that Jesus was a special baby.
Feel: Feel happy that Jesus was born.
Do: Show they are happy Jesus was born (smile, sing, tell).

Children will accomplish the goals when they:

1. Say the Bible words, "His name was Jesus."
2. Sing about Jesus' birth.
3. Tell why we are happy at Christmas. (Jesus was born.)
4. Pray, "We are happy because Jesus was born."

Let's Get Ready

For the Bible story, you will need the classroom Bible, puppet Zach, a doll and blanket, and a box with straw or a manger from a crèche.

Prepare the Art Center, the Book/Picture Center, and the Block Center. If you are the only teacher, use just the Art Center. Have materials ready for the Family Living Center to be used after the Bible story.

Learning Activities

(30 minutes, including 10 minutes presession)

Let's Get Started

Use Zach to greet each child by name. After children have hung up coats, have Zach say to a child, "Jeremy, find a sticker to put on the attendance sheet. You are big enough to do things for yourself!" Then encourage each child to get involved in one of the learning centers.

Worship and Bible Story

(15 minutes)

Let's Worship God

Let Zach tell the children, "It's time to put our things away so we can sing and pray to God." Begin singing as soon as children come to the circle. Sing "Smile, Mary, Smile" and "Jesus, You Are Special." Introduce the rhyme, "The Baby Jesus." Open your Bible and say, **We have been singing about a special baby. The Bible tells us, "His name was Jesus." Can you say that with me?** Then pray, **Thank You, God, for babies. We are happy because Jesus was born.**

Let's Learn From the Bible

Introduction: Have Zach push or pull a box of straw or the manger from the crèche and put it where everyone can see it. **Did you know cows and sheep eat out of a box something like this? It is called a manger. Where do big animals such as horses and cows sleep?** *(Outside, in barns, etc.)* **A stable is like a barn. Animals sleep there. Something very exciting happened in a stable in our Bible story. Let's find out what was so exciting.** Put Zach away. Place your Bible on your lap or at your side.

The Bible Story: An angel had told Mary some happy news. Do you remember what that happy news was? Yes! Mary was going to have a baby. And now it was almost time for the baby to be born.

Mary had to take a trip with Joseph to Bethlehem. Perhaps Mary rode on a donkey. Can you pat the floor with your hands to sound like the donkey's feet? *(Do this with the children.)* Good.

When Mary and Joseph got to Bethlehem they were very tired. They wanted to go to bed. Joseph knocked at the door of an inn. Knock-knock. *(Have children knock with you.)* Knock-knock. A tired man said, "There is no room here."

Joseph knocked at another door. Knock-knock. *(Children knock.)* "No room," said a tired woman. Finally, Joseph found a quiet stable. It was peaceful and quiet and had clean straw to sleep on.

Joseph and Mary and the donkey went into the stable with the animals. They were glad to rest. While they were staying in the stable, something wonderful happened. Do you know what happened? Yes! Jesus was born!

Mary smiled as she wrapped Jesus in soft cloths and laid Him in a manger. Maybe the animals quietly watched the tiny baby sleep. Mary and Joseph were happy that baby Jesus was born.

Let's Apply the Lesson

Place a baby doll wrapped in a blanket in the box of straw.

Can you lie down on the floor and pretend to be an animal asleep in the stable? Sh-h-h. The animals are very quiet while they sleep. Oh, now a baby is crying. What is that baby's name? Yes, Jesus. Mary and Joseph were happy Jesus was

and saw—the angel with the message about Jesus' birth, many angels praising God, and baby Jesus lying in the manger.

God sent Jesus to earth so He could teach us about God. The Bible says, "His name was Jesus." Show the children the words in the Bible. Say the verse together. Let each child who is willing hold the Bible, point to the words, and "read" them to the class.

Learning Activities

(20 minutes)

Let's Play Awhile

Stand to do the rhyme, "The Baby Jesus." Then play hide-the-blanket from the Game Center Card. If your class is large, let children who want to role-play the Bible story, do so. If your class is large, some teachers can take children back to centers used previously and allow them to repeat activities or try new ones.

Let's Go Home

Have Zach tell the children it is time to pick up the toys. As soon as the first child has finished, start the following song to the tune of "London Bridge." If you want, let two children make a bridge and others go under it.

Angels came to tell the shepherds,
Tell the shepherds, tell the shepherds.
Angels came to tell the shepherds
About baby Jesus.

Shepherds came to see baby Jesus,
See baby Jesus, see baby Jesus.
Shepherds came to see baby Jesus.
Thank You, God, for Jesus.

Make up more stanzas or repeat these. Make sure each child has her sheep to take home.

Shepherds Come to See Jesus

Luke 2:8-20

Bible Words: "His name was . . . Jesus" (Luke 2:21).

Lesson Value: An angel appearing in the night, then joined by a host of angels praising God is a fantastic way to announce the birth of the Son of God! And who received this heavenly announcement? Kings, rulers, leaders of the people? No! God chose lowly shepherds to receive this momentous news. The awestruck shepherds were so amazed at what they had seen and heard that they shared their story with everyone they met. Your children will feel a little of the wonder and excitement today as you make this story come to life for them.

Know: Know that Jesus was a special baby.
Feel: Feel happy that Jesus was born.
Do: Show they are happy Jesus was born (smile, sing, tell).

Children will accomplish the goals when they:

1. Say the Bible words, "His name was Jesus."
2. Sing about Jesus' birth.
3. Tell why we are happy at Christmas. (Jesus was born.)
4. Pray, "We are happy because Jesus was born."

Let's Get Ready

For the Bible story, you will need the classroom Bible, white cloth drape for angels, a lamb puppet or a stuffed lamb, a stick for a staff, and strips of cloth or towels to dress children as shepherds.

Prepare the Art Center, the Book/Picture Center, and the Music/Drama Center. If you are the only teacher, set up just the Art Center. Have materials ready for the Game Center to use during *Let's Play Awhile.*

Learning Activities

(30 minutes, including 10 minutes presession)

Let's Get Started

Greet each child with your lamb. If you don't have a lamb, let Zach pretend he is a lamb. Have him say, "Baa-a-a," now and then, and perhaps cover his head with cotton batting. After the children have hung up their coats, let the lamb (or Zach) help the children pick out stickers and put them on the attendance chart. Encourage each child to go to a specific learning center. **Tommy, I think you would like to go to the Art Center to make a fuzzy sheep.**

Worship and Bible Story

(15 minutes)

Let's Worship God

Have Zach say, "It's time to put away our things so we can sing and pray to God." Start singing as soon as the first child joins you. Sing "Smile, Mary, Smile," and "Jesus, You Are Special." Introduce "Jesus Is the Son of God." Then pray, **Thank You, God, for Jesus. We are happy because Jesus was born.**

Let's Learn From the Bible

Introduction: Have costume materials ready. Let Zach ask, "Boys and girls, what is a shepherd?" *(A shepherd is a person who takes care of sheep.)* **Who would like to dress up like a shepherd?** Help several children put on head gear. Have them practice looking surprised and frightened, hands and arms shielding eyes; walk to see baby; say, "Sh-h-h." **A shepherd also uses a staff like this.** Let Zach hold the staff. **It is used to help guide the sheep and protect them from danger. You are going to be the shepherds in our Bible story.**

Choose one or more older children to be angels. Drape white cloth around their shoulders. Explain to one angel that she will say with you, "Jesus is born." Have angels sit next to you. **The rest of you are going to be sheep.** Let Zach point to these children. **What do sheep say? "Baa-a-a." That's right!** Explain that they will say, "Baa-a-a," when you say, "Sheep." **I can see that all of you are ready for the story.** Put Zach away. Hold your Bible on your lap or lay it next to you.

The Bible Story: Some shepherds were quietly watching their sheep at night. Most of the sheep were asleep. Suddenly an angel appeared! *(One angel stands.)* He was bright and shining. The shepherds were surprised and scared. Can you act surprised and scared like the shepherds? Maybe they put up their hands and their arms to keep the bright light from shining in their eyes. *(Do this with the children.)* The angel said, "Don't be afraid. Jesus is born." *(Have the angel say this with you.)*

Then many angels came and praised God. *(The rest of the angels stand. Perhaps they could say, "God is good," or "Thank You, God.")* When the angels left, the shepherds went to see the special baby. They found baby Jesus lying in a manger. "Sh-h-h," the shepherds said to each other. "We don't want to wake up the baby." Can you say, "Sh-h-h," to the other shepherds? The shepherds were so excited about the special baby Jesus, they told everybody they saw about Him.

Let's Apply the Lesson

How did the shepherds feel after they saw Jesus? (Happy!) **Why are we happy at Christmas? Right! We are happy because Jesus was born. What do you think the shepherds told other people?** Help children recall things the shepherds heard

show Jesus we love Him by helping someone or giving a gift to someone. What can you do for someone who is sick? a hurt friend? someone who is sad? You may need to suggest some ideas here. If children made the cards in the Art Center, remind the children that these are gifts to give someone who is sick, etc. **We can also tell our friends, "His name was Jesus." We are happy that Jesus was born!**

Learning Activities

(20 minutes)

Let's Play Awhile

Let the children pretend to be some of the animals that might have seen Jesus. The sheep should walk slowly and say, "Baa-a-a," while the camels should sway back and forth as they clip-clop along. Add others if you have time. **These were animals that might have seen baby Jesus. How would they walk when they saw baby Jesus?** Have the children imitate the animals walking quietly and carefully. **The people who were with the animals said, "His name was Jesus."** Have the children repeat the words with you.

The Book/Picture Center will be a good place to review the stories from the past three weeks. Let the children tell you as much of the stories as they remember. If necessary, insert questions or short sentences to prod their memories. Use the other centers if you have a large class and multiple teachers.

Let's Go Home

Have Zach tell the children it is time to put the toys away. Sit in a circle. Sing songs and do action rhymes you have been using this month. Make sure children have their cards ready to take home. Let Zach tell them good-bye.

Wise Men Bring Gifts

Matthew 2:1, 2, 9-11

Bible Words: "His name was . . . Jesus" (Luke 2:21).

Lesson Value: Birthdays and Christmas are exciting. Even at this young age eyes light up at the sight of gifts. The gifts brought by the wise men were costly and meaningful. The wise men remind us that we need to look for Jesus, worship Him, and give to Him. The children should begin to see that giving gifts can be as much fun as getting them!

Know: Know that Jesus was a special baby.
Feel: Feel happy that Jesus was born.
Do: Show they are happy Jesus was born (smile, sing, tell).

Children will accomplish the goals when they:

1. Say the Bible words, "His name was Jesus."
2. Sing about the baby Jesus.
3. Tell why we are happy at Christmas. (Jesus was born.)
4. Pray, "We are happy that Jesus was born."

Let's Get Ready

If possible, have a tape of children's Christmas music and a tape player to use as children arrive. (No secular music, please!) For the Bible story, you will need your classroom Bible, Zach, and a small wrapped gift. Cut out a large star from construction paper and add glitter. Put it on a dark flannel background and place it in your story area.

Set up the Family Living Center, the Art Center, and the Music/Drama Center. Have the Book/Picture Center ready to use after the Bible story. If you are the only teacher, do just the Art Center activity first.

Learning Activities

(30 minutes, including 10 minutes presession)

Let's Get Started

Have the tape of children's Christmas music playing as children enter. After Zach has greeted each child by name, helped him with wraps and attendance sticker, gently guide the child to a learning center. **Isn't our music pretty? Would you like to sing some songs like these, or would you rather make a pretty card to give to a friend?**

Worship and Bible Story

(15 minutes)

Let's Worship God

Have Zach say, "It's time to put away our things so we can sing and pray to God." As soon as the first child is ready, begin singing "Smile, Mary, Smile." Then sing "Jesus Is the Son of God." Do the rhyme, "I Stand on Tiptoe"; then sing "Jesus, You Are Special." Take your Bible and show the children the Bible words. Have the children repeat the words with you. Do the rhyme, "The Baby Jesus"; then pray, **Thank You, God, for Jesus. We are happy that Jesus was born.**

Let's Learn From the Bible

Introduction: If your children know this story, let them do actions, such as climbing on a camel, and so forth. Have Zach hold up the wrapped gift. **I wonder what is in this package. I like to get gifts, don't you? And I like to give gifts to special people too! Whom do you like to give gifts to? What do you give for gifts?** *(Let children give answers to both questions.)* **Our Bible story is about some wise men who wanted to give gifts to Jesus. Do you have your listening ears on?** Put Zach away. Have your Bible in front of you.

The Bible Story: Some wise men who lived far away saw a big bright star in the sky one night. *(Show the star you have made.)* They said, "This star means that a special baby has been born. He is a king. If we follow the star, we will find Him." So they packed some clothes, some food, and some very special gifts. Perhaps they climbed up on their camels. Then they began their long journey.

The wise men followed the big bright star. It led them on and on. Clip-clop, clip-clop. *(Pat your legs and make the clip-clop sound of the camels.)* The camels walked and walked. Sometimes the wise men stopped to eat or to sleep or to get drinks of water. And then they would clip-clop, clip-clop along again. *(Pat legs.)*

Finally, the star stopped over a small house. The wise men climbed down off their camels. There in that house were Jesus and Mary, His mother! The wise men were very happy they had found Jesus. They bowed down to Him. Then they gave their special gifts to Jesus. They were happy that Jesus was born. And they were happy to give their special gifts to Him, because they loved Him.

Let's Apply the Lesson

Let's clip-clop like camels again. Did they clip-clop for a long time or a short time? Where were they going? Why did the wise men want to see Jesus? *(Because they loved Him. To give Him gifts. To show they were happy that Jesus was born.)* **We can**

Jesus came to earth because He loves us. We can be like the shepherds and tell others that Jesus loves them. And we can be like the wise men and give gifts to show our love for Jesus.

Learning Activities

(20 minutes)

Let's Play Awhile

If you did not use one of the learning centers listed at the beginning of the lesson, do so now. Or use a previous activity that the children particularly enjoyed.

Let's Go Home

Have Zach sing "It's Time to Put Our Toys Away." Bring children together until parents come. If time is limited, sing a couple of songs and do an action rhyme. If you have sufficient time, try this new game. To the tune of "London Bridge," sing the following words, adding appropriate motions:

Reaching, stretching, growing taller.
I'm not little, I'm so big.
God made me to grow up tall
And love my family one and all.

After singing the song a couple of times, ask a child to name a family member he could tell about Jesus. Or, let the child say the Bible words if he prefers. Sing the song again, and choose another child. Continue until all children have had a turn to answer or until most children have left with their parents. Make sure that children have their Christmas bells to take home. As you greet the parents with a smile, tell them something their children did, said, or the way they participated. Positive reinforcement helps children and encourages parents!

Thank You, God, for Jesus

Review of Lessons 1–4

Bible Words: "His name was . . . Jesus" (Luke 2:21).

Lesson Value: All of the special events surrounding the birth of Jesus help to point out the uniqueness of Jesus' birth. An angel announced His coming birth to a virgin, and then again an angel announced His birth to shepherds. Wise men brought Him expensive gifts after being led by a very bright star. Jesus' birth was indeed unique. Today we can follow the shepherds' example and tell others about the Son of God, whose "name was . . . Jesus."

Know: Know that Jesus was a special baby.
Feel: Feel happy that Jesus was born.
Do: Show they are happy Jesus was born (smile, sing, tell).

Children will accomplish the goals when they:

1. Say the Bible words, "His name was Jesus."
2. Sing a song about Jesus' birth.
3. Help tell the story of Jesus' birth.
4. Thank God for Jesus.

Let's Get Ready

For the Bible story, you will need a Bible, Zach, a baby item, and the visuals used in previous lessons.

Set up the Family Living Center, the Art Center, the

Block Center, and the Games Center. If you are the only teacher, use just the Art Center. The Family Living Center will require having a mother and baby available. Use this one either now or after the Bible story, according to the baby's schedule. If there is no baby available, use doll babies as you have done previously.

Learning Activities

(30 minutes, including 10 minutes presession)

Let's Get Started

Let Zach greet the children by name, help with their wraps, and their attendance stickers. Then guide children to the various learning centers. If the mother and baby are present, make sure all children have time to spend with them.

Brittany, I'm glad to see you today. We have a surprise, some special visitors. Look in our Family Living Center. Mrs. Blank has brought her baby, Elizabeth. Isn't she cute! I know you would like to go over and talk to baby Elizabeth and ask her mommy some questions.

Worship and Bible Story

(15 minutes)

Let's Worship God

Have Zach sing with the children, "It's Time to Put Our Toys Away." When toys are picked up and children begin coming to the story circle, start singing the songs and doing the rhymes from this unit. Hold up your Bible and show the children the words, "His name was . . . Jesus." Let the children take turns holding the Bible and "reading" the words with you. Then pray, **Thank You, God, for sending Your Son, Jesus, to earth. We are happy He was born.**

Let's Learn From the Bible

Introduction: Let Zach carry in a baby item, such as a bottle. Have Zach say, "Babies are so cute! I just saw a baby all wrapped up in a blanket. Her mother was holding her like she was special. And she is! But there was one baby who was even more special. Do you know His name? That's right, Jesus. Let's remember some of the special things that happened when Jesus was born." Put Zach away. When appropriate, hold up visuals used previously. Let children answer as many of the questions as possible (answers in parentheses).

The Bible-story Review: The Bible tells about Mary, who loved God very much. God chose Mary to be the mother of Jesus, God's Son. Who told Mary this happy news? (The angel.) Was Mary happy to hear this good news? (Yes.) *(Sing "Smile, Mary, Smile.")*

Mary and Joseph went to Bethlehem. Did they stay in a nice hotel? (No.) Where did they stay? (In a stable.) When Jesus was born, where did Mary lay Him? (In a manger.) That same night out in the country, who told shepherds that Jesus had been born? (An angel.) Then lots of angels came and praised God. When the angels left, what did the shepherds do? (They went to see baby Jesus.) Then they told everyone they saw about baby Jesus. *(Sing "Jesus, You Are Special.")*

Some wise men who lived far away saw something that told them Jesus was born. What did they see? (A big star.) They rode their camels for a long time. How did the camels sound? (Clip-clop, clip-clop.) When the wise men found little Jesus, what did they give Him? (Gifts.) *(Sing "Jesus Is the Son of God.")*

Let's Apply the Lesson

Who was the special baby we've been talking about? Help children answer, "His name was Jesus."

Who is the Son of God? "His name was Jesus."

Who did the angel tell about? "His name was Jesus."

Who did the shepherds hurry to see? "His name was Jesus."

Who did the wise men take gifts to? "His name was Jesus."

Family Living Center

Unit 1—Jesus Is Born

Items to Include:

Lesson 1
Diapers

Lesson 2
Baby bed or box
Rocking chair

Purpose: The child will know that Jesus was a special baby.

Things to Do and Say

Lesson 1

As the children hold and love the babies say, **What is the name of your baby? We treat babies gently. Who takes care of babies? That's right, mommies and daddies, and sometimes grandmas and grandpas.** Mention any others who may care for the children. **And who can help take care of the baby? Yes, you can. What can you do for the baby? What else do we need to take care of this baby?**

An angel told Mary the happy news that she was going to have a baby. The Bible tells us, "His name was Jesus." I'm happy that baby Jesus was born.

Lesson 2

Make sure you have at least one small rocking chair today. Encourage the children to get their babies ready for bed.

What are you doing with your baby right now? How do you know if your baby is tired? What do you do when she cries? That looks like a gentle way to hold the baby. God likes it when we are gentle with babies. Does your baby like to be rocked to sleep? What do you think Mary did to help baby Jesus go to sleep? Do you think Mary sang to Him? Sing "Jesus, You Are Special," as you hold a baby. **Did baby Jesus have a crib to sleep in? No, His mommy laid Him in a manger to sleep.**

Art Center

Unit 1—Jesus Is Born

Items to Include:

Lesson 1
Page 107
Wrapping paper
Cloth scraps

Lesson 2
Page 108
Sandpaper
Flannel scraps
Raffia or straw

Lesson 3
Page 109
Cotton balls

Purpose: The child will know that Jesus was a special baby.

Things to Do and Say

Lesson 1

Make copies of page 107. Two's may only want to color their pages. Three's can add shiny wrapping paper cut to fit the angel, cloth on Mary's dress, and yarn for hair.

As children color, talk about the picture. **Who is this? That's right, an angel. Who is this woman? Yes, Mary. This angel is bringing good news to Mary. The good news is from God. Do you know what that good news is? God wants Mary to be the mother of His Son, Jesus. The Bible says, "His name was Jesus."**

Lesson 2

Cut mangers from sandpaper. Glue on sheets of construction paper. Cut baby Jesus figures, blankets, and hay from construction paper. Glue outing flannel on blankets.

Let children glue hay in place, babies on the hay, and blankets on the babies. Optional: Add dots of glue to hay and let children add raffia or straw. As the children work, talk about and ask questions about the special baby, Jesus, and the events surrounding His birth.

Lesson 3

Before class, make one sheep for each child. Have cotton balls and glue ready. Put a bit

Art Center, continued

of glue on a sheep and show the child how to spread the cotton ball and place it in the glue. Three's can use glue sticks themselves.

There were lots of sheep out on the hillside the night Jesus was born. Who was taking care of them? Yes, shepherds. The shepherds were the first people to know that Jesus was born. Were they excited? Yes! Were they happy? Yes! They went to see this special baby. The Bible tells us, "His name was Jesus."

Lesson 4
Nativity pictures or stickers
Construction paper

Lesson 4

Cut construction paper in half, then fold these in half to make cards 4 1/2" x 6". On the front of each card print "His name was Jesus." Find appropriate nativity pictures or stickers. (No secular pictures!) Give each child a card and one picture at a time.

These words say, "His name was Jesus." Those are our Bible words. Who is this baby? Yes, baby Jesus. Some wise men traveled a long way to bring Him gifts. They were happy that Jesus was born. This card is going to be a gift to my friend Mrs. Jones, because she is sick. I'm happy that Jesus is born. He was a special baby!

Lesson 5
Paper cups
Jingle bells
Self-stick stickers

For all lessons
Glue
Crayons
Yarn

Lesson 5

Put bells together ahead of time like this: Poke a hole in the bottom of each cup. Thread a chenille wire from the outside to the inside. Thread the wire through a jingle bell inside the cup. Poke the wire back through another hole in the bottom of the cup. Twist the wire to make a handle. Use only self-stick stickers. Others won't hold.

We are happy at Christmas because Jesus was born. Whenever you ring your bell, you can think about the time when this special baby was born. The Bible tells us, "His name was Jesus."

Family Living Center, continued

Jesus was a special baby because He is God's Son. Thank You, God, for baby Jesus. I'm happy that He was born.

Lesson 4
Baby bottles
Bibs
Toy high chair or infant seat

Lesson 4

If possible, have a toy high chair or infant seat today. As the children feed their babies say, **What is your baby eating? What is good for your baby to eat? Can a baby eat fried chicken?** *(No, it's big-people food.)* **Why does God give mommies and daddies to babies? That's right, so they can take care of the babies. Who took care of baby Jesus? Yes, Mary and Joseph. God knew they would take good care of Him. Jesus was a special baby. I'm glad baby Jesus was born.**

Lesson 5
Real mother and baby

Lesson 5

Find a mother who feels comfortable bringing her baby to the class. You will need to caution the children on how we need to have gentle touches. Let the children ask the mother questions about the baby and how she cares for him. Find out the best time to have the baby in the classroom and fit your schedule around the baby's.

For all lessons
Housekeeping equipment
Dishes
Baby dolls
Clothes
Blankets

Book/Picture Center

Unit 1—Jesus Is Born

Items to Include:

For all lessons
Classroom Bible with Bible words highlighted and marked with a bookmark
Appropriate books on the birth of Jesus (list on page 89)
Pictures of babies, of Mary and the angel, shepherds, wise men, baby Jesus, baby Jesus with Mary and Joseph

Purpose: The child will know that Jesus is God's Son, a special baby.

Things to Do and Say

Have pictures mounted on construction paper. Cover with clear, self-adhesive plastic (optional). Display books and pictures on a table or book rack. Several pillows on the floor work well for a reading area.

Read books that have short texts, or "picture read" books—that is, look at pictures, have children point to certain people or objects, talk about them, ask who certain people are, and so forth. Also do this with your mounted pictures. Remember to use the Bible words, "His name was Jesus," often as you talk with the children.

Lesson 1

Have pictures of Mary and the angel ready. Make an enlarged copy of the picture of Mary and the angel from page 107. Add color if you wish. Talk about how Mary would have felt, what she thought, etc. Stress that the angel brought happy news from God.

Lesson 2

Have books and pictures with Mary, Joseph, and baby Jesus. Make an enlarged copy of the craft picture for Lesson 2, page 108. Add touch-and-feel effects.

Block Center

Unit 1—Jesus Is Born

Items to Include:

Large cardboard or wooden blocks
Stand-up animals made from patterns on pages 109 and 110.

Purpose: The child will know that Jesus was a special baby.

Things to Do and Say

Lessons 2 and 5

Before class, make multiple copies of the stand-up animals according to directions on pages 109 and 110. Use these in the stable(s) the children will build with your help.

As the children work on their stables say, **A stable is like a barn. It is a place where animals eat and sleep. What animals do you think were in the stable when Mary and Joseph came there to sleep? What sounds do those animals make? What do those animals eat?What do they eat out of? Yes, a manger. Let's build a manger for our animals.**

Do you know where Mary laid baby Jesus when He was born? That's right, in a manger! With all that hay it would make a soft bed for baby Jesus. Baby Jesus was a special baby. The Bible says, "His name was Jesus."

(from old take-home papers, books that are no longer fit to be used as books, etc.)

Lesson 3

If you can't find pictures of animals, use the stand-up animals from pages 109 and 110. These can be enlarged if you want, and color added.

Lesson 4

Add pictures and books that include the wise men.

Lesson 5

Use all the pictures and books as review for the unit. Let the children tell all they know about each picture. Encourage a forgetful child by asking a question or suggesting a word or two.

Game Center

Unit 1—Jesus Is Born

Items to Include:

Lessons 1 and 5
Beanbag
Tape player
Tape of Christmas music

Lesson 3
Baby blanket

Purpose: The child will say the Bible words, "His name was Jesus."

Things to Do and Say

Lessons 1 and 5

If you do not have an appropriate tape of Christmas music, have someone record the songs from this unit, using a musical instrument and/or singing.

Have the children sit on the floor in a circle. Explain that the beanbag will be passed from one child to the next while the music plays. When the music stops, the child holding the beanbag will say the Bible words, "His name was Jesus." Most 2's and some 3's will need help with this. You will need one person to start and stop the music, and one or more to sit in the circle with the children. You will need to say the words with the children the first week. After that, most will be able to say them on their own.

Use this game any time during the unit that you need an extra activity or when the children need to play awhile.

Lesson 3

As soon as the children have gathered in a circle, show them the baby blanket you will be hiding. Then have the children close and cover their eyes so you can hide the blanket. When you return to the circle, have the children guess where the blanket is hidden (or get up and find it). If you are working only with 3's, let children take turns hiding the blanket.

Music/Drama Center

Unit 1—Jesus Is Born

Items to Include:

Lesson 1
Two telephones

Lessons 3 and 4
Rhythm instruments
Tape of Christmas music
Tape player

Purpose: The child will express happy feelings because Jesus was born.

Things to Do and Say

Lesson 1

Have two play telephones set up across a table from one another. If you make the first call, the children will understand what to do. Make sure you tell the happy news that Mary heard. Let one child "call" the other one and tell him some happy news. Encourage the child to think of something fun she did that week or something she is going to do and tell that to a friend. The child can tell the happy news, "His name was Jesus." Let children take turns making the phone calls.

You can help a child know what to tell his friend by saying, **What did you do yesterday? What do you like to do? When did you do that? Can you tell your friend, Susie, about that? What happened next? Can you tell your friend the name of God's Son? That is very happy news!**

Lessons 3 and 4

If you do not have a tape of Christmas music that would be appropriate for 2's and 3's, have someone record the songs used during this unit from page 90. These could be played on a musical instrument and/or sung. Have rhythm instruments such as bells, rhythm sticks, drums, and so forth—either purchased or homemade.

Game Center, continued

Ask, **Who uses a blanket like this? That's right, a baby. Why does the baby need the blanket? Yes, to keep warm. How do you think Mary kept baby Jesus warm? Yes, she probably used a small blanket. Mary's baby was a special baby. The Bible says, "His name was Jesus."**

Music/Drama Center, continued

Tell the children they are going to be a praise band. Have the children sit in a circle. Pass out the rhythm instruments one at a time, explaining what each is. Let the child who receives the instrument play it and then set it on the floor in front of him for the next child. Have a small group so the children do not have to wait too long for an instrument. The younger the child the harder it is to sing and play at the same time, so your 2's will probably just play their instruments. After the children have had turns playing different instruments, encourage them to go to another center so that other children can participate.

We are making happy music today. I like to hear your happy voices. Why are we happy at Christmas? Yes, because Jesus was born.

This activity can be used with all lessons from this unit if you need more centers or your children especially enjoy music.

An angel told Mary she would have a baby boy. The Bible says, "His name was . . . Jesus" (Luke 2:21).

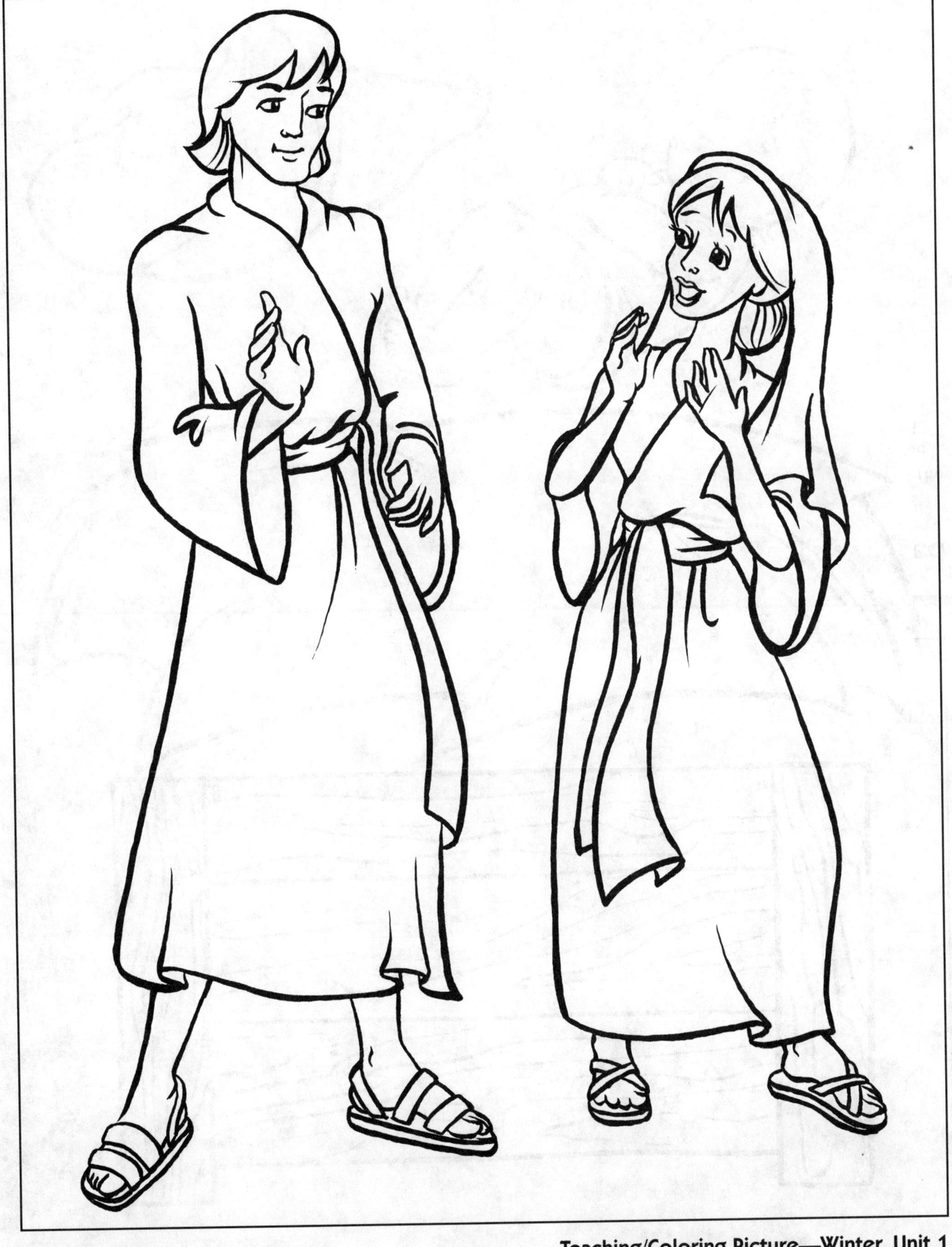

Teaching/Coloring Picture—Winter, Unit 1

Stand-up animals—Winter, Unit 1

These animals can be used all during this unit. For lesson 3, make stand-up sheep in the Art Center. Also use in the Block Center and in the Book and Picture Center for lesson 3.

Instructions

1. Photocopy animals; enlarge if you wish.
2. Color and cut out animals.
3. Tape two of each animal together at dotted lines so they will stand.
4. Let children add cotton to the sheep they make in the Art Center.

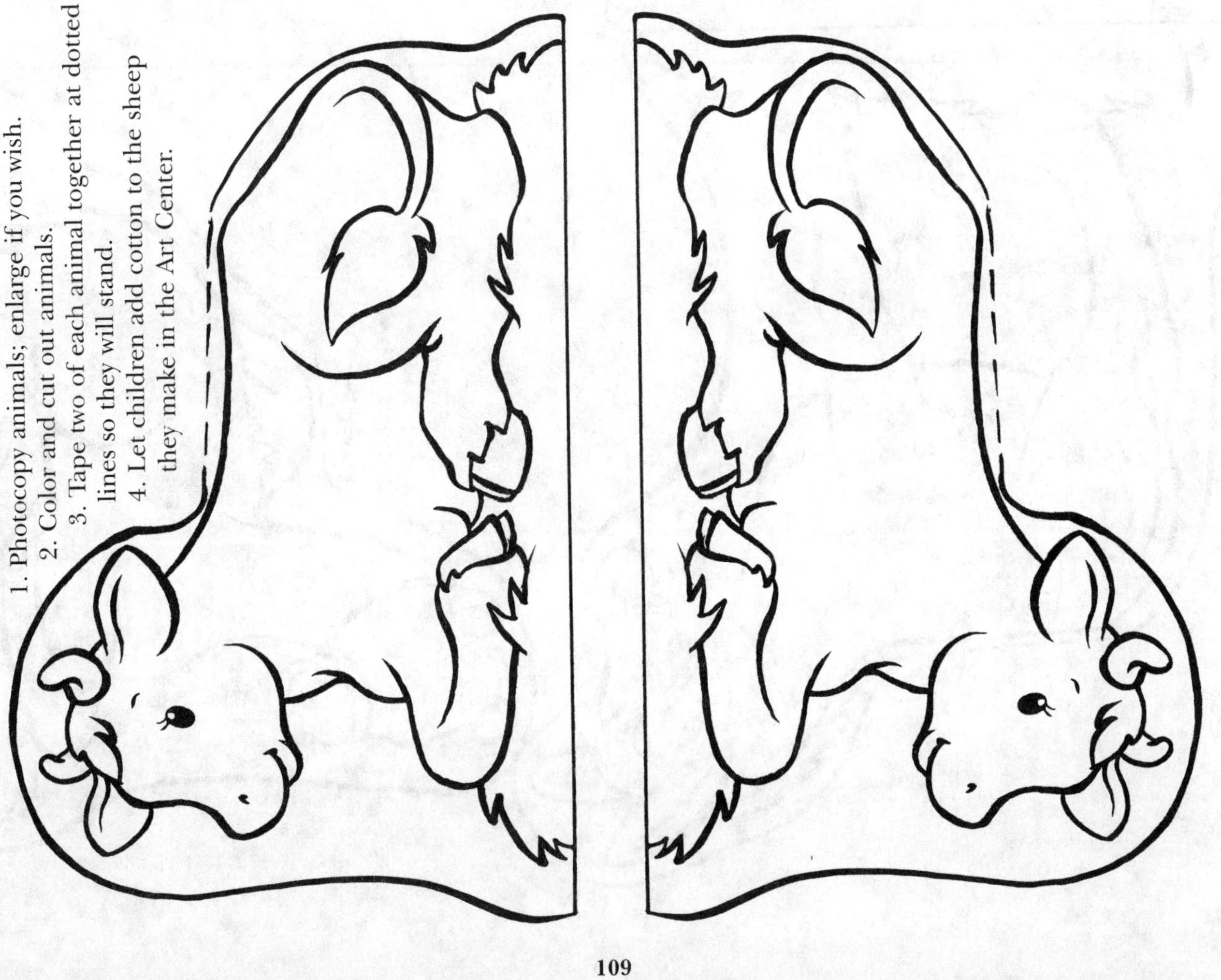

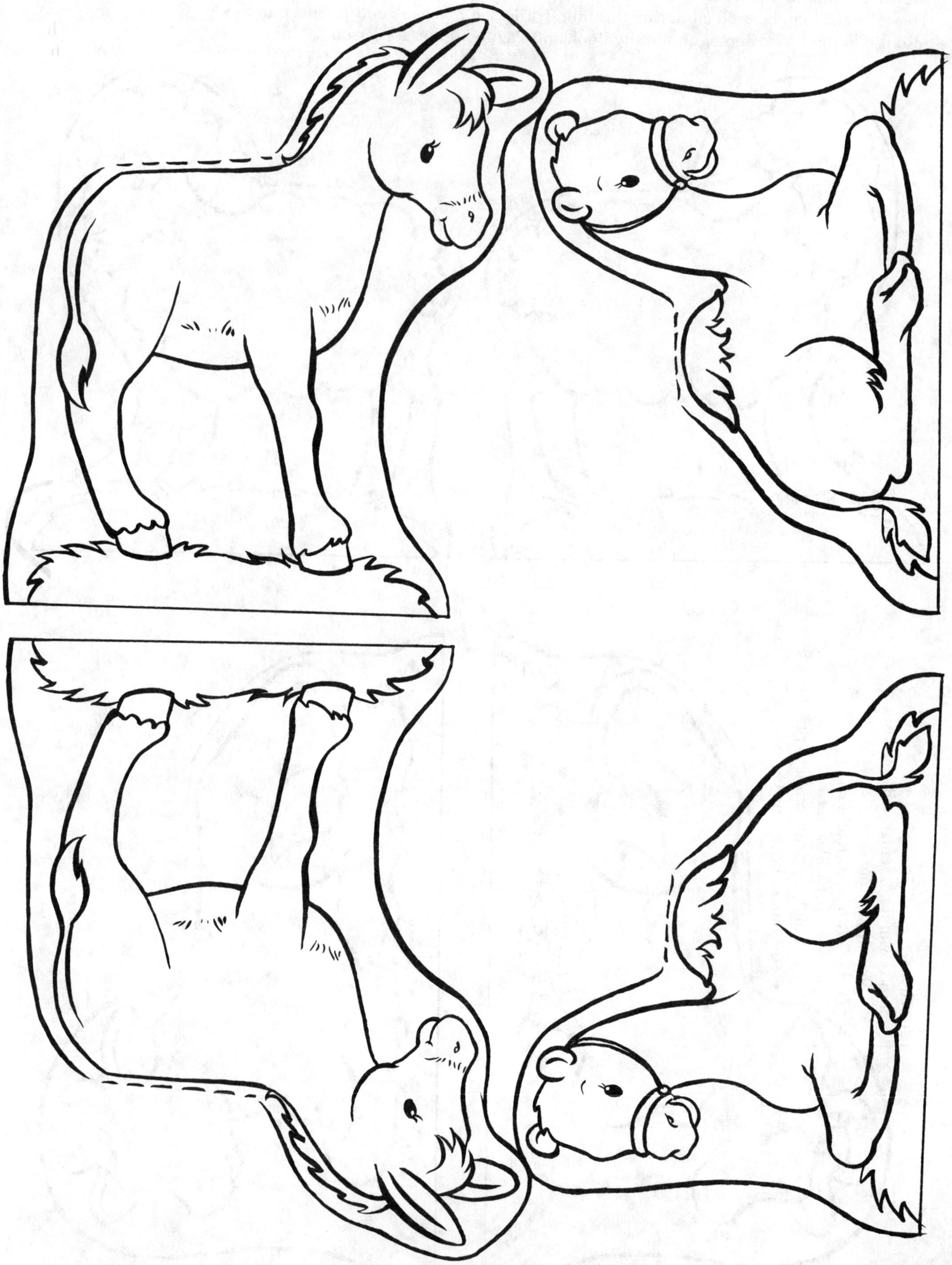

Star—Winter, Unit 1

Using this pattern, cut a star from yellow construction paper and add glitter, or from cardboard and cover with silver or gold foil. Back the star with outing flannel or fine sandpaper and use on a flannel board covered with dark blue or black cloth.

Dear Parent,

This unit your child will be learning that Jesus was a special baby. Through taking part in songs, action rhymes, varied learning activities, and the Bible stories, your child will feel happy that Jesus was born. He will learn that Jesus is the Son of God and that His birth was a special event. The titles of our lessons are:

An Angel Brings Happy News (Luke 1:26-38)
Jesus Is Born (Luke 2:1-7)
Shepherds Come to See Jesus (Luke 2:8-20)
Wise Men Bring Gifts (Matthew 2:1, 2, 9-11)
Thank You, God, for Jesus (Review of Lessons 1–4)

Here are ways to reinforce at home what your child is learning in class:

- Set up an unbreakable crèche for your child to arrange. As your child plays with the pieces, let him tell you the story. If he forgets a part, he may make up something to fill in the part he has forgotten. You can help him with the real story if that happens. For example say, "Oh, didn't the shepherds go right away to see baby Jesus?" Often all a child needs is a little reminder of what happened.
- Our Bible words are, "His name was . . . Jesus," found in Luke 2:21. Show your child the words in the Bible. Say the verse, then let her say it with you, and then by herself.
- When you are out at night, look at the sky and point out the stars. Talk about what it was like for the shepherds as they watched their sheep out on the hillside, what the shepherds would have seen, and what it would be like to see angels coming to speak to them. Talk about the wise men, perhaps riding on their camels, following one very bright star.
- The wise men brought gifts to Jesus to honor Him. We take gifts to friends and family now to show them we love them and care for them. First talk to your child about why the wise men brought their gifts to Jesus. "The wise men knew Jesus was a very special baby and they took gifts to Him to show they loved Him." Then talk with your child about who is special in his life. Encourage him to think of someone who needs some extra attention, such as someone in a nursing home, a home-bound person, a lonely neighbor. Let your child help you make a fruit plate, bake cookies, or make something for that person. Then take time to deliver the gift together.
- Enjoy this action rhyme and song with your child.

Jesus, You Are Special

(Tune: "Mulberry Bush")

Jesus was a special baby, special baby,
special baby.
Jesus was a special baby.
Jesus, You are special.

The Baby Jesus

A stable, *(Make house with hands.)*
A manger, *(Make box with hands.)*
A baby, *(Cradle baby.)*
With animals all around. *(Arms outstretched.)*
The baby is sleeping, *(Folded hands against cheek.)*
Let's tiptoe, *(Walk on tiptoe.)*
And not make even a sound. *(Sh-h-h!)*

—Dana Eynon

At this busy time of year, take time to enjoy your child, to help others, and most of all, to be happy and thankful that Jesus was born.

Your child's teacher,

Unit 2: Jesus Is God's Son

Lessons 6–9

By the end of the unit, the children will

Know that Jesus grew to be a special man.
Feel thankful Jesus is special.
Pray, "Thank You, Jesus, for being special."

Unit Bible Words

"Jesus is . . . the Son of God" (John 20:31, *NIV*).

Resources

Happy Face Stickers

Books

from Standard Publishing
Jesus Grew (24-03115)
Five Small Loaves and Two Small Fish (24-03593)
Look, I'm Growing Up (24-04233)
Jesus Is My Special Friend (24-04211)

This Unit at a Glance

6 Jesus Grows Up — **Luke 2:40-52**

The boy Jesus is old enough to accompany His parents on the long trip to Jerusalem and to learn at the temple.

7 Jesus Heals a Woman — **Mark 1:29-31; Luke 4:38, 39**

Jesus, now a man, shows that He is the Son of God by using His power to heal Peter's mother-in-law.

8 Jesus Feeds Many People — **John 6:5-13; Mark 6:32-44**

Jesus demonstrates His God-given power once again by feeding a multitude with only five small barley loaves and two small fish.

9 Jesus Does Great Things — **Review of Lessons 6–8**

Why Teach This Unit?

As you teach this unit, children will learn three valuable lessons. First, they will understand that the baby born on Christmas grew up just as they are growing. Throughout the year children will hear many stories about the *man* Jesus; this unit will help them understand that He was once *baby* Jesus.

The second lesson is that Jesus is special—the Son of God. Children will learn that God gave His Son, Jesus, special power to do wonderful things—miracles—so that all people could know that He was sent by God.

Third, this unit will help children feel thankful for this special man. They cannot understand all that Jesus has done for them but they can begin to develop an attitude of respect and thankfulness toward Him.

From the moment you greet the children, **Hello, Emily, you are growing up, just like Jesus did. The Bible tells us, "Jesus is the Son of God,"** . . . until you say good-bye, **Josh, I'm so glad you came tonight to learn that "Jesus is the Son of God,"** . . . and everywhere in between, **Rachel, who is this? Yes. Jesus. The Bible says, "Jesus is the Son of**

God," . . . in prayer, in song, in the story, in the learning centers, in conversation, use the Bible words.

Things to Do for This Unit

- Make photocopies of Parents' Letter (page 136) and the Unit Planning Sheet (pages 319 and 320).
- Prepare the bulletin board (see page 129).
- Photocopy Learning Center Cards (pages 123-128); cut pages apart on solid lines. Mount side 1 of a card on cardboard; then mount side 2 on the back of the cardboard. Laminate them for durability (optional).
- Gather materials listed on the Learning Center Cards.
- Photocopy pages 130-133 and make visual aids according to directions given on those pages.
- Find pictures of baby Jesus, the boy Jesus, and the man Jesus.
- Obtain an instant camera if possible, or use a regular camera.
- For Lesson 6, make arrangements for visitors (see God's Wonders Center).
- For Lesson 8, make copies of painting page 134.

Use These Songs and Action Rhymes During Unit 2

Jesus Grew and Grew

(Tune: "Mary Had a Little Lamb")

Jesus grew and grew and grew;
Just like me, just like you.
Jesus grew and grew and grew;
Just like me and you.

Jesus, You Are Special

(Tune: "Mulberry Bush")

Jesus was a special baby, special baby, special baby.
Jesus was a special baby. Jesus, You are special.
2. *Jesus was a special boy.*
3. *Jesus was a special man.*

Jesus Is the Son of God

(Tune: "London Bridge")

Jesus is the Son of God, Son of God, Son of God.
Jesus is the Son of God. Jesus, You are special.
2. *Jesus made a sick woman well.*
3. *Jesus fed a crowd of people.*
4. *Jesus, You do wonderful things.*

When I Pray

When I pray, I fold my hands *(Fold hands.)*
And close my eyes. *(Close eyes.)*
I think about God, and He hears me. —*Jean Katt*

Jesus

Where is baby Jesus? *(Pretend to hold baby.)*
Has He gone away? *(Puzzled look; shrug shoulders.)*
No! He's grown into a little boy,
(Raise hand to indicate growing.)
Who likes to run and play. *(Pretend to run.)*
—*Cathy Allen Falk*

Where is baby Jesus? Has He gone away?
No! He's grown into a great big man,
(Raise hands above head.)
Who likes to help and pray. *(Fold hands in prayer.)*
—*Carrie Chesnut*

Jesus Is God's Son

Can a baby listen quietly to the teachers?	No!
Could Jesus?	Yes, Jesus was a special boy!
Can a baby pray to God?	No!
Could Jesus?	Yes, Jesus was a special boy!

The Bible tells us why Jesus was a special boy. It says, "Jesus is the Son of God." Let each child "read" the verse. Then give her a happy-face sticker to place on the bulletin board. **We are happy that God's Son, Jesus, grew up and that we are growing up too! Let's pretend we are going on a trip and we are big enough to help.** Suggest actions, such as packing clothes, loading a car, putting on seat belts, riding quietly, getting out, walking, etc.

Learning Activities

(20 minutes)

Let's Play Awhile

Repeat the rhyme, "Jesus." Sing "Jesus Grew and Grew," adding these motions. Bend down each time you begin the phrase, "Jesus grew." Straighten up a little each time you say "grew." Point to yourself and to a child when appropriate. Substitute names of children for "me" and "you." **Caleb, who helped Jesus grow? . . . Who is helping you grow?**

Have materials ready for the Family Living Center. If you are the only teacher and did not begin the bulletin board project earlier, combine these two centers by having your Family Living Center near the bulletin board. Use the pictures of Jesus already on the board and take pictures of the children as they play.

Let's Go Home

Have Zach say, "Moms and dads will be coming soon for their big boys and girls. Let's clean up so we are ready." Read the Bible story from a children's picture Bible or book.

If your children are restless, have them do the action rhyme, "Jesus." Make sure each child has a copy of the Parents' Letter.

Jesus Grows Up

Luke 2:40-52

Bible Words: "Jesus is . . . the Son of God" (John 20:31, *NIV*).

Lesson Value: In this lesson, the children will learn that the special baby born on Christmas grew up to be a boy. The baby grew big enough to help, work, play, listen, learn, and pray. Your children will recognize that there are many things they can do now that babies cannot. The children will be encouraged to thank God for helping Jesus grow up to be a boy.

Know: Know that Jesus grew to be a special boy.
Feel: Feel thankful Jesus is special.
Do: Pray, "Thank You, God for helping Jesus grow up to be a boy."

Children will accomplish the goals when they:

1. Say the Bible words, "Jesus is the Son of God."
2. Sing about Jesus.
3. Point to or name Jesus as a baby and as a boy.
4. Pretend to be Jesus as a baby and/or a boy.
5. Pray, "Thank You, God, for helping Jesus grow up to be a boy."

Let's Get Ready

Wrap Zach in a blanket and tie a baby bonnet on his head. For the Bible story, prepare the story wheel (pages 130 and 131); highlight the Bible words in your classroom Bible;

have pictures of the baby Jesus and boy Jesus ready. You will also need happy-face stickers (make from page 132 or purchase some).

Set up the Block Center, the Art Center, and the God's Wonders Center. If you are the only teacher, use just the Block Center. Have the Family Living Center materials ready for use after the Bible story.

Learning Activities

(30 minutes, including 10 minutes presession)

Let's Get Started

As you greet the children, sit with Zach cradled in your arms. Smile, look each child in the eyes and say, **Look, Jacob, Zach is pretending to be a small puppy. He is lying quietly now but he will grow to be bigger and will run and play. Today we will learn how baby Jesus grew and learned new things.** Encourage each child to join an activity. Place the "sleeping" Zach near the story area in a doll-size bed.

Worship and Bible Story

(15 minutes)

Let's Worship God

Make soft, howling sounds. **Zach, our puppy, is waking up from his nap. He is lonely. Let's clean up so we can sing.**

Stand in a circle. As children arrive, quickly pick two; let them hold the pictures of baby and boy Jesus in the center of the circle. Remaining children hold hands and walk while singing stanzas 1 and 2 of "Jesus, You Are Special." Repeat several times using other children. Collect the pictures. Do verse 1 of the rhyme, "Jesus." Sing "Let's Be Very Quiet" (page 88). **Let's pray, Thank You, God, for helping Jesus grow up to be a boy.**

Let's Learn From the Bible

Introduction: Make another soft, howling sound. Pick up Zach. **What's the matter, Zach?** Continue the sounds. **Zach, I can't understand you. You sound like a puppy.** Then Zach sits up and says he is tired of being a puppy; he wants to get up and play with the "big" boys and girls. Remove bonnet and blanket. **That's great, Zach, because we are going to learn how the special baby born on Christmas grew to be a special boy.** Ask the children to name the special baby. Put Zach away. **Yes, Jesus is His name.** Show the picture of baby Jesus. **Let's find out what He can do, now that He is bigger.**

The Bible Story: *(Have your open Bible on your lap; hold up the story wheel, showing the appropriate pictures.)* "Jesus," called his mother, Mary. "We are going on a long trip. Please pack your clothes." Jesus was big enough to pack His clothes.

"Jesus," called Joseph, "We are going on a long trip. Please help me load the donkey." Jesus was big enough to help load the donkey.

Walk, walk, walk. Walk, walk, walk. The trip to the temple-church was long. Jesus was big enough to walk a long way.

Now it was time to sit quietly and listen to the teachers. Jesus was big enough to sit quietly.

Now it was time to pray to God. Jesus was big enough to pray to God. "Thank You, God, for helping Jesus, and all of us, grow up to be bigger."

Let's Apply the Lesson

Let Zach ask the following questions. Lead the children in enthusiastic response.

Who helped Jesus grow?	God helped Jesus grow!
Who helps you grow?	God helps us grow!
Can a baby pack clothes?	No!
Could Jesus?	Yes, Jesus was a special boy!
Can a baby load a donkey?	No!
Could Jesus?	Yes, Jesus was a special boy!

is the Son of God." Show the words and give each child an opportunity to say them. Give a happy-face sticker as you say to a child, **We are happy because Jesus is the Son of God; He is special.**

Learning Activities

(20 minutes)

Let's Play Awhile

Stand in a circle and sing, "If You're Happy and You Know It" (page 88). As you sing the word *face,* put on a big smile. The children will imitate your enthusiasm.

Have materials ready for the Block Center. If you did not work on the bulletin board earlier, do the block activity near the bulletin board so you can add a child's pictures and stickers while the others play with the blocks. If you have multiple teachers, open the other centers used earlier.

Let's Go Home

Children, Zach is feeling better now. Let's put our toys away so we can help him take off his bandages. Praise each child by name as you see him helping. When the children finish picking up, remove Zach's bandages. "I feel like singing now," Zach says. Sing "If You're Happy and You Know It" and other songs from this unit.

If you prefer a quiet closing, have Zach say, "I feel much better. I feel happy like the woman in our Bible story did." Let the children retell the story using the visual. Zach may help as needed.

Jesus Heals a Woman

Mark 1:29-31; Luke 4:38, 39

Bible Words: "Jesus is . . . the Son of God" (John 20:31, *NIV*).

Lesson Value: In this lesson, children will learn that the special baby, who grew to be a boy, kept on growing to become a special man. They will hear of Jesus' awesome power over sickness and His great compassion that caused Him to reach out and heal those in need. The children will begin to feel thankful for this special man, Jesus, the Son of God.

Know: Know that Jesus grew to be a special man.
Feel: Feel thankful Jesus is special.
Do: Pray, "Thank You, Jesus, for being special."

The children will accomplish the goals when they:

1. Say the Bible words, "Jesus is the Son of God."
2. Point to or name Jesus as a special baby, boy, and man.
3. Act out the Bible story.
4. Pray, "Thank You, Jesus, for being special."

Let's Get Ready

Have a basket or box for children to put their baby pictures in as they arrive. Wrap Zach's head or paw with gauze or white cloths. Write the Bible words on adhesive bandages, one per child, using a black permanent marker.

For the Bible story, you will need pictures of Jesus from last week and one of Him as a man; your Bible, the happy/sad visual aid (page 132), and happy-face stickers (page 132 or purchased).

Prepare the Family Living Center, the Art Center, and the Game Center. If you are the only teacher, use just the Family Living Center. Use the Block Center after the Bible story.

Learning Activities

(30 minutes, including 10 minutes presession)

Let's Get Started

Holding the injured Zach, greet each child. **Sarah, poor Zach is hurt. In our Bible story we will learn how God's Son, Jesus, helped a sick lady** *(look sad)* **get well** *(look glad)*. **Here is a bandage with our Bible words on it. It will remind you that Jesus is special.** Help each child put on her bandage, place her baby picture *(name on back)* in the basket, and become involved in an activity.

Worship and Bible Story

(15 minutes)

Let's Worship God

Using a feeble voice, have Zach tell the children to clean up. As the children come, do all of the rhyme, "Jesus," several times. Sing all the stanzas of "Jesus, You Are Special," as you did last week using the pictures. Then sing "Let's Be Very Quiet" (page 88) and do "When I Pray," (page 114). Pray, **Thank You, Jesus, for being special.**

Let's Learn From the Bible

Introduction: Hold up Zach and have him say sadly, "Oh-h-h-h! I feel bad." **In our Bible story, a woman felt bad too. She probably looked like this.** Show sad face. **Can you sound sad?** Have Zach lead the children in practicing the sad sound, "Oh-h-h-h!" **Great! Our Bible tells us something that happened to make her feel glad.** Show happy face. **Can you sound happy?** Practice a happy sound, "Ah-h-h-h!" **When you see the sad face, say a sad "Oh-h-h-h!" When you see the happy face, say a happy "Ah-h-h-h!"** Set Zach aside as though he is listening. Have your open Bible in your lap. Show the appropriate face as you talk.

The Bible Story: Jesus and His friends were going to visit Peter's house. *(Show happy face.)* Ah-h-h-h!

When Jesus and His friends got to Peter's house, they found a very sick woman. *(Sad face.)* Oh-h-h-h!

Her head was very hot and she was lying in bed. *(Sad face.)* Oh-h-h-h!

But someone told Jesus about the sick woman. *(Happy face.)* Ah-h-h-h!

Jesus went to the sick woman. *(Happy face.)* Ah-h-h-h!

Jesus held the sick woman's hand. *(Happy face.)* Ah-h-h-h!

Jesus told the sickness to leave. *(Happy face.)* Ah-h-h-h!

The woman felt good again. She was well. *(Happy face.)* Ah-h-h-h!

She even helped serve supper. *(Happy face.)* Ah-h-h-h!

Jesus is special. Jesus is the Son of God. *(Happy face.)* Ah-h-h-h!

Let's Apply the Lesson

Help Zach hold up the sad face as he asks, "Who was sad?" *(A woman.)* "Why was she sad?" *(She was sick.)* Turn the visual around. "What happened to make her happy? *(She was well.)* "Who made her well? *(Jesus.)* Begin singing "Jesus Is the Son of God," using both stanzas. Sing joyfully several times, encouraging the children to join you. **The Bible tells us, "Jesus**

there were twelve baskets full of food left over. Jesus is special!
Teacher: Jesus is special; He can do wonderful things!

Let's Apply the Lesson

Hold up Zach. **Zach, where is your bone?** "I want some fish and bread." **OK, here.** Place one of the cutout fish in his mouth. Call a child up to the front to hold up the other fish, then have the group count them. Do the same with the bread and baskets.

God's Son, Jesus, surely is special! He can do wonderful things! Review last week's lesson quickly, using the Happy/Sad Face visual aid. Do the rhyme, "My Bible." Let each child read or point to the words, and then give each child a happy-face sticker. **We are happy that Jesus is God's Son. We are happy He can do wonderful things.**

Learning Activities

(20 minutes)

Let's Play Awhile

Let the children stand and sing "If You're Happy and You Know It." Have materials ready for the Family Living Center. If you have several teachers, also use one or more of the earlier learning activities. If your children did not work on the bulletin board earlier, do this now.

Let's Go Home

Have Zach move from child to child whispering in each ear that it is time to clean up. For a quiet closing, read the book, *Five Small Loaves and Two Small Fish,* or read the story from a child's picture Bible. For an active closing, act out the story, using the picnic basket from the God's Wonders Center to put the fish and bread cutouts in, and the blanket as the grassy hillside. Make sure each child takes home his painting page.

Jesus Feeds Many People

John 6:5-13; Mark 6:32-44

Bible Words: "Jesus is . . . the Son of God" (John 20:31, *NIV*).

Lesson Value: In this lesson, the children will hear again how baby Jesus grew to be a man who, because He was special (God's Son), could take the lunch of one small boy and feed five thousand men, plus women and children. Your children will be encouraged to feel thankful. To show they are thankful, they will pray, "Thank You, Jesus, for being special."

Know: Know that Jesus grew to be a special man.
Feel: Feel thankful Jesus is special.
Do: Pray, "Thank You, Jesus, for being special."

Children will accomplish the goals when they:

1. Say the Bible words, "Jesus is the Son of God."
2. Point to or name Jesus as a baby, boy, and man.
3. Act out the Bible story.
4. Tell why Jesus is special. (He is God's Son; He can do wonderful things.)
5. Pray, "Thank You, Jesus, for being special."

Let's Get Ready

For the Bible story, you will need your Bible, Zach, his cardboard bone (page 127), happy-face stickers (page 132), fish crackers, two cardboard fish and five bread and twelve basket cutouts (pages 127 and 128), boy puppet (page 133), and the happy/sad face visual used last week.

Set up the God's Wonders Center, the Art Center, and the Game Center. If you are the only teacher, use just the God's Wonders Center. The Family Living Center will be used after the Bible story.

Learning Activities

(30 minutes, including 10 minutes presession)

Let's Get Started

Have a container ready in which to collect the baby pictures. Cut a dog bone from cardboard and put it in Zach's mouth *(or have him hold it in his paws)* as he greets children. **Hello, Sarah. Zach is busy eating his supper. We're going to hear a story about how Jesus, God's Son, fed lots of people their supper. Let's get your coat off and find you something fun to do.** Help as needed, and then guide the child to an activity.

Worship and Story Time

(15 minutes)

Let's Worship God

Have Zach say, "Let's clean up 'cause it's supper time; come and get it! Savannah, after these dolls are put away you may have a treat."

Give each child a handful of fish crackers and have the children sit in a circle. While they eat say, **Listen while I sing a song about Jesus, God's Son. I'll sing it once, then you can sing with me.** Sing "Jesus Is God's Son," then sing other songs from this unit. Do the rhymes "Jesus" and "I Can" (page 88). Sing "I Can Talk to God," do the rhyme, "When I Pray," and say, **Thank You, Jesus, for being special.**

Let's Learn From the Bible

Introduction: Hold up Zach with the bone still in his mouth or paws. **Zach, are you still chewing on that bone?** "Yes, I'm hungry!" **Well then, you will like our Bible story because it's about food—bread and fish.**

Put Zach away. Hold up the fish cutouts and let children count them. Do the same with the bread. **Let's open our Bible and see what happens to these two small fish and these five small loaves of bread.**

The Bible Story: *(Speak to the little boy puppet as you tell the story. Change the story where needed to fit a male teacher.)*

Boy (excitedly): Mom, Mom, you should have seen all the people who came to see Jesus today! There were moms and dads, big boys and girls, little boys and girls, grandmas, grandpas, and babies.

Teacher: It is late. Sit down and eat your supper.

Boy (still excited): Mom, you should have seen the wonderful thing Jesus did! Andrew, one of Jesus' helpers, came asking if anyone had any food. I told him I had five small loaves of bread and the two fish you gave me.

Teacher: You gave away your lunch!? You must be starving. Sit down and eat your supper.

Boy: Wait, Mom! Andrew told us to sit down on the grass and then he took my bread and fish to Jesus. Jesus thanked God for my food and then His helpers started passing out my food to everyone.

Teacher: Everyone?

Boy: Yes, everyone. We all ate until we were full. All the moms and dads, the big boys and girls, the little boys and girls, the grandmas and grandpas, and babies. So you see, Mom, I already had supper. Jesus fed me. Jesus fed everyone. Oh, and

Let's Apply the Lesson

Pick up Zach. He says, "You do know that Jesus is special because He is God's Son. Let's thank Jesus for being special." Children follow Zach's example when he prays, "Thank You, Jesus, for being special," going through these actions:

- Standing, hands raised, loudly.
- Kneeling, quietly.
- Bowed down.
- Night—turn off lights, lie down.
- Day—turn lights on, sit up.
- Give each child a turn to pray alone, if he wishes.

Let's sit in our circle and listen as our friends thank Jesus. Help as needed, and then give happy-face stickers after each child's turn. **Jesus is happy when we thank Him. We are happy too.**

Learning Activities

(20 minutes)

Let's Play Awhile

Do the rhyme, "Jesus," and sing "If You're Happy and You Know It." Have materials ready for the Family Living Center. If you have several teachers, use one or more of the other learning activities.

Let's Go Home

Have Zach signal the children that it is time to pick up. For a quiet activity, read a favorite book or story from a children's picture Bible. Let Zach help the children review the Bible stories using the visuals from Lessons 6-8.

If the children are restless, let them play a favorite game, sing songs, and do rhymes they enjoyed, or pretend to be Jesus growing up as described in the Family Living Center, Lesson 6. Include the wonderful things Jesus did as a man.

Make sure each child has his party hat and the envelope with his pictures.

Jesus Does Great Things

Review of Lessons 6–8

Bible Words: "Jesus is . . . the Son of God" (John 20:31, *NIV*).

Lesson Value: In this lesson, children will again be reminded that the special baby, Jesus, grew to be a special boy and then a special man. They will be encouraged to celebrate by thanking Jesus, God's Son, for being special and for doing wonderful things. They will pray, "Thank You, Jesus, for being special." Choose the activities the children enjoyed most during this unit.

Know: Know that Jesus grew to be a special man.
Feel: Feel thankful Jesus is special.
Do: Pray, "Thank You, Jesus, for being special.

Children will accomplish the goals when they:

1. Say the Bible words, "Jesus is the Son of God."
2. Point to or name Jesus as a special baby, boy, and man.
3. Point to or name wonderful things Jesus did.
4. Tell why Jesus is special.
5. Pray, "Thank You, Jesus, for being special."

Let's Get Ready

Decorate your classroom using streamers and balloons. Make a party hat for Zach and one for yourself using the pattern on page 135.

For the Bible story, you will need a picture of baby Jesus,

the story wheel from Lesson 6, the happy/sad face from Lesson 7, the painting page from Lesson 8, your Bible, and happy-face stickers.

Prepare the Art Center, the Game Center, and the Block Center. If you are the only teacher, use just the Art Center. The Family Living Center will be used after the Bible story.

Learning Activities

(30 minutes, including 10 minutes presession)

Let's Get Started

Have Zach greet the children. "Hello, Caleb, welcome to the celebration! That means party." Then continue, **Jesus, God's Son, has grown up and can do wonderful things. Can you remember one of the wonderful things Jesus did?** Help as needed. **Yes, Jesus healed a sick woman. Let's hang up your coat and then you can make a party hat to wear during the celebration.**

After a child makes his party hat, make sure he gets involved in another activity until time to pick up.

Worship and Bible Story

(15 minutes)

Let's Worship God

Zach says, "It's time to clean up so we can all celebrate and thank Jesus together." Sing "Jesus Is God's Son" several times, then other songs from this unit. Last, sing "Jesus Is the Son of God." Say, **Rachel, can you tell me one wonderful thing Jesus did?** Call on several children to answer; help as needed. Sing "Let's Be Very Quiet," do "When I Pray," then pray, **We thank You, Jesus, for being God's special Son and for doing wonderful things.** Then do the rhyme, "I Can," from page 88.

Let's Learn From the Bible

Introduction: Have pictures and visuals on your lap in order, with your Bible on the bottom. Hold up Zach, who says in a teasing voice, "I know something you don't know. I know something you don't know."

Say, **What, Zach, tell me.** Zach pretends to whisper in your ear. **Oh, I knew that!** Zach whispers again. **They know too.** Put Zach away as you hold up the picture of baby Jesus.

The Bible-story Review: *(Hold up pictures/visuals when indicated. Allow children to respond when appropriate.)*

(Hold up the picture of baby Jesus.) You don't know who this baby is. (Jesus!) Oh, you do know about the special baby, Jesus.

(Hold up story wheel.) Well, you don't know who this boy is. (Jesus!) Yes, Jesus is getting ready to take a trip with His family. *(Show each picture, reviewing quickly.)* You did know Jesus was helping Mary pack clothes for the trip. You did know about the boy Jesus.

(Hold up the happy/sad face with the sad face showing.) I'm sure you don't know whose face looked like this! (The sick woman.) Oh, you do. *(Show happy face.)* But you don't know who made her face look like this! (Jesus did!) You're right again. Jesus made the sick woman well. Jesus can do wonderful things!

(Hold up the painting page.) You don't know who this is. (Jesus.) Well, you're right again. This is Jesus feeding many people with a boy's small lunch. Jesus can do wonderful things!

You don't know who God's Son is. (Jesus!) You are all so smart! Jesus *is* the Son of God! Why, that sounds just like our Bible words. *(Hold up your open Bible.)* You don't know our Bible words. I'll count one, two, three, and we'll say our Bible words together. ("Jesus is the Son of God.")

Let's say them quietly. *(Do so.)* Let's say them loudly, without yelling. *(Do so.)* Let's sing them. *(Sing the first verse of "Jesus Is the Son of God.")*

Jesus can do wonderful things because He is God's Son!

Family Living Center

Unit 2—Jesus Is God's Son

Items to Include:

Child-size housekeeping equipment
Dress-up clothes (optional)
Pictures of baby Jesus, boy Jesus, and man Jesus

Lesson 7
Toy doctor kit
Cloth for bandages
Empty medicine containers

Purpose: The child will know Jesus grew from a baby to a boy to a man.

Things to Do and Say

Lesson 6

For all lessons, display pictures of Jesus in the hall at child's eye level or on a table. Laminate the pictures for durability (optional). As children play, point out the differences between what a baby can do and what an older child can do.

Holly, what is your baby eating? . . . Yes, small babies drink from bottles. When your baby gets older, she will eat food and drink from a cup. Jesus was a baby, then He grew to be a boy. Point to *(or find)* **a picture of Jesus when He was a baby. Now show me a picture of Jesus when He grew to be a boy. Very good!**

Also, let children pretend to be babies, then big boys and girls, "growing up like Jesus did." **Aaron, show me what Jesus might have done when He was a baby. . . . What do you think He did when He was a big boy, Jose.**

Lesson 7

Suggest that children take turns pretending to be the doctor who makes sick people well. Make sure you speak individually with each child, giving her an opportunity to point to the picture of Jesus, and to pray alone or with your help.

Jacob, when your baby was sick, you took her to the doctor who used medicine to help her get well. Jesus did not need any medicine to make the sick woman well

Game Center

Unit 2—Jesus Is God's Son

Items to Include:

Lesson 7
Rope, string, or yarn (5')

Lesson 8
Fish, bread, and basket cutouts (pages 127 and 128)

Purpose: The children will know Jesus is special.

Things to Do and Say

Lesson 7

Game #1: This game will be similar to "London Bridge." Sing, or play on the tape player, "Jesus Is the Son of God." Start the game by taking hold of a child's hands and making a bridge. Say, **This bridge is special. When you sing the word *special*, the bridge goes up or down.** Children go under the bridge while singing. When they sing "special," whoever is underneath will be caught. With the child between your arms, sing stanza 2, releasing her at the end and saying, **Jesus is special. He is God's Son.** Repeat as long as children enjoy the game. Have older children tell why Jesus is special.

Game #2: Tie one end of your rope to a secure place, close to the floor. Hold the other end, and as you sing "Jesus Grew and Grew," wiggle the rope and raise it very slightly. **Jesus grew taller. Our rope is getting higher too!** Let children jump (or step) over the rope, waiting on the other side till everyone has come over. You may substitute names for "me" and "you," having children listen for their names before they jump.

Lesson 8

Game #1: Play a hide-and-seek game using the cutouts of fish, bread, and baskets. Mount these on cardboard and cover with clear, self-adhesive plastic for durability. Have the children close or cover their eyes while you hide the cutouts. Children will

Family Living Center, continued

because He is God's Son. He is special. Can you find a picture of this special man? . . . That's right, Jesus. Thank You, Jesus, for being special. Jacob, you are big enough to thank Jesus too.**

Lesson 8
Play dough
Cookie cutters
Pictures from Lesson 6

Lesson 8

Help children use the play dough to make pretend meals and feed their babies.

Noah, who is this? . . . Yes, the special man, Jesus. What wonderful thing did Jesus do? . . . You're right. He made the sick woman well. We had that story last week. Our story for today tells about a time Jesus fed many people with only a little food. He could do that because He is God's Son. Jesus is special!

Lesson 9
Muffins
Plastic knives
Napkins
Icing, sprinkles

Lesson 9

Help the children spread icing on the muffins and decorate them with sprinkles. **Taylor, you have grown big enough to decorate your own muffin. You are growing up, just like Jesus grew up.**

Talk with the children as they play with the dolls and dishes, etc. Point out the pictures and ask questions. **Breena, who is this special man? . . . Yes, Jesus. Tell me a wonderful thing Jesus did. . . . Yes, He made a sick woman well and He didn't need medicine to do it. Jesus could do this because He is God's Son. Jesus is special!**

Game Center, continued

then "seek" till all the cutouts have been found. Encourage older children who find several to share with younger children who have none. **Tyler, why is Jesus special? . . . Yes, He is God's Son. He can do wonderful things like feeding many people with a little boy's lunch.**

Game #2: One child stands in the middle of a circle while the other children sing stanza 3, "Jesus was a special man," and walk around him. At the end of the song, the child in the middle tells one reason Jesus is special. (*He is God's Son; He does wonderful things; He fed many with a little lunch; He made a sick woman well.*)

Choose another child and repeat the game. Help the children as needed. **Sutton, Jesus is God's Son, right? . . . Yes, that makes Him special. He could also do wonderful things like making a sick woman well and feeding many people with a little lunch.**

Lesson 9

Play games your children enjoyed. **Kourtni, why is Jesus special? . . . Yes, He is God's Son and He can do wonderful things. Thank You, Jesus; You are special.**

Lesson 9
Items used previously

For all lessons
Tape player
Cassette of music from this unit (optional)

God's Wonders Center

Unit 2—Jesus Is God's Son

Items to Include:

Lesson 6
Classroom visitors—baby, parent, boy
Jars of baby food
Same food cut into pieces

Purpose: The child will thank God for helping Jesus grow to be a boy and a man.

Things to Do and Say

Lesson 6

Make proper arrangements to have your classroom visitors. Have baby foods such as bananas, peas, pears, and so forth, and the same foods cut into bite size pieces displayed on a low table, along with the plastic spoons.

Children, we have visitors in our class today. Introduce them, and tell their ages. Ask, **Which visitor looks like baby Jesus? . . . Who looks like the boy Jesus? . . . Thank You, God, for helping Jesus grow up to be a boy. . . . Who talks like baby Jesus? . . . Who talks like the boy Jesus? Thank You, God, for helping Jesus grow up to be a boy.**

Have the visiting parent let the children take turns sitting on his lap. **The baby needs to be held, but Mr. Blank has grown big enough to hold you.**

Show the food. **Which food will the baby eat? . . . What will a child like the boy Jesus eat? Allow children to taste the foods. Thank You, God, for helping Jesus grow up to be a boy.** Let children pray with you or thank God on their own. Sing the following song several times to the tune, "Row, Row, Row Your Boat":

God made Jesus grow; God made Jesus grow.
Thank You, thank You, thank You, God, for making Jesus grow.

Art Center

Unit 2—Jesus Is God's Son

Items to Include:

Lesson 6
Pictures of baby, boy, and man Jesus
Picture of Zach dressed as puppy, then as dog

Lesson 7
Pictures of children
Children's baby pictures

Purpose: The child will help to prepare a bulletin board and learn to say the Bible words.

Things to Do and Say

Lesson 6

Prepare the bulletin board as shown on page 129. Have your Bible *(with Bible words highlighted)* open and stickers ready. **Coleman, point to the picture of baby Jesus. Good. . . . Sutton, who is this?** *(Boy Jesus.)* **Yes, Jesus was a baby, a boy, and then He grew to be a man.** Point to each picture.

Our Bible says, "Jesus is the Son of God." Show the words in the Bible and on the board. Let each child "read" the words; then give her a sticker. **You each have a star on the board with your name on it.** Show each child her star. **I will take a picture of how you look today. Next week you will bring a picture of how you looked as a baby. We will put these on our board to show that you are growing too.** Take each child's picture.

Lesson 7

Staple pictures of the children on the board. Have your open Bible, stickers, and baby pictures ready. Point to each picture of Jesus when appropriate. **Holly, who is this? Yes, Jesus, the special baby born on Christmas. . . . Sarah, who is this? Yes, the boy Jesus. . . . Coleman, who is this? Yes, the special man Jesus.**

Do the rhyme "Jesus." Point to the board. **What do these words say? . . . Good!** Read

Art Center, continued

the words in the Bible. As each child says the words, give him a sticker. **Jesus is the Son of God; that makes us smile.** Hold up baby pictures and let children identify their own. Staple them to the board. **You are growing just like Jesus grew.**

Lesson 8

Prepare the art area. Gather the children near the bulletin board. Put up new pictures. **Breena was a baby, but God has helped her grow bigger.** Review other pictures. Let children take turns reading the Bible words and putting up stickers.

Hold up the painting page. **Our Bible words are here too.** Point to the words and read. **Let's paint and talk about the wonderful thing Jesus did.** If painting is impossible in your situation, use crayons.

Lesson 9

Cut out a party hat for each child. Gather near the bulletin board, review Bible words and Jesus pictures. Take down each child's pictures and place them in envelopes to take home. Let the children decorate their hats, write on names, and then glue them together.

Holly, our Bible words are written on our hats. Can you "read" them? Great! Here is a sticker to put on your hat. Yes, that's Jesus when He became a man. We are happy that Jesus, God's Son, could do wonderful things.

Lesson 8
Watercolor paint
Copies of page 134
Painting smocks
Large paint brushes

Lesson 9
Hat patterns (page 135)
Crayons, markers
Stickers (page 132)
Envelopes

For all lessons
Bulletin board
Bible
Happy-face stickers
Black marker
Camera (instant, if possible)
Stapler

God's Wonders Center, continued

Lesson 8
Picnic basket or paper bag
Blanket
Bread
Plastic knives
Canned tuna or salmon
Ingredients for bread

For all lessons
Napkins
Plastic spoons

Lesson 8

Place the ingredients for bread on a table where the children can see and touch them. Include small amounts of flour, oil, salt, water, yeast, and sugar. Also show the canned fish. Have fish on a plate for the children to taste. Place the bread, butter, knives, and blanket in the picnic basket or bag.

Jesus fed many people with only two small fish and five little loaves of bread. God helped Jesus grow up to be a special man who could do wonderful things! Sing the song above several times. Do the rhyme, "Jesus," from page 114. Pray, **Thank You, God, for helping Jesus grow up to be a man who did wonderful things.** Finally, allow each child to butter a piece of bread and eat it.

Patterns—Winter, Unit 2

Instructions

1. Make cardboard patterns of dog bone, loaf of bread, basket, and fish.
2. Trace around patterns on appropriate colors of construction paper.
3. Mount on cardboard.
4. Cut out.
5. Make the number indicated.

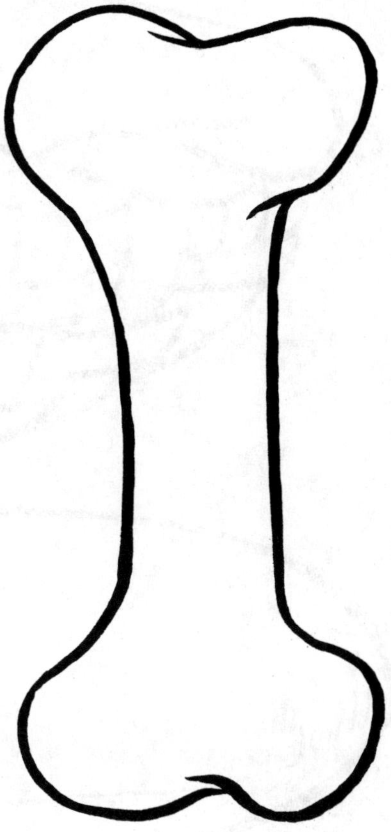

Block Center

Unit 2—Jesus Is God's Son

Items to Include:

Lesson 6
Story wheel from pages 130 and 131

Lesson 7
Saltine crackers
Towel

Purpose: The children will act out the Bible story.

Things to Do and Say

Lesson 6

Provide the story wheel for the children to handle. Divide the blocks into two groups at opposite ends of the center. Encourage the children to build Jesus' house at one end and the temple-church at the other end.

Our Bible story tells us Jesus grew big enough to take a trip with His family. Let's pretend we are Jesus going to the temple-church. Walk slowly. When you arrive, sit quietly for a moment as if listening to a teacher. **I'm glad we are big enough to come to church and learn about Jesus. Breena, show me how you look when you are happy. Thank You, God, that we are big enough to learn about Jesus.**

Return home and repeat as time and interest allow. Some children may want to build alone. **Nathan, can you build a tower as tall as you are?** Count the blocks. **You are not a small baby anymore. You are growing like Jesus did. Thank You, God, for helping Jesus and Nathan to grow.**

Lesson 7

Divide the blocks into two groups. The towel will be used as the woman's bed and the crackers will be "supper" after Jesus heals her. Encourage children to build Peter's house at one end of the center while the other children make a road leading to the house.

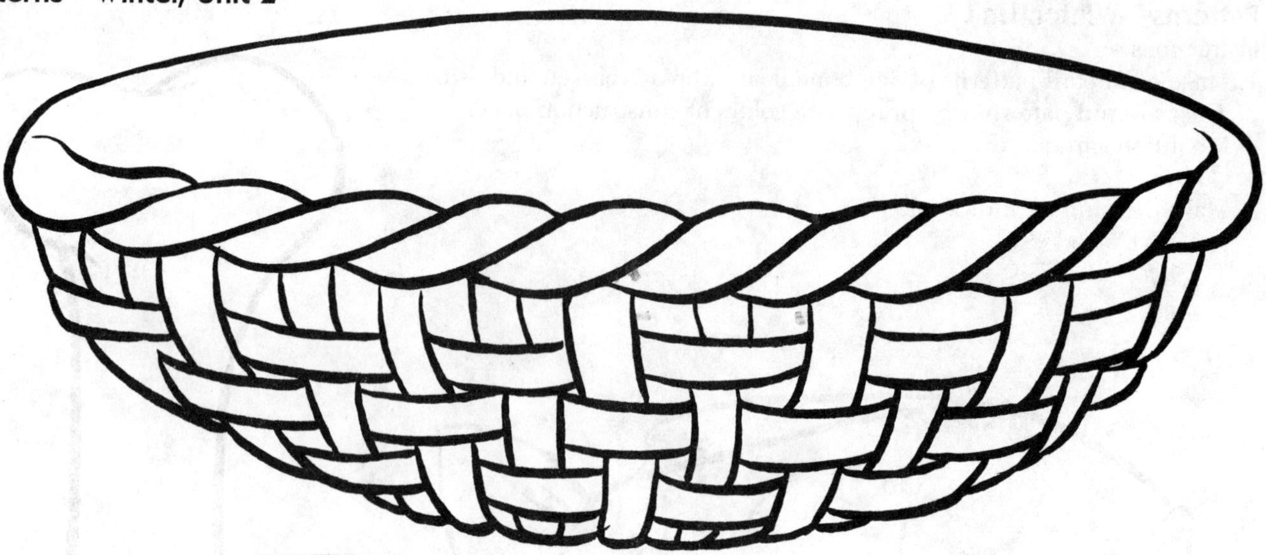

Block Center, continued

Lesson 9 Items from previous lessons Fish and bread cutouts Picnic basket Blanket **For all lessons** Large blocks

As the children work, tell the story. **Rachel, Jesus healed the sick woman in Peter's house. Jesus is special! . . . Hunter, what wonderful thing did Jesus do? Yes, He made a sick woman well. The Bible tells us, "Jesus is the Son of God."**

Act out the story giving each child an opportunity to participate. **Erin, it's your turn to be Jesus, God's Son. You can make the sick woman feel good again. . . . Sutton, lie down and pretend to be sick. After Jesus makes you well you can give out the crackers and we'll pretend to eat supper, just like Jesus did in our story.** Allow shy children to watch if they prefer.

Lesson 9

Let the children build the necessary structures. Act out the Bible stories as described in Lessons 6 and 7. Use the cutouts, picnic basket, and blanket to act out the story of Jesus feeding the 5,000.

Hunter, where is Jesus going on His long trip? . . . Yes, to the temple-church. God helped Jesus grow and God is helping you grow up too. Continue in this manner with all the stories.

Bulletin Board—Winter, Unit 2

Instructions

1. Cover bulletin board with paper/cloth of your choice and add an appropriate border. If you do not have a bulletin board, attach a piece of background paper or poster board directly to a wall at the children's eye level.
2. Print the Bible words at the bottom of the board.
3. Make a star for each child from yellow paper.
4. Add pictures of Jesus as a baby, boy, and man.
5. Add pictures of children each week, as suggested in the Art Center.

Story wheel—Winter, Unit 2

Instructions

1. Photocopy story wheel onto heavy paper. Enlarge if possible.
2. Color pictures.
3. Cut out wheel.
4. Cut cover from construction paper, using pattern on page 131.
5. Place cover on story wheel and attach in center with a paper fastener.

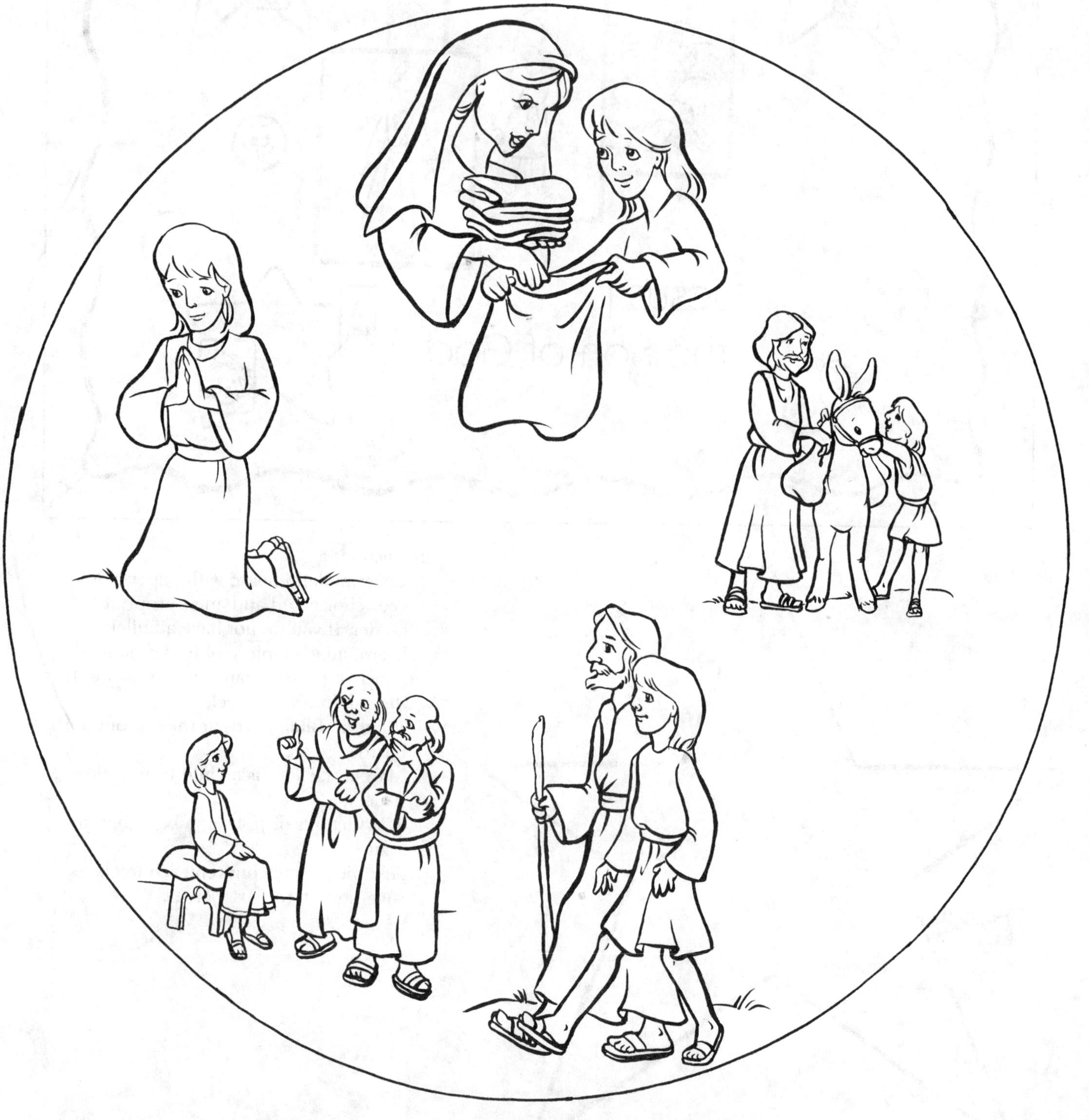

Story wheel cover—Winter, Unit 2

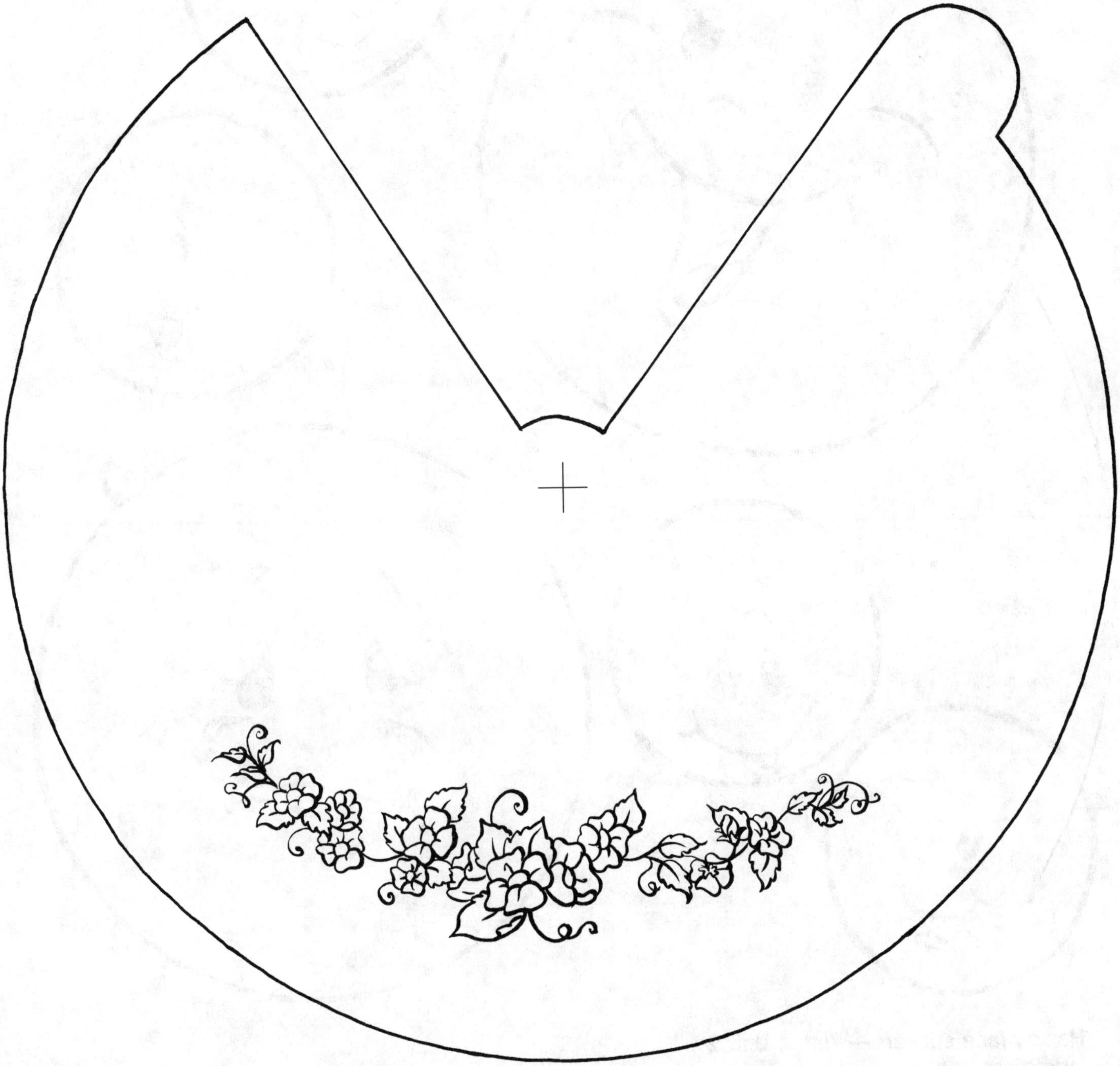

Faces—Winter, Unit 2

Instructions

1. Copy large faces onto colored construction paper. Enlarge faces.
2. Glue faces back-to-back with a craft stick between for a handle.

Happy face stickers—Winter, Unit 2

Instructions

1. Make multiple copies of the smaller happy faces on various colors of construction paper.
2. Mix two parts white glue and one part vinegar.
3. Lightly "paint" the mixture onto the backs of uncut stickers. Let dry.
4. Cut out stickers.
5. Let children use damp sponges to help attach stickers to party hats, page 133.

Puppet—Winter, Unit 2

Instructions

1. Copy page onto construction paper.
2. Add color with felt-tip pens.
3. Cut out puppet pieces.
4. Glue puppet pieces with a craft stick in between.

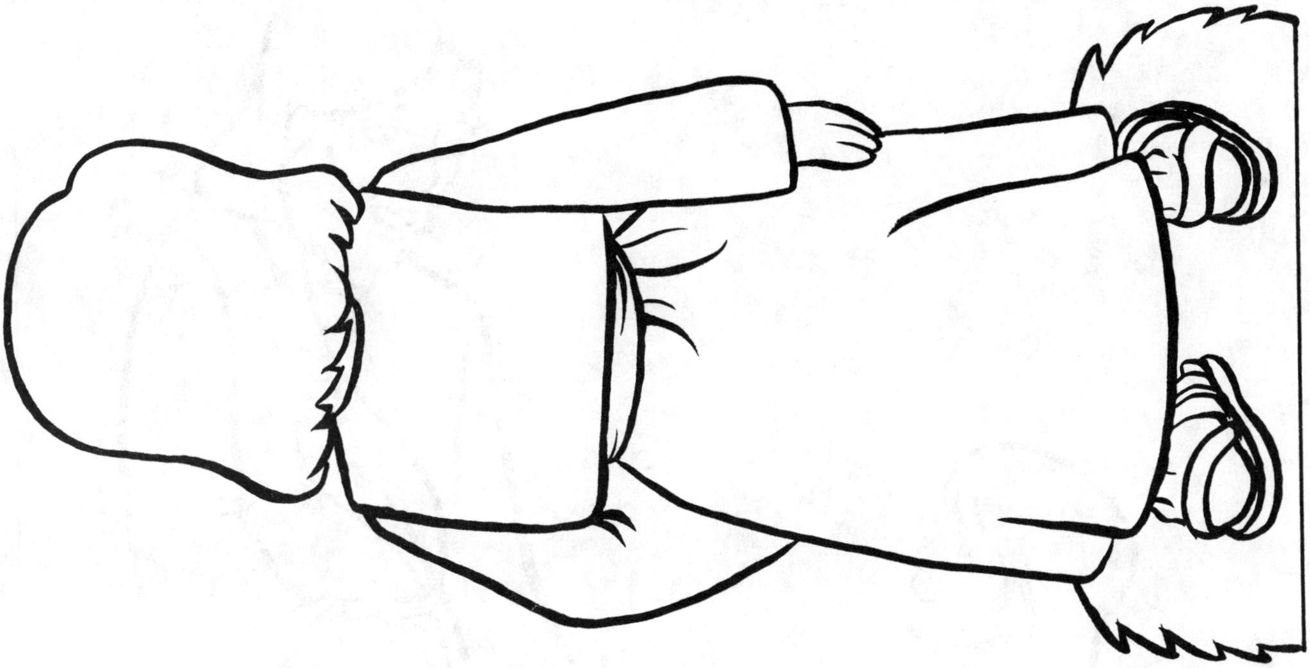

One day, Jesus fed many people with just a boy's small lunch.
Jesus can do wonderful things because He is God's Son.
"Jesus is . . . the Son of God" (John 20:31).

Party hat—Winter, Unit 2

Instructions

1. Photocopy page onto colored construction paper.
2. Cut out.
3. Children will decorate hats in class with happy face stickers (page 132).
4. Add glue and overlap edges.

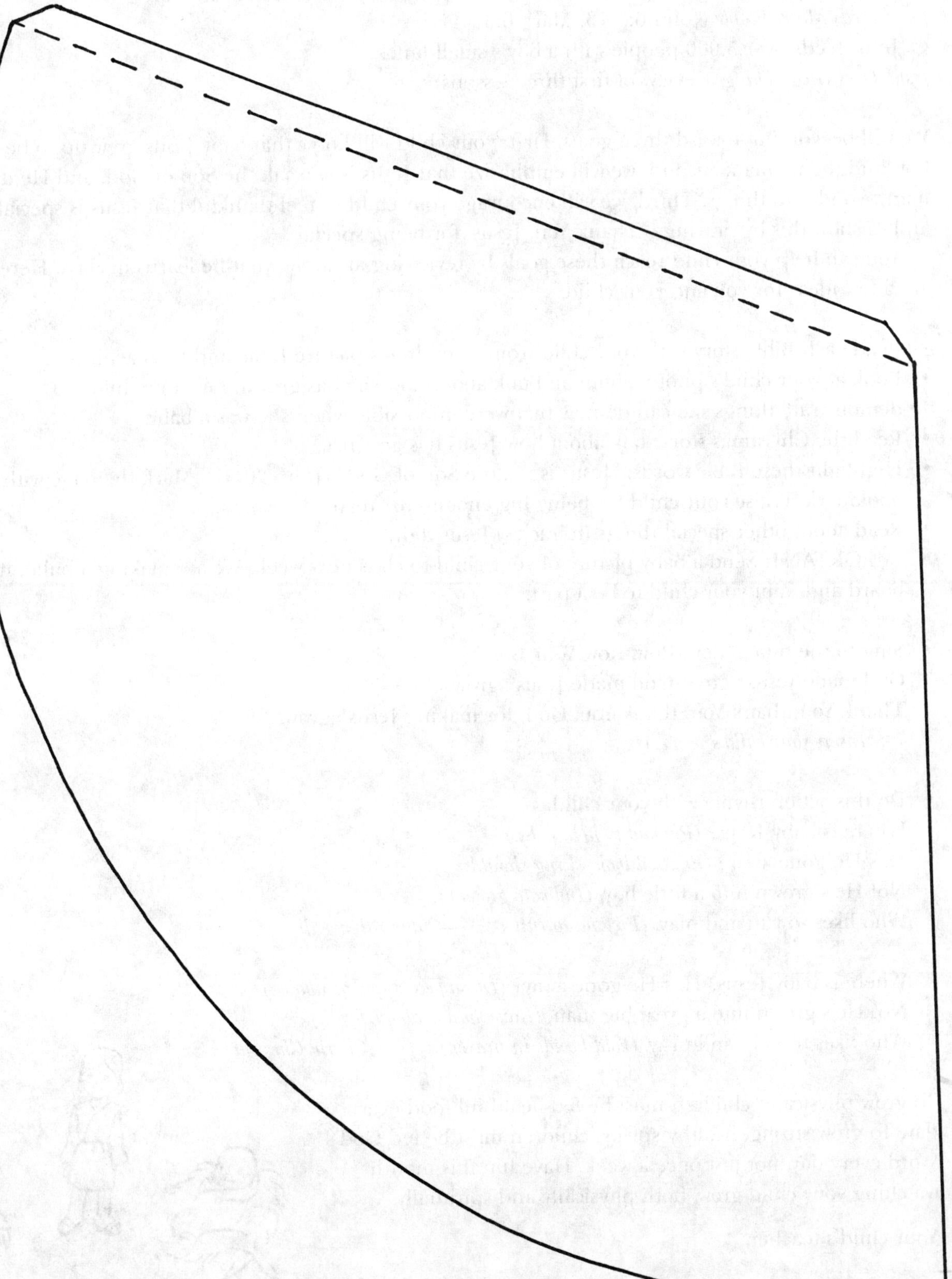

Dear Parent,

Listed below are the stories your child will be hearing in our class this month.

Jesus Grows Up (Luke 2:40-52)

Jesus grows from a baby to a boy who is old enough to go to the temple to worship God.

Jesus Heals a Woman (Mark 1:29-31; Luke 4:38, 39)

The man Jesus shows He is the Son of God by healing Peter's mother-in-law.

Jesus Feeds Many People (John 6:5-13; Mark 6:32-44)

Jesus feeds over 5,000 people with a boy's small lunch.

Jesus Does Great Things (review of first three lessons)

We will be working toward three goals. First, your child will know that baby Jesus grew up to be a boy, and then a man. Second, we will emphasize that Jesus is special, the Son of God, and He did many wonderful things. Third, we will encourage your child to feel thankful that Jesus is special, and to show this by praying, "Thank You, Jesus, for being special."

You can help your child reach these goals by reviewing at home what he learns in class. Here are a few ideas for you and your child.

- Read each Bible story with your child from a children's picture Bible and then act it out.
- Look at your child's photo album and talk about how she has grown. Let your child demonstrate things she can do now that were impossible when she was a baby.
- Read the Christmas story; talk about how Jesus has grown.
- Highlight these Bible words: "Jesus is . . . the Son of God" (John 20:31). Mark the page with a bookmark. Praise your child for being big enough to "read" the words.
- Read about other special things (miracles) Jesus did.
- IMPORTANT: Send a baby picture of your child to class next week. We are making a bulletin board and want your child to be a part.

- Sing to the tune, "Row, Row, Row Your Boat":
  God made Jesus* grow. God made Jesus* grow.
  Thank You, thank You, thank You, God, for making Jesus* grow.
  *(*Insert your child's name.)*

- Do this action rhyme with your child:
  Where is baby Jesus? *(Pretend to hold baby.)*
  Has He gone away? *(Puzzled look; shrug shoulders.)*
  No! He's grown into a little boy, *(Indicate growing.)*
  Who likes to run and play. *(Pretend to run.)* —*Cathy Allen Falk*

  Where is baby Jesus? Has He gone away? *(Do same actions as above.)*
  No! He's grown into a great big man, *(Raise hands above head.)*
  Who likes to help and pray. *(Fold hands in prayer.)* —*Carrie Chesnut*

To grow physically, children must be fed healthful food every day. To grow strong, healthy spirits, children must be fed God's Word every day, not just once a week. Have fun this month watching your child grow, both physically and spiritually.

Your child's teacher,

Unit 3: Jesus Loves Us

Lessons 10–13

By the end of the unit, the children will

Know that Jesus is their special friend.

Feel eager to show love for Jesus.

Show love for Jesus (sing and pray).

Unit Bible Words

"You are my friends" (John 15:14, *NIV*).

Children's Books

from Standard Publishing

Curlicue Caterpillar and Friends (24-03438)

Jesus Is My Special Friend (24-04211)

My Family and Me (24-03701)

Skedaddle Skunk and Friends (24-03437)

The Best Thing Is Love (24-03710)

Resources for Teachers

from Standard Publishing

Teaching Our Children to Pray (18-03217)

Tips for Teachers—Early Childhood (14-03157)

Puzzles

Children, Friends, Family, House, Tree, Church, Airport, Praying

This Unit at a Glance

10 Jesus Loves Zaccheus — **Luke 19:1-6**

Zaccheus needed a friend. He was so glad when Jesus called him down from the tree and came to his house.

11 Jesus Loves the Children — **Mark 10:13-16; Luke 18:15-17**

Jesus welcomed the children when His disciples wanted to send them away. Jesus held the children and talked to them.

12 Jesus Listens to the Children Sing — **Matthew 21:15, 16**

Jesus listened to the children and told the chief priests and scribes to listen. It was God's Word come to life.

13 Jesus Loves Me — **Review of Lessons 10–12**

The emphasis of the review is to make each child know that Jesus is his friend. We praise God for our friend Jesus.

Why Teach This Unit?

We feel very special when we have friends. Friends listen, talk, care for us, and spend time with us. We know Jesus is our friend through His Word, the power of the Holy Spirit, prayer, and fellowship with other Christians.

Young children know Jesus loves them and is their special friend through a real person they can see, touch, and trust. A teacher has the opportunity to be this real person in the classroom. As children learn they can trust and believe in your love, they will trust and believe when you teach that Jesus is your friend and their friend. Give the gentle touch and loving look that will reflect Jesus' love as you present these lessons about Jesus and the Bible people He befriended.

Let children see and hold the Bible at the offering table, in the learning centers, during the worship and Bible story time. Use special bookmarks with the verse and stories. Highlight the Bible words for children to "read."

Use Bible words frequently in conversation, prayers, and the Bible story. Emphasize the word *friend* often. **I'm glad to see my friends come to class. . . . The Bible tells us that Jesus said, "You are my friends." . . . Friends take turns with toys. . . . Thank You, God, for friends.**

Things to Do for This Unit

- Make photocopies of the Parents' Letter (page 160) and the Unit Planning Sheet (pages 319 and 320).
- Photocopy Learning Center Cards (pages 147-152); cut pages apart on solid lines. Mount side 1 of a card on cardboard; then mount side 2 on back of cardboard. Laminate for durability.
- Gather materials listed on Learning Center Cards.
- Make four bookmarks, green, blue, yellow and red. Stickers and instructions are on page 159.
- Photocopy pages 153-159 and prepare as visual aids or art activities.

Use These Songs and Action Rhyme During Unit 3

Where's a Friend?

(Tune: "Where Is Thumbkin?")

Where's a friend, where's a friend?
Here I am! *(Left thumb.)* Here I am! *(Right thumb.)*
How are you today, friend? *(Left wiggles.)*
Very well, I thank you. *(Right wiggles.)*
Jesus loves you. *(Left wiggles.)*
Jesus loves you. *(Right wiggles.)*
(Substitute: Where is [name]? Hello, friend.)

My Best Friend Is Jesus

(Tune: "Mary Had a Little Lamb")

My best friend is Jesus, love Him, love Him.
My best friend is Jesus. I love Him.

Find a Friend

(Tune: "Oh, Be Careful Little Hands")

Find a friend, everybody,
Hold his hands. *(Face friend.)*
Find a friend, everybody,
Hold her hands. *(Hold friend's hands.)*
Hold them HIGH, everybody, *(Hands up.)*
Hold them LOW, everybody, *(Hands down.)*
Drop your hands, everybody, and SIT down.

Ten Little Children

(Tune: "Ten Little Indians")

One little, two little, three little children,
Four little, five little, six little children,
Seven little, eight little, nine little children;
Ten little children come (or sing, pray).

All the children come to Jesus (or sing, pray),
All the children come to Jesus,
All the children come to Jesus.
Jesus says, "I love you."

Reach Up to the Ceiling

Reach up to the ceiling, *(Stretch arms overhead.)*
Stretch out to the walls, *(Stretch arms in front.)*
Bend to touch your knees and toes,
Sit down very small.*
**Stand up big and tall.*
Turn around, one and all.

Jesus Said, "You Are My Friends."

(Tune: "London Bridge")

Jesus said, "You are my friends,
Are my friends, are my friends."
Jesus said, "You are my friends;
I love you."

Let's Apply the Lesson

Who wanted to see Jesus? Show just the picture of Zaccheus. **Who is with Zaccheus?** *(No one.)* **That's right! Zaccheus did not have any friends. Who became Zaccheus' friend?** Unfold the picture. **How did Zaccheus feel?** *(Happy.)* **How would you feel if Jesus was your friend?** *(Happy, good.)* **Zach, choose a helper for me.** Have Zach touch or name a helper. **Daniel, would you find the red Bible marker? Thank you. Jesus says in our Bible** (point to words), **"You are my friends." Stand up and say Jesus' words, "You are my friends." Clap as you say Jesus' words, "You-are-my-friends."** Have children sit down.

Mark, can you tell me the name of a friend of yours? . . . Julie, who is a friend you are sitting by? . . . Will my friend Michael please hold this picture of Jesus and Zaccheus for me? . . . Will my friend Kori find a friend in this picture? Help several children find Jesus.

Learning Activities

(20 minutes)

Let's Play Awhile

Let's all stand up big and tall and sing about "Zaccheus." Have materials ready for the Game Center. While you wait for children to finish their binoculars, suggest things to look for. **Who can find the blocks? the dolls? a picture of Zaccheus? a friend?**

Let's Go Home

Play "Look for Jesus" as the parents pick up their children. Make sure each child has a Parents' Letter, a pair of Look-for-Jesus Binoculars, and a tree picture even if she did not paint. Remind each child to tell a friend about her special friend, Jesus.

Jesus Loves Zaccheus

Luke 19:1-6

Bible words: "You are my friends" (John 15:14, *NIV*).

Lesson Value: Children often feel alone, somewhat like Zaccheus must have felt. Jesus took time to talk to Zaccheus and visit his home. He became Zaccheus' friend. Children need to learn at an early age that Jesus is their friend too. Through your attitudes as well as your teaching, they will learn that Jesus loves them and is their special friend.

Know: Know that Jesus is our special friend.
Feel: Feel eager to show love for Jesus.
Do: Show love for Jesus (sing and pray).

Children will accomplish the goals when they:

1. Name a friend of Jesus.
2. Say Jesus' words, "You are my friends."
3. Pray, "Thank You, God, for our friend Jesus."
4. Sing to and about Jesus.

Let's Get Ready

For the Bible story, you will need your Bible marked with strips of construction paper at John 15:14 (red) and Luke 19:1-6 (green), and the visual of Jesus and Zaccheus (page 153).

Set up the Art Center, the Family Living Center, the Block Center, and the God's Wonders Center. If you are the only teacher, use just the Family Living Center now. The Game Center will be added after the Bible story.

Learning Activities

(30 minutes, including 10 minutes presession)

Let's Get Started

Help children with coats, offerings, and name tags. Have Zach say, "Hello, I'm glad to see my friend Amy. Please choose a sticker to put on the attendance chart. What friend is in this picture? *(Jesus.)* Do you see any friends to play with? Would you like to set the table for company or play with the puzzles? Two friends can work together."

Worship and Bible Story

(15 minutes)

Let's Worship God

Have Zach bark three times at each learning center. **Zach says you have three more minutes to play before we pick up.** Sing, "Time to Put Our Toys Away." As children come to the worship area, sing "Find a Friend." **Adam, what friend are you sitting by?** Ask several children. **Jesus is our special friend. Let's thank God for Jesus and for all our friends. Thank You, God, for our friend Jesus. Thank You for all our friends.** Sing "My Best Friend Is Jesus."

Let's Learn From the Bible

Introduction: Zach, did you see our friends *(name children)* **cleaning up the house and scrubbing vegetables?** Zach nods his head. **It looked like they were getting ready for company.** Zach nods his head and slurps his tongue. **We saw some friends building with the blocks too.** Zach nods his head. **Friends are fun to play with.** Zach nods his head vigorously.

I need three friends to help me now. Zach is looking for some good listeners. Have two or three children stand shoulder to shoulder facing class. Have Zach try to look between their legs, jump up over their heads, and peek around their waists. **Zach, are you having trouble seeing Michael? Can you see Katie over here? It's hard to see when you are short. Why don't you sit up here on my shoulder?** Ask the children to take their seats. **Now can you see all your friends?** Zach nods his head. **I know someone in the Bible who was like you. He was short like you. In fact, his name was Zaccheus, just like yours! But he did not have any friends.** Drop Zach's head. **Sit over here, Zach, and listen to our Bible story.** Have children say the rhyme, "My Bible."

The Bible Story: *(If most of your class has heard the story recently, have them stand and do the motions with you.)* Zaccheus heard a lot of voices. *(Hand to ear.)* Zaccheus saw a crowd of people coming down the street. *(Hand to your eyes.)* Zaccheus heard the people say *(hands to mouth)*, "Jesus is coming, Jesus is coming." Can you say that with me? "Jesus is coming, Jesus is coming." Zaccheus jumped up and stretched up tall. *(Do so.)* He looked this way *(left)* and that way *(right)*, but he could not see Jesus. *(Shake head sadly.)* There were too many people and he was too short.

Zaccheus turned and looked up and down the road. *(Do so.)* There was a tree he could climb. Down the road he ran. *(Run in place.)* He hurried up into the tree *(climbing)*. He looked up the road and there was Jesus. Zaccheus was all by himself *(sad face)*. He did not have any friends. Zaccheus probably thought *(tip head, hand and finger to chin)*, "I wish Jesus were my friend."

Just then *(surprised look)*, Jesus stopped right under the tree, looked at Zaccheus, and said *(point finger and look up)*, "I want to come to your house with you."

Zaccheus climbed down the tree. He was so happy to have Jesus come to his house and be his friend! *(Clap hands and say, "Yea!")* Zaccheus probably gave Jesus a special place to sit and said, "Sit down." *(Have the children sit down.)*

(The babies.) Have Zach whisper in your ear; nod your head. **Boys and girls, Zach wants me to tell you he is so happy you came to see him. How did Jesus feel when He saw the children?** *(Happy.)* **Who is your special friend? Yes, Jesus is!**

Ask a child to help you find the red marker. **Let's "read" Jesus' words together.** Hold hands like an open Bible. **"You are my friends."**

Sing the following words to the tune of "The Farmer in the Dell":

I have a happy face, I have a happy face.
I have a happy face today, for Jesus is my friend.

Learning Activities

(20 minutes)

Let's Play Awhile

Have the children stand as you touch their heads while singing, "Ten Little Children." Use two hands as you say one number, if necessary. Walk in place as you sing, "All the children come to Jesus." Pray, then pass out napkins and food for your picnic.

Materials should be ready for the Game Center. If you have a large group and several teachers, use other activities from this lesson.

Let's Go Home

Have Zach sing, "Ten Little Children." Make a circle. Hold a cup-phone to your mouth and ear. **Ring, ring! Hello, Jesus says, "You - are - my - friends!" Carrie, would you call a friend and tell her Jesus' words?** Alternate between individuals and the group if children are restless. Each child should have a child figure from the Art Center and a cup/phone.

As each child leaves, remind him, **Tell your family who went to see Jesus and what Jesus said.**

Jesus Loves the Children

Mark 10:13-16; Luke 18:15-17

Bible Words: "You are my friends" (John 15:14, *NIV*).

Lesson Value: Time is a precious gift. Jesus' taking time for children should teach us something about how precious little ones are to His kingdom. Jesus encouraged the children to come to Him. He talked and listened to the children. He probably held them gently on His lap as He sat at their eye level. Young children learn through repetition and imitation. Feeling the loving, unhurried touch of a teacher as she quietly tells of Jesus will help the children develop confidence and trust in Jesus and His love for them. Friends listen, talk, care, and spend time with us. Jesus is truly our special friend!

Know: Know that Jesus is our special friend.
Feel: Feel eager to show love for Jesus.
Do: Show love for Jesus (sing and pray).

Children will accomplish the goals when they:

1. Say Jesus' words, "You are my friends."
2. Pray, "Jesus, thank You for being our friend."
3. Sing to and about Jesus.
4. Point to or name someone who is a friend of Jesus.

Let's Get Ready

For the Bible story, mark your Bible words (red) and Mark

10:13-16 (blue). You will also need a picnic blanket, and the visual (page 155). Arrange a place to walk to with your picnic and blanket for story time (another room, hallway, by a window, etc.).

Set up the Art Center, the Family Living Center, the Block Center, and the Puzzle Center. Have the Game Center materials ready to use after the Bible story. If you are the only teacher, use just the Family Living Center now.

Learning Activities

(30 minutes, including 10 minutes presession)

Let's Get Started

Help children with coats, offerings, and stickers. **Zach likes to snuggle and sniff his friends. He likes to have his ears scratched and be petted.** Do so. **Jeffrey, I'm glad you came to class. The children in our Bible story went to see a special friend. Do you want to see our airport or fix a picnic?** Direct each child to a center.

Worship and Bible Story

(15 minutes)

Let's Worship God

Have Zach bark three times at each center to give children an opportunity to finish playing. Sing "Time to Put Our Toys Away." As children join you, sing "Find a Friend" and "Where's a Friend?" Have Zach help the child respond, "Here I am! Here I am," when you sing, "Where is (name), where is (name)?" Let the child stand by you and place your arm around her. At the end, sing the words, "Jesus loves you, please sit down," so other children can have a turn. **Jesus loves you. Zach wants to know who else loves you, Brian?** *(Mommy, Daddy, sister, brother, grandparents, etc.)* Put Zach down while you pray. **Let's talk to Jesus in prayer. Thank You for our families. Thank You, Jesus, for being our friend.**

Let's Learn From the Bible

Introduction: Zach starts sniffing around children to find the picnic basket from the Family Living Center. **Zach, why are you sniffing?** Zach whispers in your ear, slurps his tongue, rubs his tummy. **Oh, you are hungry and you think someone fixed a picnic. Well, you are right and we are going on a walk with our friends, just like the children in our Bible story did. Zach, choose a helper for me.** Zach names a child. **Andre, please find the blue Bible marker. Thank you; please sit down.** Open your Bible. Do the rhyme, "My Bible."

The Bible Story: "Comb your hair. Straighten your coat. Don't forget the picnic basket," said Mother.

The children were excited as they started out to see their special friend. *(If you cannot go outside, walk around your room.)* Let's walk along the road like the children did. Do you see any birds? *(Look up.)* Do you think the children saw their special friend yet? They probably skipped and hopped as they went to see their special friend. *(Do so.)* They may have climbed a big hill *(bend as if climbing)* or jumped over a puddle of water. *(Jump.)*

Then they heard people talking and saw their special friend Jesus. They hurried up behind the big people and spread out their blanket and set their picnic basket down. *(Do this.)* The children tiptoed up close to hear their special friend's voice. Just as they saw their friend Jesus, one of Jesus' helpers said, "Stop! Jesus is too tired and busy for children. Don't bother Him."

When Jesus heard this, He said, "Let the little children come to me." *(Show the picture of Jesus and the children.)* Jesus touched the babies. He wanted to talk to the children and hold them on His lap. Jesus was happy to see the children. The children were happy to see Jesus, their special friend.

Let's Apply the Lesson

Zach, you were a good listener. Zach nods his head vigorously. **Who did Jesus want to talk to?** *(The children.)* **Yes, Zach, I know you like to be petted. Who did Jesus touch?**

listened to their words, "Hosanna! Hosanna! Jesus is God's Son." Jesus liked to hear His friends sing, "Hosanna! Hosanna!"

Let's Apply the Lesson

Where did the children follow their friend Jesus? *(Into the temple-church.)* **What were the children singing? Who liked to hear the children sing?** *(Jesus, mommies, daddies.)* **What did Jesus say to the angry men?** *(Listen to the children.)* **Let's stand up and say the true words.** Raise visual. **Hosanna! Hosanna!** Now sit down and whisper the children's song *(raise visual)*, **Hosanna! Hosanna!**

Choose a helper to find the red marker. **What do our Bible Words say? "You are my friends." Who can point to our special friend? Who can point to a friend of Jesus?**

Learning Activities

(20 minutes)

Let's Play Awhile

Let's march around the room like we're singing to Jesus. Sing "Ten Little Children." Put Telling Tubes up for now. Have materials ready for the God's Wonders Center. Some children may want another turn playing hopscotch in the Game Center.

Let's Go Home

Help children set chairs back-to-back to play Musical Chairs. Place a picture of Jesus on one chair. Have Zach play his song, "Ten Little Children," as children march around and sing. Let the child who sits by the picture of Jesus hold Zach and say the Bible words (with help). Keep music short so several can have a turn. Have Listening Ears and Telling Tubes ready to go home. Tell each child good-bye. **Use your Telling Tube to sing about your special friend Jesus. Be a good listener just like your friend Jesus was.**

Jesus Listens to the Children Sing

Matthew 21:15, 16

Bible Words: "You are my friends" (John 15:14, *NIV*).

Lesson Value: The children will learn that Jesus was a friend who not only stopped what He was doing to listen to the children sing, but also told others to listen. Your children will feel important when you listen to them by stopping to look at them on their level and putting your arm around them or holding their hands. Repeating their words reinforces that you listened carefully and are their friend. They will learn that Jesus is a special friend through you, their friend who loves them and takes time to listen to them.

Know: Know that Jesus is our special friend.
Feel: Feel eager to show love for Jesus.
Do: Show love for Jesus (sing and pray).

Children will accomplish the goals when they:

1. Say and listen to Jesus' words, "You are my friends."
2. Sing and pray to Jesus.
3. Tell who listened to the children sing.
4. Pray, "Thank You, Jesus, for being our friend."

Let's Get Ready

For the Bible story, mark the Bible words (red) and Matthew 21:15, 16 (yellow). Prepare Zach with headphones and a tape recorder. Record a tape with "Ten Little Children," using the words *sing to Jesus*. Make a visual aid of the picture of Jesus on page 153, and a "Telling Tube" (page 157) for each child.

Set up the Art Center, the Family Living Center, the Block Center, and the Game Center. If you are the only teacher, use just the Art Center. Have materials ready for the God's Wonders Center after the Bible story.

Learning Activities

(30 minutes, including 10 minutes presession)

Let's Get Started

Have Zach sing, "Where's a Friend?" using the words *Hello, friend; hello, friend,* as each child arrives. Help children with coats, name tags, and attendance stickers. **Jesus was happy to see the children. Do you remember what He said?** *("You are my friends.")* **Zach sang to you today to remind us that some children sang to Jesus. Do you want to make some big "Listening Ears" first or help build a church building?**

Worship and Bible Story

(15 minutes)

Let's Worship God

Have Zach give the "three bark" signal for three minutes to play. **Has everyone made Listening Ears? We want to be good listeners like Jesus was when He heard the children sing.** Sing "Time to Put Our Toys Away." Suggest that children wear their "ears" for Bible story time. As children finish picking up, start singing, "Find a Friend." **I see many listening ears today. Stephen, what sound have you heard? Would anyone else like to tell us a sound he heard? God listens when we pray. Let's talk to God today. Dear God, thank You for listening to us. Thank You for our friend Jesus. Thank You for happy singing.**

Let's Learn From the Bible

Introduction: Have Zach move his head as he listens to headphones. **Zach, Zach, ZACH!** Remove headphones. **Zach, it's Bible story time. What are you listening to?** Nod your head. **Oh, I see. OK, let's all listen to Zach's song.** Turn on the tape recorder and have Zach touch children's heads as they listen and sing, "Ten Little Children."

Zach, did you know that Jesus likes to hear the children sing? In our Bible story, He tells everyone to listen to the children. Choose a helper to find the yellow bookmark. Give each child a Telling Tube. **Boys and girls, when I hold up this picture of Jesus** *(tube visual)* **everyone say, "Hosanna! Hosanna!" using your Telling Tube. Listen and watch. Let's try it now.** Use the Jesus visual to help children say, "Hosanna! Hosanna!" Explain to the children that they are to do this in the Bible story every time you say, "Hosanna! Hosanna!" Now put Zach away and place your Bible in your lap or beside you.

The Bible Story: Jesus smiled and remembered when the children sang to Him in the streets of Jerusalem. *(Raise Jesus visual.)* "Hosanna! Hosanna!" Jesus liked to hear the children sing *(continue to raise visual),* "Hosanna! Hosanna!" The children followed their friend Jesus into the temple-church. "Hosanna! Hosanna!" The daddies and mommies liked to hear the children sing to their friend Jesus, "Hosanna! Hosanna!" Many of the people who loved Jesus liked to hear the children sing, "Hosanna! Hosanna!" Some of the people probably helped the children sing, "Hosanna! Hosanna!" They knew Jesus was God's Son. Jesus smiled as the children sang loudly to their friend, "Hosanna! Hosanna! Jesus is God's Son."

Not everyone, however, was smiling. Some men in the temple-church did not like Jesus. They did not like what the children were singing, "Hosanna! Hosanna! Jesus is God's Son." Jesus looked at the angry men and said, "God wants these children to sing, Hosanna! Hosanna! Everyone should listen to their true words, Hosanna! Hosanna!" Jesus looked at the children and

Did Jesus say, "Sh-h-h"? No! *(Finger to lips; shake head.)*
He said, "Children, come 'round!"
(Extend arms to sides; then bring them together.)

Did Jesus say, "Sh-h-h"? No! *(Finger to lips; shake head.)*
He said, "Sing words that are true." *(Hands to mouth.)*

Jesus loves me and Jesus loves you. *(Point to self; then others.)*
Sh-h-h! Now let's pray and say, "Thank You."
(Finger to lips; folded hands.)

After the last time pray, **Thank You, Jesus, for being my friend.**

Learning Activities

(20 minutes)

Let's Play Awhile

Clap and sing, "Jesus Said, 'You Are My Friends'." Then have children go to the Puzzle Center. If children especially enjoyed an activity from this unit, you may want to repeat it. If your class is large, repeat several.

As children finish coloring their puzzle pieces, play Zach's tape, "Ten Little Children." Help the children take turns gluing the puzzle pieces. **Caleb, who was Zaccheus' friend? . . . Jacob, who told the children, "Come to me?". . . Elizabeth, who listened to the children's song? All of you tell me who your special friend is.** *(JESUS!)* Glue the picture of Jesus and the children (page 155) in the center of the heart.

Let's Go Home

Let the children get their Praise Shakers. **Let's praise Jesus for being our special friend.** Sing, shake, and march to the children's favorite songs from this unit. Make sure children have their Praise Shakers and any other projects from this unit. Give an extra hug as each one leaves. **Jesus loves you and I do too!**

Jesus Loves Me

Review of Lessons 10–12

Bible Words: "You are my friends" (John 15:14, *NIV*).

Lesson Value: Children learn by repetition. The review lesson gives you an opportunity to repeat the fact that Jesus was a friend to Zaccheus, and that Jesus talked and listened to the children. This lesson should emphasize to the children that Jesus loves them the same way He loved His friends in the Bible. The children should know that Jesus says to them, "You are my friends," through you and the Bible. Let the children hear you express your love for Jesus and for them also.

Know: Know that Jesus is our special friend.
Feel: Feel eager to show love for Jesus.
Do: Show love for Jesus (sing and pray).

Children will accomplish the goals when they:

1. Say the Bible words, "You are my friends."
2. Pray, "Thank You, Jesus, for being our friend."
3. Tell who their special friend is.
4. Sing to and about Jesus.

Let's Get Ready

For the Bible story, have all four bookmarks in place—three stories and the Bible words with the following visuals: green and tree visual for Lesson 10; blue and child figure for Lesson 11; yellow and Jesus figure and children's faces for

Lesson 12. Place a small mirror with red Bible words marker. Also have a mirror with which Zach can greet the children.

Set up the Art Center, the Family Living Center, God's Wonders Center, and the Game Center. If you are the only teacher, use just the Art Center. Use the Puzzle Center after the Bible story.

Learning Activities

(30 minutes, including 10 minutes presession)

Let's Get Started

Zach is glad to see his friend Jonathan come to class. Help with coats, offerings, and attendance sticker. **Can you think of some of Jesus' friends?** *(Zaccheus, the children, etc., or members of the class.)* **Zach has one he wants you to meet.** Help Zach hold a little mirror for a child. **What friend of Jesus do you see? Would you like to play a game about Jesus' friends first or make a Praise Shaker?** Children may stay at a center as long as it does not keep someone else from having a turn.

Worship and Bible Story

(15 minutes)

Let's Worship God

Listen, what is Zach barking about? Zach barks three times again. **Yes, we have three more minutes to play. You are good listeners.** Make sure you have everyone's attention when you explain Zach's bark. Children should help with clean-up as you start singing, "Time to Put Our Toys Away." Each teacher should supervise three or four children, if possible. Gentle encouragement and praise will set the mood for Worship and Bible Story.

Sing "Find a Friend" as children finish with clean-up. **Jesus is our friend. He loves everyone here.** Sing, "Jesus Loves Me." **I see some friends of Jesus.** Point to and name several children. **Let's fold our hands and bow our heads and pray now. Thank You, Jesus, for being my friend. I love You.**

Let's Learn From the Bible

Introduction: Zach, let's count Jesus' friends. Let Zach touch heads as you count children and teachers. **The Bible tells me about many friends of Jesus. Let's open our Bible and see who they are.** Say the "My Bible" rhyme.

The Bible Story: Zach, would you choose two friends to help me? *(Nods his head and touches two children.)* Maria, please find the green bookmark. Thank you. You may sit down. Drew, what do you see in our Bible? *(The child removes the tree and shows the class.)* Thank you. You may sit down. Jesus found a friend up in a tree. What was his name? (Zaccheus.) What did Jesus say to him? (Come down. I'm going to your house.)

Zach, please choose two more helpers. *(Have one child find the blue bookmark and the second child take out the child figure.)* Show us what you have. What did the helpers say to the children? (Jesus is tired and busy.) What did Jesus say to the children? (Come to me.)

Zach, we need three more helpers. *(The first child finds the yellow bookmark, and second and third children will remove Jesus and the singing children visuals.)* Show us the picture of Jesus. Who did Jesus listen to? Show us the children singing. Hold Jesus up high. Do you remember what the children sang? (Hosanna! Hosanna!) What did Jesus say to the angry men? (Listen to the children.)

OK, Zach, two more helpers. Can you find the red bookmark? Thank you. *(Second child will remove mirror.)* Show us what you found! Do you see someone Jesus loves? What is her name? *(Take the mirror to each child and say, "Who does Jesus love?")* Help the child say his or her name.

Let's Apply the Lesson

Have children stand and repeat the following rhyme several times.

Did Jesus say, "Sh-h-h"? No! *(Finger to lips; shake head.)*
He said, "Zaccheus, you come down!" *(Motion to come down.)*

Game Center

Unit 3—Jesus Loves Us

Items to Include:

Lesson 10
Toilet-paper tubes
Yarn/clear tape
Jesus stickers (page 159)
4 1/4" x 11" paper
Picture of Jesus (page 153)

Lesson 11
Styrofoam cups
String
Crayons or markers

Purpose: The children will learn Jesus' words, "You are my friends."

Things to Do and Say

Lesson 10

For each set of binoculars, glue two toilet-paper tubes together and glue or tape a yarn neck strap on the sides. Children will decorate their papers and add Jesus stickers; then help them wrap their papers around their binoculars and apply tape. **Who climbed up in the tree to see Jesus? Yes, Zaccheus. Who can see Jesus in our room?** Point out pictures or stickers. **What did Jesus say to Zaccheus? What do our Bible words say? "You are my friends."**

Use the binoculars to play "Look for Jesus." Have the children kneel down and close their eyes. Move the picture of Jesus and let the children "Look for Jesus." When they find the picture, they bring it to you and everyone says the Bible words.

Lesson 11

To make a phone, connect two Styrofoam cups with a 24" string with knots inside the cups. Each child will decorate a "telephone." Play "Ring, Ring" with the phones.

Who will you call on your phone? What will you say? What did Jesus say to His helpers? What did the helpers say to the children? What did Jesus say to the children? Can you tell a friend Jesus' words? Name a friend sitting by you. What is your teacher's name? Jesus is my friend too.

Art Center

Unit 3—Jesus Loves Us

Items to Include:

Lesson 10
Aprons/paint shirts
Copies of tree, page 154
6" sticks
Green tempera paint

Lesson 11
Child figure, page 156
1" cloth squares
Glue/glue sticks

Purpose: The children will know that Jesus is their friend.

Things to Do and Say

Lesson 10

Copy a tree for each child. Cut sturdy but flexible (not brittle) sticks to paint with. Place sticks on paper plate. Put an apron on each child. Let the children add their Bible words stickers before they paint. Pour a quarter-size circle of paint on each child's tree. Add paint as needed.

Which friend do you want to sit by while you paint? . . . Can you move the paint around with the stick? . . . Have you ever climbed a tree? Zaccheus climbed a tree to see Jesus. Jesus went to Zaccheus' house. Jesus was Zaccheus' friend. He is your friend too.

Lesson 11

Give each child a copy of page 156. Place the 1" cloth squares on paper plates and have two children share a plate. Use glue sticks or a very small amount of liquid glue in a section of egg carton; apply with cotton swabs or craft sticks. Have the children glue cloth on the clothing of their figures. Add the Bible words stickers to each picture.

What colors do you like? What do you wear to your friend's house? In our Bible story, some children went to see Jesus. They probably wanted to look very nice. Jesus liked to talk to all the children. Jesus was their friend. Jesus is your friend too.

Art Center, continued

Lesson 12
Ear pattern, page 158
Adding machine paper
Stickers from page 159

Lesson 13
Crayons
Rice/bowls
Teaspoons
Colored tape

For all lessons
Clean-up supplies
Bible words stickers (page 159)
Stapler
Paper plates to hold supplies

Lesson 12

Cut a set of ears and staple 5" to 6" apart on a 24" headband (adding machine paper) for each child. Give the children the stickers from page 159. Use paper plates to hold the stickers. When a child finishes decorating his or her ears, staple the band to fit the child's head.

Would you like to decorate your "Listening Ears" with stickers? How does a bird sound? What sounds can you make? . . . Did you hear any sounds as you came to class? Jesus wanted the children to sing. He liked what they sang. Jesus says, "You are my friends."

Lesson 13

For each child, staple together the sides of a folded paper plate, leaving a large opening. Place rice in a sturdy bowl with several teaspoons. Watch that children do not put rice in their mouths.

Review stories and the Bible words. **We're making "Praise Shakers." Decorate yours and we'll have a parade for our friend Jesus. How was Zaccheus a friend to Jesus? . . . How might you have felt if you had gone to see Jesus the way the children did in our Bible story? . . . What do you suppose the children sang to Jesus? What would you like to sing to Jesus? How did Jesus feel when the children sang to Him?** Help each child put 3 or 4 spoons of rice inside his or her plate. Staple the opening in the plate and cover staples securely with colored tape. Make sure the children add their Bible words stickers.

Game Center, continued

Lesson 12
Hopscotch court

Lesson 13
Shoe boxes
Set of review visuals
Beanbags

For all lessons
Crayons
Markers
Masking tape

Call a friend and say, **Hello, Jesus says, "You are my friends."** Help children who have difficulty doing this.

Lesson 12

Make a hopscotch court with masking tape—one block, two blocks, one, and end with two. Draw toes on a strip for start.

Children will say the Bible words as they hop. "You - are - my - friends." **Jump, turn around, hop back.** Set chairs along the court for other children to watch, wait, and help with the verse. **You are all waiting so quietly. I like it when you take turns. Jesus liked to hear the children sing. I know He likes to hear you say His words. Perhaps the children jumped and hopped as they went into the temple singing.**

Lesson 13

Make copies of tree, Jesus/Zaccheus, Jesus/children, singing children. Mount each visual on cardboard or tape to wall behind a shoe box. Use small beanbags to toss at boxes. Mark the start line with masking tape close to the boxes.

Can you toss the beanbag into a box? Tell me about the picture. Who did Zaccheus want to see? . . . What did Jesus do when the children and babies came to see Him? . . . Who sang to Jesus? Did Jesus like their song? Jesus is our friend. Can you say the Bible words?

Family Living Center

Unit 3—Jesus Loves Us

Items to Include:

Lesson 10
Cleaning tools
Sweeper
Tablecloth
Party plates and cups

Lesson 11
Basket, napkins
Bread, cheese slices
Paper plates
Cookie cutters
Sandwich bags

Purpose: The children will feel eager to show love for Jesus.

Things to Do and Say

Lesson 10

Show the children how to use dust cloths, feather dusters, and hand sweepers, and set the table with a party cloth, plates, and cups.

Let's pretend that Jesus is coming to our house. We need to get our house cleaned up. Eric, would you like to dust or sweep? . . . Rosa, do you pick up your toys when your friends come to visit? Do you share them with your friends? . . . Sarah, let's put these pretty plates and cups on the table. In our Bible story, Jesus went to Zaccheus' house. How happy that must have made Zaccheus. . . . What would we say if Jesus were coming to see us? Maybe we'd say, "Jesus, we love You." Maybe we'd say thank-you to Jesus for being our friend.

Lesson 11

Choose simple cookie cutters that fit a slice of bread. Children will place bread and cheese on paper plates to cut with the cutters and make sandwiches. They may eat the edges now. Have an enlarged picture of Jesus and the children (page 155) set up where you can "go to see Him."

We're going on a pretend trip today. The children in our Bible story went to see Jesus. Jesus loved the children. He wanted them to come. . . . Let's pretend that we

Block Center

Unit 3—Jesus Loves Us

Items to Include:

For all lessons
Blocks
People
Cars

Lesson 10
Houses
Trees

Lesson 11
Airport
Airplanes/helicopters
Airline hats (optional)

Purpose: The children will know Jesus is their friend wherever they are.

Things to Do and Say

Lesson 10

If you do not have the props suggested, make your own. Make houses out of boxes; cut people from catalogs and tape to blocks or cans. Put twigs in spools to make trees. Use blocks to build houses, sidewalks and streets.

What people live in your house? Who drives the car in your family? Zaccheus had to walk to his house. No one lived there but him. Sometimes he was very lonely. He wanted a friend.

As children play with the blocks, people, and cars, talk about their friends and family. **Do you have company sometimes? Do you have a swing on a tree? Do you know who climbed a tree to see Jesus? Jesus went to Zaccheus' house. Jesus was his friend. Jesus is your friend too, at church, at home, or wherever you are.**

Lesson 11

Use boxes as hangers and terminals. Build a short runway. Children will pretend blocks are planes if you do not have any.

Have you ever flown in an airplane? Who did you go see? Some children walked with their mommies to see Jesus. Wherever you go Jesus is your friend. Jesus says, "You are my friends." . . . How did Jesus take a trip? If children can't answer this,

Family Living Center, continued

For all lessons
Dolls,
Telephones

are going to see Jesus. We want to take our lunch. Would you like to cut your bread or cheese first? What cookie cutter will you choose? Let's pack our picnic basket and save it for our trip. We're happy Jesus is our friend.

Bethany, would you like to get the dolls ready to go with us or call a friend who would like to go see Jesus?

Lesson 12
Dress-up clothes
Unbreakable mirror

Lesson 12

Have a variety of dress-up clothes: men's ties, shirts, blouses, hats, jewelry, purses, billfolds, etc. Pieces of fabric can be draped and tied. **Let's get ready to go to church. What would you like to wear? What friends do you see at church? What do we do at church?** *(Play, sing, pray, learn about Jesus.)* **I like to go to church. My friends are there, and I can hear stories about my friend Jesus. That makes me happy! . . . Thank You, Jesus, for being my friend.** Encourage children to pray alone. Use a telephone to invite a friend to go with you.

Lesson 13
Aprons
Towels
Dish pans
Sponges
Cotton swabs
Empty baby powder cans

Lesson 13

Place large bath towels on the tables to absorb spills. Put just 1" of water in pans. Lay dolls on small towels with sponges and cotton swabs. Teachers (example) and children (imitation) wear aprons. If your dolls are not waterproof, use just a slightly damp wash cloth to wipe their hands and faces.

Choose a baby to wash. Do you have a baby at your house? What did Jesus do with the babies? *(Touched and held them.)* **Let's sing a song about Jesus to our babies.** Suggest a song, or let children choose one. **Who listened to the children's song in the temple-church?** Encourage children to feed and rock their babies so others can have a turn to wash.

Block Center, continued

remind them that sometimes Jesus went in a boat, but most of the time He walked.

As children play, talk with them about places they go. **Do you go to the grocery store with your mommy or daddy? Where else do you go?** *(Church, park, doctor, swimming, relatives, friends.)* **Jesus will be your friend wherever you are. . . . Jesus wanted the children to come and see Him. He liked the little babies too. He was the children's friend. He is your friend too.**

Lesson 12
Small furniture and playground toys (from doll house)
Bell

Lesson 12

Small furniture and playground toys can be used to talk about the various areas in your church building. Help the children use the blocks to make an outline of your church building. Put the furniture inside the outline. Let the children ring the bell to call the people to church. **Where do the babies sleep in our church building? Where does the preacher work? . . .This can be our room. And this is the room where your mommies and daddies have class.**

Do we have a refrigerator or stove in our church? Have you ever eaten dinner in the church building? The children in our story followed Jesus into the temple-church. They were singing to Jesus. Would you like to sing a song to Jesus? Sing "My Best Friend Is Jesus." **I'm glad Jesus is our friend. Thank You, Jesus, for being our friend.**

God's Wonders Center

Unit 3—Jesus Loves Us

Items to Include:

Lesson 10
Dish pans/towels
Vegetable brush
Aprons
Vegetables/fruits

Lesson 12
Small containers
Rice/beans/macaroni

Purpose: The children will sing to and about Jesus.

Things to Do and Say

Lesson 10

Have teacher and children wear aprons. Put just 1" of water in a pan. Have a large towel under the pan to absorb spills. Place vegetable brushes in the water. Let children scrub the carrots and celery. Then you cut the vegetables into small strips and peel the apples, if necessary. Let the children cut the bananas and apples into slices using a plastic table knife.

Let's pretend we're having company. We'll all work to get the food ready. In our Bible story, Zaccheus had company. Do you know who came to his house? Yes, Jesus. What kind of food do you suppose Zaccheus served Jesus? . . . Where was Zaccheus when Jesus first saw him? *(In a tree.)* **Let's sing while we prepare our food.** Sing the song, "Zaccheus." Show the children how to arrange the food on paper plates and then let them taste the fruits and vegetables.

Lesson 12

Have a variety of small containers, two of each kind. Put the same items in the identical cans so they will make the same sounds. Use the same size jingle bells. Glue on lids. Have one cardboard circle or lid to hold each set of containers.

Puzzle Center

Unit 3—Jesus Loves Us

Items to Include:

Lesson 11
Copies of page 155
Old teaching pictures
Coloring book pictures
Construction paper or cardboard
Glue
Clear, self-adhesive plastic (optional)

Purpose: The children will show love for Jesus (sing, pray, share).

Things to Do and Say

Lesson 11

Make several puzzles using copies of the picture of Jesus and the children. Glue the pictures to construction paper or cardboard. Color the pictures, then cover them with clear, self-adhesive plastic for durability (optional). Do the same with the picture of Jesus on page 153, and with any appropriate teaching pictures or other pictures you find. Cut the puzzles into 3 or 4 pieces for 2's and 5 or 6 pieces for 3's. Do not cut across faces, or facial features. To save the puzzles, have envelopes to store the pieces when the children have finished with them. Help children with the puzzles only when they ask for help. Make sure a child finishes one puzzle before working another one or leaving the table.

Who is that in your puzzle, Aaron? Yes, it's Jesus with the children. Look how He is holding the baby. He loved the children. He loves you too! He is your friend. . . . That boy in your puzzle looks like he could be a friend of Jesus, Tony. Jesus is your friend too! . . . You have a puzzle of a mommy. Did she take her children to see Jesus? Jesus loved the children. He loves you, Ashley. The Bible tells us that Jesus said, "You are my friends."

God's Wonders Center, continued

Nuts/bolts/ pennies
Bells
Lids or cardboard circles
Glue

David, shake this can. Now shake this larger one. Do they sound alike? No! Can you find one that sounds like the first one? When a child makes a match, he may put the set on a lid. **Now let your friend Josh shake one. Can you match the one Josh is holding?**

After children have had fun shaking and matching sounds, use the shakers as you sing to Jesus. **Our shakers make happy sounds when we sing. Jesus heard a happy sound when He went into the temple-church. Do you know what the sound was? Children were singing to Him! Jesus liked their singing. The children were His friends. Jesus is our friend too. Thank You, Jesus, for being my friend.** Sing "My Best Friend Is Jesus."

Lesson 13
Plastic pans
Shower curtain
Sand
Scoops
Spoons, etc.

For all lessons
Small wash pan
Plastic drop cloth
Hand towels
Soap

Lesson 13

Spread a shower curtain on the floor and place dishpans or boxes lined with plastic in the center. Allow ample room for this activity. Pour about 2" of sand in the pans/boxes. Use small scoops, tablespoons, berry baskets, and assorted strainers and containers for the children to mix and pour. Store sand in a plastic bucket when you have finished.

Do you have a sand pile at your house? What friends come over to play? Thank you for sharing the spoon, Carlos. It makes your friend happy when you share. It makes Jesus happy too. The Bible tells us that Jesus said, "You are my friends." Jesus was a friend to Zaccheus, to the children who came to see Him, and to those who sang to Him. He's our friend too! I'm glad, aren't you? Sing the following words to the tune of "Farmer in the Dell":

I have a happy face, I have a happy face.
I have a happy face today, for Jesus is my friend.

Puzzle Center, continued

Lesson 13
Two large hearts, one cut into puzzle pieces
Red crayons
Glue sticks
One copy of the picture on page 155
Tape player

For all lessons
Board puzzles of children and adults

Lesson 13

Draw a large heart on a piece of poster board. Cut it out and trace it on a piece of paper. On the first heart draw enough puzzle pieces for each child in your class to have one. If your class is large, make more than one puzzle. Make the pieces as large and unique as possible. As you cut the pieces out, trace the lines on the second heart. Hang the second heart on the wall to use as a guide when you assemble the puzzle.

As children color the pieces, review the Bible stories and Bible words. **Who did Jesus see in a tree? Where did He go? Who is your special friend? Who did the children go to visit? Did He want to see them? What did Jesus' helpers say? Who did Jesus want to talk to? Let's talk to God right now. Thank You, God, for our friend Jesus. Does anyone have a song he or she wants to sing? Jesus likes to hear your singing.**

When the heart is assembled, sing, "Jesus Said, 'You Are My Friends,'" and glue the picture of Jesus and the children in the center.

Visual—Winter, Unit 3

Instructions

1. For lesson 10 visual, copy picture; fold Jesus back.
2. For lesson 12, copy just Jesus. Tape figure to paper-towel tube.
3. For lesson 13, copy Jesus. Place figure in Bible with yellow bookmark.
4. For lesson 13, Game Center, copy full page; mount on cardboard.

When Jesus saw Zaccheus up in the tree, He said, "Come down, Zaccheus. I want to go to your house with you." Zaccheus became Jesus' friend.

Jesus said, "You are my friends."

Teaching picture—Winter, Unit 3

Art activity—Winter, Unit 3

Instructions

1. Make copies of page for each child.
2. Have 1" square scraps of cloth and glue ready.
3. Children will glue cloth on their figures.

When the children came to see Jesus, He was glad.
Jesus loved the children. He said, "You are my friends."

Friends—Winter, Unit 3

Instructions for lesson 12 Telling Tubes

1. Make multiple copes of the page on colored paper.
2. Cut apart on solid lines.
3. Tape each strip around a toilet-paper tube.
4. Make one for each child in your class.
5. For lesson 13 visual, copy the page; cut apart on outside lines. Place in Bible with yellow bookmark.
6. For lesson 13 game, copy; mount on cardboard.

"You are my friends" John 15:14.

"You are my friends" John 15:14.

"You are my friends" John 15:14.

"You are my friends" John 15:14.

"You are my friends" John 15:14.

"You are my friends" John 15:14.

"You are my friends" John 15:14.

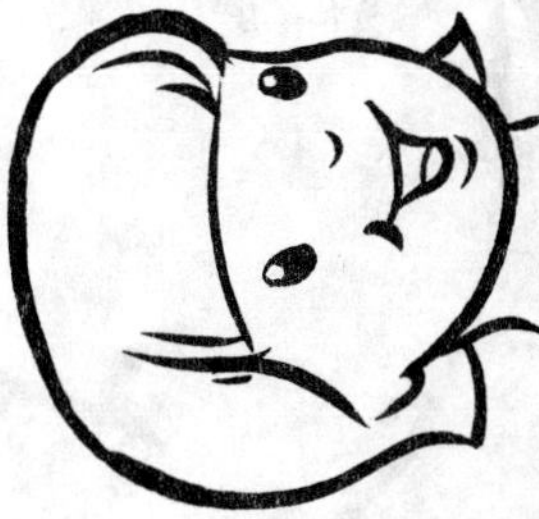

"You are my friends" John 15:14.

Art activity—Winter, Unit 3

Instructions

1. Make a copy of this page for each child. Use construction paper.
2. Cut out ears. Staple ears 5" to 6" apart on adding machine paper, 24" long.
3. Give children the stickers from page 159 to put on their ears.
4. Staple bands to fit children's heads.

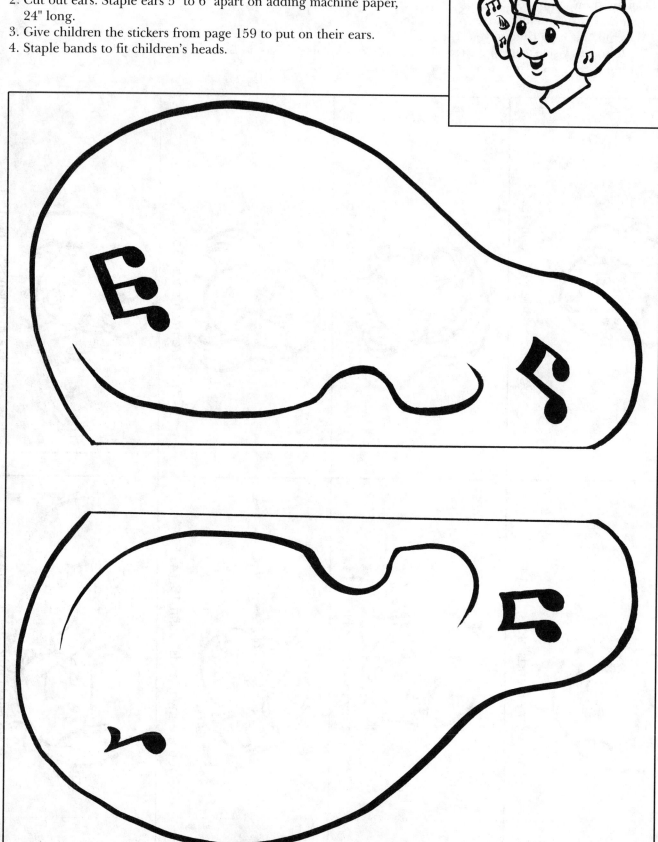

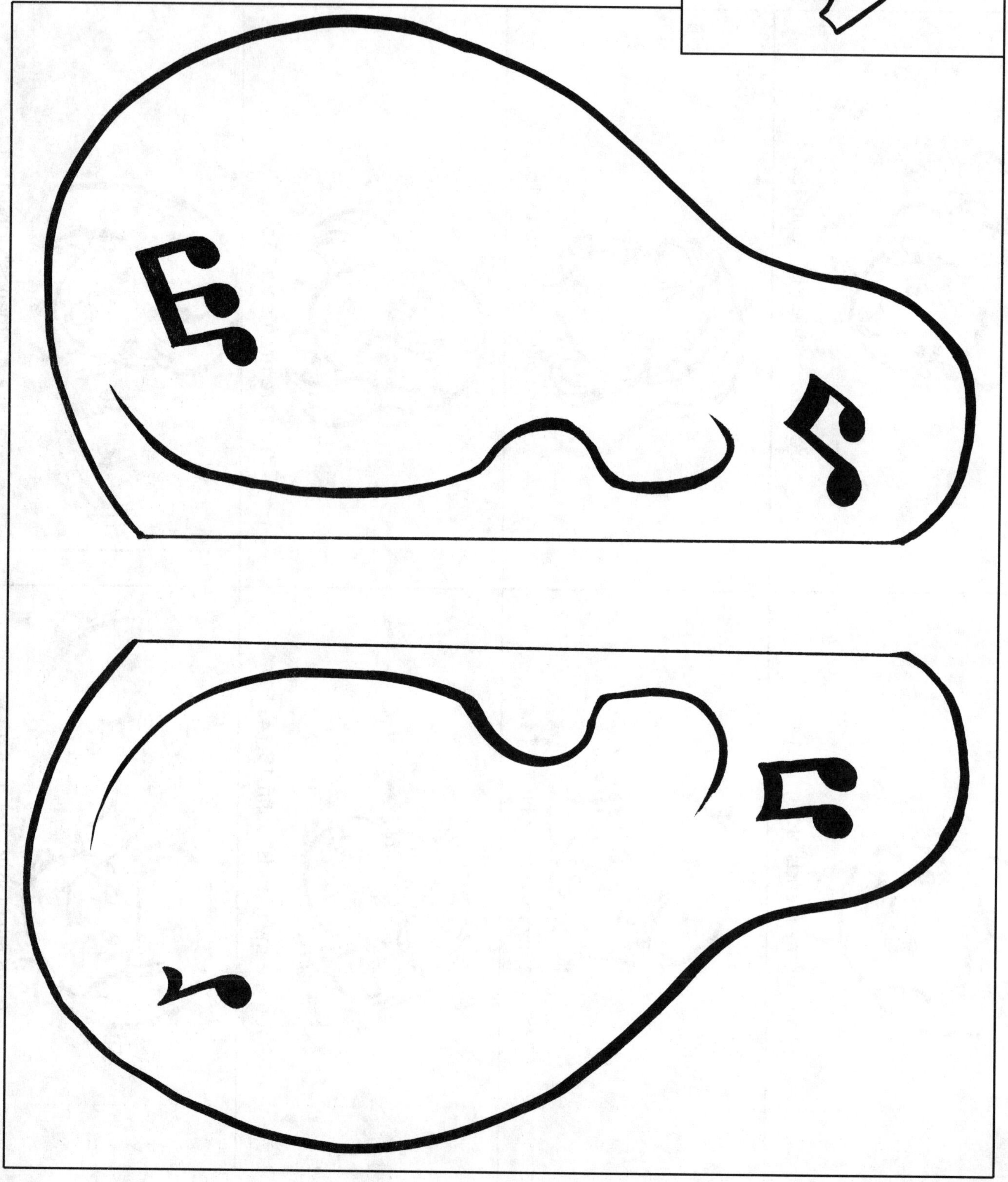

Stickers—Winter, Unit 3

Instructions to make stickers

1. Make multiple copies of page on manila paper or flesh colored construction paper.
2. Mix two parts white glue and one part vinegar.
3. Lightly "paint" mixture onto backs of uncut stickers. Let dry.
4. Let children color stickers; then cut out stickers.
5. Use damp sponges to attach stickers.

Instructions to make bookmark

1. Make multiple copies of page on manila paper or flesh colored construction paper.
2. Cut strips of construction paper 9" x 2" (one green, one blue, one yellow, one red).
3. Glue the tree on the green strip, Jesus and child on the blue one, children singing on the yellow one, and Jesus on the red strip. Use as suggested in lessons.

Stickers for Art Center—Winter, Unit 3

Sticker for Game Center—Winter, Unit 3

Stickers for bookmark—Winter, Unit 3

"You are my friends."—John 15:14

"You are my friends."—John 15:14

Dear Parent,

Thank you for bringing your child to learn about Jesus. Our unit theme is "Jesus Loves Us." Your child will learn of Jesus' love through the following lessons:

Jesus Loves Zaccheus (Luke 19:1-6)
Jesus Loves the Children (Mark 10:13-16; Luke 18:15-17)
Jesus Listens to the Children Sing (Matthew 21:15, 16)
Jesus Loves Me (Review of Lessons 10–12)

We emphasize that Jesus is our friend, as we learn about Bible friends. The following activities will introduce and reinforce the lessons. (Suggestions for ways to talk to your child are printed in **boldface.**) You have a wonderful opportunity to teach daily about Jesus' love in your home. How exciting it will be for a child to share, "I heard that story at home," when he or she hears it in class.

- Take a walk and use binoculars to look at different kinds of trees. **What kind of trees would be easy to climb? Zaccheus climbed a tree to see Jesus.**
- Wash rubber dolls. Sponges, cotton swabs and powder add to the fun. **Jesus held the babies and talked to the children.**
- Listen to music through earphones. **Jesus heard the children sing in the temple-church. He listened. He liked the children's songs.**
- See if your child can match sounds made with safe kitchen items. **Thank You, God, for our ears. Friends use their ears to listen to our words.**
- Draw a hopscotch court. Make 6" squares: one, two, one, ending with two. Say, **"You - are - my - friends,"** as the child jumps. Try it and then invite a friend over to play.
- Fix a "little" picnic. Sit on a beach towel in a sunny spot in the house if you cannot go outside. **Jesus went to Zaccheus' house to eat. . . . Some families probably packed lunches when they went to see Jesus.**
- Cut a big heart from a shirt box lid. Paste a picture of Jesus on the outside bottom of the box. Trace a second heart on the inside bottom of the box. As you cut the "lid" heart into 5 or 6 pieces trace them on the second heart. Color pieces and assemble in the box. Tape to hold in place. Cut a piece of clear wrap twice the length of the box. Lay it over the heart and turn the box over. **Surprise! Jesus loves you!**
- Sing to and about Jesus. Use these songs and action rhyme often with your child.

Where's a Friend?

(Tune: "Where Is Thumbkin?")

Where's a friend*, where's a friend?
Here I am! *(Left thumb.)* Here I am! *(Right thumb.)*
How are you today, friend? *(Left wiggles.)*
Very well, I thank you. *(Right wiggles.)*
Jesus loves you. *(Left wiggles.)*
Jesus loves you. *(Right wiggles.)*
**Insert your child's name.*

Jesus Said, "You Are My Friends."

(Tune: "London Bridge")

Jesus said, "You are my friends,
Are my friends, are my friends."
Jesus said, "You are my friends; I love you."

My Bible

This is my Bible; *(Palms held together.)*
I'll open it wide *(Open hands; keep them touching.)*
And see *(or say)* what is written
On the inside! *(Say Bible words: "You are my friends.")*
—*Jean Baxendale*

In the love of Jesus, your child's teacher,

Spring Quarter

Learning What God Wants Us to Be

Each unit of this quarter is planned to help you teach your 2's and 3's about a special quality God wants His children to have.

The special quality in Unit 1 is *thankfulness.* "Let the peace that Christ gives control your thinking. You were all called together in one body to have peace. Always be thankful" (Colossians 3:15, *ICB*). Two's and 3's can learn to be thankful for food, for the love and care of parents and others, and for their friend Jesus.

Unit 2 centers on *helpfulness.* Learning to be helpful teaches 2's and 3's to be aware of the needs of others. Two's and 3's are beginning to be able to tell others, "Jesus loves you!" and "Come to church," the special thrust of this unit.

Jesus said, "Love your neighbor as you love yourself" (Matthew 19:19, *ICB*). *Self-confidence* is the special quality that is stressed in Unit 3, "Learning About Me." Two's and 3's will learn just how important they are in the eyes of God because He made each one with wonderful capabilities.

As a result of these lessons, 2's and 3's will

KNOW

Know that God wants them to be thankful; that they help Jesus when they say, "Come to Sunday school" or "Jesus loves you!"; and that God made them.

FEEL

Feel thankful (for Jesus, caregivers, and food); feel good about themselves because God made them.

DO

Say thank-you to God and to people; help Jesus in two ways (saying "Come to Sunday school" and "Jesus loves you!"); thank God for making them.

Use these songs and action rhymes throughout the quarter, along with those specifically mentioned in the units.

I Can Talk to God

Head and Shoulders

(Tune: "London Bridge")

Head and shoulders, knees and toes, knees and toes, knees and toes.
Head and shoulders, knees and toes.
Thank You, God, for making me.

For Unit 3:
Eyes and ears, nose and mouth, nose and mouth, nose and mouth.
Eyes and ears, nose and mouth.
Thank You, God, for making me.

Angry, mad, happy, sad; happy, sad, happy, sad.
Angry, mad, happy, sad.
Thank You, God, for making me.

The Busy Fingers

Busy little finger people, *(Hold up fists.)*
Who will put the toys (blocks, etc.) away?
(Look at fists.)
"I will," "I will," "I will," "I will," "I will,"
All the fingers say.
(Raise fingers one at a time, both hands at the same time, beginning with index fingers.)
—*Louise M. Oglevee*

My Eyes, My Ears

My eyes, my ears, my nose, my mouth,
My hands and feet so small,
My arms, my legs, my tummy, my head—
I know God made them all!
(Point to each part of the body as you name it.)
—*Sylvia Tester*

Spring Party Suggestions

March—Music Makers Mayhem

Purpose:	To provide a fun time of praise and worship
When:	During class time
Activity:	Make musical instruments (see page 317); then go to another class and give a concert.
Games:	Musical Chairs (Don't take out chairs for this age.); Musical Circles (Children sit in two circles and pass balls while the music plays. When the music stops, the children holding the balls switch circles.)
Food:	Cookies and/or bite-size pieces of fruit
Bible Story:	Children Sing to Jesus, or David Plays the Harp for King Saul

April—Easter Celebration

Purpose:	To help children focus on the Easter story
When:	During class time
Activity:	Play "Hide and Go Seek Jesus" (Take children from room to room looking for the risen Jesus. Have "tomb" set up in the last area. "He is not here, He is risen!" Sing songs and praise God!)
Food:	Cupcakes decorated with jelly beans
Game:	Muffin Toss (toss jelly beans into muffin tins)
Bible Story:	The Easter Story

May—Mother's Tea

Purpose:	To help children do something special for Mom
When:	During class time or on a Saturday morning or afternoon
Preparation:	Tell moms and kids to dress up!
Craft:	Take instant pictures of moms and children, mount on craft-stick frames decorated by children.
Food:	Special cookies and punch (tea for moms, if you want)
Game:	Dress-up relay (use a hat, purse, shoes, and a necklace large enough to slip over the head)
Bible Story:	Mary and Baby Jesus (Talk about how she would have cared for Him.)

Reminder: If you are using the year-round attendance chart, order *Spring* seals (22-01775—216 seals) now.

Unit 1: Being Thankful

Lessons 1–5

By the end of the unit, the children will

Know that God wants us to be thankful.

Feel thankful (for Jesus, caregivers, food).

Say "thank you" to God and to people.

Unit Bible Words

"We . . . thank God" (2 Thessalonians 1:3).

Happy Day Books

The Little Lost Sheep 24-04232

Saying Thank You Makes Me Happy 24-04220

A Child's Story of Jesus 24-04217

God Made Me Special 24-04205

The Unit at a Glance

1 **The Lost Sheep** — **Luke 15:3-7**
Jesus tells how important each sheep is.

2 **One Man Is Thankful** — **Luke 17:11-19**
A man thanks Jesus for healing him.

3 **Jesus Is Thankful** — **Luke 22:7-19**
Jesus gives thanks for juice and bread.

4 **Thank You, God, for Jesus** — **Luke 19:29-38**
Crowds of people give thanks for Jesus.

5 **Breakfast With Jesus** — **Based on John 18–21**
Jesus shares breakfast with His friends.

Why Teach This Unit?

Being thankful is basic to anyone's relationship with God. In fact, it can go a long way in building any relationship.

This unit teaches the art of being thankful. Through the use of stories of Jesus' thankfulness as well as the thankfulness of others to and for Jesus, the unit makes the very personal point that each child should be thankful because he or she is special to Jesus. The children will learn to show thankfulness verbally, through art, and through action.

You will find many suggestions for using the Bible words throughout the hour. Practice doing this until it becomes natural to incorporate them into your conversations and prayers. For example, "We . . . thank God" for beautiful flowers. . . . "We . . . thank God" that we can talk to Him.

Have a Bible with the words highlighted or underlined, placed where the children can see it. Make sure your classroom Bible is small enough that the children can handle it respectfully.

Things to Do for This Unit

- Photocopy Learning Center Cards (pages 175-180); cut pages apart on solid lines. Mount side 1 of a card on cardboard; then mount side 2 on back of cardboard. Laminate for durability.
- Gather materials listed on the Learning Center Cards.
- Make copies of Parents' Letter (page 188) and the Unit Planning Sheet (319 and 320).
- For Lesson 1, make lambs of white wool fabric, or a similar fabric, using pattern on page 181.
- For Lesson 2, make ten copies each of pages 182 and 183. Color and cut out the figures and glue one of each back to back.
- For Lesson 3, make visual of Jesus, cup, and bread (see pages 181, 184, and 186).
- For Lesson 4, make visual of Jesus on donkey, and cut coats and palm leaves (all patterns on page 185).
- For Lesson 5, photocopy page 187 and add color.

Use These Songs and Action Rhymes During Unit 1

We Thank You, God in Heaven

I Love Jesus

My Bible

This is my Bible;
(Hands held out in front, palms together.)
I'll open it wide
(Open hands, but keep them touching.)
And see (or say) what is written
On the inside! *(Say Bible verse together.)*
—*Jean Baxendale*

I Can

I can stand up straight and tall, *(Do so.)*
I can curl up like a ball,
(Squat with arms around knees.)
I can spread out like a tree,
(Arms high, spread out.)
I can sit down quietly.
(Place finger to lips and then sit down.)
—*Dorothy Fay Richards*

Let the children name people—parents, grandparents, other caregivers, doctors, fire fighters, etc. **Thank You, God, for taking care of each one of us.**

Learning Activities

(20 minutes)

Let's Play Awhile

If possible take the children outside for the Game Center activity. If time allows, the children might enjoy repeating this activity or doing one of the other learning activities not used earlier in the hour.

Let's Go Home

Have Zach gather the children and lead them in a favorite song. Make sure each child has his or her self-portrait from the Art Center as well as a woolly lamb. See that parents get their letters too.

The Lost Sheep

Luke 15:3-7

Bible Words: "We . . . thank God" (2 Thessalonians 1:3).

Lesson Value: Since it is normal for every 2- and 3-year-old to think that the world revolves around him, some would think it unnecessary to teach these children about Jesus' concern for the individual. When we stop to remember that we are not living in a normal world, we realize that it is a very necessary lesson. Many preschoolers have had their every desire given in to while their most basic needs have been ignored. Even the most self-centered 2- or 3-year-old needs to know that Jesus cares about him as a person. That is truly something for which he needs to be thankful.

Know: Know that God wants us to be thankful
Feel: Feel thankful.
Do: Say thank-you to God and to people

The children will accomplish the goals when they:

1. Say the Bible Words, "We thank God."
2. Pray a thank-you prayer.
3. Sing thank-you songs.
4. In a play situation, say thank-you to God and to people.
5. Express thankfulness in non-verbal ways.

Let's Get Ready

For the Bible story, you will need a white wool lamb for each child and yourself, made from the pattern on page 181. You will also need your classroom Bible with the new Bible words highlighted, and a chalkboard with 100 chalk circles drawn on it.

Prepare the Family Living Center, the Art Center, and the Book and Picture Center if you have enough teachers. If you are the only teacher, use just the Family Living Center. Use the activity suggested in the Games Center after the Bible story.

Learning Activities

(30 minutes, including 10 minutes presession)

Let's Get Started

Have Zach greet each child enthusiastically by name. As you help each child put away his personal belongings and place his offering in the container, say, **Do you know that you are very important to Jesus?** Encourage the children to choose an activity by suggesting two possibilities. Say, **Would you rather draw a picture of yourself or look for pictures of sheep in these books?**

Worship and Bible Story

(15 minutes)

Let's Worship God

Give the children a warning that clean-up time is coming, before Zach gives the clean-up signal. As the children gather, begin singing. Use the song, "Jesus Loves Me." Also use the rhyme, "My Eyes, My Ears" (page 162). **Our Bible words say, "We thank God." Each one of you is special to Jesus (God).** Call each child by name and encourage her to say thank-you to Jesus. Say, **Abbie, you are special to Jesus (God). Let's say thank-you to God right now.**

Let's Learn From the Bible

Introduction: Place the white wool lambs in a covered box or basket. Have Zach say, **There are some lambs missing around here. Can you help me find them?** Let Zach sniff around until he comes to the container where they are. Let Zach call each child by name to come up and choose a lamb to hold during the Bible story. Encourage the children to stroke the rough cloth. Place one in your Bible. Have one hundred circles drawn on a chalkboard or poster board. **The Bible tells us that Jesus taught people about how import each person is to Him.**

The Bible Story: Jesus told a story about a shepherd who had a hundred sheep. Now, that is a lot of sheep! One day, one little sheep got lost. *(Erase one circle.)* If the shepherd had one hundred and lost only one, he would still have a lot of sheep. Do you think the shepherd worried about that one little sheep? *(Pick up your sheep and stroke it.)*

Of course he did! Even one little sheep is important! Jesus said, "The shepherd left all of these *(point to circles)* to go after that one little lost sheep." *(Replace missing circle.)* Then the shepherd carried the little sheep home on his shoulders. The shepherd was happy. He had found his one little lost sheep. I'm glad God made shepherds to take care of the sheep.

Then Jesus said that is how God feels about every person. He loves each one. Each one is very important to Him. Thank You, God, for loving each of these children.

Let's Apply the Lesson

Have the children hold up their sheep and count them. Say, **We have __ sheep. Are they all important?** Let the children respond. **Would any of you like to lose your sheep?** Let the children respond. Have the children stand up. Count them. Say, **We have __ children. Are you all important to Jesus?** Let the children respond. **That's right. Each of you is important to Jesus. . . . Who takes care of the sheep? Yes, God made shepherds to take care of the sheep. Who takes care of you?**

thank-you to Jesus. Jesus likes for us to say thank-you to Him. Who else should you thank? Wait for children to name others, such as parents, grandparents, friends, teachers, etc. **Saying thank-you to these people makes them happy too!**

Learning Activities

(20 minutes)

Let's Play Awhile

Have the children stand and sing the song, "We Thank You, God in Heaven." Let them suggest people and things for which to thank God. If the children need some exercise, sing "Head and Shoulders" (page 161) before starting the activity suggested for the Art Center. You may need to help the children think of things to write thank-you notes about.

Let's Go Home

Have Zach encourage the children to clean up the Art Center and come together. Until parents arrive, lead the children in some songs and rhymes used during this unit and previous ones. Make sure each child has his or her thank-you card from the Art Center. Tell parents what the cards are for so they can help the children follow through on this project.

One Man Is Thankful

Luke 17:11-19

Bible Words: "We . . . thank God" (2 Thessalonians 1:3).

Lesson Value: One of the first lessons in good manners a young child receives is, "Now say thank-you." I am sure many a child has thought, "Can't they see I'm thankful? I turned three cartwheels when they gave me the gift."

The nine lepers may have felt the same way. They may have thought, "Jesus will know how thankful we are. We are healed!" Excitement over the gift, however, is not the same thing as gratitude to the giver of the gift. Two's and 3's can learn, from Jesus' delight in the expression of thankfulness from the one leper who returned, that gratitude to the giver is important.

Know: Know that God wants us to be thankful.
Feel: Feel thankful.
Do: Say thank-you to God and to people.

Children will accomplish the goals when they:

1. Say the Bible words, "We thank God."
2. Pray a prayer of thanksgiving.
3. Sing thank-you songs.
4. Name or point to people who say "thank-you."
5. Express thankfulness in verbal and non-verbal ways.

Let's Get Ready

The Bible story will require ten copies each of the men on pages 182 and 183. Cut out each and glue one well man to the back of each sick man. If you have more than ten children, make one figure for each child. You will also need your classroom Bible.

For learning activities prepare the Family Living Center, the Block Center, and God's Wonders Center. If you are the only teacher, use just the Family Living Center. Have materials ready for the Art Center learning activity after the Bible story.

Learning Activities

(30 minutes, including 10 minutes presession)

Let's Get Started

Use Zach to greet each child when he arrives. Give each child the choice of two centers by asking, **Would you rather build some words with blocks or see some things God made that we can be thankful for?**

Worship and Bible Story

(15 minutes)

Let's Worship God

Give the children a warning about two minutes before you have Zach tell them it is clean-up time. Begin singing as the first children come to the story circle. Sing "Jesus Loves Me" and "We Thank You, God in Heaven" from page 164. Use the rhyme, "My Bible" (page 164) and end with the Bible words. Pray, **Thank You, God, for letting us talk to You and tell You thank-you for all the good things You give us.** Do an action rhyme to get out "the wiggles" so the children can listen to the Bible story.

Let's Learn From the Bible

Introduction: Encourage the children to come one by one and give Zach a pat on the head. Have Zach say thank-you to each one. Ask the children to hold up their ten fingers and count out loud: 1, 2, 3, 4, 5, 6, 7, 8, 9, 10. Give each child at least one sick/well man that you made ahead of time.

The Bible Story: The Bible tells us about ten men who were sick with leprosy. That means they had sores all over their bodies. Can you show me the ten men with leprosy? *(Let children hold up the ten men with leprosy.)* This sickness made the men feel bad and sad at the same time. They hurt and they had to stay away from other people so they did not pass the sickness on. No one wanted to have leprosy!

One day Jesus was walking near where the ten sick men lived. They called out, "Jesus, please make us well!"

Jesus said, "Go show the priest. You are well!"

Can you make your men begin to walk away? *(Let children pretend to walk men.)* When the men had gone a little way, they felt different. They looked at themselves. They were well! Can you turn your men so we can see the well men? They were so happy. Maybe they jumped up and down for joy. Can you make your men jump? Then 1, 2, 3, 4, 5, 6, 7, 8, 9 of them went on to show themselves to the priest.

May I borrow your man, Emily? *(Hold up the man so the children see the well side.)* But one man had something special to do. Do you know what it was? Yes, he went back to say thank-you to Jesus for making him well. *(Return Emily's man.)*

Let's Apply the Lesson

How many men remembered to say thank-you? Let the children respond. Can you imagine that! Just one man remembered to say thank-you to Jesus! Do you think that man made Jesus happy? I'm sure he did!

Which of the ten men do you want to be like? Let the children respond. Yes, like the man who came back to say

two things did Jesus say thank-you for? Allow children to respond. **Do you say thank-you to God for your food each meal? What do you say?** Let children tell you if they can. **Yes, we say, "Thank You, God, for this good food."** If the children seem interested, thank God for favorite foods the children suggest.

Do you think Jesus was also thankful for His friends who were with Him that special night? Can you name some people you are thankful for? Allow children to respond. Take time to thank God for the people mentioned.

Learning Activities

(20 minutes)

Let's Play Awhile

Have the children stand and do an action rhyme and/or a song, then begin one of the games suggested for this week on the Game Center Card. If you have several teachers and a large class, also use activities from earlier in the session.

Let's Go Home

Have Zach remind the children to tell God thank-you many times in the days to come and remind them that there are people all around them who would like to hear a thank-you also.

After the children have put the room in order and you have said thank-you to them, make sure they have their paper plates from the Art Center and a sample of the bread they baked to take home.

Jesus Is Thankful

Luke 22:7-19

Bible Words: "We . . . thank God" (2 Thessalonians 1:3).

Lesson Value: Even though many of your preschoolers may be in the habit of saying a blessing before meals, they probably take most of the necessities of life for granted. In this lesson they see Jesus, who could have had anything He wanted, giving thanks. The children will be encouraged to think about what they are thankful for before praying prayers of thanks.

Know: Know that God wants us to be thankful.
Feel: Feel thankful.
Do: Say thank-you to God and to people.

Children will accomplish the goals when they:

1. Say the Bible words, "We thank God."
2. Pray a prayer of thanks.
3. Experience some concrete things for which they are thankful.
4. Name someone or something they are thankful for.
5. In a play situation, say thank-you to God and to people.

Let's Get Ready

For the Bible story, you will need a Bible, the visual aid of Jesus (page 184), the cup (page 181), and the loaf (page 186); some grapes, and bread—matzos would be ideal. You will need a basket of fruit immediately after the Bible story.

Make arrangements for the Family Living Center, the Art Center, and God's Wonders Center. If you can have only one center, use the Family Living Center. Have materials ready for the Game Center after the Bible story.

Learning Activities

(30 minutes, including 10 minutes presession)

Let's Get Started

Remember to use the words *thank, thanks, thankful,* and *thank you* often during this lesson. Use the words in your conversation and in prayers. Thank the children for the things they do to help, for sharing with someone, for being extra attentive, whatever you notice, but do be genuine about it. Modeling what you want the children to learn is the best way to teach.

Let Zach help you greet each child by name. Help that child take care of his or her personal business before getting involved in learning centers. Say, **Krista, I'm thankful you are here today. Would you rather see some fruits God made or paint with grapes? . . . You want to paint? That's a good choice. Today we will learn that Jesus was thankful for something made from a type of fruit.**

Worship and Bible Story

(15 minutes)

Let's Worship God

Give the children about a two-minute warning before it is time to clean up. Have Zach issue the clean-up command itself. Begin singing as soon as the first children arrive at the story circle. Sing "We Thank You, God in Heaven" and "I Love Jesus." Also include the song, "Head and Shoulders," and the action rhyme, "My Eyes, My Ears," from page 162.

Do the rhyme, "My Bible." Let each child tell one thing or person he or she is thankful for, then tell God thank-you for that person/thing. **Thank You, God, for Eric's mommy. . . . Thank You, God, for giving Sarah a new baby sister.** Simple, one-sentence prayers are easy for children to say and understand.

Let's Learn From the Bible

Introduction: Have the visual aid of Jesus, the cup, and the loaf ready. Give each child a grape to hold in one hand and a small piece of bread to hold in the other. Have Zach question them. "Can you hold up a grape? Good. Can you hold up a piece of bread? Good. You will hear these things mentioned in the Bible story today. When you hear one of them mentioned, hold that one up and look at it carefully." Put the puppet away.

The Bible Story: *(Pick up your Bible.)* The Bible tells us about many times when Jesus gave thanks. Let me tell you about one of those times. *(Hold up Jesus visual.)*

It was a very special night. Jesus and His friends were eating a special dinner. They were eating in a special room. Special foods had been prepared. Special prayers had been prayed. Jesus and His friends had spent a lot of time talking to each other.

Near the end of the meal Jesus stood up. Jesus picked up a cup of juice made from grapes. *(Put cup in hands of Jesus.)* Jesus said thank-you to God for that juice. Then Jesus picked up a piece of bread. *(Put bread in hands of Jesus.)* Jesus broke the piece of bread and shared it with His friends. Jesus said thank-you to God for the bread too.

Let's Apply the Lesson

Whom did Jesus pray His thank-you prayer to? Let children respond. **That's right, Jesus prayed to God. What**

What an exciting day it was! Everyone was so thankful for Jesus *(wave leaf or clothing)*.

Let's Apply the Lesson

How did the people show that they were thankful for Jesus on that special day? Let the children respond. **Would you like to have been there?** Let the children respond. **What are some ways we can show God that we are thankful for Jesus ?** After the children have responded, suggest the additional possibility of waving some type of flag. Then say, **We are going to make some flags in the Art Center.**

Learning Activities

(20 minutes)

Let's Play Awhile

After making their flags in the Art Center, have the children hold their flags and wave them gently as they sing the following words to the tune of "London Bridge."

All the people gave thanks, gave thanks, gave thanks.
All the people gave thanks to God for Jesus.

We can also give thanks, give thanks, give thanks.
We can also give thanks to God for Jesus.

Let's Go Home

Gather the children for a short closing prayer. If time permits repeat some of the songs or action rhymes used in today's lesson.

Make sure that each child has his or her belongings before parents arrive. Remind the children to be very careful carrying their flags as they take them home.

Thank You, God, for Jesus

Luke 19:29-38

Bible Words: "We . . . thank God" (2 Thessalonians 1:3).

Lesson Value: Two's and 3's grasp the big concepts much better than the fine ones. Today's lesson stresses one of those big concepts, being thankful for Jesus. Not only will it provide a motivation for the children's feelings of thankfulness, it also will teach them specific ways to express that thankfulness.

Know: Know that God wants us to be thankful.
Feel: Feel thankful.
Do: Say thank-you to God and to people.

Children will accomplish the goals when they:

1. Say the Bible words, "We thank God."
2. Pray a prayer of thanks for Jesus.
3. Sing thank-you songs.
4. Explore other ways of expressing thanksgiving.

Let's Get Ready

For the Bible story, you will need a Bible, and the visual aid of Jesus riding on a donkey, many construction-paper palm leaves, and pieces of clothing all cut from the patterns on page 185.

For the learning activities set up the Family Living Center, the Blocks Center, and the Book and Picture Center. Remember to limit your centers to the number of adults you have. If you are the only teacher, use just the Family Living Center. Have materials ready for the Art Center to use after the Bible story.

Learning Activities

(30 minutes, including 10 minutes presession)

Let's Get Started

Have Zach enthusiastically welcome each child by name. Say, **I think Zach is really glad to see you, Troy. Today we are going to learn about some people who were really glad to see Jesus. Before we do that would you rather play in the Family Living Center or build a special road with our big blocks?** Offer other children a choice of one of these two or the Book and Picture Center.

Worship and Bible Story

(15 minutes)

Let's Worship God

Give the children notice beforehand that it is almost time for clean-up. This will allow the children to finish their work in an unhurried way. Let Zach tell them when to put their work away and come to the story circle. When the first child arrives, begin singing. Today be sure to use the songs, "We Thank You, God in Heaven" and "I Love Jesus." You may want to provide real or construction-paper palm leaves for the children to wave as they sing.

The Bible words say, "We thank God." We thank God for Jesus. Ask the children to say Jesus' name when you pause in the following prayer. **Dear God, we especially want to thank You today for** *(pause and wait for the children to join you in saying "Jesus")*. **We love Him.** Before the Bible story, do the rhyme, "I Can."

Let's Learn From the Bible

Introduction: Have Zach question the children. "How many of you have ever waited for someone special to come? Were you excited? How did you show that you were excited?" Give each child a construction-paper palm leaf or a piece of clothing. Make sure you hold one yourself. **I want you to help me tell the story by waving whatever you have in your hand when you hear the name *Jesus*.** Now put Zach away and have your visual aids and Bible ready.

The Bible Story: *(Hold your Bible in your hand as you tell the story. Place the visual of Jesus in your lap until it is time to mention Him in the story.)* The Bible tells us about one exciting day when Jesus *(wave leaf or clothing)* was coming to town.

We do not know how people knew Jesus *(wave leaf or clothing)* was coming. There were no televisions or radios back then to give the news. Perhaps someone ran through the crowds and from house to house shouting, "Jesus *(wave leaf or clothing)* is coming."

Many of the people had heard about Jesus *(wave leaf or clothing)*. Many of the people had seen Jesus *(wave leaf or clothing)* do wonderful things. Many of the people knew Jesus *(wave leaf or clothing)* was very special!

When Jesus *(wave leaf or clothing)* passed by *(place figure of Jesus on the donkey on the block road and scatter some construction-paper palm leaves and garments in front of Him)*, the Bible tells us that the people laid down palm leaves and even their clothing on the road in front of Him to show how special they thought He was. The people cried out, "Hosanna! Hosanna! We love Jesus!"

to Jesus. They just enjoyed being with Jesus. How thankful they must have been for this special quiet time to be with their special friend Jesus.

Let's Apply the Lesson

Why were Jesus' friends sad? Show the black construction paper. Let the children respond. **What made them happy?** Show the yellow construction paper. Let the children respond. **What happened one special morning that made them feel so content and thankful?** Let the children respond.

Can we spend quiet times like that with Jesus? Well, we can't eat breakfast with Him on the beach, but we can find quiet places to go to think about Him and thank God for Him. We can look at the beautiful things in God's world and be reminded of Jesus. Let's be quiet for just a few seconds and think about Jesus now. Pause. **You just spent a special time with Jesus.**

Learning Activities

(20 minutes)

Let's Play Awhile

For the activity in God's Wonders Center, take the children outside if possible. If the weather is bad, use a porch or simply arrange some plants and other items from God's creation for a special atmosphere. The children will need to stretch their legs, so even if you must have the activity inside your classroom, take the children on a walk inside the building first. If you have extra children, use the Book and Picture Center also.

Let's Go Home

Have Zach gather the children. Lead them in some of the songs they have sung during this unit. Make sure each child has his or her flower arrangement from the Art Center. Say, **When you see these flowers, remember to give thanks for Jesus and for all of God's other gifts.**

Breakfast With Jesus

Based on John 18–21

Bible Words: "We . . . thank God" (2 Thessalonians 1:3).

Lesson Value: By the time we become teachers, most of us have come to cherish special times with special people because we have experienced the loss or near loss of other special people. Most 2's and 3's, even if they have experienced loss, have not developed that ability to cherish those special times. They may be enthusiastic about the appearance of those they love. They may cling to someone they are afraid will leave. They need guidance in quietly enjoying the companionship of someone special. In today's lesson they will be shown ways of enjoying fellowship and worship, and ways of expressing companionship and thanksgiving.

Know: Know that God wants us to be thankful.
Feel: Feel thankful.
Do: Say thank-you to God and to people.

Children will accomplish the goals when they:

1. Say the Bible words, "We thank God."
2. Pray a prayer of thanksgiving.
3. Sing thank-you songs.
4. Express thankfulness in non-verbal ways.

Let's Get Ready

The Bible story will require the picture from page 187, and a sheet of black and a sheet of yellow construction paper. Enlarge the picture if possible, and add color to make it attractive to the children.

NOTE: Five learning centers have been suggested for this lesson. You may choose to use four at the beginning and one at the end, or three and two. Choose what you think will work best in your situation.

For the learning activities, you will need to prepare the Family Living Center, the Block Center, and the Art Center. The God's Wonders Center or the Book and Picture Center will be used after the Bible story. If you are the only teacher, use just the Family Living Center now.

Learning Activities

(30 minutes, including 10 minutes presession)

Let's Get Started

Tell each child that you are glad he or she came to spend time with you to learn about God and His Son Jesus. Have Zach guide the children in the routine things of hanging up wraps, giving their offerings, and choosing learning centers. Have Zach say, "Amy, would you like to go to the Family Living Center to discover some ways of showing love to people? Or would you rather build a bonfire and 'cook' some fish?"

Worship and Bible Story

(15 minutes)

Let's Worship God

Give the children a two-minute warning before Zach tells them it is time to clean up and go to the story circle. Once the first children arrive, begin singing. Use "We Thank You, God in Heaven" and "I Love Jesus."

Do the action rhyme, "My Bible." **Our Bible words say, "We thank God."** Show the words in the Bible. Let the children take turns holding the Bible and "reading" the words. Then invite the children to pray after you, **Dear God, thank You for Jesus and for all of the good things You give us.** If you pause after every few words, and have another teacher repeat your words, the children will soon pray after you.

Let's Learn From the Bible

Introduction: Have Zach ask, "Can you show me a sad face?" Let children do so. "Can you show me a happy face?" Let children do so. "Can you show me a contented face?" Let children do so, though they may have more trouble with this one. You may need to demonstrate it for them. Have Zach say, "Can you use those faces when your teacher says those words during the story today? Very good!" Now put Zach away.

The Bible Story: *(Fold your story picture from page 187. Place a piece of black construction paper on one side and a piece of yellow construction paper on the other. Place this inside your Bible and hold the Bible as you tell the story.)*

The Bible tells us about the feelings of some of Jesus' friends. There were a few days when they felt very sad. *(Look sad and hold up black piece of construction paper.)* Some bad people had killed Jesus. Jesus' friends thought they would feel sad forever. They thought all good times were over.

One day something happened to make them feel very happy! *(Show yellow piece of construction paper and smile.)* Jesus came back to life. Some of His friends saw Him. Some of them talked to Him. They were happy and excited! Jesus was alive!

Then one morning something *very* special happened. Some of Jesus' friends had been fishing. When they finished they saw Jesus on the shore waiting for them. Jesus had cooked their breakfast on a fire right there by the lake. *(Sigh, look contented, and open picture.)* Jesus' friends went to Jesus. They ate breakfast with Jesus. They talked quietly with Jesus. They listened carefully

Art Center

Unit 1—Being Thankful

Items to Include:

Art smocks
Clean-up supplies

Lesson 1
Drawing paper
Crayons or markers

Lesson 2
Construction paper
Stickers
Pretty pictures
Glue

Purpose: The child will learn to express thankfulness through various art forms.

Things to Do and Say

Lesson 1

Have the drawing paper and crayons ready on your art table. Also have a sample of a very simple drawing of a child. Encourage each child to draw a self-portrait. Don't be alarmed if younger children leave out the trunk.

If your children are too young to do this, help them with their self-portraits. Draw a very simple outline of a child, with or without features, and photocopy it. Then let the children fill in as many details as they can.

Talk about each child's similarities: two hands, two arms, one body, two legs, etc., and differences—hair color and length, eye color, height, skin.

God made each of us different. He and His Son Jesus know each of us very well. And each of us is very important to God and to Jesus. We can be thankful for that.

Lesson 2

Let each child decorate the front of a folded piece of construction paper with stickers or pretty pictures. Write down a dictated thank-you message from the child. Say, **If you will tell me what to write, I will write a thank-you message for you to give to someone.**

Game Center

Unit 1—Being Thankful

Items to Include:

Lesson 1
Toy lambs
Pictures of lambs

Lesson 3
Basket
Fruits, or
Canned foods

Purpose: The child will say thank-You to God in play situations.

Things to Do and Say

Lesson 1

Hide one lamb or picture of a lamb per child. Tell each child to find a lamb and come back to you. Talk about how each lamb is different. Say, **A good shepherd knows about each of his sheep. And each sheep is special. God knows about each one of us, and we are all special to Him. I'm so glad He loves each one of us! Thank You, God, for loving us.**

Lesson 3

Place an empty basket in the middle of the floor. Have the children form a circle around it. Ask them to pass an apple from one to another around the circle as you sing the following words to the tune of "The Farmer in the Dell."

Thank You, God, for apples. *(Repeat.)*
Thank You, thank You, thank You, thank You.
Thank You, God, for apples.

When the song is finished, let the child holding the apple place it in the basket. Give the next child another fruit and sing again. Encourage the children to sing with you. Use as many fruits as possible.

If you do not have fresh fruits, play this game. Hide several cans of food around the

Art Center, continued

Lesson 3
Paper plates
Blue or purple tempera paint
Grapes
Shallow bowls, sponges

Lesson 3

Print the words, “We thank God,” in the middle of paper plates. Put small amounts of paint into shallow bowls and place sponges in the paint. Show the children how to dip their grapes into the tempera paint and make prints around the words.

I'm glad we can use art to show God how thankful we are for His blessings. The Bible says Jesus gave thanks for the grape juice. You may want to have extra grapes for the children to eat.

Lesson 4
White fabric
Dowel rods
Markers
Glue

Lesson 4

Before class, make flags by cutting the white fabric into 8" x 12" pieces. Have glue ready to glue the flags to short dowel rods as the children finish their decorating.

In our Bible story, people probably waved palm leaves as Jesus passed by them. They were happy to see Jesus. Today we might wave welcome flags.

Lesson 5
Spring flowers
Leaves
Praying hands from page 186
Glue
Drinking straws

Lesson 5

Using the pattern on page 186, copy and cut a pair of praying hands for each child. Mount the hands on straws. Allow each child to arrange some of the flowers and leaves as a love gift to someone special. As the children arrange their flowers, help them decide to whom they will give their flowers.

The pretty spring flowers and new leaves remind me that God made Jesus alive again. How happy His friends must have been! They loved Jesus very much. We often give gifts of flowers to people we love. Let's make these gifts of flowers to express our love to our friends.

Game Center, continued

room. Let the children find them and bring them back to the basket. Say, **You have found a lot of good food. Let's see what you have.** Discuss the various foods. **In our Bible story, Jesus thanked God for food. Let's do that now. Thank You, God, for so many good foods.** If the children seem interested, thank God for each food represented.

Lesson 4
Sack
Objects
Pictures

Lesson 4

Fill a sack with many objects and pictures of things and people (parents, grandparents, friends, etc.) the children can be thankful for. Let each child walk to the sack and draw out one object or picture. Then have him say with you the Bible Words + for + the object or picture. For example, “We thank God' for mommies.” If the children get to have second turns, they may be able to say this alone. When you finish, ask, **Can you point to someone who is thankful?**

Family Living Center

Unit 1—Being Thankful

Items to Include:

Table and chairs
Play stove
Dolls
Doll bed

Lesson 1
Family pictures

Lesson 2
Tea set

Lesson 3
Flour, oil, water
Flat baking tray
Bowl, spoon
Loaf of bread

Purpose: The child will have opportunities to say thank-you to God or to people, in play situations.

Things to Do and Say

Lesson 1

Before class call each child's family and ask for a framed (if possible) picture of the child with his family. Let the children arrange the pictures around the family living center. Talk to each child about his family. Say, **Jesus (God) cares for each of us in many ways. He has given us families who care for us. Thank You, God, for our families.**

Lesson 2

Show the children good manners and times to say thank-you to others. **Let me show you how to pass a tray of cookies.** Do so. **When someone passes you the cookies, you say, "Thank you." One man in our Bible story said thank-you to Jesus. Jesus likes for us to say thank-you to Him and to the people we know.**

Lesson 3

Let the children mix 1 cup flour, 2 Tbl. oil, and 6 Tbl. water to make flat bread. Help them place this in a shallow baking pan. If possible, bake the bread in a toaster oven so the children can see and smell it. (Make sure the children can't reach the oven.) Or, have someone take it to the church kitchen to bake it.

Book/Picture Center

Unit 1—Being Thankful

Items to Include:

Bookmarks

Lesson 1
Picture books about sheep

Lesson 4
Books and pictures of Jesus' life

Purpose: The child will learn through the use of books and pictures to express his or her thankfulness for Jesus.

Things to Do and Say

Lesson 1

Tell the children to find pictures of sheep and mark them. Read at least one short book that tells about the behavior of sheep. Say, **Sheep need a shepherd to care for them. Who cares for us? . . . Yes, Jesus (God) does. He loves each one of us. We are all special to Him! "We thank God" for Jesus.**

Lesson 4

If your books and pictures include the triumphal entry, mark these with bookmarks. Let the children discover these pictures. Ask, **How do the people look in the pictures? Do they look happy? Do they look excited? What do they have in their hands? . . . These people were glad to see Jesus. They must have thanked God for Jesus. "We thank God" for Jesus too!**

If you have just picture books about other times in Jesus' life, look at the pictures and talk about the people (children) who came to see Jesus because they loved Him, or point out how much Jesus loved the people who were His friends, and so forth. Lead the children to say, "We thank God" for Jesus.

Family Living Center, continued

Show already baked bread. **Would you be thankful if this were your dinner? Jesus was. The Bible says He broke the bread and gave thanks for it. Jesus was thankful for all food. Let's say thank-you to God for our bread.** Let each child taste the bread.

Lesson 4
Bible-times dress-ups
Picture of Jesus on donkey
Small garments
Palm branches (optional)

Lesson 5
Flowers
Tea set

Lesson 4

Encourage the children to get their babies ready to go see Jesus. **In our Bible story, many people came out to greet Jesus as He rode into town on a donkey. They were glad to see Jesus. Let's play like Jesus is coming to our town. Let's go greet Him. We love Jesus. He loves us too!**

If possible, have a picture of Jesus riding on a donkey. Let the children lay garments and palm branches on the ground in front of the picture. Lead the children to say, "Hosanna! Hosanna! We love You, Jesus! . . . Thank You, God, for Jesus."

Lesson 5

Say, **I want you to look for ways to show love to people without using words. You can practice on each other.** You may need to demonstrate or suggest some ways such as giving a flower, taking someone a cup of tea, or giving a hug. As a child receives a flower, help her say, "Thank you for the flower."

Blocks Center

Unit 1—Being Thankful

Items to Include:

Large cardboard blocks

Lesson 2
Small wooden blocks
Shelf paper

Lesson 4
Visual from page 185
Palm branches
Clear self-adhesive plastic

Purpose: The child will have opportunities to say thank-you to God and to people in play situations.

Things to Do and Say

Lesson 2

Before class, outline the words THANK YOU in large block letters on a sheet of shelf paper. Ask the children to help you build the words with blocks by placing the blocks on the lines. Read the words to the children.

Todd, please hand me a small block. Thank you. Repeat with another child. The children may want to take over when they grasp what you are doing. When they finish, say thank-you. Ask, **Can you point to someone who is thankful** (self or another)? **Can you point to someone who should always remember to say thank-you?**

Lesson 4

Let the children construct a road with the large blocks. Have it end in the story circle. Cut many construction paper branches from the pattern on page 185. Let them play with the visual from page 185 which you have covered with clear self-adhesive plastic. They can "walk" the visual aid down the road as they put the branches on the road.

The people in our Bible story laid palm branches on the road in front of Jesus to show that they loved Him. Maybe they said, "Thank You, God, for Jesus." Let's say thank-you to God for Jesus right now.

God's Wonders Center

Unit 1—Being Thankful

Items to Include:

Lesson 2
Basket of nature items

Lesson 3
Several types of fruits
Juice of same fruits
Juicer
Pitcher and glasses
Clean-up supplies

Purpose: The child will feel thankful for some of God's wonders.

Things to Do and Say

Lesson 2

Remove one item at a time. Let the children pass it around and carefully look at it. As they do, sing these words to the tune of "Row, Row, Row, Your Boat." Repeat the song for each item.

Thank You, thank You, God.
Thank You, thank You, God.
Thank You, thank You, God for flowers.
Thank You, thank You, God.

Lesson 3

Let the children match the fruits with their juices. Let them squeeze the juice from at least one type of fruit. Oranges would perhaps be the easiest. Say, **The Bible tells us about Jesus giving thanks for the juice of grapes. What juice are you most thankful for? Let's tell God, "Thank You, God, for good orange juice."**

Blocks Center, continued

Lesson 5
Small wooden blocks
Paper fish

Lesson 5

Let the children build a campfire with the blocks. Provide paper fish for them to cook. (The pattern is on page 186.)

Isn't it fun to spend time with people we love? In the spring we can begin going on picnics together or having cookouts. The food is not the most important thing. Spending time with special people is the important thing. Jesus met with His special friends and cooked fish for them on a fire something like ours. Jesus' friends were very happy to see Him! They were thankful that Jesus was alive!

God's Wonders Center, continued

Lesson 5
Plants
Nature items,
Newspapers

Lesson 5

Locate a quiet outside place. If the grass is damp, provide newspapers to sit on. Say, **God's world in the spring is so beautiful! Let's be quiet and listen for sounds of life.** After a minute ask, **What did you hear? A bird? Thank You, God, for birds that sing. . . . Can you gently touch a blade of grass (violet)? How does it feel? Thank You, God, for soft grass (violets). . . . Close your eyes and take a deep breath. What do you smell? Thank You, God, for flowers that smell good.**

If you must stay indoors, have a variety of nature items to look at, feel, smell, and listen to (a seashell or a tape of birds singing, for example). Encourage the children to thank God for each item.

Visuals—Spring, Unit 1

Instructions

1. Photocopy page.
2. Add color (crayons, markers).
3. Cut out visual on solid lines.
4. Fold on dotted lines; glue onto large-size gelatin box.

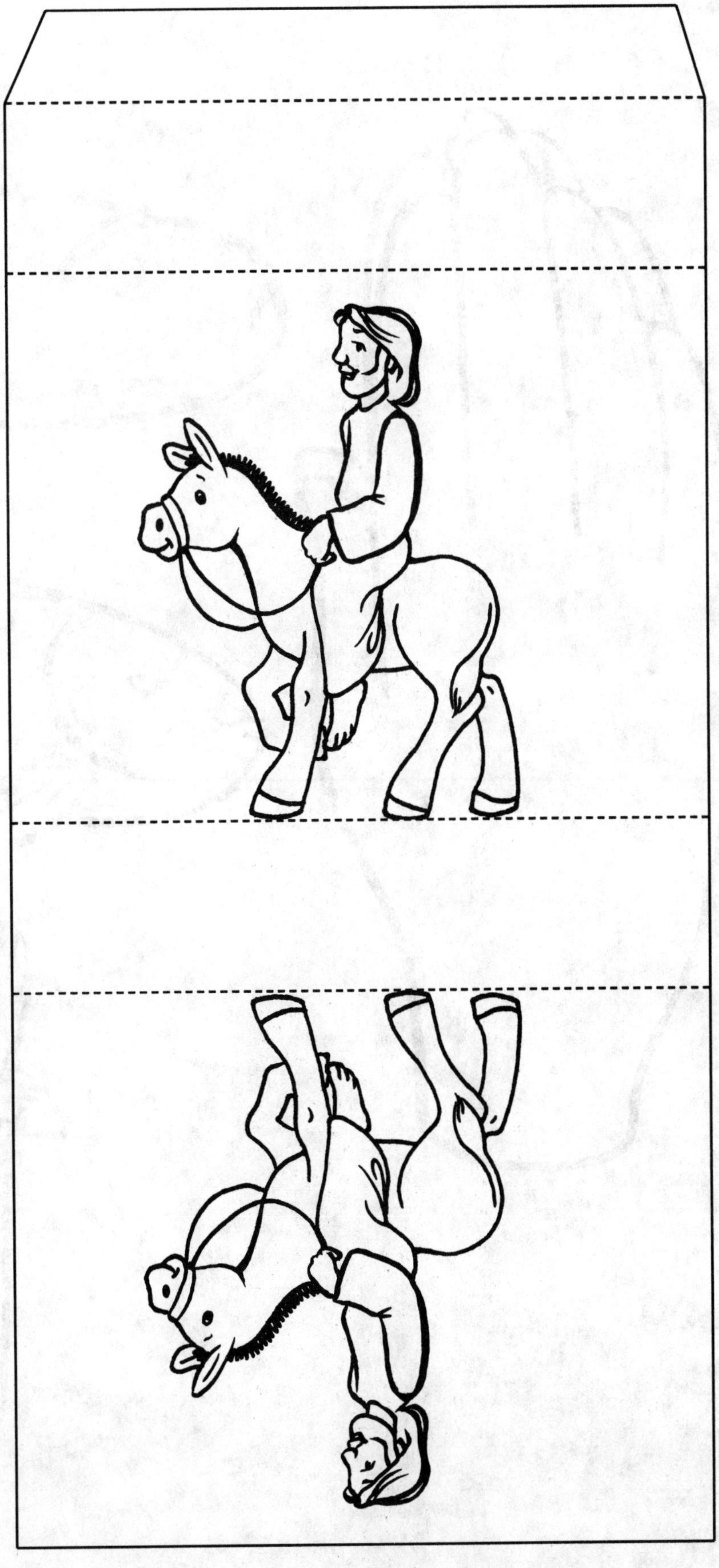

Praying Hands Art Project—Spring, Unit 1

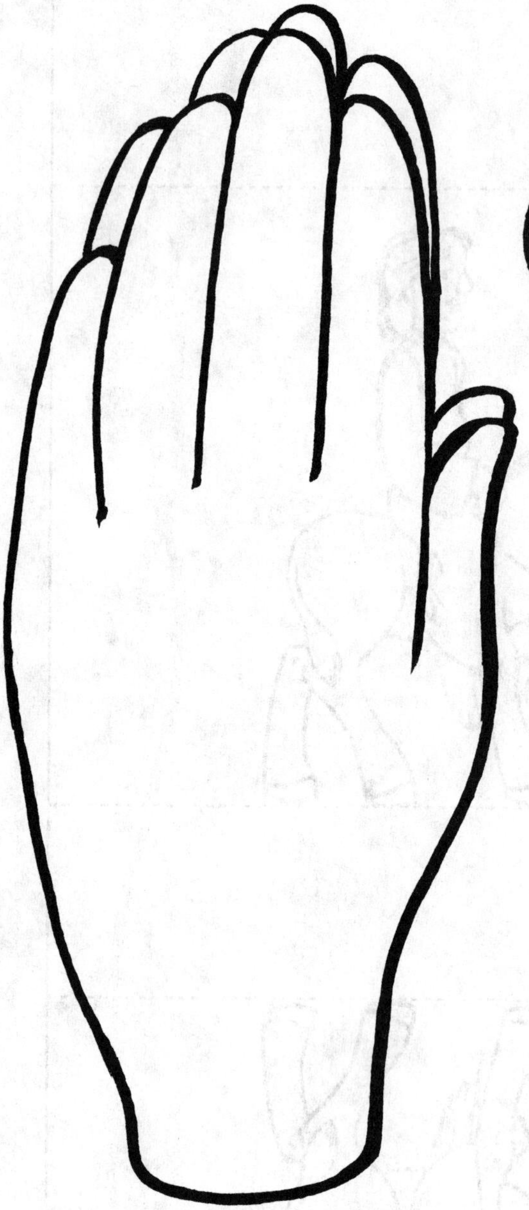

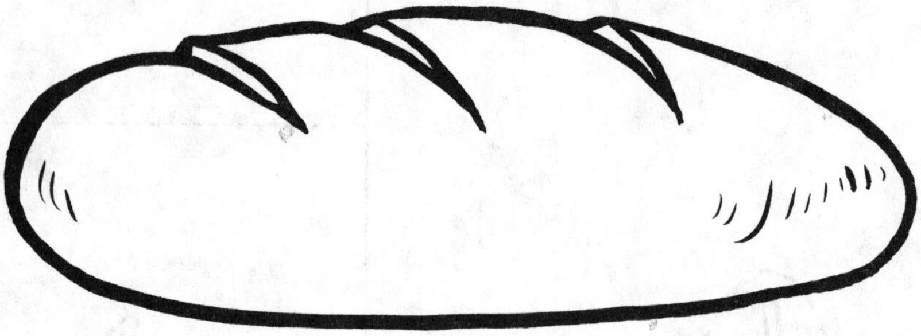

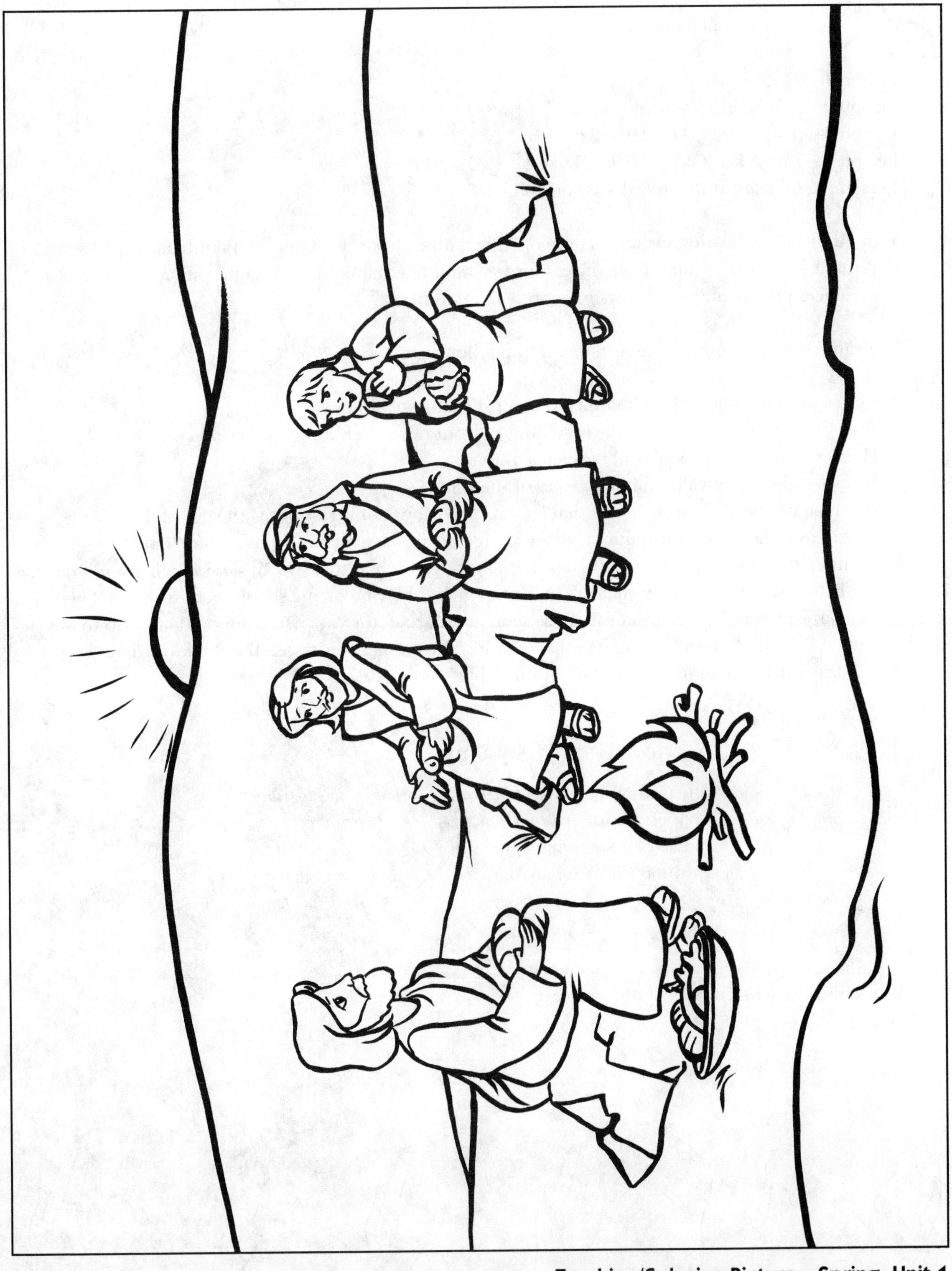

Teaching/Coloring Picture—Spring, Unit 1

Dear Parent,

During this unit your child will be learning about being thankful. Here are the Bible stories we will be using.

Lesson 1—*The Lost Sheep* (Luke 15:3-7)
Lesson 2—*One Man Is Thankful* (Luke 17:11-19)
Lesson 3—*Jesus Is Thankful* (Luke 22:7-19)
Lesson 4—*Thank You, God, for Jesus* (Luke 19:29-38)
Lesson 5—*Breakfast With Jesus* (based on John 18–21)

Your child will be hearing examples of people, including Jesus, who were thankful and expressed that thanks. We will be talking about reasons we should be thankful. Your child will be experiencing many times and ways to express thankfulness.

You can reinforce these lessons at home in the following ways:

- Be sensitive to your child's attempts to express thanks to you.
- Seek opportunities to say thank-you to and in front of your child.
- Help your child deliver special messages of thanks.
- Be especially attentive to family prayers of thanks.
- Incorporate the Bible words, "We thank God," into your conversations with your child.
- Since Easter falls within this unit, take advantage of special activities in your church or community to worship and give thanks. If you take your child to a special service, talk to him or her before you arrive about what will be going on and how he or she should behave. Say, "If you have any questions I will answer them as soon as we are in the car." Don't forget that a trip to an animal exhibit can also be a time of thanksgiving. Just remember to use the Bible Words.
- Use this rhyme to remind your child of the Bible Words.

My Bible

This is my Bible; *(Hands held out in front, palms together.)*
I'll open it wide *(Open hands; keep them touching.)*
And see (or say) what is written
On the inside! *(Say the Bible words: "We thank God.")*
—*Jean Baxendale*

Your child's teacher,

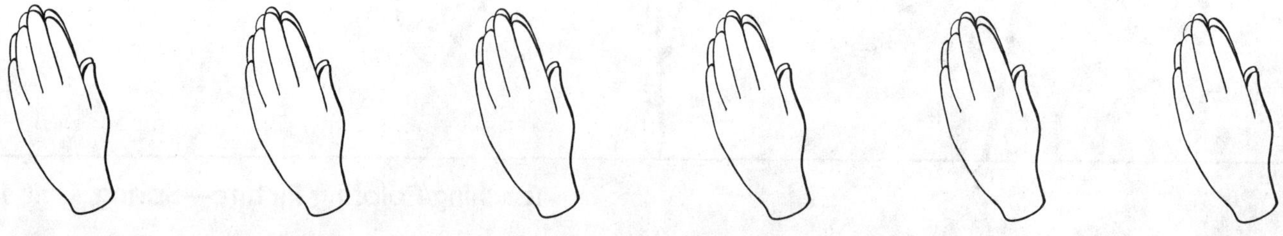

Unit 2: Helping Jesus

Lessons 6–9

By the end of the unit, the children will

Know that we help Jesus when we say, "Come to church," or "Jesus loves you!"
Feel eager to help.
Help Jesus in two ways ("Come to church," and "Jesus loves you!").

Unit Bible Words

"We . . . are helpers" (2 Corinthians 1:24).

Books

from Standard Publishing
I Like Sunday School 24-03830
A Child's Story of Jesus 24-04217
Jesus Makes Me Happy 24-04213
All About Hands 24-03591
Busy Feet 24-03592

The Unit at a Glance

6 Peter Becomes a Helper — **John 1:40-42**
Andrew is a helper when he takes his brother to meet Jesus.

7 Paul and Timothy Are Helpers — **Acts 16:1-5**
Paul asks Timothy to help him tell the Good News to others.

8 Lydia Learns to Be a Helper — **Acts 16:11-15**
Paul and Timothy share the Good News; Lydia and her family are happy to hear the Good News.

9 I Can Help — **Review of Lessons 6–8**

Why Teach This Unit?

When this unit is over your children will know that Andrew, Paul, and Timothy were helpers for Jesus. The children will have heard that telling others, "Come to church," and "Jesus loves you!" are ways in which they can be helpers for Jesus too. They also will have been given the opportunity to practice "helping" ways and recognizing themselves and others in their class as Jesus' helpers. This is information your children will have because of what you teach.

There is another goal for your children that can only be reached because of the *way* in which you teach. Teach in such a way that your children will add *your* name to those of Andrew, Paul, and Timothy. Demonstrate in your teaching and in your example that you also are Jesus' helper. The final step in teaching this unit is communicating an excitement and a desire about being helpers for Jesus. We are effective only when our skills match our enthusiasm about being helpers for Jesus.

The Bible words should be used over and over, in your conversation, in the Bible stories, at the learning centers, and in your prayers. For example, **"We are helpers" when we pick up and put away our toys! "We are helpers" when we sing about Jesus!**

Things to Do for This Unit

- Photocopy Learning Center Cards (pages 199-204); cut pages apart on solid lines. Mount side 1 of a card on cardboard; then mount side 2 on back of cardboard. Do this for all cards. Laminate them for durability.
- Gather materials listed on the Learning Center Cards.
- Make lunch-sack puppets of: Andrew, Peter, Paul, Timothy and Lydia (pages 205-209).
- Make copies of Parents' Page (page 212) and the Unit Planning Sheet, pages 319 and 320.
- Make play dough for Lesson 8 (recipe on Learning Center Card).
- Find pictures and books of people and children helping, working, worshiping, etc.
- Find river scene pictures. Copy scene on page 210, mount on construction paper, and cover with clear, self-adhesive plastic.

Use These Songs and Action Rhymes During Unit 1

I Can Help

(Tune: "Three Blind Mice")

I can help. *(Point to self.)*
You can help. *(Point to another.)*
We can help Jesus today. *(Spread arms wide; point upward.)*
Let's say, "Come with me to Sunday school."
(Stop; say words aloud.)
Let's say that "Jesus loves you too!"
(Stop; say words aloud.)
I can help. *(Point to self.)*
We can help. *(Spread arms wide.)*

Jesus Loves You!

(Tune: "Jesus Loves Me")

"Jesus loves you!" we can say, *(Point to mouth.)*
Helping Jesus every day. *(Point upward.)*
Come to church and sing with me,
(Beckon others to come.)
Jesus' helpers we will be.
We're helping Jesus. *(Point upward. Repeat line twice.)*
Like Jesus wants us to. *(Point to self.)*

I Want to Help Every Day

(Tune: "If You're Happy and You Know It")

I want to help every day. *(Clap, clap. Repeat line.)*
With ears and eyes, *(Point to ears; then to eyes.)*
With mouth and hands *(Point to mouth; then open hands.)*
I'll be a helper today.

Come to Sunday School

"Hi, Bobby."
"Hi, Joe."
(Hold up both index fingers. Wiggle first left; then right.)
"Want to come to our Sunday school?"
(Wiggle left index fingers.)
"Yes, but I'll have to go home and ask."
(Wiggle right index finger.)
"OK."
(Wiggle left finger. Then jog right finger toward the right, and back again.)
"Yes, I can go."*(Wiggle right finger.)*
"Good! Let's go to Sunday school!"
(Wiggle left finger; then jog both together toward left.)

The Cleanup Song

(Tune: "I'm a Little Teapot")

I can be a helper every day,
By doing what my teachers say.
I can be a helper every day,
By keeping my playthings put away.

I Want to Help

I want to help in every way!
With ears, and eyes, and mouth, *(Point to each.)*
With feet, *(Bend down and touch feet.)*
And hands. *(Clap hands.)*
I want to help today. *—Dorothy Fay Richards*

tell Zach about a helper for Jesus? Yes, Mary! Andrew was a helper for Jesus! He was a helper when he took Peter to meet Jesus. Zach, can you be a helper for Jesus? Zach will say, "Randy, Jesus loves you!" Say, **I want to be a helper too! Zach, will you come to church with me?** Zach will nod yes. **Now it's your turn to be helpers! Let's help Zach say our Bible words, "We are helpers."**

Learning Activities

(20 minutes)

Let's Play Awhile

Sing "Head and Shoulders" (page 161) with appropriate actions. Lead the children in doing the rhyme, "Come to Sunday School" (page 190). Use the activity suggested in the Game Center for this session.

Let's Go Home

Use Zach to ask the children to be helpers by getting ready to leave. Children should pick up and put away toys or activities at this time. Sing "I Can Help," from page 190. Make sure each child has a Parents' Letter to take home.

Optional Activity

On a piece of poster board print the Bible words, "We are helpers." Attach this to a wall or door in your classroom. Ask children to bring pictures of themselves or take pictures of them during Lesson 6. Frame the Bible words with the developed pictures of the children. Use the poster board to ask, **Who is a helper for Jesus?** Children can point to themselves and to others.

Peter Becomes a Helper

John 1:40-42

Bible Words: "We . . . are helpers" (2 Corinthians 1:24).

Lesson Value: In this story the helper helps by doing something your 2's and 3's can do: he uses his mouth! Telling about Jesus is an important job. The boy or girl who learns to say, "Come to church," or "Jesus loves you!" should be recognized as Jesus' special helper. Two's and 3's love to help and feel as if they are doing a special and important job. As the teacher, your very important job is to make the children feel special when they talk about Jesus.

Know: Know that I help Jesus when I say, "Come to church," or "Jesus loves you!"
Feel: Feel eager to help.
Do: Help Jesus in two ways: ("Come to church." "Jesus loves you!")

Children will accomplish the goals when they:
1. Say the Bible Words, "We are helpers."
2. Pray, "Dear God, help us be helpers for Jesus."
3. Sing about helping Jesus.
4. Name or point to Jesus' helpers in the class (self, others).
5. Act out being a helper for Jesus.

Let's Get Ready

For the Bible story you will need to prepare the lunch-sack puppets of Peter and Andrew made from patterns found on pages 205 and 206. You will also need the classroom Bible with the new Bible words highlighted, and Zach, the class mascot. If you do not have a "Zach" puppet any animal puppet may be used.

Set up the Book and Picture Center, the Family Living Center, and the Music Center. If you are the only teacher use just the Family Living Center. The Game Center will be used after the Bible story.

Learning Activities

(30 minutes, including 10 minutes presession)

Let's Get Started

As children arrive greet each one by name. **Zach is being a helper today. He wants to tell you, "Jesus loves you!"** Zach can say, "Jesus loves you, Kathy!" Help children with coats and offerings. Direct each child to a learning center. Say, **Ashley, we are going to learn how to be helpers for Jesus today! You may dress up and visit Abby to tell her, "Jesus loves you!" Or you may learn a new song in the Music Center.** Two's and 3's learn by making choices. Make sure that you can accept either choice a child makes.

Worship and Bible Story

(15 minutes)

Let's Worship God

Use Zach the puppet to say, "Let's be helpers! Helpers pick up and put away their toys! When you have finished being a helper with your toys we will sing and pray to God." Begin singing as soon as the first child sits in the circle with you. Sing a well-known song, such as "Jesus Loves Me," then sing a new one, "I Can Help," from page 190. Use the action rhyme, "I Want to Help," also found on page 190. Show the children the Bible words in your Bible. Then pray, **Dear God, help us be helpers for Jesus.**

Let's Learn From the Bible

Introduction: Use Zach to help you introduce the story. Say, **Zach, can you find a helper for me?** Zach whispers the name of a child sitting quietly. **Yes, Sarah is a helper when she listens quietly. If we all listen quietly to our Bible story we will hear how to be helpers for Jesus!** Put the puppet away.

The Bible Story: (*Hold your Bible on your lap, open to this story. Hold up sack puppets as they are introduced. Puppets should "speak" when appropriate.*)

This is Andrew. Andrew had a special friend, Jesus. Andrew had a brother. His name was Peter. Andrew wanted to be a helper for Jesus.

"Come with me, Peter," said Andrew. "Come with me to meet my friend Jesus. I want you to know Him. You will like Him."

"Yes," Peter said. "I will go with you to meet Jesus." (*Ask children to nod their heads "yes" with Peter.*) Peter and John started walking together to see Jesus. (*Children may "walk" quietly with their hands. Then use hands spy-glass fashion to "look" for Jesus.*) They found Jesus!

Jesus smiled. He was glad Andrew brought Peter to see Him. (*Ask children to smile like Jesus!*)

Peter smiled. He was glad to know Jesus. (*Say, "Smile if you're glad to know Jesus!"*) Andrew smiled. He was glad to be a helper for Jesus. Andrew was glad to bring Peter to see Jesus. (*All helpers for Jesus smile!*)

Let's Apply the Lesson

Place Zach on one hand and the Andrew puppet on the other. Have Zach look at the Andrew puppet. Say, **Who will**

Learning Activities

(20 minutes)

Let's Play Awhile

Do the rhyme, "I Want to Help," with the children. If they are particularly restless, also do the song, "Head and Shoulders." Have materials ready for the Music Center. You may also wish to use the Block Center again if time permits.

Let's Go Home

Use Zach to begin the rhyme, "The Busy Fingers" (page 162). This will tell children it is time to clean up their activity areas. Gather children in a circle to sing "I Want to Help Every Day," the song used in the Music Center for this session.

As parents arrive to pick up their children, tell something helpful each child did during the session, including telling others, "Jesus loves you!" and/or "Come to church." Parents like to know that their children are doing well in class. Praise for good behavior encourages more of that behavior!

Paul and Timothy Are Helpers

Acts 16:1-5

Bible Words: "We . . . are helpers" (2 Corinthians 1:24).

Lesson Value: The helpers in this lesson bring the simple message that "Jesus loves you!" Paul and Timothy brought this message to many people, both Jews and Gentiles. The message was profound in that Jesus loves you, no matter who you are. Children listening to today's story should be touched in two directions. Not only will *they* be helped by hearing "Jesus loves you!" but they will be encouraged to *help* by practicing what Paul and Timothy did in telling that message to others.

Know: Know that I help Jesus when I say, "Come to church," or "Jesus loves you!"
Feel: Feel eager to help.
Do: Help Jesus in two ways. ("Come to church." "Jesus loves you.")

Children will accomplish the goals when they:

1. Say the Bible Words, "We are helpers."
2. Pray, "Dear God, help us be helpers for Jesus."
3. Sing about helping Jesus.
4. Name or point to Jesus' helpers in the class (self, others).
5. Act out being a helper for Jesus.

Let's Get Ready

For the Bible story you will need a toy phone, your classroom Bible, and the Paul and Timothy sack puppets made from patterns on pages 207 and 208. The puppet Zach is used to introduce the Bible story.

Set up the Book and Picture Center, the Family Living Center, and the Block Center. If you are the only teacher use just the Block Center. Have materials ready for the Music Center to use after the Bible story.

Learning Activities

(30 minutes, including 10 minutes presession)

Let's Get Started

Use Zach to greet each child by name. "I see helper Luke! I'm glad you came to help today." Assist children with coats and offerings. **Jessica, we're building a house today in our block area. Would you like to help us build our house? We want to practice saying, "Come to church!" Or would you prefer to read a book in the Book and Picture Center?**

Worship and Bible Story

(15 minutes)

Let's Worship God

Zach can say, "I need helpers to clean up toys and books. Who will be a helper? It's time to sing and pray to God." Begin singing as soon as the first child sits in the circle with you. Sing "Jesus Loves You!" and "I Want to Help Every Day" (both on page 190). Do the rhyme, "Come to Sunday School," using "church" in place of "Sunday school." After the rhyme thank children for being helpers with the blocks and other learning center materials. Pray, **Thank You God for hands that help. Help us be helpers for Jesus.**

Let's Learn From the Bible

Introduction: Let Zach use the toy phone to call the children. Say, "Hello, Chelsey? Will you come to church?" When the child nods, Zach can say, "That makes me happy!" Zach may also call and say, "Hello, Chad? Jesus loves you! Good bye!"

Ask the children to help Zach say, "Jesus loves you!" Then say, **Good-bye Zach! It's time for our Bible story.**

The Bible Story: *(Use the Paul and Timothy puppets to speak for those characters during the Bible story. Hold your Bible open to this story on your lap.)*

This is Paul. *(Display Paul puppet.)* Paul is walking down the road. Let's walk with Paul. *(Children may "walk" their hands on the floor in front of them.)* Paul is being a helper for Jesus. Paul says, "Jesus loves you."

Paul has a friend. His name is Timothy. *(Display Timothy puppet.)* Paul says, "Timothy, you can be a helper for Jesus. Do you want to tell people, 'Jesus loves you'?"

Timothy says, "I want to be a helper for Jesus. I want to tell people, 'Jesus loves you.'"

Paul says, "I'm glad you want to be a helper for Jesus, Timothy. Let's go tell people, 'Jesus loves you.'"

Paul and Timothy are walking down the road. Let's walk with them. *(Children "walk" with hands.)* Paul and Timothy have something important to tell. They tell many people, "Jesus loves you!"

Paul and Timothy were good helpers for Jesus.

Let's Apply the Lesson

Place Paul and Timothy puppets on your hands. Say, **Who sees a helper?** Let the children respond. **Who can show how to be a helper?** If no one responds have Zach say, "Teacher, Jesus loves you!"

God is happy when we tell others that Jesus loves them. Our Bible words are, "We are helpers." Let's say our Bible words together.

helpers. Give each child who desires it an opportunity to use the puppets. Put puppets on your hands and ask younger children to point to Jesus' helpers and to the one they helped (Lydia).

Children who remember the Bible words may whisper them to Zach. Say, **Zach wants to know our Bible words. Who can whisper them in his ear?** Use Zach to praise each child for remembering the Bible words. Say them together as a class.

Learning Activities

(20 minutes)

Let's Play Awhile

Before class make a path on your classroom floor with masking tape. The path may wind, zigzag, or circle around; make it interesting, but not too difficult. Ask the children to follow the path with you as you sing the following words to the tune of "Row, Row, Row, Your Boat:"

We will help today; we will help today.
We are Jesus' helpers; we will help today.

Have materials ready for the Music Center. If time permits you may wish to allow children to use the Art Center again.

Let's Go Home

Use Zach to tell the children it is time to pick up their toys and get ready to leave. Gather children in a circle. Do the rhymes, "I Want to Help" and "Come to Sunday School," using "church" in place of "Sunday school."

Gather children's Bibles and coats to help them get ready to leave.

Lydia Learns to Be a Helper

Acts 16:11-15

Bible Words: "We . . . are helpers" (2 Corinthians 1:24).

Lesson Value: In this lesson the children learn yet another example of how Paul and Timothy were helpers for Jesus. Although the message remains the same, the identities of those who *receive* the message become specific. This week the story includes the name and some very visual details about who received the Good News. Use the puppet visuals to paint an exciting picture for your children about telling others Jesus' Good News.

Know: Know that I help Jesus when I say, "Come to church," or "Jesus loves you!"
Feel: Feel eager to help.
Do: Help Jesus in two ways. ("Come to church." "Jesus loves you!")

Children will accomplish the goals when they:
1. Say the Bible words, "We are helpers."
2. Pray, "Dear God, help us be helpers for Jesus."
3. Sing about helping Jesus.
4. Name or point to Jesus' helpers in the class (self, others).
5. Act out being a helper for Jesus.

Let's Get Ready

For the Bible story you will need the lunch-sack puppets of Paul and Timothy used in Lesson 7, and the puppet of Lydia from page 209. You will also need your classroom Bible, Zach the puppet, and a fishing pole for Zach to use. A stick with yarn and a paper clip will serve as a fishing pole for Zach. You will also need a roll of masking tape to use during Let's Play Awhile.

Set up the Book and Picture Center, the Art Center, and the Block Center. If you are the only teacher use just the Art Center. You will need to have the materials prepared for the Music Center to be used after the Bible story.

Learning Activities

(30 minutes, including 10 minutes presession)

Let's Get Started

Use Zach to say, "Hi Alicia! Jesus loves you! I'm glad you're here!" Help children with coats and offerings. Interest each child in a learning center. **Anna, would you like to go to the Art Center to use the modeling clay to make a helper? Make someone who looks like you! You are Jesus' helper! Or would you rather play with the blocks?**

Worship and Bible Story

(15 minutes)

Let's Worship God

Use Zach to sing "The Cleanup Song" (found on page 190). Tell children that Zach is asking them to clean up their activities and come to the worship area. Begin singing as soon as the first child sits in the circle with you. Sing "I Can Help" and "I Want to Help Every Day." Do the rhyme, "Come to Sunday School," using "church" in place of "Sunday school." Pray, **Thank You, God, for giving us hands, arms, legs, and mouths so we can be helpers. Help us to be helpers for Jesus.**

Let's Learn From the Bible

Introduction: Display Zach holding his "fishing pole." Ask, **Children, what is Zach going to do?** Allow children to respond. Zach may say, "We're going to a river for our Bible story today. While you tell the story to the children, I'm going to fish!" Tell Zach good-bye and lay him aside. **Who can tell where our story takes place today?** *(By the river!)* **Let's listen!**

The Bible Story: *(For this story you will need three hands. Hold Lydia and Paul puppets while another teacher, or an older child, holds the puppet of Timothy next to you. Hold up the puppet who is talking during the story.)*

My name is Lydia. Today is a spring day and I'm glad to be outdoors! I'm glad you're here with me. I like to feel the sun on my face *(Ask the children to put their hands on the sides of their faces.)*, and the cool breezes from the river. Let's be cool breezes. *(Sway back and forth.)* I talk to God when I sit by the river. *(Ask the children to fold their hands and close their eyes as if praying.)*

One day as I was praying beside the river, Paul and Timothy came. *(Children may "walk" their hands as you hold up the puppet of Paul and a teacher or child holds Timothy near Paul.)* Paul and Timothy said, "We have happy news for you. Jesus loves you!"

That happy news made me smile! *(Ask the children to smile with you.)* I'm happy to know that Jesus loves me. *(Have Lydia talk to Paul and Timothy.)* Thank you for being a helper for Jesus.

I was glad to learn about Jesus. I was glad that Paul and Timothy were good helpers for Jesus. I was so happy that I invited Paul and Timothy to come to my house. Let's go to my house now! *(Children will "walk" with their hands to Lydia's house.)* Let's talk more about our friend Jesus.

Let's Apply the Lesson

Hand a child one of the lunch-sack puppets. Ask the child to use the puppet to show how Paul and Timothy were hand mirror in front of each child. Ask, **Who is in the mirror?** Ask each child to say his or her name aloud. **Bethany is a helper for Jesus when she says, "Jesus loves you!"** Encourage each child to say the helping words, "Jesus loves you!" or "Come to church!"

Use the Bible to show the Bible words. Ask the class to say the Bible words with Zach.

Learning Activities

(20 minutes)

Let's Play Awhile

Sing "I Want to Help Every Day." Have materials ready for the Art Center. If time permits you may wish to use the Block Center as well.

Let's Go Home

Have Zach hold the hand mirror as he says, "I'm looking for helpers who are picking up their toys! Thank you, Tim for being a helper by putting that block away." Pointing out specific good behavior helps the child know just what he has done right and encourages him to repeat that behavior. Gather children in a circle to sing "Head and Shoulders."

Make sure the children have their invitations to send or give to friends and/or families.

I Can Help

Review of Lessons 6–8

Bible Words: "We . . . are helpers" (2 Corinthians 1:24).

Lesson Value: This session reviews Lessons 6-8. Make use of every opportunity to praise children for being helpers. Hearing their names associated with being helpers will please them and increase their desire to repeat the actions being praised. Invite them to practice "helping" often, as you teach them about the many opportunities they have for telling others about Jesus' love.

Know: Know that I help Jesus when I say, "Come to church," or "Jesus loves you!"
Feel: Feel eager to help.
Do: Help Jesus in two ways. ("Come to church." "Jesus loves you!")

Children will accomplish the goals when they:

1. Say the Bible words, "We are helpers."
2. Pray, "Dear God, help us to be helpers for Jesus."
3. Sing about helping Jesus.
4. Name or point to Jesus' helpers in the class (self, others).
5. Act out being a helper for Jesus.

Let's Get Ready

To review the Bible stories you will need the sack puppets from Lessons 6-8, the classroom Bible, an unbreakable hand mirror, and Zach the puppet.

Prepare the Game Center, the Music Center, and the Block Center. If you are the only teacher use just the Game Center. Have the materials for the Art Center ready to be used after the Bible story.

Learning Activities

(30 minutes, including 10 minutes presession)

Let's Get Started

Use Zach to say, "I see a helper! This helper's name is Kendall!" Repeat this procedure with each child's name. Assist children with coats and offerings. Interest each child in a learning center. **Kayla, we're going to play a fun game about being Jesus' helper. Would you like to play with us or would you prefer to sing some songs in the Music Center?**

Worship and Bible Story

(15 minutes)

Let's Worship God

Use Zach to sing "The Cleanup Song" to signal children that it is time to pick up activities and come to the worship area. Begin singing as soon as the first child sits in the circle with you. Sing "Jesus Loves You!" used in the Music Learning Center for Lesson 8, as well as the other songs used this unit. Show the children the Bible words in your Bible. Let the children take turns holding the Bible and "reading" the words. Then ask them to say the Bible words with you. Pray, **Dear God, help us to be helpers for Jesus.**

Let's Learn From the Bible

Introduction: Hold up Zach. **Who can be a helper for Jesus? What can we tell Zach?** Invite the children to say, "Jesus loves you, Zach! Come to church, Zach." **Thank you for being helpers for Jesus! Jesus is happy when we are helpers. Good-bye Zach!** Lay Zach aside during the Bible-story review time.

The Bible-story Review: *(Use sack puppets from Lessons 6-8 to review the Bible stories.)* The Bible tells us about people who were helpers for Jesus. *(Display Bible.)* Here are some people who were helpers for Jesus.

(Display Peter and Andrew puppets). Who are these helpers? That's right, Peter and Andrew! What did Andrew tell Peter? Yes! Andrew said, "Come see Jesus!" *(Allow children to use Andrew puppet to tell Peter about Jesus.)* Let's sing about Andrew the helper! *(Sing "I Can Help," substituting Andrew's name for "I.")* Andrew is a helper. He says, "Jesus loves you!"

(Display Paul and Timothy puppets.) Who are these helpers? You are right if you said Paul and Timothy! What did Paul ask Timothy? (Do you want to be a helper for Jesus?) What did Paul and Timothy tell people? (Jesus loves you!) Let's sing about the helpers named Paul and Timothy. *(Sing "I Can Help," substituting Paul's name for "I.")*

(Allow children to use the puppets to "tell" about Jesus.)

(Still using the Paul and Timothy puppets ask,) What did Paul and Timothy tell Lydia? (Jesus loves you!) Who were helpers for Jesus? Yes, Paul and Timothy. *(Sing "I Can Help," this time substituting Timothy's name for "I.")*

(Allow children to take turns holding the puppets to "tell" or sing about Jesus.)

Let's Apply the Lesson

Use Zach to whisper a question in your ear. Nod to Zach. Tell the children, **Zach wants to find helpers for Jesus. Where are helpers, Zach?** Have Zach "hold" an unbreakable

Music Center

Unit 2—Helping Jesus

Items to Include:

Rhythm instruments such as oatmeal-box drum, sand blocks, triangle and stick, tambourine, shakers (any sealable container filled with beans, dried peas, sand, etc.)

Purpose: The child will sing about helping Jesus.

Things to Do and Say

Lesson 6

Teach the children the song, "I Can Help," from page 190. After you have gone over it several times say, **Thank you for singing about being Jesus' helpers! All of us are Jesus' helpers when we say, "Jesus loves you!"**

Before singing the song again, demonstrate how to use several rhythm instruments. To avoid confusion, it may help to specify which instrument each child may play. **Melissa, you can help us with our song by playing this drum. David, you play the triangle. We want to sing about being Jesus' helpers!** After the song, allow children to trade instruments.

Lessons 7 and 9

Teach the children the song, "I Want to Help Every Day," found on page 190. After the children are familiar with the song, stop when you reach the word *mouth*. Ask, **What can our mouths say to be helpers for Jesus?** (Jesus loves you! Come to church.) Repeat the song, using rhythm instruments as available.

Make the song more interesting to your children by varying the volume and speed with which you sing. Say, **I want to sing this helping song again. Can you help me sing it very softly? Good! You are learning to be good helpers for Jesus!**

Block Center

Unit 2—Helping Jesus

Items to Include:

Large cardboard blocks
Cars and trucks

Lesson 8
Construction equipment—hats, nail aprons, gloves, toy tools, flannel shirts, tape measure, etc.

Purpose: The child will act out being a helper for Jesus.

Things to Do and Say

Lessons 7 and 9

Help the children build houses and a church building. Three's may build fairly good structures, while 2's may put a few blocks on top of one another and call it a house. What you say as the children play is far more important than how or what they build.

Encourage a child to "drive" to another child's house to ask that child to come to church. Sit near the entrance to the church and say, **Thank you, Tony, for asking Rachel to church today! When we ask our friends to come to church we are being Jesus' helpers!** Ask children to choose a song to sing at church.

Lesson 8

Tell the children that today they are going to "work." They will use the blocks to build a church building. Show them how to build the outline of a building large enough for the group to fit inside. Allow the children to dress up for "work."

Thank you, boys and girls, for helping me build a church building today! We are doing good work. Thank you for sharing that block, Shannon. Jesus is happy when we help others. When the church building is finished say, **I like the church building we have built! Let's practice being Jesus' helpers and ask someone to come to church. When we ask someone to come to church with us we are being Jesus' helpers.**

Block Center, continued

What else can we say to practice being Jesus' helpers? Let children respond, "Jesus loves you!" Seat the children in a circle in the church building. Say the Bible words together. Ask children to choose a song to sing for Jesus. End the time by asking the group to say, "Jesus loves you!"

Music Center, continued

Lesson 8
Tape recorder
Blank tape

Lesson 8

If the children have not already learned "Jesus Loves You!" from page 190, teach it to them today. If they know the song, go through it once. Then say, **I see a helper! When Karen sang, "Jesus loves you!" she was being a helper for Jesus. I see another helper! When Nathan sings, "Come to church," he is being a helper for Jesus too! Let's all practice being helpers for Jesus again.**

Use the tape recorder to record the song as children sing it again. Play the tape for the children. Say, **I hear helpers for Jesus!** Repeat any songs learned earlier in the unit, making use of rhythm instruments as desired. If you have time and the children enjoy hearing themselves, tape more songs.

Family Living Center

Unit 2—Helping Jesus

Items to Include:

Dress-up items such as hats, scarves, purses, belts, ties, jewelry, shoes
Unbreakable mirror
Phone
Dolls, etc.

Purpose: The child will have opportunities to act out being a helper for Jesus.

Things to Do and Say

Lesson 6

Encourage the children to dress up to go visiting. Explain that they will practice being helpers for Jesus by visiting their friends to tell them, "Jesus loves you!" and "Come to church."

Who are you visiting today, Jenny? How will you be a helper for Jesus? Yes, you can tell Eric, "Jesus loves you!" That's being a helper for Jesus.

Call a child on the phone to invite him to come to church with you. **Hello, Andy! Jesus loves you! I want you to come to church with me. . . . Brian, can you call and invite a friend to come to church? . . . Michelle is being a helper for Jesus when she calls Chaelyn and asks her to come to church.**

Lesson 7

Ask children to call their friends. Ask them to be helpers for Jesus when they talk on the phone. Children may invite their friends to church and tell them, "Jesus loves you." Show the children where the "church" is. Suggest that a child go to his friend's "house" to take that friend to church. As the children come to church say, **I'm so glad you came to church today, Jason! Who did you bring with you? You were being a helper for Jesus when you asked Kevin to come to church with you.**

Art Center

Unit 2—Helping Jesus

Items to Include:

Lesson 8
Play dough
Boy and girl or gingerbread man cookie cutters

Purpose: The child will name or point to Jesus' helpers in the class (self, others). Act out being a helper for Jesus.

Things to Do and Say

Lesson 8

Give each child a portion of play dough. Suggest that the children make boy and girl figures "just like them." Observe the children's dough people as they work. Say, **I see the girl Julie is making. She looks like you, Julie! Mark, that is a fine-looking boy you have made. I think he can be a helper for Jesus.**

When the children have finished encourage them to use their dough people to say to each other, "Come to church," and "Jesus loves you!" **Who can point to a helper for Jesus?** Point to a child. **When Jeremy invites someone to church he is being a helper for Jesus. Who can point to another helper for Jesus?** Allow children to respond. Repeat this procedure for all children.

Play Dough Recipe:

1 cup flour	1/2 cup salt	1 cup water
1 tsp. cream of tartar	1 Tbs. oil	food coloring

Mix ingredients in a pan. Cook over medium heat until mixture pulls away from sides of

Art Center, continued

pan and becomes doughy in consistency. Knead until cool. Make as many colors as desired. This dough is not edible. It keeps three months unrefrigerated if kept in an airtight container.

Lesson 9
Copies of page 211
Crayons
Stickers from page 204
Damp sponges

Lesson 9

Make photocopies of page 211 and cut off the excess paper. Fold each card where indicated. Copy and prepare stickers as directed on page 209.

In class, let the children color the stickers before they are cut out. Show a completed card. **Do you know what this says?** Point to the words on the front of the card. **That's right, "Come to church." Now, see these words? What do you suppose they say? "Jesus loves you!" Very good!**

Help the children put their stickers in place, but don't do it for them. **Who will you give your invitation to, Jeffrey? You're going to send it to your grandma. That's a good idea. You are all going to be helpers for Jesus when you send or give your cards to your friends.**

Book/Picture Center

Unit 2—Helping Jesus

Items to Include:

Books from list on page 189

Other books and pictures that show children helping

Lesson 7

Teacher-made book of church people helping (Church pictorial directory could be used here.)

Purpose: The child will learn that helpers for Jesus say, "Jesus loves you!" and "Come to church."

Things to Do and Say

Lesson 6

Have a special reading area with a table and chairs, or an area rug and perhaps pillows to make the place inviting. Display books and pictures in a rack, or spread them on the floor or table.

Join the children in looking at pictures and reading books. As children look and listen, encourage them to tell about ways they see children helping. Ask, **How is this child helping? How do you think she feels about helping? How do you help at home? . . . I like the way you put the books back on the shelf. You are a good helper at church. We are helpers for Jesus when we say, "Jesus loves you!" or "Come to church."**

Lesson 7

Display the picture book of church helpers (church directory). Say, **This is Mr. Bridgman. He is our minister. He tells people, "Jesus loves you!" He is a helper for Jesus. Here is a picture of Miss Barbie, a Sunday school teacher. She says, "Come to church!" She is a helper for Jesus.** Repeat this procedure for other pictures in the book. Ask, **What does this helper do? Who is helping in this picture? Who can be a helper?** (I can!)

Game Center

Unit 2—Helping Jesus

Items to Include:

Large ball

Purpose: The child will name or point to Jesus' helpers in the class (self, others).

Things to Do and Say

Lessons 6 and 9

Seat children in a circle. Ask each child to say his or her name. Start the game by rolling the ball to a child. Say, **Felicia, come to church with me!** Then say, **Boys and girls, who was a helper? Mrs. Hatfield was a helper!** Encourage Felicia to roll the ball to someone in the circle. Assist Felicia in saying the helping words, "Come to church," or "Jesus loves you!" Ask the class, **Who was a helper? Yes, Felicia was a helper!** Continue with all the children in the circle. If time permits ask the class to say the Bible words with you. After the children are familiar with the Bible words, ask for a volunteer to say them. Roll the ball to that child. The child will say the Bible words and roll the ball back to you. Continue with other volunteers.

This game can be played each week if you have time and sufficient teachers to do this along with the suggested learning activities. Playing a game is a good way to relieve the "wiggles" that are so prevalent with 2's and 3's. After using their large muscles for awhile, children are usually ready to take part in a quieter learning time. Varying activities is very important when working with young children.

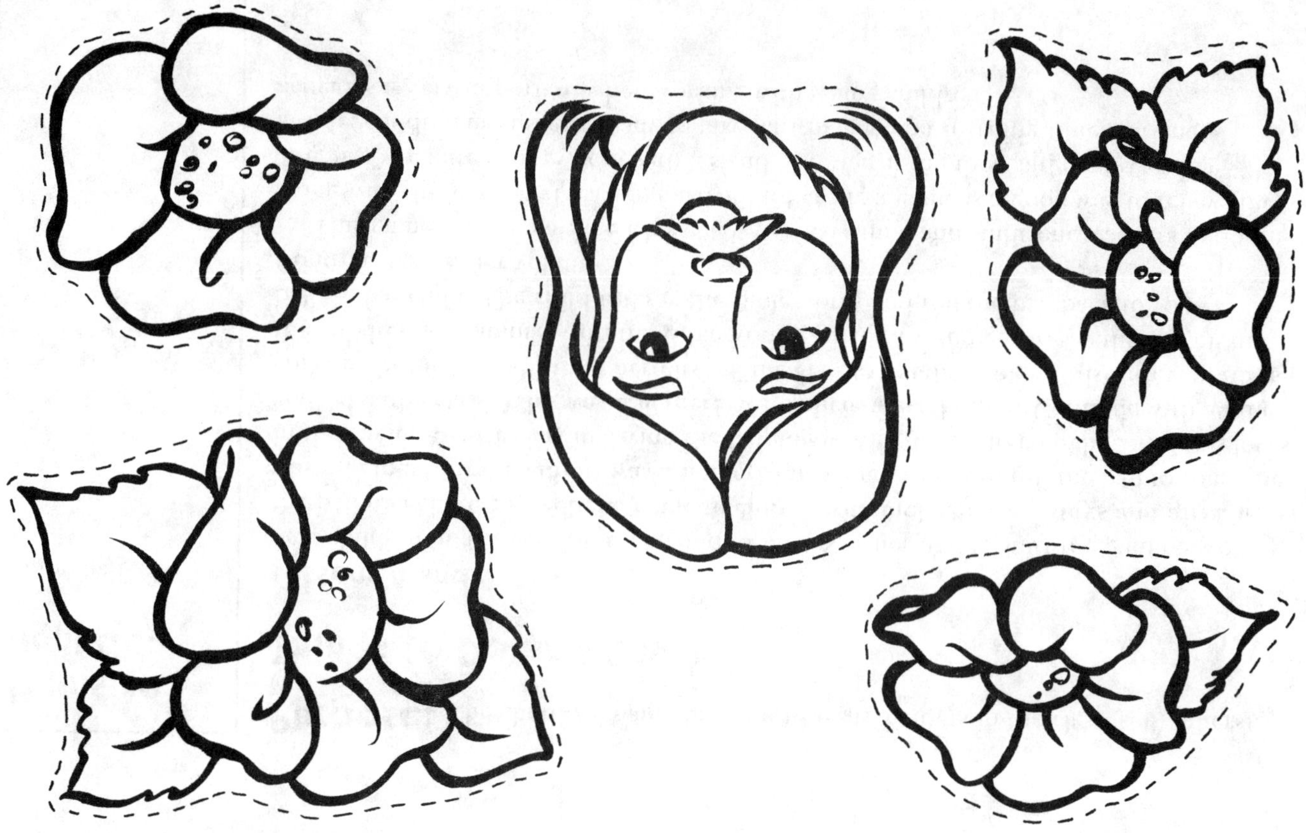

Book/Picture Center, continued

Lesson 8 River scene made from page 210 Other river scenes

Lesson 8

Photocopy page 210; color the picture. Pictures that are mounted on cardboard or construction paper and covered with clear, self-adhesive plastic can be used over and over. Display the river scenes along with books and pictures used previously.

One day, Paul found some people by a river. He told the people, "Jesus loves you!" Paul was being a helper for Jesus! Ask children to point to helpers in books and pictures provided. Pray, **Dear God, help us be helpers for Jesus.**

Andrew Puppet—Spring, Unit 2

Instructions

1. Photocopy page.
2. Add color (crayons or markers).
3. Cut on heavy lines.
4. Glue upper portions of head on bottom of lunch-size paper bag (see sketch).
5. Glue lower portion on bag as shown.

cut here

cut here

cut here

cut here

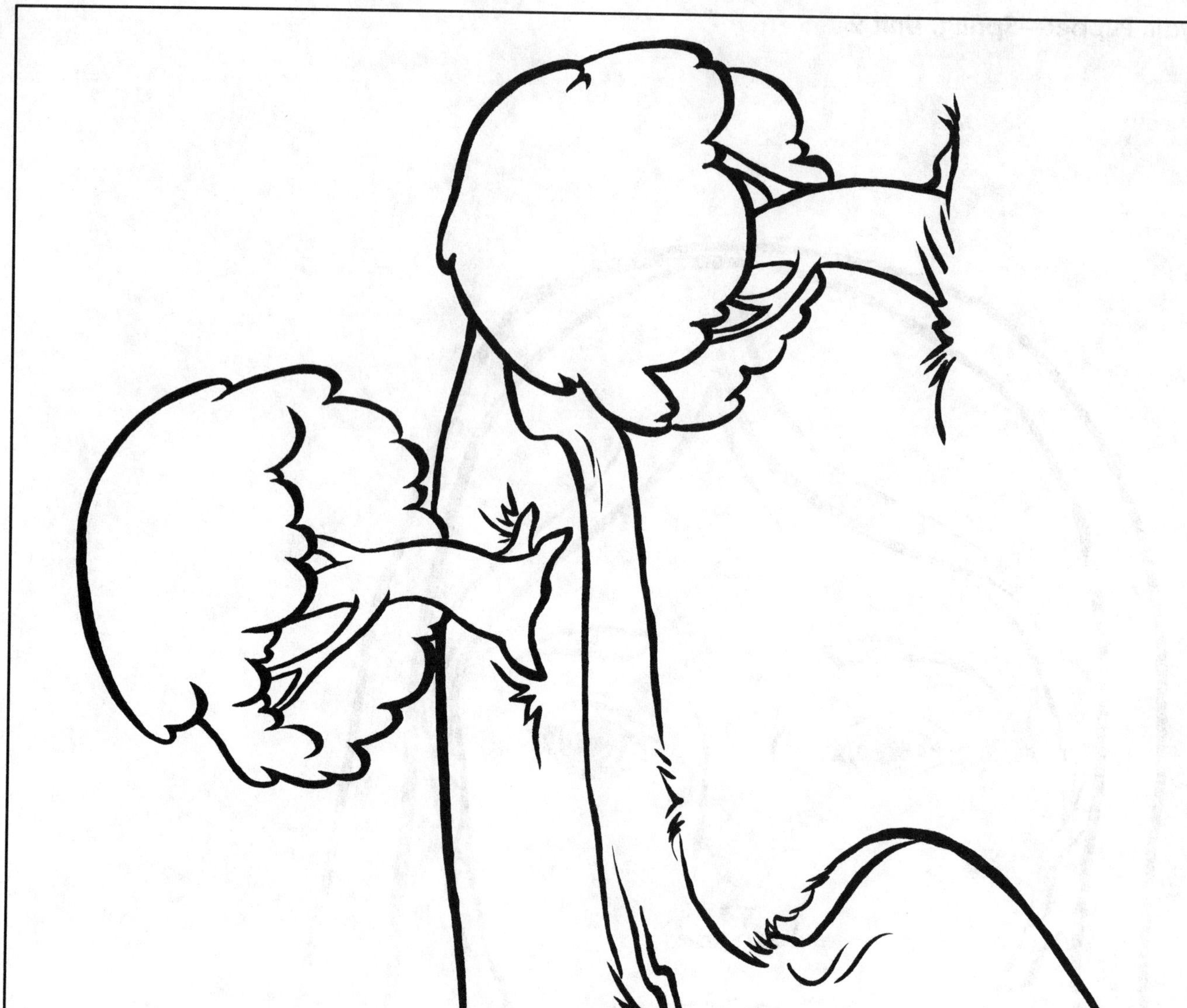

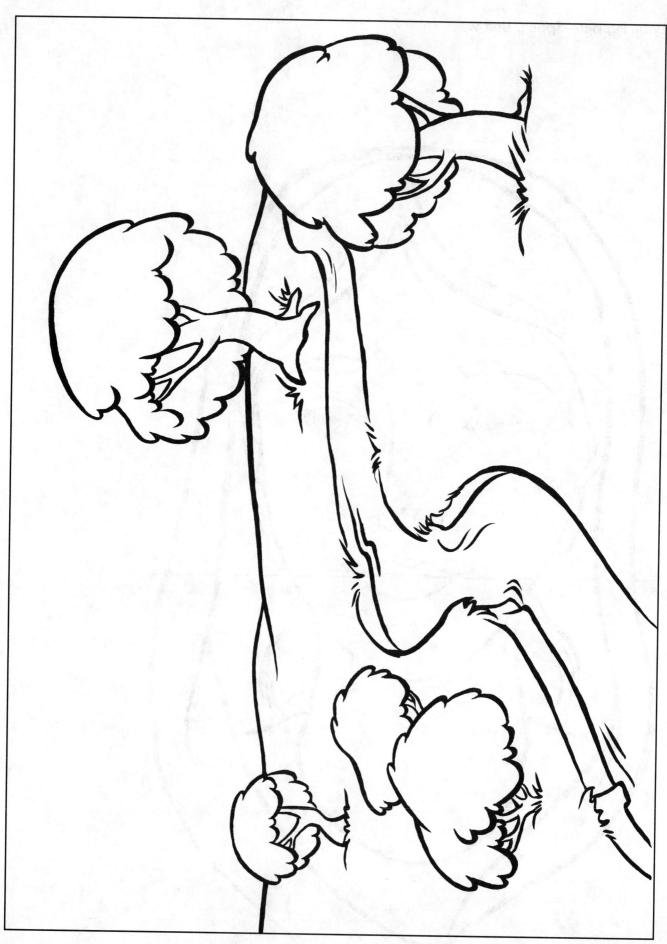

Teaching Picture—Spring, Unit 2

Invitation to Church—Spring, Unit 2

Instructions

1. Photocopy this page for each child.
2. Cut on the solid lines.
3. Fold on the dotted line so that the words are on the front of the cards.
4. Let children color what they want on the card.
5. Copy and cut out stickers from page 204.
6. Ahead of time, coat backs of stickers with a mixture of 2 parts white glue and 1 part vinegar. A few drops of peppermint extract can be added if you want. Let this dry. Before cutting out stickers, let children color them. Then cut out stickers and let children add them wherever they want inside the cards.

Jesus Loves You!

Come to Church

Dear Parent,

In this unit your child will be learning to be a helper for Jesus! We will use these Bible stories.
Lesson 6—*Peter Becomes a Helper* (John 1:40-42)
Lesson 7—*Paul and Timothy Are Helpers* (Acts 16:1-5)
Lesson 8—*Lydia Learns to Be a Helper* (Acts 16:11-15)
Lesson 9—*I Can Help* (Review of Lessons 6–8)

The goal for these lessons is to teach the children that they are helpers for Jesus when they say, "Come to church," and "Jesus loves you!" Through the activities and songs introduced in this unit your child will not only learn how to be a helper for Jesus but be excited to practice what he or she has learned! Here are ways to reinforce these lessons at home:

- Play "house" with your child. Ask him or her to call you on the phone and use the "helping" words, "Come to church," or "Jesus loves you!"
- When your child plays "dress-up" encourage him or her to invite you to go to church. Go to "church" and sing a song about Jesus together. (Note: While adults know that Christians are the church, 2's and 3's consider the building "the church." They think in "concrete" terms, not abstract. They will learn about the church as they grow up.)
- Say the Bible words, "We . . . are helpers," (2 Corinthians 1:24) with your child every day. Show your child the words in the Bible.
- Write the Bible words, "We are helpers," on construction paper. Put the paper on the refrigerator with a picture of your child. Point to the picture and ask, "Who is a helper?" (I am!)
- Praise your child when he or she is a helper.
- Use the following songs and rhymes during the week:

The Cleanup Song

(Tune: "I'm a Little Teapot")

I can be a helper every day,
By doing what my teachers say.
I can be a helper every day,
By keeping my playthings put away.

I Want to Help

I want to help in every way!
With ears, and eyes, and mouth, *(Point to each.)*
With feet, *(Bend down and touch feet.)*
And hands. *(Clap hands.)*
I want to help today.

—Dorothy Fay Richards

Jesus Loves You!

(Tune: "Jesus Loves You")

"Jesus loves you!" we can say, *(Point to mouth.)*
Helping Jesus every day. *(Point upward.)*
Come to church and sing with me, *(Beckon others to come.)*
Jesus' helpers we will be.
We're helping Jesus. *(Point upward. Repeat line twice.)*
Like Jesus wants us to. *(Point to self.)*

The Busy Fingers

Busy little finger people,
(Hold up fists.)
Who will put the toys (blocks, etc.) away?
(Look at fists.)
"I will," "I will," "I will," "I will," "I will."
All the fingers say.
(Raise fingers one at a time, both hands at the same time, beginning with index fingers.)

—Louise M. Oglevee

Your child's teacher,

Unit 3: Learning About Me

Lessons 10–13

By the end of the unit, the children will

Know that God made them.

Feel good about themselves because God made them.

Thank God for different parts of their bodies.

Unit Bible Words

"God . . . made us" (Psalm 100:3, *NIV*).

Happy Day Books

All About Hands 24-03591
Busy Feet 24-03592
I'm Glad I'm Me 24-04209
God Made Me Special 24-04205
Look, I'm Growing Up 24-04233
God Made Me 24-04230

The Unit at a Glance

10 Learning About My Body — **Genesis 1; Psalm 139:13-15; Matthew 19:19**
God made Adam and Eve in His image.

11 Learning About My Senses — **Genesis 1; Psalm 139:13-15; Matthew 19:19**
God gave us eyes, ears, noses, mouths, and fingers.

12 Learning About My Feelings — **1 Samuel 16:11-13; Psalms 23; 31:9, 14, 15; 56:3, 4**
God made our emotions.

13 I Am Wonderfully Made — **Review of Lessons 10–12**
This lesson reviews the three previous lessons and reinforces the fact that God made each person, and each is unique and special.

Why Teach This Unit?

The human body is truly a masterpiece of God! Each part was perfectly fit together by Him to work for the good of the whole.

Two's and 3's are interested in their bodies and how they work. This unit provides an opportunity to build on that interest by emphasizing to children that God created each of them. Not only did He make each part to accomplish an important task, He also made each person unique and special. Children need to be aware of how special and important they are because God, their Heavenly Father, made them in His own image.

It is important for children to understand that the Bible words are God's words, and that God's words are always true. Refer to the Bible frequently throughout the unit as a means of reinforcing the theme. Say, **We know God made our eyes, because the Bible says, "God made us."**

Make sure your classroom Bible is on hand at all times in the classroom. The Bible words should be highlighted and the page marked, so children can "read" the words themselves.

Things to Do for This Unit

- Photocopy the Learning Center Cards (pages 223-228); cut pages apart on solid lines. Mount side 1 of a card on cardboard; then mount side 2 on back of cardboard. Laminate for durability.
- Gather/prepare materials listed on the Learning Center Cards.
- Make copies of Parents' Letter (page 236) and the Unit Planning Sheet (319 and 320).
- For Lesson 10, photocopy the puzzle backgrounds on pages 229 and 230, making the appropriate number for boys and for girls. Photocopy the "body parts" found on page 231. Add color to these or just copy them onto various pastel shades of construction paper.
- For Lesson 11, photocopy the picture on page 232. Use this as an extra activity or in place of the art activity, or as a coloring sheet to take home.
- For Lesson 12, make a copy of the shepherd's scene on page 233 for each child. Make five cotton-ball sheep for each child by drawing two black dots on each cotton ball.
- For Lesson 13, make a copy of the certificate on page 235 for each child. Add color to the certificates, or copy them onto pastel shades of construction paper. Give these out at the end of the lesson.
- Even though no Book and Picture Center is suggested, you may want to have a supply of appropriate books to look at and read at times when you need an extra activity.

Use These Songs and Action Rhymes During Unit 3

I'm So Happy Today

D. F. R. DOROTHY FAY RICHARDS

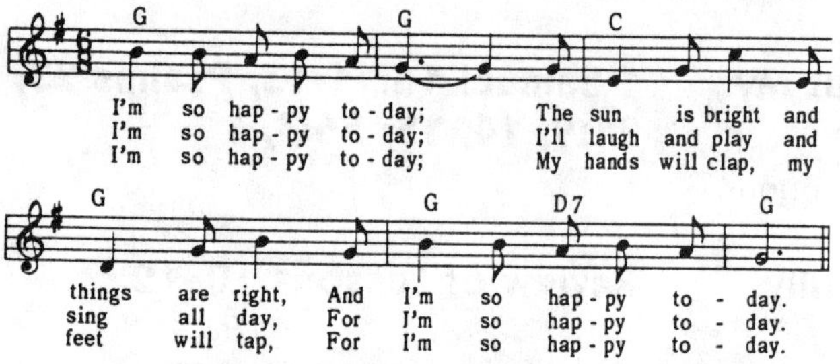
G G C
I'm so hap-py to-day; The sun is bright and
I'm so hap-py to-day; I'll laugh and play and
I'm so hap-py to-day; My hands will clap, my
G G D7 G
things are right, And I'm so hap-py to-day.
sing all day, For I'm so hap-py to-day.
feet will tap, For I'm so hap-py to-day.

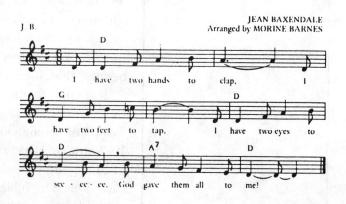

I Have Two Hands

S. T. SYLVIA TESTER

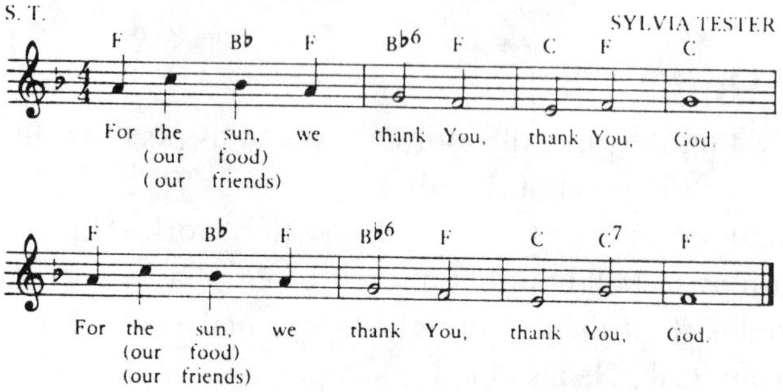
F Bb F Bb6 F C F C
For the sun, we thank You, thank You, God.
(our food)
(our friends)
F Bb F Bb6 F C C7 F
For the sun, we thank You, thank You, God.
(our food)
(our friends)

I Can

I can stand up straight and tall, *(Do so.)*
I can curl up like a ball, *(Squat with arms around knees.)*
I can spread out like a tree, *(Arms high, spread out.)*
I can sit down quietly. *(Place finger to lips and then sit down.)*

—*Dorothy Fay Richards*

I'm Me

God made me special. *(Point up; point to self.)*
There's only one of me. *(Hold up finger; point to self.)*
One nose like mine, *(Squeeze nose.)*
One mouth like mine, *(Touch mouth with finger.)*
One chin like mine, *(Tap chin.)*
Two eyes like mine, *(Touch eyes with finger.)*
Two ears like mine, *(Wiggle ears with fingers.)*
Two hands like mine, *(Shake hands at sides.)*
Two feet like mine, *(Shake feet.)*
There's only one of me. *(Hold up finger; point to self.)*
I'm special as can be! *(Point to self; smile.)*

—*Karen M. Leet*

We Thank You, Thank You, God

JEAN BAXENDALE
Arranged by MORINE BARNES
J. B.

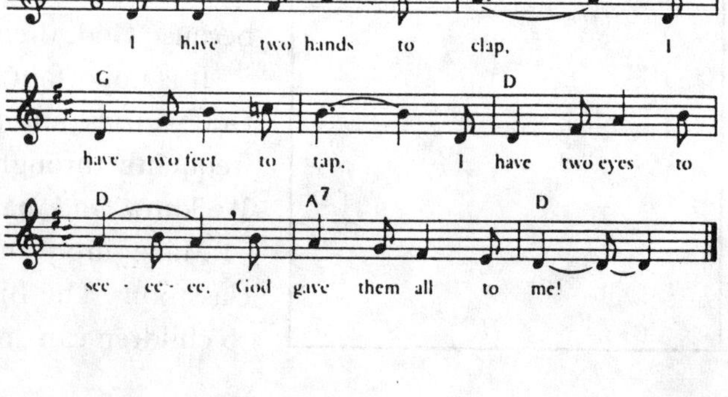
D
I have two hands to clap, I
G D
have two feet to tap. I have two eyes to
D A7 D
see-ee-ee. God gave them all to me!

legs to their puzzles.) And God made feet for Adam and Eve so they could stand up. *(Finish puzzles by adding the feet.)* God made Adam and Eve, and He made each one of us. He made each of our bodies special with arms and legs, hands and feet!

Let's Apply the Lesson

You did a good job putting your puzzles together. You all used your hands and arms very well. Thank You, God, for hands and arms. . . . Take your puzzles apart now, and let's put them together again while someone else tells the Bible story. Ask for volunteers. If the child has trouble remembering, maybe Zach could help in prompting. **The Bible tells us who made our bodies. It says, "God made us." Let's say those Bible words together, so we can remember them. Now let's stand up and use our legs and feet awhile. Thank You, God, for legs and feet.**

Learning Activities

(20 minutes)

Let's Play Awhile

Have the children stand up and do stretching exercises with you. If you can, have Zach lead these exercises. Focus on using the arms, legs, hands, and feet (touch your toes, hop on one or both feet, do jumping jacks, jog in place, etc.). Have materials ready for the Game Center. If your class is large and there are several teachers, learning activities from before can be used as well.

Let's Go Home

Have Zach tell the children that it is time to clean up the room. Gather children together and do the action rhyme, "My Eyes, My Ears" (page 162). Make sure that each child has his puzzle, body tracing, and a Parents' Letter to take home.

Learning About My Body

Genesis 1; Psalm 139:13-15; Matthew 19:19

Bible Words: "God . . . made us" (Psalm 100:3, *NIV*).

Lesson Value: All too often today, we see children who grow up believing they are "bad." They frequently put themselves and others down. The job of the Christian teacher should be to change these negative attitudes toward self by words of encouragement and by teaching two important Biblical truths:

—We were each made by the hand of God himself, not by a human hand (Psalm 100:3).

—Of all the different creatures God made on the sixth day of creation, only the one called "man" was made in His own image (Genesis 1: 27).

Children and adults alike should be thankful for and marvel at the wonder of God's creation!

Know: Know that God made me.
Feel: Like myself because God made me.
Do: Thank God for different parts of me.

Children will accomplish the goals when they:

1. Say the Bible words, "God made us."
2. Pray, "Thank You, God, for making my arms, legs, hands, and feet."
3. Label and thank God for each body part as it is being used.
4. Sing songs to thank God for the bodies He made.

Let's Get Ready

For the Bible story, you will need the classroom Bible with the new Bible words highlighted or underlined. Prepare a puzzle for each child. Run copies of the "body parts" from page 231 on colored construction paper, then cut out the pieces. Place puzzles in individual envelopes, so children can take them home. Also copy the puzzle backgrounds (pages 229 and 230). These will guide children in placing their pieces. Have Zach ready for use.

Set up the Family Living Center, the Art Center, and the Music/Drama Center. If you are the only teacher, use just the Family Living Center. The Game Center will be used after the Bible story. All materials needed and directions for what to do and say are included on the Learning Center Cards (pages 223-228).

Learning Activities

(30 minutes, including 10 minutes presession)

Let's Get Started

Have Zach welcome each child by name and help the child to take off his or her wraps, hang them up, and add an attendance sticker. Also make a point of using Zach's arms to shake hands with, wave to, pat on the back, or hug each child. Say, **I'm glad God gave us arms so we can hug each other, Jordan.** Offer a child a choice between two of the learning activities. Children learn by making choices. Just make sure that the choices you give him are acceptable to you. **Would you like to play "doctor" or sing a song now?** Then direct each child toward the learning center of his choice.

Worship and Bible Story

(15 minutes)

Let's Worship God

Have Zach encourage the children to clean up. Have him say, "I want to see who can use their arms, legs, hands, and feet to help clean up." Sing the action song, "Head and Shoulders" (page 162), making sure you put plenty of action into it. Introduce the song, "I Have Two Hands" (page 214). Lead children in the rhyme, "I'm Me" (page 214). Open the Bible and read the Bible words, then say them together. Then pray, **God, thank You for the bodies You made for us. Thank You for our arms, legs, hands, and feet.**

Let's Learn From the Bible

Introduction: Zach can help to introduce the story by saying the following: "How many of you have arms and hands? Show them to me. What do you use your arms and hands for?" Let the children respond, then ask the same question about legs and feet. **You know, boys and girls, we could not do any of those things if God had not given us our arms, legs, hands, and feet.** Be sensitive to the needs of a physically handicapped child, if you have one in your class. Try to say something positive about his or her body in some way as you teach this lesson and the following ones in this unit.

Pass out the puzzle backgrounds and the "body parts."**As I am telling the Bible story, you can put the body parts I talk about on your puzzle background.** Now put Zach away and have your Bible on your lap or at your side.

The Bible Story: God made the whole world. He made the sky and the oceans and the ground. He made the sun, moon, and the stars. God made trees and flowers and animals.

When God was finished making the world, He made people. He made the people to be like Him, instead of like the animals. First God made a man named Adam. Then He made a woman named Eve.

God gave Adam and Eve arms so they could stretch and reach. *(Have children add the arms to their puzzles.)* God also gave them hands so they could touch the things He made, like the flowers and the animals. *(Help the children put the hands on.)* God gave Adam and Eve legs to walk and run. *(Children can add the*

Bible tells us who made our bodies. It says, "God made us." Let's say those words together. Allow the children to hold the classroom Bible. Help them point to the highlighted words and "read" them aloud.

Learning Activities

(20 minutes)

Let's Play Awhile

Have the children stand and play a short game of "Zach Says" (instead of "Simon Says"). **Zach says to touch your nose. Zach says to wiggle your fingers. Blink your eyes.** Have materials available for the Art Center. Learning activities from before can be repeated if there are too many children for one center and you have a multiple staff of teachers.

Let's Go Home

Zach can tell the children when it is time to stop playing and to clean up the room. Sing the action song, "Head and Shoulders," with the children while they wait for their parents. Make sure each child has his play dough in a plastic bag, ready to take home. Take time to tell parents something good their child has done during this session. **Adam did a good job of putting away the "doctor" equipment we used earlier!**

Learning About My Senses

Genesis 1; Psalm 139:13-15; Matthew 19:19

Bible Words: "God . . . made us" (Psalm 100:3, *NIV*).

Lesson Value: Everyone needs to be loved. Without love a person's life is meaningless and empty. Unfortunately in our society, the word *love* has been distorted. Many children grow up believing that they must earn love from parents, teachers, and friends by doing certain things or by looking a certain way.

Children need to know that God's love for them is not based on how they act or how they look. His love is absolutely unconditional. It is a precious gift that needs only to be accepted. A Christian teacher not only needs to share verbally about this gift, but also needs to show the children by example how to love each other in this same unconditional way.

Know: Know that God made me.
Feel: Like myself because God made me.
Do: Thank God for different parts of me.

Children will accomplish the goals when they:

1. Say the Bible words, "God made us."
2. Pray, "Thank You, God, for making me special."
3. Sing songs to thank God for the bodies He made.
4. Label and thank God for each body part as it is used.

Let's Get Ready

For the Bible story, you will need a small apple for each child, your classroom Bible, and the Zach puppet.

Set up the Family Living Center, the Game Center, and the God's Wonders Center. If you are the only teacher, use just the God's Wonders Center. Have the Art Center materials ready to be used after the Bible story.

Learning Activities

(30 minutes, including 10 minute presession)

Let's Get Started

Use Zach to greet each child as he or she comes in. Talk about how the children use their eyes, ears, and mouths to respond to Zach. Say, **I'm glad God gave us eyes so we can see each other, Lara. He also gave us ears and a mouth so we can talk to each other.** Then give each child an opportunity to choose a learning center. **Maria, would you like to play a listening game or take a "texture walk"?** Then direct each child to the learning activity he or she has chosen.

Worship and Bible Story

(15 minutes)

Let's Worship God

Have Zach warn the children that they have only a few minutes left to play, then let him encourage the children to clean up. Gather the children in a group and sing the action song, "Head and Shoulders." Sing "We Thank You, Thank You, God" (page 214), inserting parts of the body ("For our hands, we thank You . . . ") Do the action rhyme, "I'm Me." Then pray, **God, thank You for the bodies You made. Thank You for our eyes, noses, hands, mouths, and ears.**

Let's Learn From the Bible

Introduction: Hold up an apple for the children to see. **How many of you know what this is?** Let the children respond. **Of course, it's an apple. God made apples for us to enjoy. But how do we know this is an apple? God gave us eyes, noses, hands, mouths, and ears so we can learn about and enjoy things. Zach is going to give each of you an apple so we can use our bodies to learn about them.** Have Zach give an apple to each child. **Now hold your apple and I will tell you what to do with it.** Put Zach away now.

The Bible Story: God made the whole world. He made all people. He made each one of us different and special, because He loves us.

God made our eyes. You can use your eyes to look at your apple. What does it look like? (It is red. It is round, like a ball.) My apple looks good to eat, does yours?

God made our noses, too. You can use your nose to smell your apple. It smells delicious!

God also made our hands and fingers. You can use your hands and fingers to touch your apple. How does it feel? (It is cool. It is smooth.)

And God made our mouths and tongues. You can use your mouth to bite into and taste your apple. How does your apple taste? Is it sweet and juicy?

God also made our ears. You can use your ears to hear your apple when you bite into it and chew it. It is crunchy.

I am so glad that God gave us eyes, noses, hands, mouths, and ears so we can enjoy His beautiful world!

Let's Apply the Lesson

Children may finish eating their apples if they so choose. You may need to cut apples into quarters for 2's and even peel them for very young 2's. **We learned a lot about our apples. What body parts did we use? What do we use our eyes for?** Continue asking what each part is used for as it is named. **The**

them were there. He had not lost any sheep. David felt happy again.

Let's Apply the Lesson

You did a good job taking care of your sheep, just like David did. What were some of the feelings David had in our story? Why did David feel happy (sad, angry)? Do you think David was afraid of the lion? . . . When are you afraid (happy, sad, angry)? It is OK to have lots of different feelings, because God made our feelings. Our Bible words say, "God made us." Thank You, God, for giving us feelings.

Learning Activities

(20 minutes)

Let's Play Awhile

Have the children stand and try a short game. **How would you walk if you were feeling happy (sad, angry, afraid)?** Show the children how you would walk and look if you were feeling these emotions. Be prepared at this time to do the Family Living Center. If there are several teachers, earlier activities may be repeated.

Let's Go Home

Let Zach tell the children that it is time to put away the toys and activities. When the children are gathered, sing "I'm So Happy Today" and "I Have Two Hands." Make sure each child has his shepherd's scene and sheep to take home.

Learning About My Feelings

1 Samuel 16:11-13, 18; Psalms 23; 31:9, 14, 15; 56:3, 4

Bible Words: "God . . . made us" (Psalm 100:3, *NIV*).

Lesson Value: The Bible speaks frequently about the various emotions or feelings that human beings experience. David especially speaks of his emotions in the songs he wrote and sang to God, recorded in the book of Psalms. Anger, fear, sadness, and joy are probably the ones mentioned the most. These are also the feelings that children deal with the most. Unfortunately, children sometimes get the false impression that feelings of anger, fear, and sadness are wrong. Christian teachers can express to their class that true joy comes only from God, yet no one can feel happy all the time. Every person feels angry, afraid, or sad at some time. These feelings are made by God and are not wrong, unless they cause us to hurt other people.

Know: Know that God made me.
Feel: Like myself because God made me.
Do: Thank God for different parts of me.

Children will accomplish the goals when they:

1. Say the Bible words, "God made us."
2. Pray, "Thank You, God, for giving me feelings."
3. Label and thank God for feelings of happiness, sadness, anger, and fear.
4. Sing songs about the feelings God made.

Let's Get Ready

For the Bible story, make a copy of the shepherd's scene, page 233, for each child (these may be colored by the teacher or the children). Prepare five "sheep" for each child by drawing two black dots for eyes on each cotton ball. Have Zach ready to use.

Set up the Art Center, the Music/Drama Center, and the God's Wonders Center. The Family Living Center will be used after the Bible story. If you are the only teacher, use just the Art Center now.

Learning Activities

(30 minutes, including 10 minutes presession)

Let's Get Started

Have Zach welcome each child into the classroom. Let him comment on the emotions children might be feeling as they enter. "Mollie, I can tell by your smile that you are happy to be here. . . . Brandon, it's OK to feel sad when mommy leaves. She will feel happy to see you when she comes back." Direct children toward the learning centers and see that each one gets involved in an activity.

Worship and Bible Story

(15 minutes)

Let's Worship God

Encourage children to put the toys and activities away neatly. **Zach feels happy because he sees everyone picking up and helping each other.** Sing "Head and Shoulders," focusing on the stanza about feelings. Then introduce the song, "I'm So Happy Today." Do the rhymes, "I'm Me" and "I Can." Open the Bible and read the Bible words, then say them together. Let each child hold the Bible and "read" the words if there is time. Pray, **Thank You, God, for our bodies. Thank You for giving each of us feelings.**

Let's Learn From the Bible

Introduction: Zach can help introduce the story. "When I look at your faces, I can tell how some of you are feeling. Show me your happy faces. Very good! Now show me your sad (angry, scared) faces."

Some of you know about a man in the Bible who felt just like we do. Sometimes he was happy or sad. Sometimes he was afraid or angry. His name was David. Pass out a shepherd's scene and five cotton-ball sheep to each child. **As I tell the story, I want you to pretend to be David and these** (hold up cotton balls) **are your sheep. Put your sheep in the pen on your picture. Then listen so you will know when to move your sheep around on your picture.**

The Bible Story: David was a shepherd. His job was to take care of his father's sheep. Every morning David would lead his sheep out of their pen to the green pasture. David felt happy as his sheep hopped and skipped and jumped *(show children how to move their "sheep" to the pasture).*

When the sheep were finished eating the green grass, they needed a drink. So David would walk the sheep over to the water *(children walk "sheep" to water)* and they would drink. Then the sheep would lie down in the grass and sleep *(move "sheep" to sleep),* while David played his harp and sang songs to God. David felt very happy *(speak quietly, then pause).*

Suddenly a lion came out of the bushes and tried to catch one of David's sheep! David felt angry! He took a stone and his sling and chased the lion away.

David and his sheep started to walk home *(children walk their "sheep" toward the pen).* Oh, no! One of the sheep got caught in the thorns and was hurt. David felt sad for the sheep.

Finally David and his sheep were safely back home *(put all "sheep" in the pen and count).* David counted his sheep and all of

Who can help tell the stories again? Have three children come up and hold the visuals. Have them tell all they can about each story or answer your questions about the stories. **We know who made our bodies, because our Bible words say, "God made us." Thank You, God, for making all the parts of our bodies.**

Learning Activities

(20 minutes)

Let's Play Awhile

Have the children stand and do exercises with you. Focus on using as many body parts as possible (jumping jacks, toe touches, knee bends, sit ups, etc.). Be prepared at this time to do the Game Center. If there are several teachers, other learning activities can be repeated.

Let's Go Home

Sing "We Thank You, Thank You, God," inserting "hands, arms, legs, feet," and so forth, as the children put the toys away. Then gather the children and sing "I'm So Happy Today" and "I Have Two Hands," as well as favorite songs and/or action rhymes of the children. Take the children, one at a time, to the door as parents arrive.

I Am Wonderfully Made

Review of Lessons 10–12

Bible Words: "God . . . made us" (Psalm 100:3, *NIV*).

Lesson Value: This lesson is a review of the previous three lessons. The children should be aware of the simple, yet extremely important, fact that the One who made them is God. It is necessary to remind 2's and 3's often that no matter what we look like or how we feel, God loves us. When we work hard to make something, we think it is special and we like it. God feels the same way toward His creation.

Know: Know that God made me.
Feel: Like myself because God made me.
Do: Thank God for different parts of me.

Children will accomplish the goals when they:

1. Say the Bible words, "God made us."
2. Pray, "Thank You, God, for making all the parts of my body."
3. Label and thank God for each body part.
4. Sing songs to thank God for the bodies He made.

Let's Get Ready
For the Bible story, you will need the visuals from the past three lessons: the child's body puzzle (with pieces glued in place), an apple, and the shepherd's scene, with five cotton-ball sheep glued on. Zach should be ready to use.

Set up the Family Living Center, the Music/Drama Center, and the God's Wonders Center. If you are the only teacher, use the Music/Drama Center. The Games Center will be used after the Bible story.

Learning Activities
(30 minutes, including 10 minutes presession)

Let's Get Started
Have Zach greet each child by name as he or she comes in. Shake hands with or hug each child. **We are using our bodies to say hello, Ryan. We know that God made our bodies special.** Guide children toward the learning centers and make sure they all get involved. A child who is just an onlooker will usually cause problems in a short while.

Worship and Bible Story
(15 minutes)

Let's Worship God
Zach can ask the children to straighten up the room. "Let's use our bodies to be helpers." Sing the action song, "Head and Shoulders." Sing "I'm So Happy Today." Do the rhymes, "I'm Me" and "My Eyes, My Ears." Open the Bible and say the Bible words. "Sing "We Thank You, Thank You, God." Then pray, **Thank You, God, for making all the parts of our bodies. Thank You for loving us. We love You.**

Let's Learn From the Bible
Introduction: Zach wants to play a game with you. He will tell you about a person in this room and you can guess who it is.

"Boys and girls, I'm thinking about a boy who has blue eyes and curly black hair. He has freckles on his nose and he wears glasses. Who is it?" After the children guess several names, continue with the lesson. Put Zach away and have your Bible open on your lap.

The Bible-story Review: God made the world. He made trees and flowers and animals. Then God made people to be like Him. The first people were Adam and Eve. *(Show children the completed puzzle.)* Adam and Eve had bodies like ours. God has given us arms and hands, so we can reach and touch. He has also given us legs and feet, so we can stand and walk. (If you have a handicapped child in class, make sure you point out that "God has given Mark strong arms so he can make his wheelchair go," or whatever you can say to make the child feel that God has blessed him in a special way.)

When God made people, He made them with special bodies. *(Hold up the apple.)* He gave us eyes so we can see that this is a red apple. He gave us noses to smell, ears to hear, and fingers to touch. And He gave us tongues so we can taste. *(Demonstrate each action, using the apple. If there is time, cut the apple into slices and give one to each child.)*

When God made our bodies, He made them with feelings. We know about a man in the Bible who had feelings like ours. *(Hold up shepherd's scene.)* David was a shepherd. He felt happy when he took care of his sheep. He felt angry when a lion tried to catch one of his sheep. He felt sad when one of his sheep got hurt. But he felt happy again when all of his sheep were safe at home.

Let's Apply the Lesson
We have learned a lot about our bodies. We know that we are all very special, because God made us and loves us.

Art Center

Unit 3—Learning About Me

Items to Include:

Lesson 10
Butcher paper
Scissors
Masking tape
Washable markers
Rubber bands

Lesson 11
Peanut butter
Powdered milk
Large bowl and spoon

Purpose: The child will know God made everyone and each person is special to Him.

Things to Do and Say

Lesson 10

Roll out and cut the butcher paper into pieces large enough for children to lie on. If the paper curls, tape the edges to the floor with masking tape. Have children lie still on their papers and trace around them with a washable marker.

We just made a picture of your body, Stephanie. Who made your body? The Bible says, "God made us." Let the children use the washable markers (or crayons) to fill in the features on their bodies. **Look at the pictures of your friends. There are some things that are the same. All of you have arms and legs, hands and feet. But do you see some things that are different? Yes, David's legs are longer than Lauren's legs. I'm glad God made us special!** Roll up tracings and secure with rubber bands for taking home.

Lesson 11

For this lesson, make play dough that will affect most of the senses. Mix powdered milk with peanut butter in a large bowl until the play dough is thick enough to handle. Give each child a lump of dough to play with and explore. Children can share plastic knives and cookie cutters. **What does your play dough smell like, Travis? What does it feel**

Game Center

Unit 3—Learning About Me

Items to Include:

Lesson 10
Newspapers
Masking tape
Large paper sacks

Lesson 11
Wind-up alarm clock

Purpose: The children will identify and use their body parts.

Things to Do and Say

Lesson 10

Wad up full sheets of newspaper and wrap masking tape around the wads several times to make balls. Fold down the tops of paper sacks to keep them open.

Let each child have a ball and a sack. Show the children how to stand a few feet away from the sack and throw the ball in the bag. **Brad, you can use your arms and hands to throw the ball in the sack. I'm glad God made our arms and hands, so we can play games. Thank You, God, for making our arms and hands.**

Lesson 11

Before you begin this game, let the children hear the clock ticking. Then set the alarm on the clock for three or four minutes and hide the clock in the room. (The children will need to cover their eyes.) Let the children search for the clock by listening for the ticking.

God gave us ears so we can hear things. Can you hear the clock ticking, Adam? See if you can find it before the alarm goes off. Try the game several times.

Art Center, continued

Plastic sandwich bags
Plastic knives
Cookie cutters
Permanent marker

Lesson 12
Shaving cream
Wet towels

like? Do you like the taste of it? God made our noses to smell, our fingers to touch, and our tongues to taste. Thank You, God, for our fingers (tongues, noses, etc.).

When the children have finished with their play dough, put it in plastic bags for them to take home. Make sure you put the child's name on the bag with a permanent marker, and label it "Peanut Butter Play Dough (edible)" so parents know what it is.

Lesson 12

Put a small amount of shaving cream on the table in front of each child. Encourage children to spread the shaving cream around on the table, then use their fingers to draw faces. You will need to show them how to make an easy happy and sad face.

Sometimes I feel happy and my face has a smile like this. But sometimes I feel sad and I want to frown like this. . . . What makes you feel sad, Donnie? . . . When are you happy, Casey? God knows when we are happy or sad, because He made us. He loves us and we are all special to Him.

Game Center, continued

Lesson 13
Construction paper
Clear, self-adhesive plastic
Masking tape
Tape player
Tape of children's songs

Lesson 13

Cut out ten circles from various colors of construction paper. Each circle should be large enough for one child to stand on. Cover the circles with clear, self-adhesive plastic.

Arrange the circles in a circular pattern on the floor and tape them down. As you play music, the children will walk from circle to circle. **When the music stops I want you to put your elbow (nose, hand, head, etc.) on your circle. God gave us all kinds of special body parts, Lacey!** Children might also use their eyes to identify the colors they stop on.

Music/Drama Center

Unit 3—Learning About Me

Items to Include:

Lessons 10 and 13
- Tape player
- Tape of children's upbeat songs

Lesson 12
- Cardboard harp
- Bathrobe
- Staff (large stick)
- Cardboard blocks

Purpose: The child will use his body to make music and to show his emotions.

Things to Do and Say

Lesson 10

Play the music and practice clapping in time with it. Then let the children decide what other body parts they could use to keep a beat to the music. They might snap their fingers, tap their toes, pat their heads, click their tongues, or a combination of several.

God made your feet, Randi. Can you tap your feet with the music? . . . God made your lips and mouth, Blake. Can you hum with the music? . . . Thank You, God, for making our bodies. And thank You for music that makes us feel good.

Lesson 12

Children can help build a sheep pen from the blocks. Choose one child to be David (he wears the bathrobe and carries the staff), one to be the lion, and the rest will be the sheep. Role play the Bible story, emphasizing the emotions David felt while watching his sheep.

David felt happy when all of his sheep were safe inside their pen. What makes you happy, Dillan? Let children trade roles and act out the story again.

Family Living Center

Unit 3—Learning About Me

Items to Include:

- Dress-up clothes
- Baby dolls
- Strips of cloth for bandages
- Toy doctor's kits
- Mats or cots.

Purpose: The child will learn about the bodies God made.

Things to Do and Say

Lessons 10 and 13

Set up the area as a doctor's office. Let the children choose which role they will play. **Today let's pretend we need to take our babies to the doctor.** Show children how a doctor uses his instruments to check heartbeat and blood pressure, and to give shots. Also, use strips of cloth to bandage arms, legs, hands, and feet.

Grace, let's pretend I hurt my arm. You can be the doctor and bandage it. God has given us doctors to help our bodies feel better when we are hurt or sick. Thank You, God, for doctors who help us feel better. Thank You for our bodies.

Lesson 11

Keep the area set up as a doctor's office. Encourage the children to try different roles (doctor, nurse, patient, patient's mom or dad). Focus more on checking eyes, noses, mouths, and reflexes.

Can you see that picture across the room, Amy? God gave us eyes so we can see. Doctors check our ears and mouths so the bodies God made will stay healthy and strong. Thank You, God, for making our bodies.

Music/Drama Center, continued

Lesson 13

Use this center the same way you did in Lesson 10. Talk more about emotions in order to reinforce the lesson on feelings.

Family Living Center, continued

Lesson 12

Continue to use the area as a doctor's office. This time focus the conversation on how each person might be feeling.

Are you afraid to go to the doctor and get a shot, Katie? . . . It's OK to feel afraid sometimes. God can help us feel brave. . . . Matthew feels sad because his baby doll is sick. God made our feelings. He knows when we feel sad. He can help us to feel happy again.

God's Wonders Center

Unit 3—Learning About Me

Items to Include:

Lessons 11 and 13
Sandpaper
Carpet square
Wool blanket
Foam mat
Tub of water

Lesson 12
Unbreakable hand-held mirrors

Purpose: The child will discover that God made our body parts to do many different things.

Things to Do and Say

Lesson 11 and 13

Line up various items in a row for a "texture walk." The items listed are only suggestions. Use whatever you might have available for the children to walk on. Things chosen should have an interesting or varied texture (smooth, bumpy, rough, soft, etc.) for the children to feel with their feet and toes. Have the children remove their shoes and socks. Walk each child through the "texture walk," pausing at each item briefly so the child can tell you how it feels.

God made our skin so we can touch and feel things. We can use our hands and fingers to touch. And we can also feel things with our feet. How does the blanket feel, Tommy?

Lesson 12

Provide a small unbreakable mirror for each child. Have the children study their faces in the mirrors. As the teacher makes a statement, encourage the children to make a facial expression in reaction to it.

Show me the face you would make if today was your birthday . . . if your mom gave you spinach for lunch . . . if you just got in trouble . . . if your friend hit you . . .

God's Wonders Center, continued

if you were going to the park. Let children suggest some events. **I can tell by your smile that you feel happy about going to the park, Annie. . . . Bobby, you would feel angry if your friend hit you. We know that God gave us our feelings, because our Bible words say, "God made us."**

Boy Puzzle—Spring, Unit 3

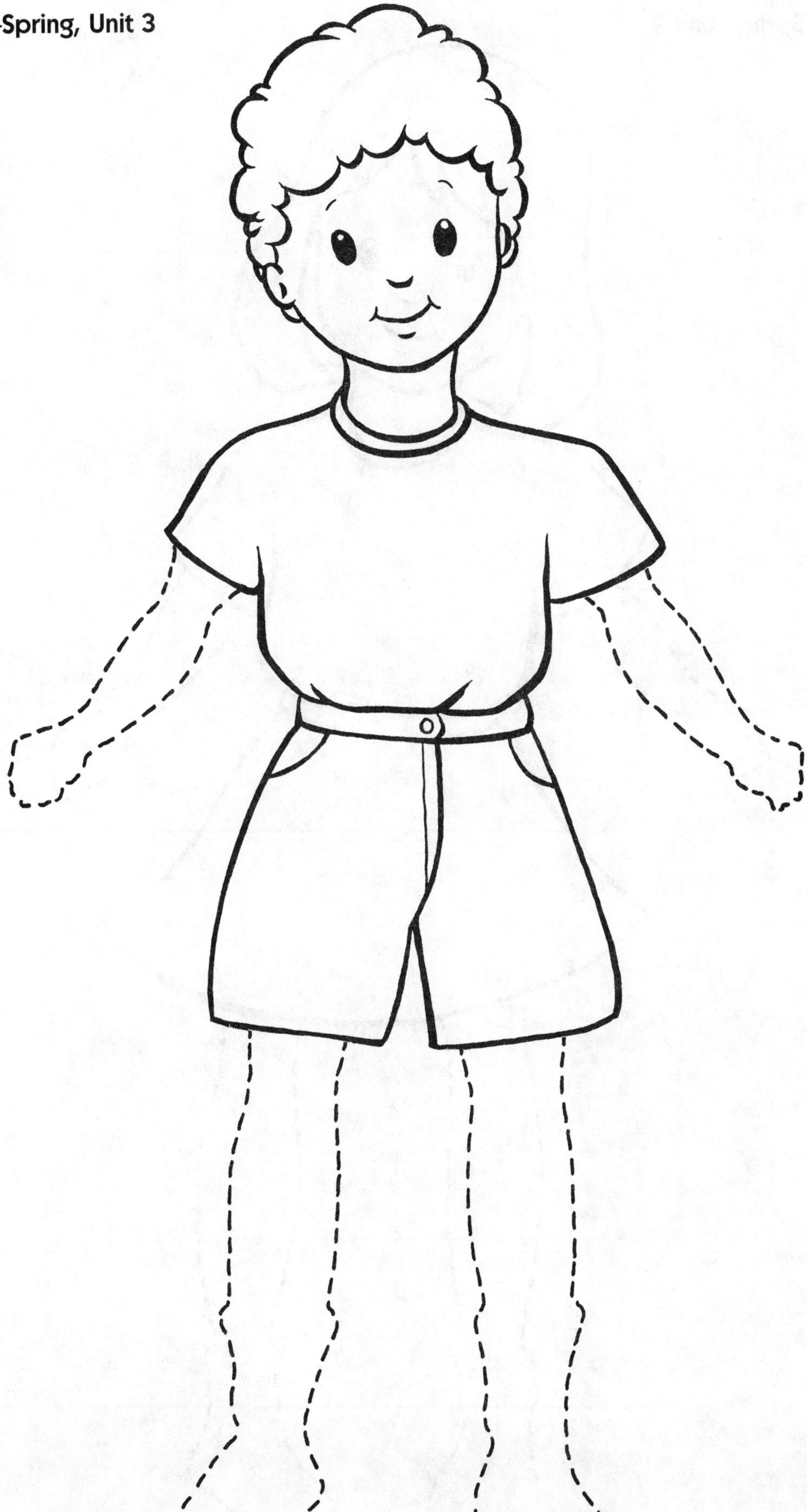

Girl Puzzle—Spring, Unit 3

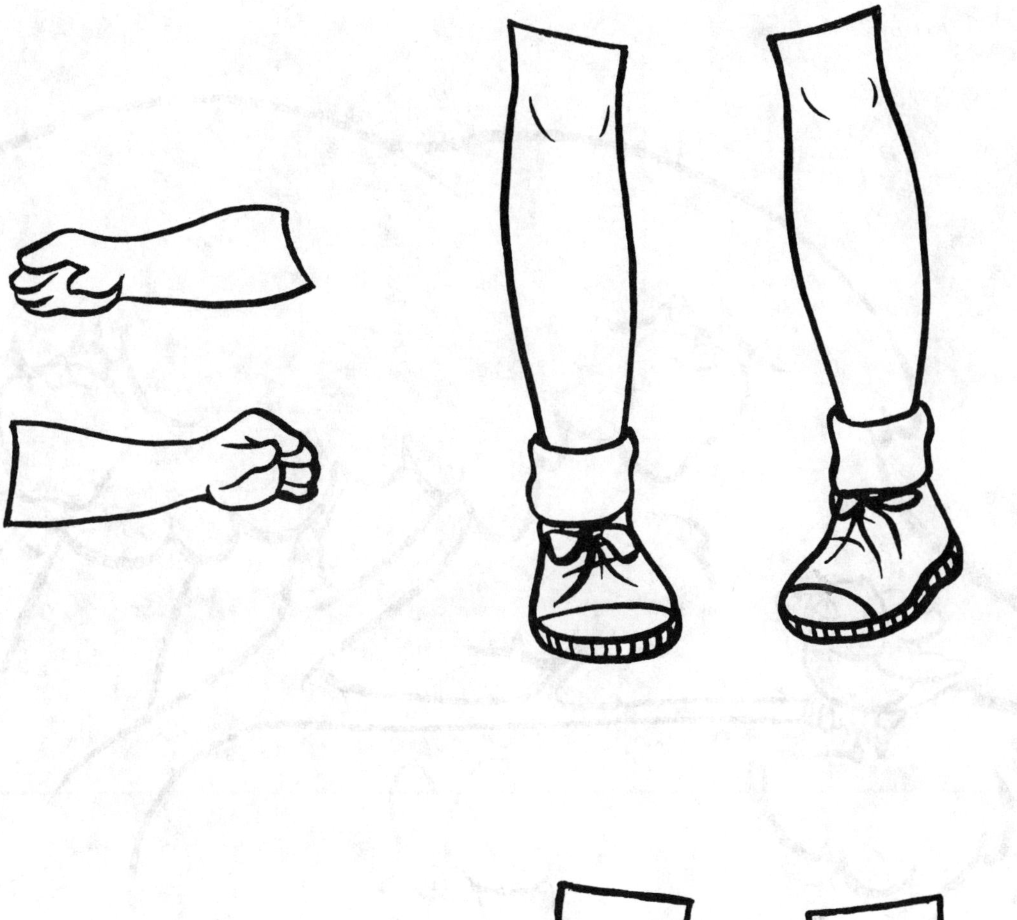

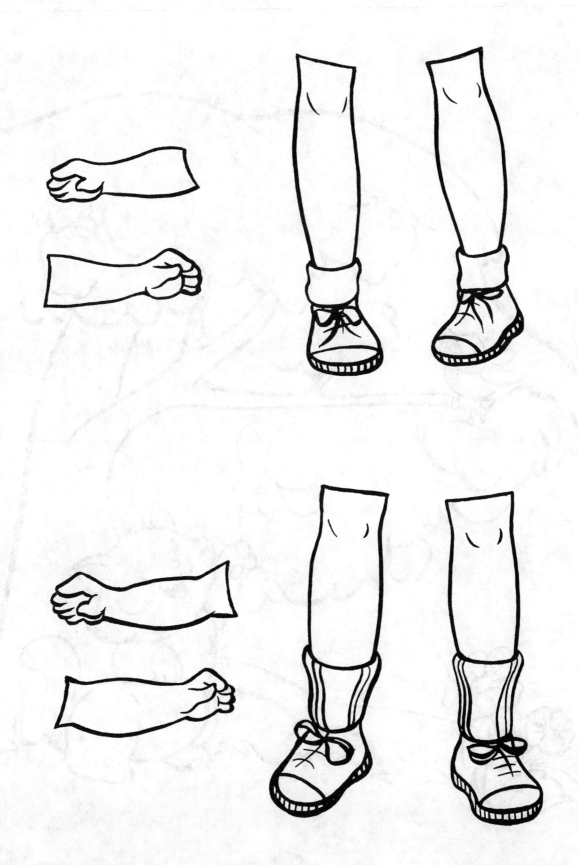

Thank You, God, for ears to hear, eyes to see, a nose to smell, hands to feel, and mouths to taste.

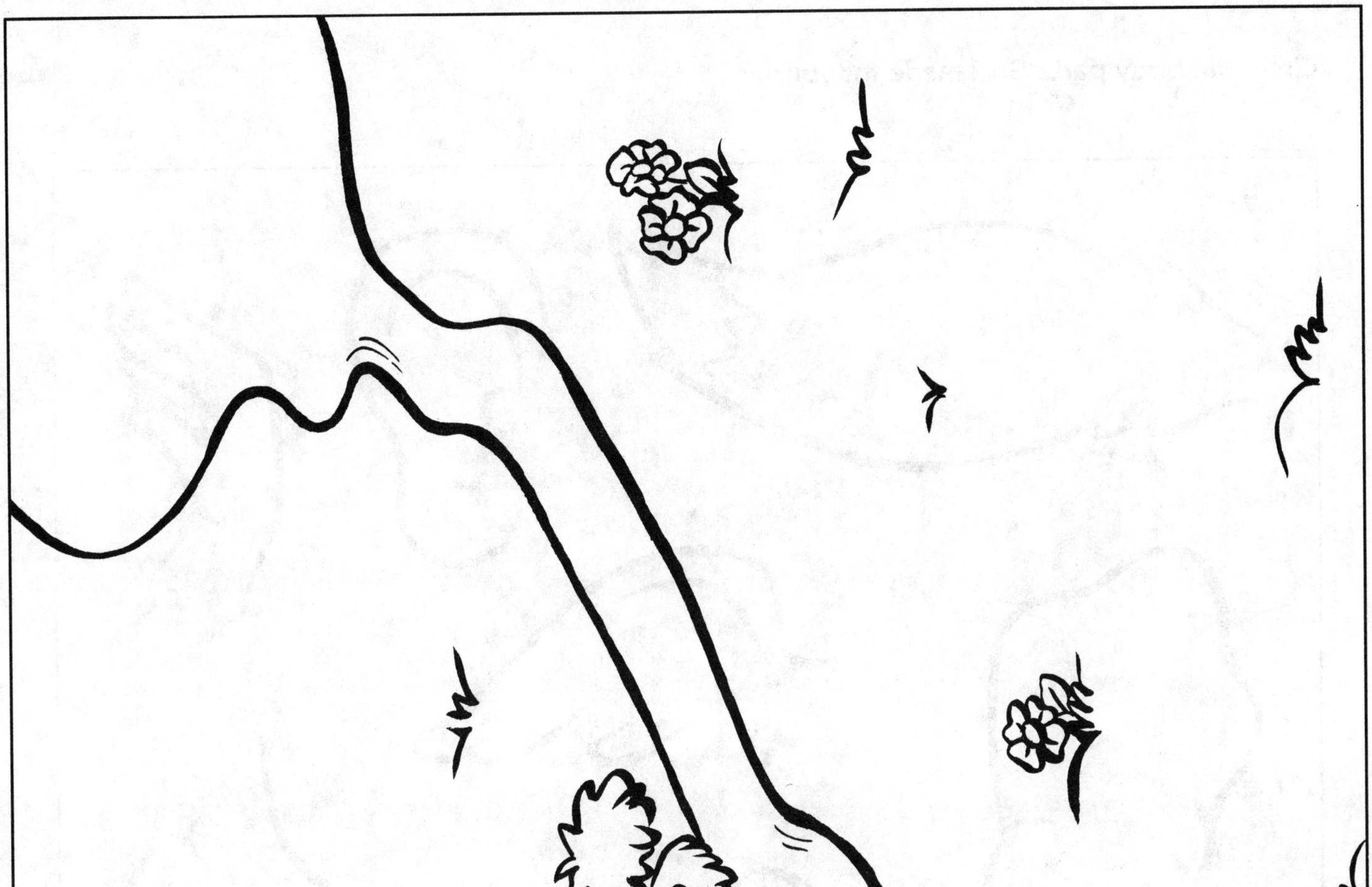

Circle the body parts God made for you.

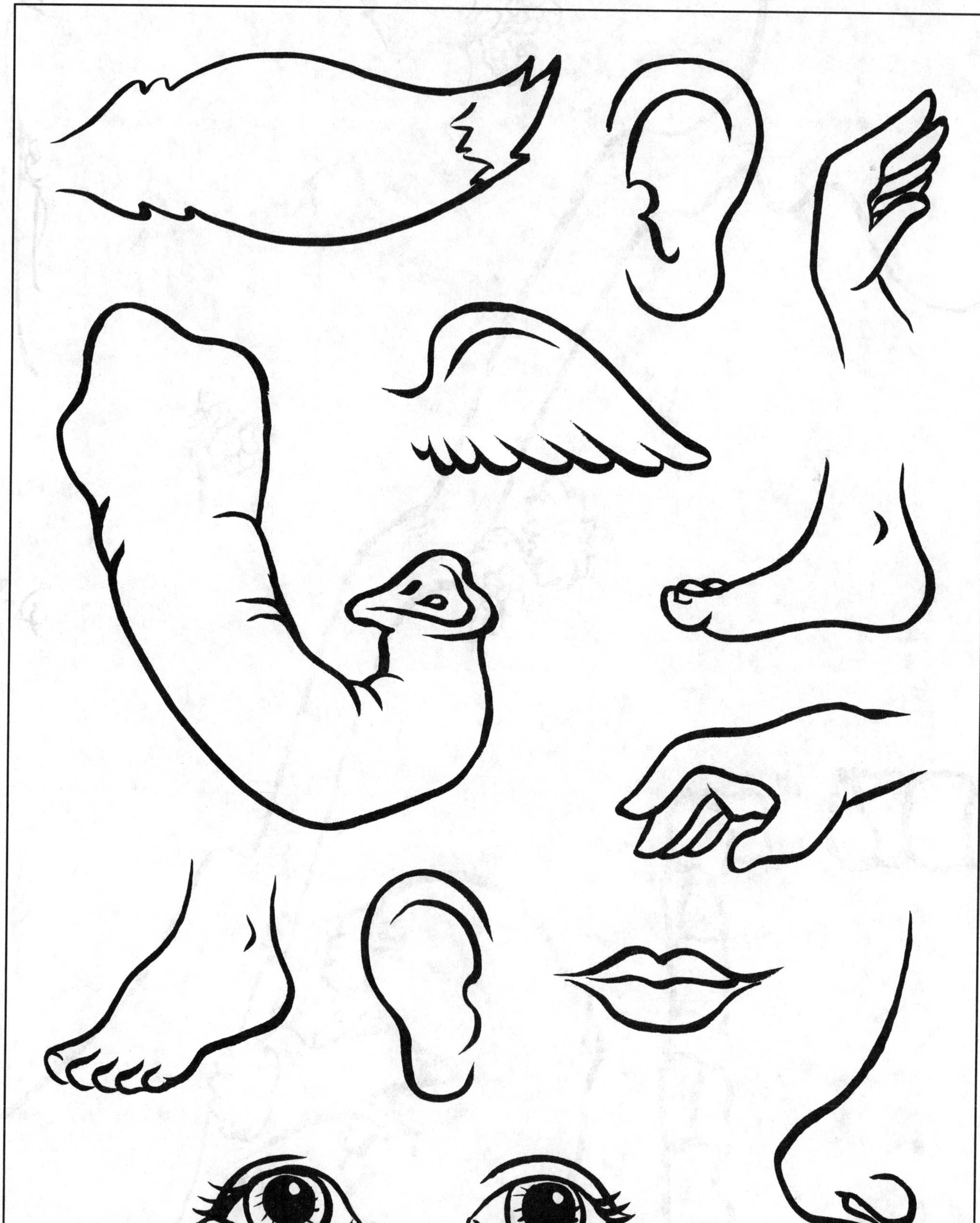

"______________

was wonderfully made

by GOD!"

(from Psalm 139:14)

Dear Parent,

During this unit your child will be learning that God made our bodies. This theme will be developed in these four lessons.

Learning About My Body (Genesis 1; Psalm 139:13-15; Matthew 19:19))
Learning About My Senses (Genesis 1; Psalm 139:13-15; Matthew 19:19)
Learning About My Feelings (1 Samuel 16:11-13, 18; Psalms 23; 31:9, 14, 15; 56:3, 4)
I Am Wonderfully Made (review of previous three lessons)

Our goals for this unit are

- to teach your child that God made each person's body;
- to help your child like himself because God made him special;
- and to encourage your child to thank God for his body.

There are a number of ways that you can reinforce these lesson themes at home with your child.

- Play "Simon Says" with your child and do exercises, focusing on using and identifying various body parts.
- Say the Bible words, "God . . . made us," from Psalm 100:3, with your child daily.
- Encourage your child to look closely at himself or herself in a mirror. Let your child find similarities and differences between herself and you (and/or other family members).
- Make handprints and footprints of you and your child by tracing them or using finger paint. Compare prints and talk about the fact that God made our hands and feet.
- Talk about the five senses. Use them in these ways:
  —Take a walk together and point out everything you see and hear.
  —Do a taste test. Taste something sweet, salty, sour, etc.
  —Have your child guess items in a paper sack by closing her eyes and touching the items in the sack.
  —Do a smelling test. Have your child close his eyes and guess what you hold under his nose.
- Talk about the feelings your child experiences during the week (happiness, sadness, fear, anger).
- Sing this song with your child *(Tune: "London Bridge")*.
  Head and shoulders, knees and toes, knees and toes, knees and toes.
  Head and shoulders, knees and toes. Thank You, God, for making me.
  (Also use "Eyes and ears, nose and mouth.")
- Use this action rhyme with your child.

My Eyes, My Ears

My eyes, my ears, my nose, my mouth,
My hands and feet so small,
My arms, my legs, my tummy, my head—
I know God made them all!
(Point to each part of the body as you name it.)
—*Sylvia Tester*

Sincerely, your child's teacher

Summer Quarter

Learning to Show Our Love for God

Two's and 3's are not too young to learn that if we truly love God, we will desire to know what He says to us. Through the lessons in Unit 1, "Learning From the Bible," your 2's and 3's will learn that the Bible is a special book from God in which He speaks to us. Make sure that you have a classroom Bible that looks like a Bible, that the children can handle (carefully), point to the highlighted words, and "read" with your help. Have the Bible on your lap or at your side as you teach, and wherever you talk to the children. Also have a Bible in each learning center for this unit.

Unit 2, "Talking to God," emphasizes prayer. Some of your children may have learned to pray "prayer rhymes" already, while others have not begun to pray. This unit will give the children many opportunities to express their own feelings and thoughts to God. Your example will encourage the children to do so. Use the words *prayer, praying,* and *talking to God* often during the course of each lesson. And make sure that you take advantage of special moments to incorporate spontaneous prayers into your teaching. Your prayer "attitude" may teach the children more than the lessons you prepare.

"Helping Others," Unit 3, is important to 2's and 3's because they are just becoming aware of the fact that they can do things for others. The children will build self-confidence as well as learn good values. The Bible people in these lessons set good examples of helpfulness. Participating in helpful actions in the classroom will encourage the 2's and 3's to make helping others a part of their lives.

As a result of these lessons, 2's and 3's will

KNOW

Know that the Bible is a special book God gave to us; that God hears us when we pray; and that helping shows we love God.

FEEL

Enjoy using the Bible in various activities; be eager and willing to talk to God; and be happy and eager to help others.

DO

Read and listen to and handle the Bible carefully; pray in many situations and activities; and help in a variety of ways.

Use these songs and action rhymes throughout the quarter, in addition to those specifically mentioned in the units.

I Can Talk to God

G. S. GERTRUDE SHANNON

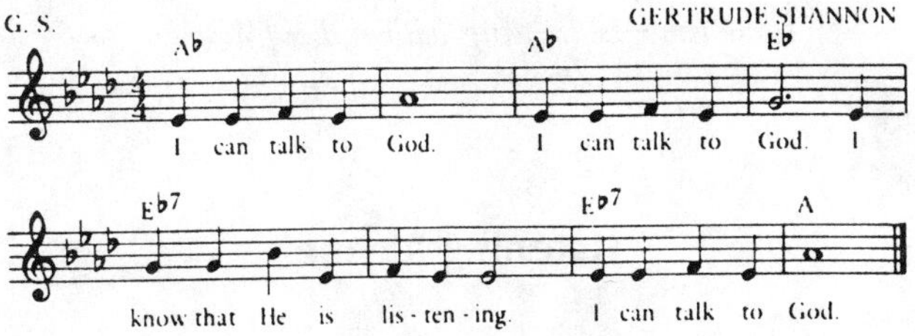

The Marching Song

D. F. R. DOROTHY FAY RICHARDS

Here Is the Bible

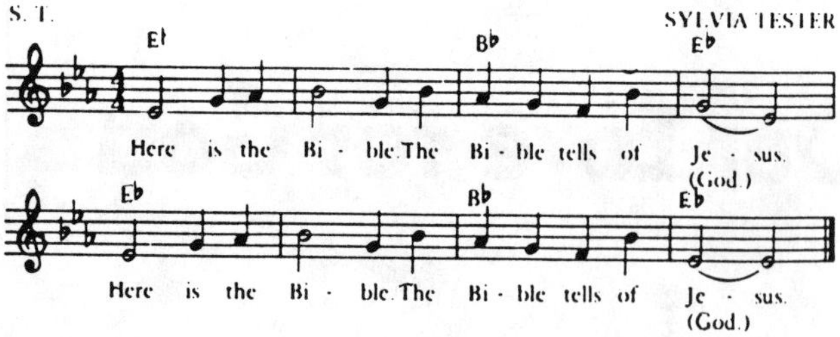

Let's Be Very Quiet

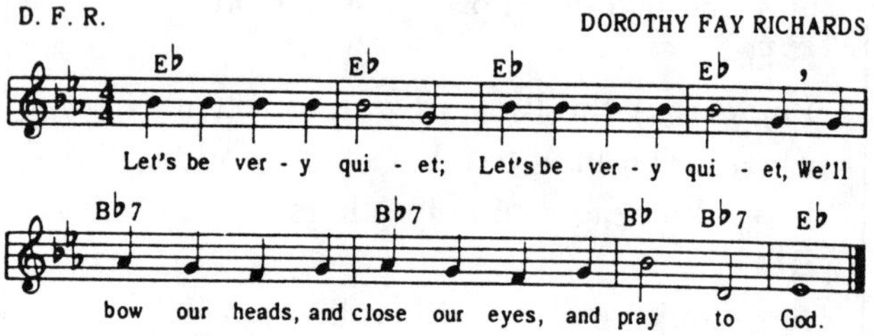

The Busy Fingers

Busy little finger people, *(Hold up fists.)*
Who will put the toys (blocks, etc.) away?
(Look at fists.)
"I will," "I will," "I will," "I will," "I will,"
All the fingers say.
(Raise fingers one at a time, both hands at the same time, beginning with index fingers.)

—*Louise M. Oglevee*

Listening Rhyme

First our feet go tap-tap-tap, *(Tap feet on floor.)*
Then our hands go clap-clap-clap. *(Clap hands.)*
We look with both our eyes,
(Make glasses by circling fingers around eyes.)
We hear with both our ears,
(Cup hands behind ears.)
And then our hands fall in our laps.
(Fold hands in lap.)

—*Dorothy Fay Richards*

Summer Party Suggestions

June—Father's Day Fun

Purpose:	To help the children do something special for dads
When:	During class time or on a Saturday morning or afternoon
Craft:	Take an instant picture of Dad and child and mount on poster board; add a memo pad to the bottom; let child decorate.
Game:	Dress-up relay (use hat, shirt, tie, shoes)
Food:	Sandwich quarters and root beer
Bible Story:	Jacob and Joseph

July—Pool Party

Purpose:	Fun!
When:	During class time or on a Saturday or Sunday afternoon
Activities:	Small wading pools; buckets with water and brushes to "paint" the building; sponge-toss games
Food:	Ice cream cone cupcakes
Bible Story:	Peter Walks on the Water

August—Graduation

Purpose:	To say good-bye to this year's class
When:	During class time or whenever it is convenient for all those involved
Preparation:	Send invitations to moms and dads (children decorate these in class a week before graduation).
Activity:	Make simple hats and diplomas; have a short ceremony with a few songs and action rhymes the children perform for moms and dads.
Game:	Play "Pin the Diploma on the Graduate" (Draw around a child on large paper and fasten to the wall; put circles of tape on the backs of "diplomas.")
Food:	Special cake and punch
Bible Story:	Heaven

Reminder: If you are using the year-round attendance chart, now is the time to purchase *Summer* seals (22-01776—216 seals).

Unit 1: Learning From the Bible

Lessons 1–5

By the end of the unit, the children will

Know that the Bible is a special book God gave us.

Feel happy to use the Bible in various activities.

Read and listen to and handle the Bible carefully.

Unit Bible Words

"Love . . . God" (Mark 12:30).

The Unit at a Glance

1 **Ezra Reads From the Bible** — **Nehemiah 8:1-12**
Ezra reads the law to the people.

2 **Jesus Reads About God** — **Luke 4:14-21**
Jesus reads a prophecy in the synagogue.

3 **Timothy Hears Bible Stories** — **2 Timothy 1:5; 3:15**
Timothy's mother and grandmother teach him Bible stories.

4 **Philip's Friend Learns From the Bible** — **Acts 8:26-40**
Philip talks to the Ethiopian man about the Bible.

5 **I Learn From the Bible** — **Review of Lessons 1–4**
The Bible still teaches us about God just as it taught Bible people.

Why Teach This Unit?

In a recent school discussion on "truth," the teacher made such statements as, "Truth doesn't exist. . . . Truth changes depending on who you are talking to." To that teacher, truth is relative.

This class had come through a system called values clarification that teaches students to determine their own values. While it is good to know what you believe, the system makes a silent statement that truth is up to the individual. Right and wrong are not something you are taught, but something you choose. Our personal sense of values replaces God's Law.

Despite what people believe, however, God's law doesn't change. There is a source of truth, and it is revealed to us in God's Word. Children need to recognize at an early age that the Bible is our authority and is to be respected.

Place a Bible in each learning center, and use it during story time and while you work on the Bible words (memory verses). Highlight or underline the words and keep a bookmark at that place. Refer to the Bible often during guided conversation. Point to the words in your Bible so that the children can see where they come from.

Explain to the children that you learn to love someone as you get to know the person. The Bible helps us to love God as we learn more about Him. Bible people also learned to love God by reading and hearing about Him.

Things to Do for This Unit:

- Make copies of Parents' Letter (page 265).
- Photocopy the Learning Center Cards (pages 251-256); cut pages apart on solid lines. Mount side 1 of a card on cardboard; then mount side 2 on back of cardboard. Laminate for durability.
- Gather/prepare materials listed on the Learning Center Cards.
- Photocopy the teaching pictures (pages 261-264); add color and mount on cardboard or large construction paper. These pictures also can be made into coloring pages.
- Make a scroll for Lesson 1. See Book and Picture Center for directions.
- Purchase or find children's books about the Bible. Also have Bible storybooks.

Use These Songs and Action Rhymes During Unit 1

We Read the Bible

(Tune: "The Farmer in the Dell")

_____* reads her Bible.
Yes, ____* reads her Bible.
She reads her Bible every day.
Yes ____* reads her Bible.
*(*Insert each child's name in the blank as you sing around the circle.)*

I Love God

(Tune: "Are You Sleeping?")

I love God. I love God. Yes, I do. Yes, I do.
The Bible says to love Him. *(Repeat.)*
And I do. And I do.

Every Day

(Tune: "This Old Man")

Every day, on my way.
I will read God's book and say,
"The Bible shows me what our God can do."
And it says, "He loves me too!"

When I Pray

When I pray, I fold my hands *(Fold hands.)*
And close my eyes; *(Close eyes.)*
I think about God, and He hears me. *—Jean Katt*

God Gave Me a Special Book

(Tune: "London Bridge")

God gave me a special book.*
Special book. Special book.
God gave me a special book.
The Bible is its name.

*It teaches me to love our God.

Clean Up Song

(Tune: "Mulberry Bush")

It's time to put our things away,
things away, things away.
It's time to put our things away,
And run to get our Bibles.

My Bible

This is my Bible;
(Hands held out in front, palms together.)
I'll open it wide
(Open hands, but keep them touching.)
And see (or say) what is written on the inside!
(Say the Bible words together.)

—Jean Baxendale

and you could hardly wait to open it? Maybe it was a special letter from your grandma or grandpa or a friend. Allow the children to respond. **That's exciting isn't it! God has sent us a very special letter called the Bible. In it He tells us about himself and how much He loves us. When we read this exciting book, we feel happy. We learn to know God better and to love Him. The Bible says, "Love God."** Have the children look at the words in your Bible and repeat the Bible verse.

Learning Activities

(20 minutes)

Let's Play Awhile

Sing the following words to "God Gave Me a Special Book" (tune: "London Bridge"):

Ezra read a special book, special book, special book.
Ezra read a special book. The Bible was its name.

They listened to the special book, special book, special book.
They listened to the special book. The Bible was its name.

It taught them how to love their God, love their God,
love their God.
It taught them how to love their God. The Bible was its name.

Have the children sit in a circle and play "Book, Book, Bible," from the Game Center Card. If you have two teachers, form several circles or repeat one of the previous learning centers.

Let's Go Home

As his parents arrive, gently tap a child on the shoulder and lead him to the door while the other children continue to play. Make sure each child has his picture from the Art Center and a copy of the Parents' Letter.

Ezra Reads From the Bible

Nehemiah 8:1-12

Bible Words: "Love . . . God" (Mark 12:30).

Lesson Value: Preschoolers are interested in communication processes. The mail, telephone, radio, tape recorder, etc., are all still amazing things at this age, and every preschooler is thrilled to be the recipient of communication.

Communication takes several things—someone who wants to send a message, the message itself, and a person who receives the message. In the story of Ezra, we witness the fact that God (the message sender) gives His message (the Bible) to a group of eager listeners (the receivers).

God still wants to communicate today—with your preschoolers. This is a great opportunity to make young minds realize that they are so important to God that He wants to know them and have them know Him.

Know: Know that the Bible is a special book God gave us.
Feel: Feel happy to use the Bible in various activities.
Do: Read and listen to and handle the Bible carefully.

Children will accomplish the goals when they:

1. Say the Bible words, "Love God."
2. Pray, "Thank You, God, for our Bible."
3. Use a Bible in the classroom.
4. Sing about the Bible.
5. State that the Bible is a special book.

Let's Get Ready

You will need a Bible in each center. For the Bible story, you will need the picture from page 261, a Bible-scroll, and the Zach puppet.

Prepare the Art Center, the Book Center, and the Block Center. If you are the only teacher, use just the Art Center. The Game Center will be used after the Bible story. See pages 251-256 for the Learning Center Cards.

Learning Activities

(30 minutes, including 10 minutes presession)

Let's Get Started

Welcome time is very important because 2's and 3's are often anxious about leaving Mom and Dad. The children will feel more secure if there is a familiar person at the door who calls them by name while touching them on the arm or shoulder. Take a few moments to talk with each child. Church should be a safe, secure place where love is experienced as well as talked about. Taking a moment to notice the child and his or her feelings and to describe what is going to happen in class will help to reassure him or her. Use Zach to do some of this. He should already be a friend. Give the child a choice between two learning centers, and make sure each child becomes involved in an activity.

Worship and Bible Story

(15 minutes)

Let's Worship God

Use the "Clean Up Song" to signal the children that it is time to get ready for worship. Sing songs from the unit introduction as the children begin to join you in the circle. Use the action rhyme, "When I Pray," then pray, **Thank You, God, for giving us the Bible.**

Let's Learn From the Bible

Introduction: Let's play a game to see how well you can pay attention. I'm going to tell a story and do some motions with my body at the same time. I want you to watch and listen and do exactly what I do.

Practice by doing silly motions so that the children learn to mirror what you do. Now put Zach aside and hold your Bible in your lap. Have the teaching picture and scroll ready to show.

The Bible Story: If you were a boy or girl in Israel a long time ago, you would have seen a very special day. Your mother would have gotten you out of bed early in the morning. You would have hurried through breakfast *(pretend to eat)* and then, off you would have gone until you saw a large gate in a very big wall *(put your hands over your eyes to look).*

You might sit down on the cold ground *(shiver and hug yourself)* and wait for the sun to come up. And you wouldn't be alone! *(Put hands over eyes and look.)* You would see *(say these as fast as you can)* —mothers and fathers and sisters and brothers, aunts and uncles and cousins and friends. There were *(use your hands)* tall people, short people, fat people, skinny people. Some were excited and some were quite shy. And everyone would be looking at a man named Ezra. *(Point to Ezra in the teaching picture.)* Ezra unrolled a piece of paper *(unroll the scroll),* but this wasn't just any paper! All the people had come because Ezra was going to read from God's special book—the Bible-scroll!

Ezra read God's words. He read about what God wanted the people to do. The people listened. They wanted to hear every word God was saying to them. They were happy to hear God's words from the Bible-scroll.

Let's Apply the Lesson

How did the people feel when they heard Ezra read from the Bible-scroll? Yes, they were happy. Why were they happy? They were hearing God's words, weren't they!

Did you ever get a letter or maybe a package in the mail,

with me? "Love God." Let the children hold the Bible and "read" the words.

Learning Activities

(20 minutes)

Let's Play Awhile

Have the children sing "God Gave Me a Special Book" as they did in Lesson 1, substituting "Jesus" for "Ezra." Then guide the children to the Art Center. Remember to use paint shirts and washable paint. If you have time, let the children act out the Bible story using the box and your scroll as props.

Let's Go Home

Sing the "Clean Up Song," from page 240, as the children pick up.

You may want to have the children sing "God Gave Me a Special Book" again as parents arrive. If you did the Music Center, you can use the scarves or instruments as you sing.

Jesus Reads About God

Luke 4:14-21

Bible Words: "Love . . . God" (Mark 12:30).

Lesson Value: This story shows the uniqueness of the Bible and its importance in our lives. The Bible was so special that Jesus, himself, took the time to read and teach from it. He often quoted from it as the source of authority on what was right and wrong.

Young children need to realize that they must do the right thing, not just because Mommy or Daddy or a teacher or a friend says it is right, but because God says it is right. He tells us what is right in the Bible. People may be wrong, but we can always go to the Bible to know what God says.

Know: Know that the Bible is a special book God gave us.
Feel: Feel happy to use the Bible in various activities.
Do: Read and listen to and handle the Bible carefully.

Children will accomplish the goals when they:

1. Say the Bible words, "Love God."
2. Pray, "Thank You, God, for the Bible."
3. Sing about the Bible.
4. Use a Bible in the classroom.
5. Name or point to Jesus and the scroll in the teaching picture.

Let's Get Ready

For the Bible story, you will need a Bible, the scroll made last week, and the teaching picture from page 262.

Set up the Book Center, the Block Center, and the Music Center. If you are the only teacher, use just the Book Center. The Art Center should be ready for use after the Bible story.

Learning Activities

(30 minutes, including 10 minutes presession)

Let's Get Started

Have Zach greet each child by name. Ask a child about her day, new shoes, anything that helps her to feel that this is a good, safe place to be where people are interested in her. Guide the child to the learning centers. **Which center would you like to start with, Brittany? Would you like to sing some songs, or build with the blocks?**

Worship and Bible Story

(15 minutes)

Let's Worship God

Use the "Clean Up Song" to signal to the children that it is time to put everything away and come to worship. Praise them in between stanzas for the good job they are doing. **Josh is picking up the paper on the floor. Thank you for being a good helper. Zach and I see many helpers!** Have Zach touch each child on the shoulder and mention her by name as she helps. Then sit in the circle and begin your music time as the children come. Pray, **Thank You, God, for giving us the Bible.**

Let's Learn From the Bible

Introduction: Have the children stand up and start walking in place as you begin to talk. Move your arms like a jogger so that you appear to be in a hurry. **Do you know where I'm going in such a hurry? My name is Ruth (or Joab) and I live in a city called Nazareth. Today a special person is coming to our town. His name is Jesus. Have you heard of Him? Everyone for miles around is talking about Him! They say He makes sick people well. And you should hear Him when He talks! He tells the best stories! At least that's what people say. Whoa! I'm tired. It's a good thing we're at the synagogue. This is where Jesus is coming to teach. Maybe we could sit down and wait for Him.** Sit down and place your Bible in your lap. Have the teaching picture and scroll handy.

The Bible Story: Do you think people might have talked like that the day Jesus came to town? The Bible says that they were very excited about Jesus coming. When Jesus came to their city, He went to the synagogue, a place like our church building, where people went to learn about God.

Do you know what Jesus did first? He didn't talk to His friends and He didn't walk around. He went to the front of the room and took a Bible-scroll, something like this one. *(Hold up your scroll.)* The Bible-scroll had God's words written on it. Jesus stood up and read the words from God's special Bible-scroll, and *all* the people listened. No one talked. No one even whispered. And no one looked away. They all listened as Jesus read God's words. *(Show the teaching picture. Have the children point to Jesus and to the Bible-scroll He is reading.)*

Let's Apply the Lesson

People in Bible times didn't have books. Instead, they had scrolls—long rolls something like this. Show the children your scroll and allow them to pass it around and look at it. **Then they could unroll it and read their favorite Bible story. Do you have a favorite Bible story? Mine is ________. It is good to read God's words on a scroll or in a book like the Bible I have in my lap. I can use my Bible to read words like our Bible words, "Love . . . God." Can you say those words**

that has so many terrific stories in it! Thank You, God, for giving us the Bible, Your Word.

Let the children help you retell the story. Have them take turns pointing to the Bible-scroll and pointing to and/or naming Timothy.

Learning Activities

(20 minutes)

Let's Play Awhile

Have materials ready for the Art Center. Children will complete their projects at different times, depending on their interest level and abilities. Have the Game Center ready to use in case some children finish early. You also may want to keep a supply of Bible picture books available for the children to look at once they've finished.

Let's Go Home

Allow Zach to remind the children that they need to pick up materials and help the teachers clean up the tables.

Make sure the children take their scrolls and their Bible cards home with them.

Timothy Hears Bible Stories

2 Timothy 1:5; 3:15

Bible Words: "Love . . . God" (Mark 12:30).

Lesson Value: The story of Timothy is one that tells the message that God wants to speak to children. God loves children and wants them to learn about Him and talk to Him, just as He wants to talk to them.

This story also offers an opportunity to stress the fact that the Bible is enjoyable. It is full of adventure stories that appeal to minds of all ages. Timothy's grandmother and mother enjoyed teaching him as much as he must have looked forward to learning. Who wouldn't enjoy the story of David and Goliath or the saga of Noah on a pitching sea? Emphasize to your children that the Bible holds many surprises and exciting hours of reading. Help them begin a habit that they will enjoy for a lifetime.

Know: Know that the Bible is a special book God gave us.
Feel: Feel happy to use the Bible in various activities.
Do: Read and listen to and handle the Bible carefully.

Children will accomplish the goals when they:

1. Say the Bible words, "Love God."
2. Pray, "Thank You, God for the Bible."
3. Name or point to Timothy in the teaching picture.
4. Use a Bible in the classroom.
5. Sing about the Bible.

Let's Get Ready

For the Bible story, you will need your classroom Bible, a Bible picture book, the teaching picture from page 263, and a paper bag with the following items in it: big mixing spoon, plastic bowl, toy hammer, pet bowl, toy broom, dust cloth, sponge, etc.

Set up the Book and Picture Center, the Game Center, and the Family Living Center. If you are the only teacher, use just the Family Living Center now. Have the Art Center ready for use after the Bible story.

Learning Activities

(30 minutes, including 10 minutes presession)

Let's Get Started

Greet each child by name as he arrives. Take time to ask about his week or significant events going on in his life. Help visitors feel comfortable by introducing them to other children and teachers. Describe the centers and allow the children to choose ones that interest them.

Worship and Bible Story

(15 minutes)

Let's Worship God

Use the "Clean Up Song" again this week. Once all the children are seated, begin singing songs from this unit, found on page 240. Do an action rhyme or sing an action song, then do the rhyme, "When I Pray," and then have prayer. **Thank You, God, for giving us the Bible. Help us always to read it.**

Let's Learn From the Bible

Introduction: Have each child take a turn picking an object out of your paper bag and telling how he or she would use it at home to help. Include these items in the story, and have the children demonstrate how Timothy might have used them as they hear them named.

Do you like to do things around the house with your mommy and daddy? You probably like to bake cakes or water the garden or feed your pet. Boys and girls usually like to help. That's true today, and it was true a long time ago, in Bible times.

The Bible Story: The Bible tells us about a young boy named Timothy. Timothy lived with his mother and his grandmother. He probably liked doing some of the same things you like to do. Maybe he liked to help his mother make bread. Perhaps he helped her make butter sometimes.

Timothy probably had to sweep the floor every day for his mother. Maybe he even had to feed the animals.

When the day's work was done, most families sat on the flat roofs of their houses and told stories. The stories Timothy's mother and grandmother told him were very special ones, because they came from the big Bible-scroll. Timothy heard about David and Moses, and about Noah floating in the big ark-boat. The stories were all exciting and true! They came from God's book. When Timothy heard the stories, he knew that God was very great. He learned to love God. *(Show the teaching picture.)*

We can read those same stories in our Bible. The stories are still exciting and true. The Bible also teaches us to love God. Our Bible words are, "Love God." Can you say those Bible words with me? "Love God."

Let's Apply the Lesson

Do you ever read stories out of your Bible with your mommy or daddy, or one of your grandparents? . . . How do you like to read stories? Do you like to curl up on a couch or rock in the rocker when you read? How many of you like to hear stories at bedtime? . . . What do you think was Timothy's favorite story? . . . Isn't it wonderful that God gave us a book

Who did the man in the chariot read about? Jesus! That's right! I'm sure the man was glad that he had ears to hear about Jesus. I'm also sure that Philip was glad he had a mouth to tell about Jesus. Have the children point to the man who used his ears to hear and to the man who used his mouth to tell.

Who could you tell about Jesus? Help the children think of people—mom and dad, grandparents, friends at nursery/day care, playmates, and so forth. **I'm so glad God has given us a special book that teaches us to love Him. Let's say our Bible words, "Love God."** Let the children take turns holding the Bible and "reading" the highlighted words.

Learning Activities

(20 minutes)

Let's Play Awhile

Have materials ready for the Family Living Center. This activity gives the children a chance to learn through several of their senses—sight, touch, smell, and taste, which is the way they learn best. If there is extra time, have the children color copies of the visual from the story (page 264).

Let's Go Home

Put away any materials. If the children did not do the coloring page, give each child a copy to take home, along with the craft. Suggest that they use their pictures to tell the story to others.

Philip's Friend Learns From the Bible

Acts 8:26-40

Bible Words: "Love . . . God" (Mark 12:30).

Lesson Value: This lesson shows that the message of the Bible is something to share. Preschoolers are the world's worst keepers of secrets. Just let them discover what someone's Christmas gift is and the secret's out of the bag! Good news, bad news, and things you would rather your hairdresser didn't know are soon spread over the neighborhood. Preschoolers are a journalist's dream! So, take advantage of this age and show them how they can share something really special—the good news of Jesus Christ! Even the youngest child can tell a simple story or talk about a friend. In the story of Philip the children can see an example of someone else who just couldn't keep the good news inside.

Know: Know that the Bible is a special book God gave us.
Feel: Feel happy to use the Bible in various activities.
Do: Read and listen to and handle the Bible carefully.

Children will accomplish the goals when they:

1. Say the Bible words, "Love God."
2. Pray, "Thank You, God for giving us the Bible."
3. Sing about the Bible
4. Use the Bible in the classroom.
5. Name or point to Philip and to his friend in the teaching picture.

Let's Get Ready

For the Bible story, you will need your Bible and the teaching picture from page 264.

Set up the Art Center, the Block Center, and the Music Center. If you are the only teacher, use just the Block Center. Prepare the Family Living Center for after the Bible story.

Learning Activities

(30 minutes, including 10 minutes presession)

Let's Get Started

Have Zach help you greet each child. "Hello, Michael. Boy, am I excited about what we are going to talk about today!" Say, **I promised Zach that we were going to talk about cars and trucks and chariots. He has ridden in cars and trucks but never in a chariot. Which center would you like to start with, the Block Center or the Music Center?**

Worship and Bible Story

(15 minutes)

Let's Worship God

Sing the "Clean Up Song" as you pick up in the learning centers. Have Zach send children to the worship time as they finish cleaning up. After the children are seated sing songs from the unit. End with prayer. **Thank You, God, for giving us the Bible, and for giving us mouths to tell other people about You.**

Let's Learn From the Bible

Introduction: What is your favorite way to travel? Do you like cars? How about a plane? Some of us have ridden on bicycles or wagons. We may have ridden in vans or trucks, but none of us has ever ridden in a chariot! Show the coloring picture of the chariot. **In Bible times, a chariot was used for traveling. It had two wheels and was pulled by a horse. You had to be rich or very important to have a chariot. Otherwise, you used these.** Point to your feet.

Show me how fast your feet go. Run in place. **Do you think your feet could help you catch up to a chariot? I know about someone whose feet did! I'll tell you the story and every time I say "chariot," you make your hands go around like wheels.** Practice doing this. **Whenever I say "feet," you make your feet move like they are running.** Practice once or twice. Put Zach away and place your Bible on your lap.

The Bible Story: The Bible tells us about a man who came from far away. He was an important man, so he had a chariot. While he was riding, he was trying to read God's book, the Bible. He was having a hard time, because he was reading about Jesus, and he had never heard about Jesus before. He needed help, so God helped him.

God sent a man named Philip to teach him. Now Philip was not a rich man. He didn't have a chariot, but he did have his feet, and he wanted to teach about Jesus. So, when God told him to go, Philip used his feet and began to run. He ran through the desert area, over a hill, and down the road. And when the important man looked down from his chariot, he saw Philip running beside him on very fast feet.

"Do you understand what you are reading?" asked Philip.

"No," said the man in the chariot. "I need someone to teach me."

So Philip climbed up into the chariot and taught his new friend about Jesus. *(Show the teaching picture.)*

Let's Apply the Lesson

Isn't it good that God gave Philip such fast feet so he could catch up with the man to teach him about the Bible. God gave us eyes to read the Bible. What else does He give us to help us learn? (Ears to hear the story, a mouth to tell the story and ask questions.)

which ones we liked best. If you are not teaching the next unit, tell about this to the teacher who is teaching.

Learning Activities

(20 minutes)

Let's Play Awhile

To further review all the stories, play the "What's Missing?" game. If the children need more physical action now, hide the halves of the game around the room ahead of time and have them hunt for the pieces before playing the game.

Let's Go Home

Have Zach touch each child on the shoulder and tell him, "Good-bye, Jeffrey. I'll be looking forward to hearing about your favorite story next week." Explain to the parents that the children are going to try to read a Bible story every day. Make sure the children have their crafts to take home.

I Learn From the Bible

Review of Lessons 1–4

Bible Words: "Love . . . God" (Mark 12:30).

Lesson Value: This lesson puts the unit all together. It is a chance to review how God wants to communicate with us, and how He has given us a special, unique book that is our source of authority on matters of right and wrong. It also offers another opportunity to discuss how God feels about children and how much He loves them. Lastly, it is an opportunity to talk about ways to share what we know about God with others. Use this time as an overview of the unit. It is a last chance to correct wrong impressions and make some lasting ones.

Know: Know that the Bible is a special book God gave us.
Feels: Feel happy to use the Bible in various activities.
Do: Read and listen to and handle the Bible carefully.

Children will accomplish the goals when they:
1. Say the Bible words, "Love God."
2. Pray, "Thank You, God, for the Bible."
3. Sing about the Bible.
4. Use the Bible in the classroom.
5. Identify pictures of those who read God's Word.

Let's Get Ready

For the Bible story you will need a Bible, a scroll, and the pictures from Lessons 1-4.

Set up the Art Center, the Book Center, and the Block Center. If you are the only teacher, use just the Art Center. After the Bible story, do the review game in the Game Center.

Learning Activities

(30 minutes, including 10 minutes presession)

Let's Get Started

Have Zach greet each child by name as he or she arrives. With Zach on your hand, stoop down so that you have eye contact with the child. This is a nonverbal way of saying that the child has your full attention because she is important to you. **I'm glad to see that you brought your Bible, Jenny. God's book is very important. We're going to talk about it today. Where do you want to go first, the Art Center or the Block Center?**

Worship and Bible Story

(15 minutes)

Let's Worship God

Have the children sing the "Clean Up Song" as they pick up. Let Zach send the children to the worship area. Sing songs from this unit and end with prayer. **Dear God, thank You for the Bible, and thank You for teaching us to "love God" like the Bible says.**

Let's Learn From the Bible

Introduction: Lay the scroll and a Bible down in the story circle. **Who can tell me what these are? Great. Which one did they use in Bible times? That's right, a Bible-scroll. How do you open a scroll? Can you pretend to do that with me? Show me how you would open your Bible. Today, we are going to look at stories with Bible-scrolls or Bibles in them. Instead of telling you which one was read, I am going to stop when I get to the word and have you show me which one you think it was.**

The Bible-story Review: *(Show the appropriate picture at the end of each review.)* The first story we studied was about Ezra. God told Ezra to gather all the people and read God's words. Ezra had all the people stand in front of the temple. All day long they listened as Ezra read from the ________.

One day, Jesus came to town. Everyone was very excited to hear Him! The people came and sat down in the synagogue. Jesus stood up in front and read to them from a ________.

Timothy's mother and grandmother told Timothy stories about God while they were working together or talking in the evenings. Timothy liked to hear Bible stories. His mother and grandmother read God's words to him from the ________.

God sent Philip to the desert where a chariot was going down the road. He could see a man in the chariot who was reading a ________. Philip had to run hard to catch up, but he did! He asked the man if he understood what was written on the ________. The Ethiopian man asked Philip to teach him, so Philip got in the chariot and taught the man about Jesus.

Every day God wants us to listen to Him. One of the ways we can do that is to take out our ________ and read God's words!

Let's Apply the Lesson

Which of the stories we studied today did you like best? I think my favorite is the one about Philip because he not only read the Bible, he also shared it with someone else. There are so many exciting stories! . . . I'm sure there is someone in your family who would enjoy reading those stories too. Do you think you could find someone who would read a story with you every day this week? See if your mom or dad or sister or grandfather will read stories with you. Next week we'll tell

Book/Picture Center

Unit 1—Learning From the Bible

Items to Include:

Bible
Crayons
Yarn

Lesson 1
Toy telephones
Stamped, addressed envelopes
A newspaper
Paper
Radio
Books
Tape recorder

Lesson 2
Bible storybooks
Bible story

Purpose: The child will know that the Bible is a special book God gave us.

Things to Do and Say

Lesson 1

Display the various means of communication you have gathered. Introduce the children to the books, including the Bible. Have the Bible words highlighted and the page identified with a bookmark.

There are many ways to tell people things you want them to know. Point out the letter and the telephone. **There are also many ways for us to learn things.** Show the tape recorder, the radio, and the newspaper. Then hold up the Bible. **God uses the Bible to tell us things we need to know. The Bible is a special book God gave us. One of the things the Bible tells us is to "love God." Those are our Bible words. Can you say them with me?**

Lesson 2

Have several Bible storybooks available for the children to look at and to have read to them. Also, have a magnetic photo album along with Bible pictures you have cut from old take-home papers and worn-out books that are no longer being used. Trim these pictures and have them ready for the children to put into the photo album. Label the album, "Our Bible Storybook."

Which book would you like to read, Brian? Good. I like that one too. It is about baby

Art Center

Unit 1—Learning From the Bible

Items to Include:

Paint shirts
Pie plates
Construction paper
Tagboard

Lesson 1
Patterns (257)

Lesson 2
Large appliance box
Small, square sponges
Brown tempera paint

Purpose: The child will learn that the Bible is the special book God gave us.

Things to Do and Say

Lesson 1

Follow the instructions on page 257 to prepare materials.

Ask a child, **Why are these people happy? Can you think of a reason everyone is smiling? What is Ezra holding? Yes, a Bible-scroll. Are you happy when it is time to read the Bible? The Bible is a special book that God gave us.**

Lesson 2

Cut a large door and window in the box. Have newspapers under the box. Pour a small amount of paint in a pie plate. Show the children how to dip the sponge and scrape off excess paint, then print bricks on the "church building."

What did we make today? Yes, a church building. What special book do we read here? Yes, the Bible is the special book God gave us. Let's go inside our church building and read a story from the Bible. Where could you read the Bible at home?

Lesson 3

Follow instructions on page 258 to prepare materials.

Who was excited about reading the Bible in our story today? Timothy! The Bible is the special book God gave us. Thank You, God, for the Bible. What stories would

Book/Picture Center, continued

pictures
Magnetic photo
album

Lesson 3
Dowel rods
Paper
Tape

Lesson 5
Large-brimmed hat
Paper punch
Patterns from pages 259 and 260
Tagboard

Jesus. The Bible is the special book God gave us. It tells about the baby Jesus too. . . . Here are some pictures to put in our Bible storybook. I'd like for you to help me put them in place, Mark. Whose picture is that? Yes, it's David the shepherd boy. Perhaps when Jesus was a boy He heard His mother read the story of David from the Bible-scroll.

Lesson 3

Tape the bottom and top of a piece of paper to two dowel rods to form a scroll. Turn the scroll sideways and print on it, "Love God." Use a piece of yarn to tie the scroll together. Have it beside the classroom Bible, along with books used previously.

Show the scroll. **What is this? Yes, it is a Bible-scroll.** Let a child open the scroll. **Do you know what those words say? "Love God." Those are our Bible words. People such as Ezra and Jesus would unroll their Bible-scrolls and read the words of God, and people who heard the words would go home and repeat them to their families.**

Our Bible story is about a boy named Timothy. His mother and his grandmother probably read to him from a Bible-scroll. . . . Here is our Bible. It is a special book that God gave us. Have a child open to the Bible words. Help him "read" the words.

Lesson 5

Copy the patterns onto colorful tagboard, punch a hole in the top of each, and tie them onto foot-long pieces of yarn. Punch holes in a broad-brimmed hat and tie each tag onto the hat to make a story hat. Have the children choose a tag; then retell the story. The children may help tell the story.

Bible stories are exciting! Each of the objects on my hat reminds me of something wonderful that I learned from the Bible. Do you see something familiar? Lakeisha, pick something on the hat; then we'll see what story it has to tell.

Art Center, continued

Lesson 3
Bible (258)
Brushes
Colored tissue paper

Lesson 4
Patterns (258)
Paper clips
Spring clothespins
Small sponges

Lesson 5
Bible, scroll, chariot, temple patterns

you want to read? What message could I write on your card about the Bible?

Lesson 4

Make stencils of the Bible and the scroll from page 258. (Keep the cutouts for Lesson 5.) Paper clip a stencil over a piece of construction paper. Pour small amounts of tempera in pie plates. Give each child a sponge held by a spring clothespin. Show how to paint inside the stencil.

What is this? Yes, a Bible-scroll like Ezra read from. This one is a Bible like the one we have here in our classroom and like yours at home. The Bible is the special book God gave us. It tells us that God loves us.

Lesson 5

Have cutouts of the Bible, scroll, chariot, and temple. Tape patterns to a table. Lay white paper over the cutouts. Have the children use the sides of their crayons to make rubbings.

Can you tell me what your picture is? Yes, Amy, yours is a temple-church. That reminds me of Ezra. What did he do? He read from the Bible-scroll and all the people listened. We read from a Bible like the one in your picture, Jason. The Bible is the special book God gave us.

NOTE: If your time is limited, use the teaching pictures (pages 261-264) for coloring pages in place of the art activities suggested.

Block Center

Unit 1—Learning From the Bible

Items to Include:

Lessons 1 and 2
Large cardboard blocks
Bible
Scroll

Lesson 4
Rice table or large pan
Rice
Small cars and

Purpose: The child will use large muscles to recreate scenes from the Bible.

Things to Do and Say

Lessons 1 and 2

Ahead of time, make a scroll using the directions on the Book and Picture Center Learning Card (under Lesson 3). In class, help the children build a church building and a temple-church. Two's and 3's build very simply. Several blocks stacked together may be what they build. Have your classroom Bible next to the church building, and a scroll next to the temple-church. Let the children take turns reading the Bible words from the Bible and/or the scroll.

You've done a good job on your buildings! You all worked together. . . . Ezra (Jesus) read from a Bible-scroll that looked something like this. God's words were on the Bible-scroll. Our Bible-scroll says, "Love God." Those are God's words. . . . Today, we read from our Bible. Here are those same words, "Love God." Bethany, would you like to hold the Bible and read those words with me?

Lesson 4

Ahead of time, make a chariot following the directions on page 260. If you have a toy horse of the right size, use chenille wires to fasten it to the chariot. You will need several chariots and horses for a large group. Put about 2" to 3" of rice in a large pan. Have the children mold the rice into hills, valleys, and roads. Bend chenille wires into the figures

Music Center

Unit 1—Learning From the Bible

Items to Include:

Tape player
Tape of unit songs (optional)

Lesson 2
Scarves or strips of colored fabric
Rhythm instruments (optional)

Purpose: The child will use his or her voice and body to sing and respond to various songs about the Bible.

Things to Do and Say

Lesson 2

If possible, make (or have someone else make) a tape of the unit songs to use for both lessons.

In class, give each child a scarf to wave. Let children march around the room and wave their scarves in an arc over their heads as they sing songs from this unit. For an extra activity, add rhythm instruments and shake them in time to the music. If you don't have any, make some by putting rice or dry beans inside containers and sealing them with glue. Use salt boxes, plastic eggs, or two paper plates that are taped together around the edges.

Did you know that long ago people took words from the Bible and used them in songs? When we sing "I Love God" we are singing our Bible verse. Isn't it nice to be able to sing about God and His special book? . . . Which song is your favorite, Joel? I like that one too.

Lesson 4

Start the activity by talking about what legs can do. Besides the usual ideas of walking, running, jogging, etc., add a few new ideas such as marching, galloping, crawling,

Music Center, continued

hopping, tiptoeing, walking like a duck or other animal. Have a child pick one action and then sing one of the songs in the unit doing "leg aerobics" at the same time. **What kinds of things did our legs do today? Legs can do some very important things can't they! They can carry you to the table to eat or outside to play. What are some things your legs did for you this week? Today we are going to learn about a man who used his legs so he could teach someone else about God and His special book.**

Block Center, continued

trucks
Chariot pattern, page 260
Individual-size cereal box(es)
Chenille wires
Toy horse(s)
Tape

Lesson 5
Small cars and trucks
Crayons
Large sheet of paper

of Philip and the Ethiopian man.

Can you make your car travel on this road? That's how we get from one place to another isn't it? We use the car or a bus or plane to go long distances. What other ways can we travel? . . . People in Bible times used chariots. How is this chariot different from your car? . . . Do you talk to people when you are traveling? In our Bible story, a preacher named Philip met a man who was traveling in a chariot. Philip talked to the man about the Bible. I'll tell you the whole story in a little while.

Lesson 5

Use a large piece of paper to cover a table; then draw a colorful map of your community on the paper. Draw streets and parking lots. Include places the children would recognize, such as the church building, the grocery store, the fire station, and the mall.

Have the children add trees, their houses, and so forth, to the map. Let the children drive their cars or trucks from their homes to a place where they could go to hear about God (the church building). Then have them drive to a place(s) where they could go to tell others about God.

Why did you go to church to hear about God? Who would tell you about God there? . . . Sara decided to go to the library. Who is your special friend at the library? What could you tell her about God? Could you share something special with her like Philip shared with the man in the chariot? Who else talked about God's book with someone else?

Family Living Center

Unit 1—Learning From the Bible

Items to Include:

Table and chairs

Lesson 3
Bible pattern, page 259
Dishes
Bread
Plastic table knives
Cheese spread

Lesson 4
Cookies cut in Bible shapes
New, very small paintbrushes
Egg yolk paint

Purpose: The child will feel happy to use the Bible in various activities.

Things to Do and Say

Lesson 3

Using the Bible pattern on page 259 as a guide, cut out bread in the shape of a Bible so there are one or two pieces per child. Have the children put cheese spread on the bread to make a "Bible" snack.

Our Bible story is about a boy named Timothy, who liked to hear the Bible stories his mother and grandmother read to him. . . . This snack looks good! Do you think that Timothy ever ate bread and cheese with his family? Bread and cheese are good for you. They help make you strong. . . . What shape is your bread? Yes, it looks like a Bible. Our Bible words are, "Love God." Adam, what could you do to show you love God? (Pray, read the Bible, tell others, etc.) Ask other children the same question.

Lesson 4

Cut out tagboard patterns of the chariot, scroll, and Bible from pages 259 and 260. You may want to reduce the size of the chariot. Make sugar cookie dough from your favorite recipe and roll the dough out as thin as possible. Use the patterns to cut out one of each shape per child.

Make the paint by combining an egg yolk with 1/4 tsp. water and a little food coloring. Put paint shirts on the children and let them paint the cookies. When the paint

Game Center

Unit 1—Learning From the Bible

Items to Include:

Lesson 3
Tagboard or cardboard
Glue
Bible and scroll patterns, page 259
Fabrics and papers

Purpose: The child will know that the Bible is a special book God gave to us.

Things to Do and Say

Lesson 1

Have the children sit in a circle. The child who is chosen to be "It" runs around the outside of the circle touching each child gently on the head and saying the word *book* as he passes. Eventually, he will touch one child and say, "Bible," instead of "book." The child who is touched will then get up and chase the child who is "It." If "It" can reach the empty spot on the floor and sit down before he is tagged, the chaser becomes "It," and the game repeats. Two's may have difficulty with this game. Keep your group(s) small for better results.

When we say, "Book," we could be talking about any book—perhaps a fairy tale or a nursery rhyme book. Do you have a favorite book? When we say, "Bible," we are talking about a very special book because the Bible is the book God wrote so He could talk with us.

Lesson 3

Using the patterns on page 259, cut Bibles and scrolls from various materials and/or papers and back them with tagboard or cardboard. Cut each pattern in half so that you have two matching halves. Place these on the table and scramble the pieces. Have the children take turns trying to find matches.

Family Living Center, continued

Water in paper cups
Bowls
Paper towels
Paint shirts
Small plastic bags

is dry, they may eat the cookies for a snack or take them home in plastic sandwich bags. Or, if you prefer, let the children spread ready-made frosting with plastic knives to frost the cookies.

Can you tell me about the cookies you are painting? One looks like a Bible-scroll and one is a Bible. The last cookie is used for traveling. It doesn't look like a bus or a truck or a plane, does it? It's called a chariot and a long time ago people rode in chariots that were pulled by horses. Can you paint some wheels on your chariot?

Game Center, continued

We have Bible-scrolls and Bible-books here. Which one did people read from long ago? Yes, the Bible-scroll. Which do we read from today? Which one tells us God's words? That's right, they both do.

Lesson 5
Patterns of temple, Bible, scroll, Timothy, grandmother, chariot from pages 257-260
Construction paper
Tray
Cloth

Lesson 5

Make six cards, each with one of the patterns from pages 257-260. (Use just the large Bible and scroll.) To do this, photocopy each pattern onto construction paper. Cut out objects and glue them onto tagboard or cardboard. Place the cards on a tray and let the children discuss each item and review its story. Cover the tray and remove one card. Scramble the cards and have the children determine which card is missing. Repeat.

Which card is missing? That's right—the temple-church. Do you remember a story where someone read a scroll in the temple-church? I'll name all the stories and you see if you can tell me where the people were when they heard God's words.

Summer, Unit 1

Instructions

1. For each child, photocopy a temple on one side of a sheet of construction paper.
2. Photocopy the sun onto yellow paper, one per child.
3. Photocopy the people onto various colors of construction paper. Mix these so the child will have a variety of colors and sizes.
4. Make stickers of the sun and people by painting the backs of the sheets with a mixture of 2 parts white glue to 1 part vinegar. (Peppermint flavoring can be added but is not necessary.) Allow sheets to dry, then cut out the figures.
5. Use the stickers in the Art Center for Lesson 1.
6. The temple pattern will also be used in the Art Center for Lesson 5.

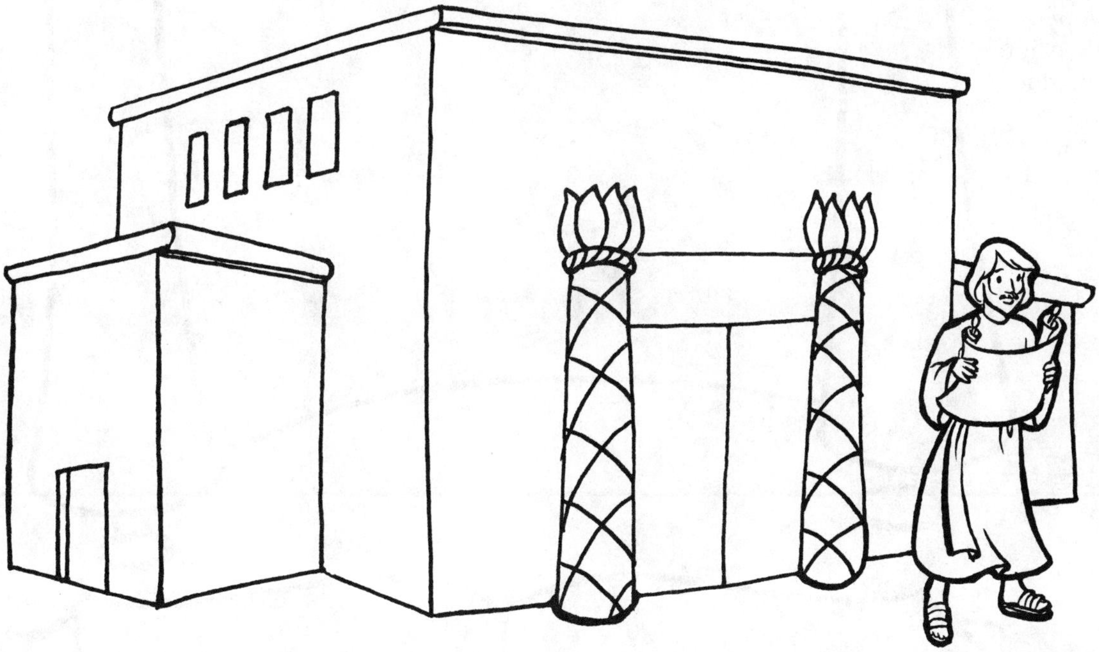

Summer, Unit 1

Instructions

1. Fold black construction paper in half to make cards.
2. Copy Bible pattern on front of each card and cut out, keeping frame intact.
3. Mix equal portions of water and white glue in small paper cup.
4. Cut pastel shades of tissue paper into small squares.
5. Have children open cards and thinly paint inside page with glue.
6. Help children place tissue squares over glue, overlapping to make a "stained-glass" Bible.

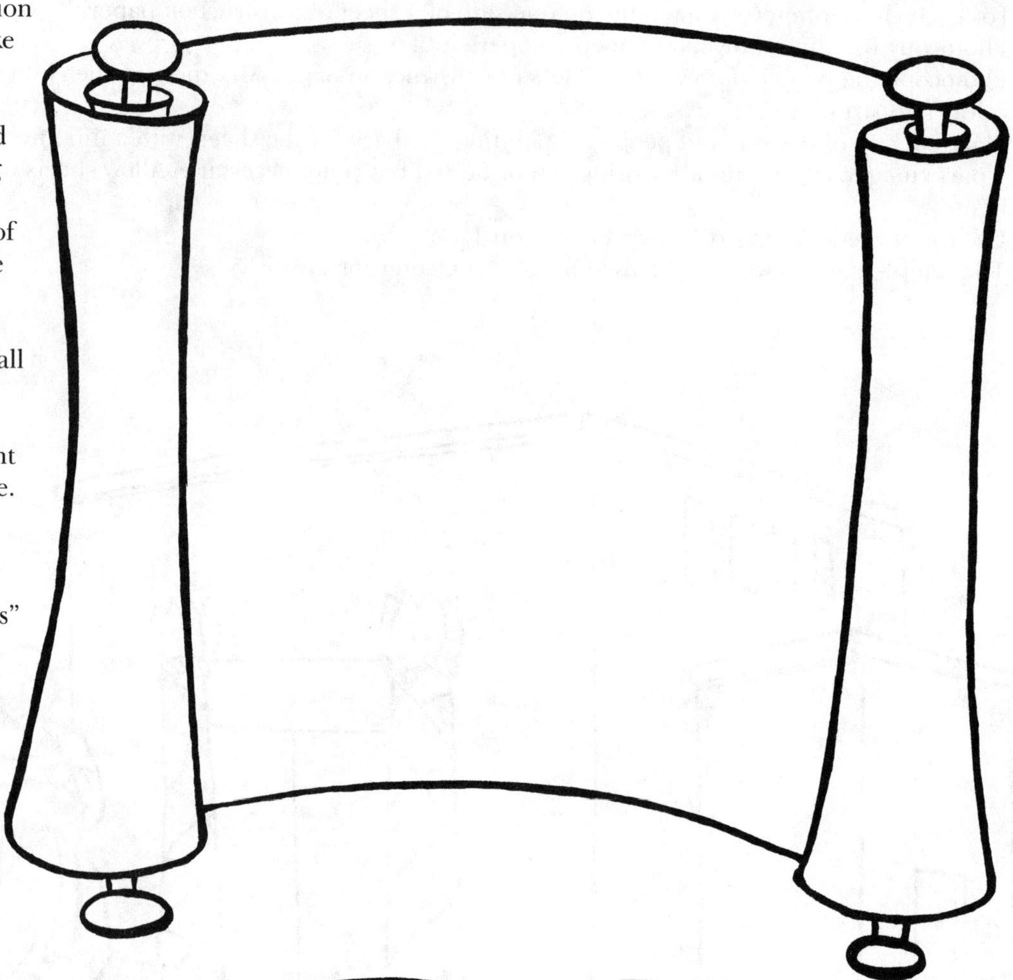

Summer, Unit 1

Instructions

Use the scroll and Bible patterns for the Game Center in Lesson 3, and the Family Living Center in Lesson 4. The patterns of Timothy and his grandmother are for the Game Center in Lesson 5.

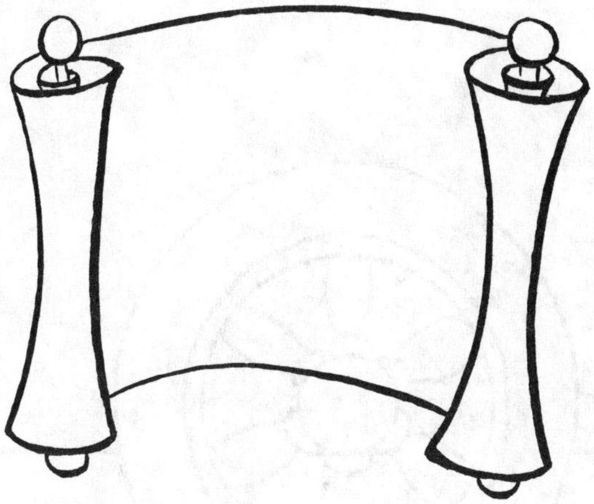

Summer, Unit 1

Instructions for making a chariot:

1. Photocopy the page onto construction paper.
2. Add color if you wish.
3. Cut out on solid lines; fold on dotted lines.
4. Glue onto a large gelatin box or an individual-size cereal box.
5. If you have a toy horse of the right size, use chenille wires to fasten it to the chariot.
6. Use the chariot in the Block Center for Lesson 4.

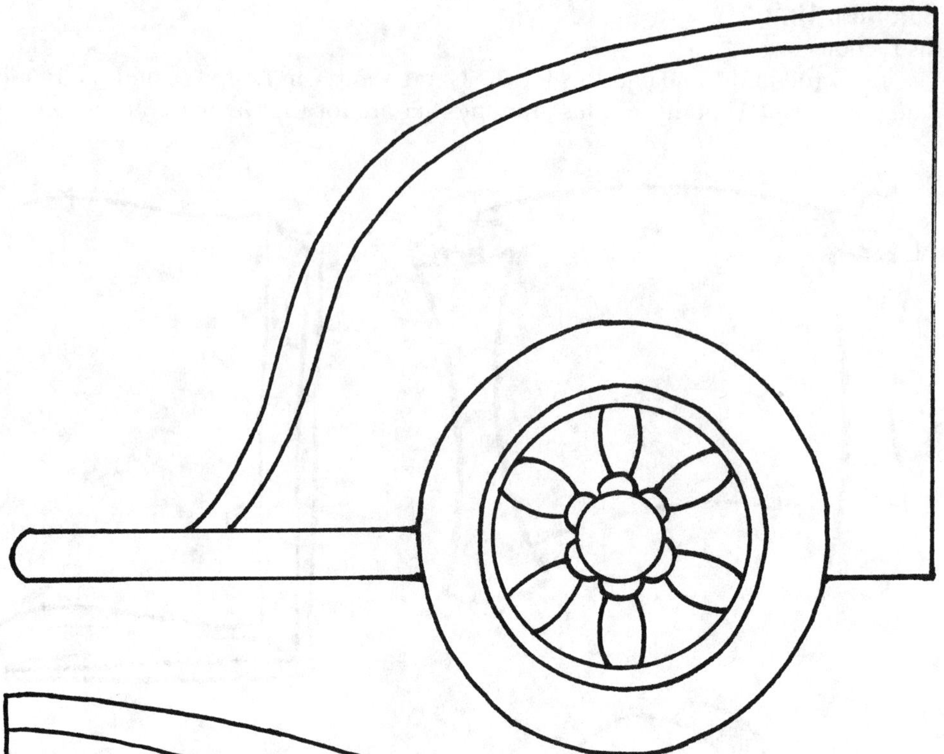

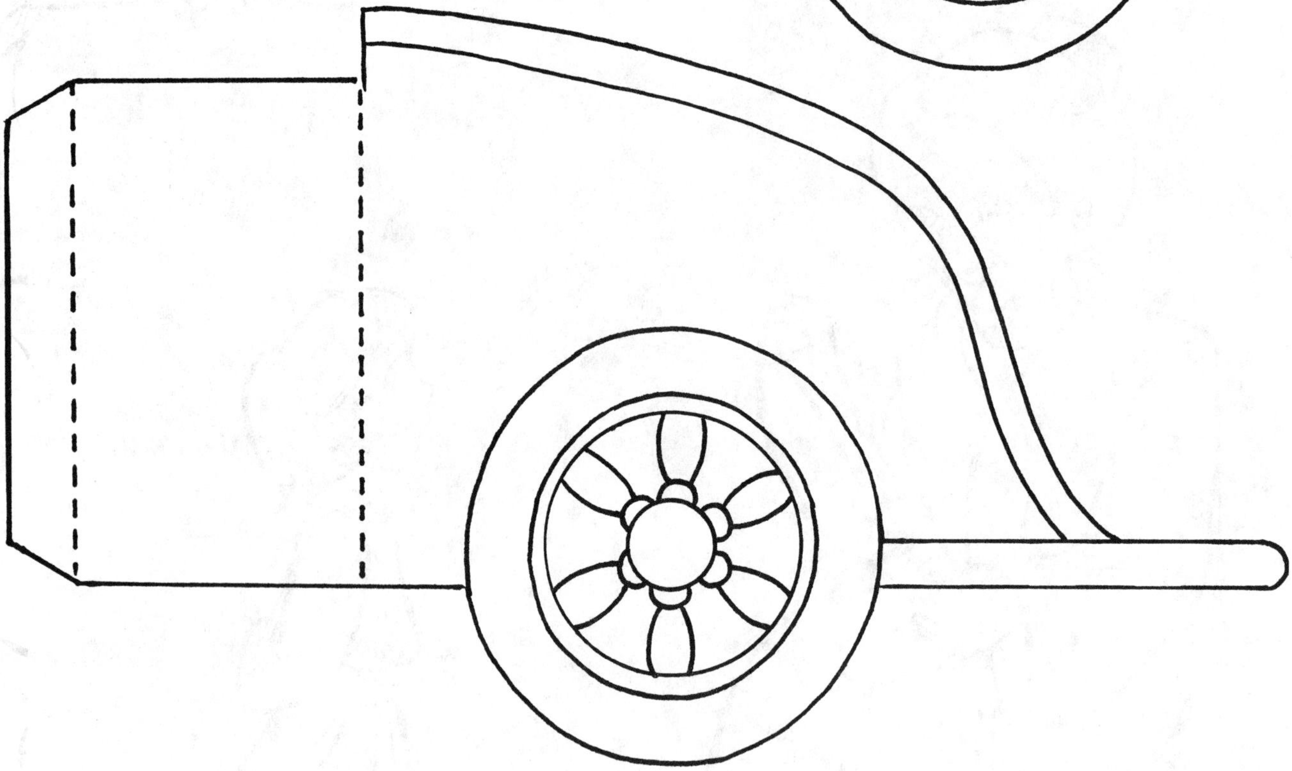

Ezra read from the Bible-scroll. The people were happy to hear God's words.

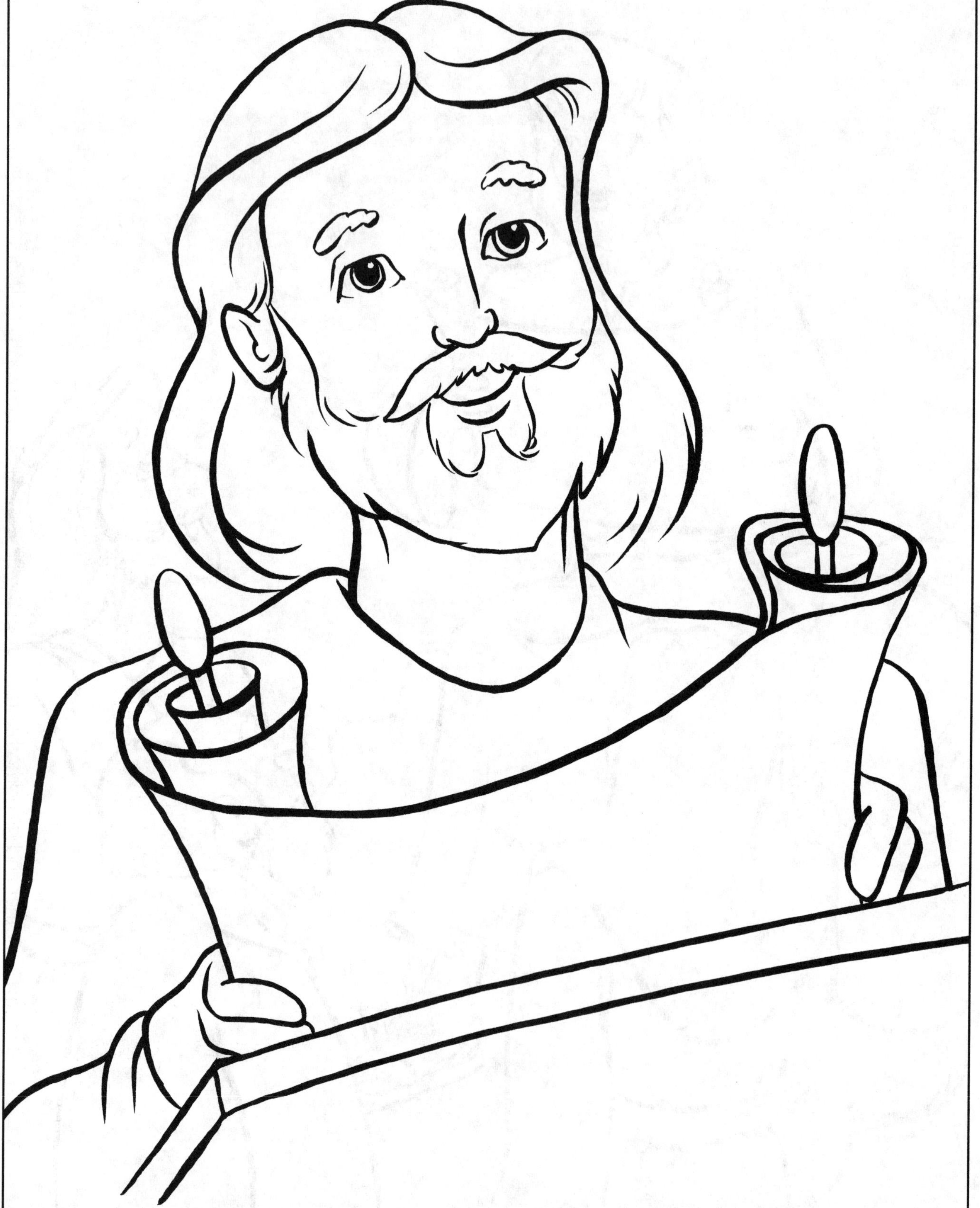

Jesus read from the Bible-scroll. All the people listened to God's words.

Timothy's mother and grandmother read from the Bible-scroll. Timothy liked to hear the stories.

Philip used his mouth to tell about Jesus. The man in the chariot used his ears to hear about Jesus.

Dear Parent:

This quarter your child will be studying about the greatest book the world has ever known —the Bible! We are doing five lessons that will introduce the children to God's Word:

Ezra Reads From the Bible (Nehemiah 8:1-12)
Ezra reads the law to the people after the rebuilding of the wall around Jerusalem.

Jesus Reads About God (Luke 4:14-21)
Jesus reads a prophecy in the synagogue.

Timothy Hears Bible Stories (2 Timothy 1:5; 3:15)
Timothy's mother and grandmother teach him Bible stories.

Philip's Friend Learns From the Bible (Acts 8:26-40)
Philip talks to the Ethiopian eunuch about the Scriptures.

I Learn From the Bible (Based on Lessons 1–4)
The Bible still teaches us about God just as it taught Bible people.

You play a very important part in your child's Christian education. Things that are learned at school or church, and that are used only at school or church, are seen by children as being irrelevant. When the things they learn are viewed as having an important place in the lives of those they love, however, preschoolers view them with respect. How you view the Bible and how often you use it will determine your child's attitude toward it.

- This is a good time to begin reading some of the great adventure stories in the Bible with your child. Use an easy-to-understand Bible, such as the *International Children's Bible,* and let your voice reflect the emotion and excitement of the stories!
- Also invest in some true-to-the-Bible children's storybooks, if you have not already done so. Take time each day to read a storybook or two to your child. Reading aloud to your child is one of the most important things you can do for him or her.
- Emphasize the fact that the Bible is God's way of talking to us and guiding us, and that we know when something is right or wrong because the Bible tells us so. You will not always be there to guide your child. Someday he or she will leave home, and it will be good to know that you pointed your child to the book that is always available to help in any situation.
- Have your child teach you songs he is learning in class, and share ones you know.
- Review the Bible words, "Love . . . God" (Mark 12:30), and use the teachable moments in your child's life to teach him or her how to show love for God. As your communication with God increases you will find that your child's does too!
- Here is a song and an action rhyme to do with your child.

(Tune: "The Farmer in the Dell")

(Child's name) reads his/her Bible.
Yes, (Child's name) reads his/her Bible.
He/she reads the Bible every day.
Yes, (Child's name) reads his/her Bible.
(Also use "Mommy" or "Daddy," in place of your child's name.)

My Bible

This is my Bible; *(Hands held out in front, palms together.)*
I'll open it wide *(Open hands, but keep them touching.)*
And see (or say) what is written on the inside!
(Say the Bible words together, "Love God.")
—Jean Baxendale

Sincerely, your child's teacher

Zach

Zach is a cute, short-legged dog. His full name is Zaccheus. He is the mascot for this course. He will be helping with many of the activities in the classroom. To make him even more appealing to the children, you may want to make a pretend doghouse, such as the one below. Make this on a large piece of cardboard or poster board. If you are not artistic, enlist the aid of someone who is.

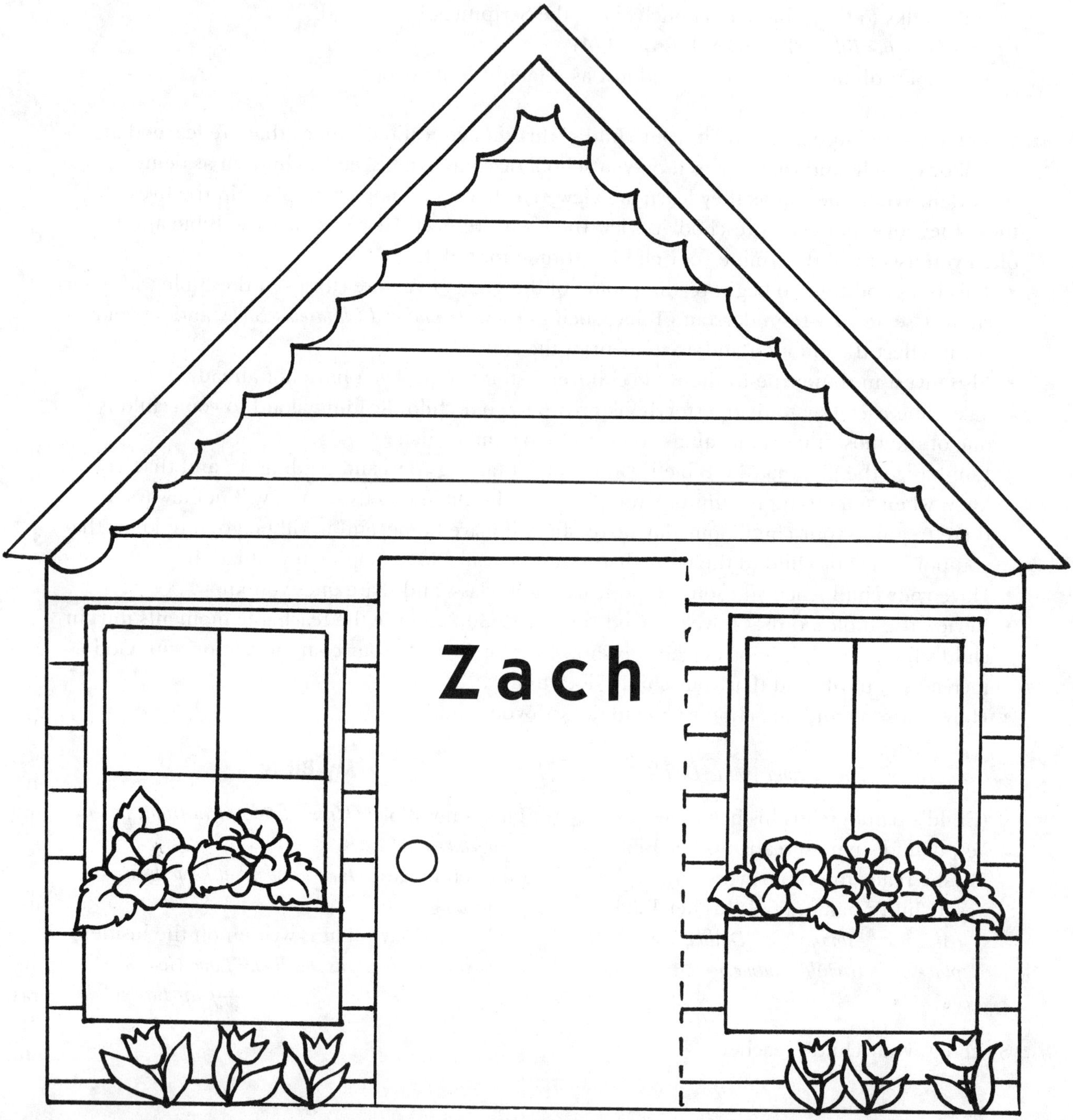

Unit 2: Talking to God

Lessons 6–9

By the end of the unit, the children will

Know that God hears us when we pray.
Feel eager and willing to talk to God.
Pray in many situations and activities.

Unit Bible Words

"I pray to God," 2 Corinthians 13:7.

Books

Now the Day Is Over 24-03146
Thank You, God 24-03820
Picture Word Prayers 24-03612
Two Prayers for Patches 24-03887
I Can Pray to God 24-04208

Just for Teachers

Teaching Our Children to Pray 18-03217

The Unit at a Glance

6 Jesus Talks to God — **Mark 1:35; Matthew 14:22, 23; John 17**

Jesus talked to God in the morning and in the evening. He prayed with His friends. He prayed for himself and for His friends.

7 A King Talks to God — **1 Kings 3:3-14**

King Solomon asked God to help him be a good king.

8 Peter's Friends Talk to God — **Acts 12:1-17**

Peter's friends prayed for him when he was in jail. God heard their prayers and freed Peter from jail.

9 I Talk To God — **Review of Lessons 6–8**

We can talk to God. He hears our prayers.

Why Teach This Unit?

Prayer is absolutely essential to the Christian life. A child cannot be too young to begin to pray and build a foundation for a lifetime of prayer.

Preschoolers can understand this complex form of communication in simple terms. It is talking to God, and preschoolers love to talk! This unit will give children confidence that they can pray to God.

The Bible stories in this unit give examples of Bible people who prayed. They show how God heard the prayers of the Bible people. This unit will teach 2's and 3's that God does indeed hear their prayers.

Use the Bible words over and over, in the Bible stories, at the learning centers, and in your prayers. For example, **Jesus prayed to God. "I pray to God." . . . The Bible tells us of many people who prayed to God. "I pray to God." . . . Our Bible words say, "I pray to God." . . . "I pray to God" every day. Thank You, God, that we can talk to You.**

Have a classroom Bible where the children will see it. Keep it on your lap or at your side as you tell the Bible story. Highlight or underline the Bible words so the children can see them and "read" them.

Things to Do for This Unit

- Photocopy the Learning Center Cards (pages 277-282); cut pages apart on solid lines. Mount side 1 of a card on cardboard; then mount side 2 on back of cardboard. Laminate for durability.
- Gather/prepare materials listed on the Learning Center Cards.
- For Lesson 9, copy page 288; cut figures apart on solid lines, and glue craft sticks on the backs.

Use These Songs and Action Rhymes During Unit 2

I Pray to God

(Tune: "Whisper a Prayer")

Jesus prayed in the morning.
Jesus prayed at noon.
Jesus prayed in the nighttime.
He prayed and He talked to God.

I pray to God in the morning.
I pray to God at noon.
I pray to God in the nighttime
I pray and I talk to God.

I Pray, God Hears

(Tune: First two lines of "Old MacDonald Had a Farm")

In the morning, (child's name) prays.
(Yawn, stretch; fold hands in prayer.)
He prays. He prays. He prays. *(Fold hands in prayer.)*
(Child's name) prays, "Thank You, God." *(Hold out hands.)*
He prays. He prays. He prays. *(Fold hands in prayer.)*

In the nighttime (child's name) prays.
(Pretend to sleep. Then fold hands in prayer.)
He prays. He prays. He prays. *(Fold hands in prayer.)*
(Child's name) prays, "Thank You, God." *(Hold out hands.)*
He prays. He prays. He prays. *(Fold hands in prayer.)*

God hears (child's name) when he/she prays.
(Cup hands behind ears.)
God hears. God hears. God hears.
(Child's name) prays, "Thank You, God."
God hears. God hears. God hears.

God Hears Me When I Pray

(Tune: "Farmer in the Dell")

I pray to God. I pray to God.
God hears me when I pray.* I pray to God.

*Any time of the day.

I'm Very Special to God

(Tune: "Hickory, Dickory, Dock")

I'm very special to God. He hears me when I pray.
I pray to God. He hears my words.
I'm very special to God.

I Will Pray Today

I will pray today. *(Fold hands in prayer.)*
I will say, "Good morning." *(Yawn and stretch.)*
I will say, "Good night." *(Pretend to sleep.)*
I will say, "Thanks," for my lunch. *(Pretend to eat.)*
I will pray today. *(Fold hands in prayer.)*

I will pray today. *(Fold hands in prayer.)*
I will say, "Help me do right." *(Nod head.)*
I will say, "Keep me from wrong." *(Shake head.)*
I will say, "Thanks for listening." *(Cup hands behind ears.)*
I will pray today. *(Fold hands in prayer.)*

I will pray today. *(Fold hands in prayer.)*
I will say, "Help my family." *(Hug self.)*
I will say, "Help my friends." *(Hug a friend.)*
I will say, "Thanks for helping." *(Look toward Heaven.)*
I will pray today. *(Fold hands in prayer.)*

What did Jesus talk to God about in the morning and at nighttime? He prayed for many things. He prayed for himself. He asked God to help Him. He prayed for His friends. He asked God to take care of His friends and watch over them. Jesus asked God to help everyone—even you and me.

Let's Apply the Lesson

Have Zach ask the children, **When did Jesus pray? Yes, He prayed in the morning** *(yawn and stretch),* **and He prayed at nighttime** *(pretend to sleep).*

Have Zach lead the children in singing "I Pray to God," from page 268. After you sing the song several times, ask, **When can you pray?** (In the morning, at noon, at night, anytime.)

Learning Activities

(20 minutes)

Let's Play Awhile

Our Bible words say, "I pray to God." Have children say the Bible words with you. Then have the children stand and do the action rhyme, "I Will Pray Today," using just the first verse.

Have materials ready for the God's Wonders Center. This will allow children to use their senses of touch, taste, sight, and smell. If you have several teachers, also use one or more of the learning activities from the beginning of the session.

Let's Go Home

Have Zach tell the children that it's time to clean up after their snack. Direct them to the wastebasket with their napkins. Use wet wipes or a damp cloth to clean hands and faces. Then gather the children in a circle. Lead them in saying the Bible words. Use the action rhyme, "Listen to Me."

Since this is the first lesson of the unit, give each child a Parents' Letter. Also make sure children have their artwork from the art center.

Jesus Talks to God

Mark 1:35; Matthew 14:22, 23; John 17

Bible Words: "I pray to God" (2 Corinthians 13:7).

Lesson Value: In this lesson children will learn that prayer was very important to Jesus. Jesus prayed often. This lesson looks at a time Jesus prayed in the morning and a time He prayed at night. Preschoolers are very familiar with these two times of day. They can learn to pray when they wake up in the morning and when they go to bed at night.

Know: Know that God hears us when we pray.
Feel: Feel eager and willing to talk to God.
Do: Pray in many situations and activities.

Children will accomplish the goals when they:

1. Say the Bible words, "I pray to God."
2. Pray, "Thank You, God, that we can talk to You."
3. Sing about prayer or sing a prayer.
4. Point to Jesus who prayed to God.
5. Tell what Jesus might say to God.
6. Pretend to be Jesus praying to God.

Listen to Me

Listen to what I can say.
I've learned some Bible words today.
(Say the Bible words, "I pray to God.")

Let's Get Ready

For the Bible story, you will need your classroom Bible with the new Bible words highlighted. Have Zach ready to help you.

Set up the Music Center, the Puzzle Center, and the Art Center, If you are the only teacher, use just the Art Center. The God's Wonders Center will be used after the Bible story. Learning Center Cards are on pages 277-282.

Learning Activities

(30 minutes, including 10 minutes presession)

Let's Get Started

Have Zach greet each child by name. Thank God for each child by name. Let Zach lead children to the offering container and attendance chart.

Direct each child to get involved in one of the learning activities. **Rachel, would you like to paint or put a puzzle together? You'll paint a bright morning scene. We're going to have a Bible story about something that Jesus did in the morning.**

Worship and Bible Story

(15 minutes)

Let's Worship God

Have Zach tell the children, "It's time to put away our things so we can sing and pray to God." Begin singing as soon as the first child sits in the circle with you. Sing songs from the unit pages or have children suggest songs to sing. Use the action rhyme, "When I Pray" (see Lesson 8). Then pray, **Thank You, God, that we can talk to You.**

Let's Learn From the Bible

Introduction: Jesus liked to pray. When did Jesus pray? If children heard the Bible story during Sunday school, have them answer.

I'm going to do some actions that describe when Jesus liked to pray. You tell me what part of the day someone would do them. Watch closely. Yawn and stretch as if you were just getting out of bed in the morning. Have Zach stretch. **What time of the day do people usually yawn and stretch?** Morning time. **Let me see how you yawn and stretch.**

Now, watch me again. Put palms of hands together and place hands against your cheek. Lay your head to the side as if sleeping. Have Zach pretend to sleep. **What time of day do people sleep?** Nighttime. **Let me see how you sleep.**

Now you know when Jesus liked to pray. Now you are ready to help me tell the Bible story. When you hear the word *morning,* I want you to yawn and stretch. When you hear the word *nighttime,* I want you to pretend to sleep. Put Zach aside. Have your open Bible on your lap or beside you.

The Bible Story: Jesus liked the morning time *(children yawn and stretch).* The morning was a good time to pray. Jesus prayed in the quiet morning time. One morning, Jesus got up before the sun was up. He walked from the house to find a very quiet place outside. Jesus got up early this morning to pray. Jesus liked to talk to God in the morning. He talked to God at the beginning of the day.

Jesus also liked the nighttime *(children pretend to sleep).* He liked the nighttime because it was a good time to pray. Jesus prayed in the quiet nighttime. One night, Jesus told His friends to get into their boat and go across the lake. He told the other people to go home. Jesus did this because it was time for Him to pray. Jesus climbed into the hills. Jesus prayed. Jesus liked to talk to God at nighttime. He talked to God at the end of the day.

Sometimes Jesus prayed by himself. Sometimes Jesus prayed with His friends. Jesus prayed in the morning and at nighttime.

prayer? Yes, God heard king Solomon's prayer, and God answered it.

Do you pray at nighttime? What do you say to God at night? Does God hear your prayers? Yes, God hears you when you pray.

Lead children in singing these words to the tune, "The Farmer in the Dell":

Solomon prayed to God.
Solomon prayed to God.
God heard him when he prayed.
Solomon prayed to God.

Learning Activities

(20 minutes)

Let's Play Awhile

Our Bible words say, "I pray to God." Have children say the Bible words with you. Then have the children stand and do the action rhyme, "I Will Pray Today," using just the middle verse. *(See page 268.)*

Get the children ready for the God's Wonders Center walk. This will allow children to use their large muscles and their senses of touch, sight, and smell. Involve all the children in this center since it involves a walk outside. If the weather doesn't permit outside activity, adapt the activity for a walk in Solomon's palace.

Let's Go Home

Have Zach tell the children that it's time to return to the classroom. In the room, gather the children in a circle. Lead them in singing "God Hears Me When I Pray," on page 268.

A King Talks to God

1 Kings 3:3-14

Bible Words: "I pray to God" (2 Corinthians 13:7).

Lesson Value: Today's story about Solomon will introduce children to the concept that they can pray about anything. God asked Solomon to ask him for anything. Preschoolers can begin now to build confidence in God knowing that they can pray to Him for anything.

Know: Know that God hears us when we pray.
Feel: Feel eager and willing to talk to God.
Do: Pray in many situations and activities.

Children will accomplish the goals when they:

1. Say the Bible words, "I pray to God."
2. Pray, "Thank You, God, that we can talk to You."
3. Sing about prayer or sing a prayer.
4. Tell what Solomon might say to God.
5. Pretend to be Solomon praying to God.

Let's Get Ready

Make a paper crown for Zach using the pattern on page 285. If you are not portraying King Solomon yourself for the Bible story, ask another adult to do so. Have a crown and some type of garment for the king to wear.

Set up the Game Center, the Family Living Center, and the Book Center. If you are the only teacher, use just the

Game Center. Prepare the God's Wonders Center to be used after the Bible story.

Learning Activities

(30 minutes, including 10 minutes presession)

Let's Get Started

Put the paper crown on Zach. Have Zach greet each child by name. Have Zach say, **Jenny, can you tell me what kind of people wear crowns? Kings and queens wear crowns. Our Bible story today is about a king. The king's name was Solomon.**

Direct the children to get involved in one of the learning activities. Say, **Michael, would you like to play a game or play house? You'll learn what the king named Solomon did.**

Worship and Bible Story

(15 minutes)

Let's Worship God

Have Zach tell the children, "It's time to put away our things so we can sing and pray to God." Begin singing as soon as the first child sits in the circle with you. Sing songs from the unit pages or have children suggest songs to sing. Sing the first stanza of "I Pray to God." Then pray, **Thank You, God, that we can talk to You.**

Let's Learn From the Bible

Introduction: Have Zach and a teaching assistant announce the arrival of King Solomon. Say, **Boys and girls, let's get ready. We have a very special guest coming to visit us today. What should we do to welcome our guest?** Take some suggestions. **When our guest arrives, let's cheer and clap to welcome him. Here he comes now. Let's welcome his majesty, King Solomon.** Lead the children to cheer and clap as King Solomon walks into the room.

The Bible Story: *(Have King Solomon do the following first-person presentation.)* Hello, boys and girls. I am King Solomon. I want to tell you about a time that God heard my prayer. I want to tell you how God answered my prayer.

I was away from my palace. I had taken a trip to a special place where I could worship God. One night while I was sleeping, God said to me, "Solomon, ask me for whatever you would like me to give you."

"Wow!" I thought. I could ask for anything! If you could ask for anything, what might you ask for? *(Have children name a few things.)* I didn't ask for any of these things. I needed something more important than these things. I was the king of God's people. I didn't know how to be a king. So I prayed, "O God, help me to know what is right and do it. Help me to know what is wrong and not do it. Show me how to be a good king."

God was pleased with my prayer. God said, "I will give you what you asked for. I will help you know what is right and do it. I will help you know what is wrong and not do it. I will show you how to be a good king." God was so happy that I asked for these things that He gave me other good things too.

God heard my prayer. God gave me what I asked for. Some people call me the wisest king who ever lived. They call me this because God taught me what to do and helped me do it. God taught me what not to do and helped me not do it. God showed me how to be a good king. Thank You, God, that we can talk to You and that You hear us when we pray.

(If children have any questions for King Solomon, let them ask. Then tell King Solomon good-bye as he exits.)

Let's Apply the Lesson

What was the name of the king who prayed to God? What part of the day did king Solomon pray? What did king Solomon pray at nighttime? Did God hear King Solomon's

Our Bible words say, "I pray to God." Have the children say the Bible words with you. Then have the children stand and do the last verse of the action rhyme, "I Will Pray Today."

Learning Activities

(20 minutes)

Let's Play Awhile

Before the last activity, sing the song, "I'm Very Special to God," from page 268. Have children clap along.

Peter's friends prayed for him. Sometimes we need to pray for other people. We can pray for our families. We can pray for our friends. Have materials ready for the Art Center. If you have several teachers, also use one or more of the learning activities used earlier.

Let's Go Home

Have Zach tell the children that it's time to clean up. Gather the children in a circle. Have Zach lead them in saying the rhyme, "Listen to Me" (see Lesson 6), ending with the Bible words.

Then have Zach give each child a section of paper chain. **Let's pretend to be Peter.** Have children sit and drape paper chains over their feet. **Peter was in jail. He was in chains. Peter's friends prayed for him. The chains fell off of Peter's feet.** Remove chains. **God freed Peter. God heard the prayers of Peter's friends. This chain will help to remind you that Peter's friends prayed for him when he was in jail. God heard their prayers, and God freed Peter from jail!**

Peter's Friends Talk to God

Acts 12:1-7

Bible Words: "I pray to God" (2 Corinthians 13:7).

Lesson Value: In this lesson, children will look at the important fact that God hears them when they pray. It will help them understand that God listens to what they say to him. Peter's friends prayed for him when he was in jail. Children will know that God heard Peter's friend's prayers because God sent His angel to free Peter.

Know: Know that God hears us when we pray.
Feel: Feel eager and willing to talk to God.
Do: Pray in many situations and activities.

Children will accomplish the goals when they:

1. Say the Bible words, "I pray to God."
2. Pray, "Thank You, God, that we can talk to You."
3. Sing about prayer or sing a prayer.
4. Tell what Peter's friends and Rhoda might say to God.
5. Pretend to be Peter, his friend, or Rhoda praying to God.

When I Pray

When I pray, I fold my hands *(Fold hands.)*
And close my eyes; *(Close eyes.)*
I think about God, And He hears me. —*Jean Katt*

Let's Get Ready

For the Bible story, prepare a paper chain from black construction paper for Zach. If you are not portraying Peter for the Bible story, ask an adult to do so. Peter should be dressed in a very plain robe of some kind with sandals on his feet. If you are not offering the Drama Center, make a paper chain for each child according to the instructions in that center.

Prepare the Game Center, the Drama Center, and the Family Living Center. If you are the only teacher, use just the Family Living Center. Have the Art Center ready to be used after the Bible story.

Learning Activities

(30 minutes, including 10 minutes presession)

Let's Get Started

Drape a paper chain around Zach. Have Zach say, "Alex, where is someone when he has chains around his feet? Yes, he is in jail. Our Bible story today is about a time when Peter was in jail. He had chains around his feet."

Direct the children to the offering center. Then direct them to get involved in one of the learning activities. Say, **Aja, would you like to match some pictures or pretend to be Peter in jail?**

Worship and Bible Story

(15 minutes)

Let's Worship God

Have Zach tell the children, "It's time to put away our things so we can sing and pray to God." Begin singing as soon as the first child sits in the circle with you. Sing songs from the unit pages or have children suggest songs to sing. Sing, "God Hears Me When I Pray." Then pray, **Thank You, God, that we can talk to You.**

Let's Learn From the Bible

Introduction: Have Zach show the paper chains, and say, "I've never been in chains, and I've never been to jail. Our guest today was put in jail by someone who hated Jesus. Peter is here today to tell us what happened. Let's welcome Peter." Peter enters room. He should greet each child with a hug, handshake, or pat on the head.

The Bible Story: *(Have Peter present the following first-person story.)* Hi, boys and girls. I am Peter. I want to tell you about a time that I was put in jail. King Herod wanted to hurt people who loved Jesus. He put me in jail. He put me in chains. I was guarded by sixteen men. *(Count the number of children in the room and relate sixteen to the number present, that is more, less, or same.)*

While I was in jail, my friends prayed for me. They knew that God was the only one who could help me. So they prayed. What do you think my friends might have prayed? My friends asked God to help me. They did not know how God would help me, but they knew that God heard their prayers.

Nighttime came. The guards fell asleep. I fell asleep too. Suddenly, there was an angel who was sent by God. The light from the angel lit up the prison cell. No one woke up. The angel told me to get up. The chain fell off of me. I got my clothes and sandals and followed God's angel. I thought I was dreaming. God's angel led me past the guards, out of the prison, and into the city. Then the angel was gone. That was when I knew that I wasn't dreaming. I knew God had rescued me!

I ran to tell my friends. They were still praying for me. I knocked on the door. A servant girl named Rhoda came to the door. She ran to tell her friends I was at the door. They couldn't believe it was me. When they saw me, they knew that God had heard their prayers.

Let's Apply the Lesson

If the children have any questions for Peter, allow them to ask him. Then help the children say good-bye to Peter.

Jesus (Solomon, Peter's friends) prayed to God.
Jesus (Solomon, Peter's friends) prayed to God.
God heard him (them) when he (they) prayed.
Jesus (Solomon, Peter's friends) prayed to God.

Learning Activities

(20 minutes)

Let's Play Awhile

Our Bible words say, "I pray to God." Have the children say the Bible words with you. Then have the children stand and do the action rhyme, "I Will Pray Today."

Have materials ready for the Art Center. This center will allow children to see themselves while they say, "I pray to God.

Let's Go Home

Have Zach tell the children that it's time to clean up.

Gather the children in a circle. Ask them to bring their mirrors. Lead them in saying the Bible words using the following action rhyme.

I look in the mirror. What do I see? *(Look in the mirror.)*
I see someone who talks to God. *(Point up.)*
That someone is me! I pray to God. *(Point to self.)*

I look in the mirror. What do I see? *(Look in the mirror.)*
I see someone God hears when he prays. *(Point up.)*
That someone is me! I pray to God. *(Point to self.)*

I Talk to God

Review of Lessons 6–8

Bible Words: "I pray to God" (2 Corinthians 13:7).

Lesson Value: This lesson reviews the previous lessons on prayer. Children have a chance to remember the examples of the Bible people who prayed. This lesson will reinforce to children that they can pray in many situations and activities and at many times. They will be reminded that God hears their prayers. This alone will make them eager and willing to talk to God.

Know: Know that God hears us when we pray.
Feel: Feel eager and willing to talk to God.
Do: Pray in many situations and activities.

Children will accomplish the goals when they:

1. Say the Bible words, "I pray to God."
2. Pray, "Thank You, God, that we can talk to You."
3. Sing about prayer or sing a prayer.
4. Point to the people who prayed to God.
5. Tell what they might say to God.
6. Pretend to be Jesus, Solomon, or Peter praying to God.

Let's Get Ready

Put the crown from Lesson 7 on Zach. Prepare the pictures of Jesus, Solomon, and Peter from page 288. Make one set for each child. Glue a craft stick to each picture.

Set up the Game Center, the Drama Center, and the Family Living Center. If you are the only teacher, use just the Game Center. After the Bible story you will be using the Art Center.

Learning Activities

(30 minutes, including 10 minutes presession)

Let's Get Started

Have Zach put on his crown from Lesson 7. Let Zach greet the children and ask, "What was the name of the king who prayed to God?" You continue, **Yes, his name was King Solomon. We can be like King Solomon and pray to God. Our Bible words say, "I pray to God."**

Direct the children to get involved in one of the learning activities. Say, **Michael, would you like to act like a Bible person who prayed or go on a picnic?**

Worship and Bible Story

(15 minutes)

Let's Worship God

Have Zach tell the children, "It's time to put away our things so we can sing and pray to God." Begin singing as soon as the first child sits in the circle with you. Sing songs from the unit pages or have children suggest songs to sing. Sing the song, "I'm Very Special to God." Then pray, **Thank You, God, that we can talk to You.**

Let's Learn From the Bible

Introduction: We have learned about some Bible people who prayed to God. One man prayed in the morning and at nighttime. One man wore a crown. And one man was in jail. Who were these Bible people? If the children have trouble remembering, let Zach give them hints. Then put Zach away and have your open Bible on your lap or beside you.

The Bible-story Review: *(Pass out a Jesus puppet to each child.)* Jesus liked to talk to God. He prayed in the morning and at night. He prayed by himself and He prayed with His friends. He asked God to help Him and to help His friends.

(Pass out King Solomon puppet to each child.) King Solomon liked to talk to God. Once God asked King Solomon to ask Him for whatever he wanted. King Solomon asked God to help him be a good king, to do right and to keep from doing wrong. God was happy with King Solomon's prayer. He helped King Solomon be a good king.

(Pass out Peter puppet to each child.) Peter was in jail. He hadn't done anything wrong. He was put in jail by someone who hated Jesus. Peter's friends were worried. They prayed to God. They asked God to help Peter. God sent an angel to free Peter from jail. God heard the prayers of Peter's friends.

Let's Apply the Lesson

Jesus, Solomon, and Peter's friends prayed to God. Show me your Jesus puppet. What might Jesus pray to God? Show me your King Solomon puppet. What might King Solomon pray to God? Show me your Peter puppet. What might Peter's friends pray to God?

Our Bible words say, "I pray to God." Show me the puppets of the Bible people who prayed to God.

Lead children in singing these words to the tune, "The Farmer in the Dell." Have them hold up the appropriate puppet for each Bible person.

Art Center

Unit 2—Talking to God

Items to Include:

Lesson 6
- Finger paints (yellow, blue, green)
- Finger paint paper
- Art smocks or adult-size shirts
- Sink or tub with soapy water and towels
- Stickers (page 284)

Lesson 8
- Drawing paper
- Doll patterns (page 285)
- Markers

Purpose: The child will feel eager and willing to talk to God.

Things to Do and Say

Lesson 6

Prepare stickers by following the directions on page 284. If you prefer, the children may paint with watercolors, or use crayons or washable markers for the background. You may want to draw a line across each paper for the horizon so children can color the sky one color and the ground another.

While the children color/paint their backgrounds, ask, **What are some things you see in the morning? What are some things you hear in the morning? I see the bright yellow sun. I hear blue birds sing. I like the morning. Jesus liked the morning. Let's make a picture of the morning.**

Jesus liked to talk to God in the morning. Let's add our picture of Jesus praying to God. . . . Now we can put a sun in the sky. Help the children add their stickers but don't do this for them. **Tell me what Jesus might be saying to God.**

Lesson 8

Accordion-style fold the drawing paper in fourths. Use the paper doll patterns from page 285. Trace a boy and a girl on the top layer of the folds. Cut them out. Make girl sets for the girls and boy sets for the boys. In class, have children add clothing, hair, and faces to the paper dolls to look like their friends.

Book/Puzzle Center

Unit 2—Talking to God

Items to Include:

Lesson 6
- Copies of page 283
- Poster board
- Glue
- Scissors

Lesson 7
- Picture books for children (*See list on page 267.*)

Purpose: The child will know that God hears us when we pray.

Things to Do and Say

Lesson 6

Make several sets of puzzles. Each set needs two copies of the puzzle on page 283. Use one copy for the puzzle base. Glue the second copy to a piece of sturdy poster board. Make sure the glue completely covers the paper. Cut the puzzle apart along the puzzle lines. Children will use the uncut copy as a guide and place the puzzle pieces on top of it.

As children work on the puzzles, ask, **What is the picture on this puzzle piece? Who is in this picture? Point to Jesus. What is Jesus doing in this picture? When is Jesus praying? Point to the sun that tells us it is morning. Jesus prayed in the morning. What might Jesus be saying to God? God heard Jesus when Jesus prayed. Let's pretend we are Jesus. What might we say to God? God hears us when we pray.**

Lesson 7

Have books displayed on a table or in a book rack. If you don't have tables and chairs in this area, have a large rug and/or pillows on the floor. Make the area inviting. When you are seated with a book in your hand, 2's and 3's are going to be interested. If a book has too much story for young children, "picture read" it. That is, look at the pictures, talk about them, ask children questions, and have them point to specific things or people.

Art Center, continued

Scissors
Transparent tape

As children work, talk about friends. **Our friends are important people. Do you like to play with your friends? We can do lots of things with our friends. . . . Jesus liked to pray with His friends. Peter liked to pray with his friends too. Peter's friends prayed for him when he was in jail. What might Peter's friends pray? What might you pray for your friends. Thank You, God, for friends.**

Lesson 9
Poster board
Glue, scissors
Aluminum foil
Pattern (page 287)
4" squares of tissue paper

Lesson 9

Prepare "mirrors." Cut mirror shapes from poster board and glue aluminum foil to one side.

In class, have children crumble the squares of tissue paper into balls. Glue them close together on the back sides of the mirrors. Help them add their Bible-words stickers to the handles.

Our mirrors will tell us something very important. They will show us who can pray to God. Look in your mirror. Who do you see? Who can pray to God? Molly can pray to God. Our Bible words say, "I pray to God."

Book/Puzzle Center, continued

Do you like to talk? God wants us to talk to Him. We can talk to God about anything. God asked King Solomon to ask Him for anything. Our Bible words say, "I pray to God." We can talk to God about anything because we know that God hears us when we pray.

As the children look at the books, ask them to tell what they might talk to God about in the picture. **What can we say in a prayer to God?**

Game Center

Unit 2—Talking to God

Items to Include:

Lesson 8
Copies of page 286
Scissors

Purpose: The child will say the Bible words, "I pray to God."

Things to Do and Say

Lesson 7

Jesus liked to talk to God in the morning. King Solomon liked to talk to God at nighttime. Any time of the day is a good time to pray. Our Bible words say, "I pray to God." Let's say our Bible words, "I pray to God."

Let's play a game. When I say, "Jesus prayed in the morning," you stretch and yawn. When I say, "Solomon prayed at night," you lie down on the floor and pretend to sleep. When I say our Bible words, "I pray to God," you say, "I pray to God" and take a giant step with each word you say. Direct the children to start at one end of the room. When they all reach the finish point, have them turn around and go back to the starting point.

Lesson 8

Make a copy of page 286 and cut the cards apart. If you have a large group you may want to have several sets of games cards.

It's fun to have friends, isn't it. I'm glad I have friends, aren't you glad you have friends? Peter had friends. Peter's friends prayed for him when he was in jail. God heard their prayers and freed Peter from jail. Peter was glad he had friends.

This is Peter. Show picture. **Here are some pictures of Peter's friends. This is**

Family Living Center

Unit 2—Talking to God

Items to Include:

Lesson 7
Dolls, doll beds
Dishpan of warm water
Wash cloths
Towels and soap
Toothbrushes
Hair brushes

Lessons 8 and 9
Paper plates
Blanket
Plastic spoons/forks
Napkins
Paper cups
Paper grocery bags

Purpose: The child will pray in many situations and activities.

Things to Do and Say

Lesson 7

Have children get the dolls ready for bed, pray with them, and put them to bed. Encourage the children to thank God that they can pray to Him.

Jesus prayed to God at night. Solomon prayed to God at night. Our Bible verse says, "I pray to God." We can talk to God at night. What do we do at night? Yes, we sleep. We get ready for bed. What do you do to get ready for bed? I take a bath, brush my teeth, and brush my hair. Before I crawl into bed, "I pray to God."

Lessons 8 and 9

To prepare a paper bag picnic basket, cut the top off of a paper grocery sack. Fold the top down 1 or 2 inches and cut "fringe." Cut a handle from the top half and glue it to the sides of the basket. Cut food pictures from magazines and glue "meals" to the paper plates. Set out the baskets, plates of food, napkins, forks/spoons, and the blanket in the center.

Say, **Who has been on a picnic? What did you do? What did you eat? Where did you go for your picnic?** Show the paper basket. **Did you take your food in a basket?** Show the blanket. **Did you sit on a blanket and eat?**

A picnic is a good time to pray to God. What might we say to God on a picnic? We

Game Center, continued

Lesson 9
Masking tape
Bell

Rhoda. Show picture. **This is Mary. This is John Mark. These are more of Peter's friends.**

Give each child one picture. Lay the matching picture face up on the table or floor. When you say "Go," encourage the children to find the matching pictures. When they do they should shout, "I pray to God."

What might Peter's friends pray to God? What could you pray to God for your friends?

Lesson 9

Use masking tape to make three large shapes (circle, triangle, square) on the floor. Keep them close together.

Jesus liked to pray to God. He asked God to help Him and to help His friends. King Solomon liked to pray to God too. He asked God to help him be a good king. When Peter was in prison, his friends prayed. They asked God to help Peter. God heard their prayers.

Our Bible words say, "I pray to God." We can pray to God and He will hear us. Let's play a game to help us remember that when we pray to God, He hears us.

Each child starts out in one shape. At the sound of the bell, the children say the Bible words, "I pray to God," and then they hop to another shape. When they stop hopping, they say, "And He hears me!" Repeat several times.

Family Living Center, continued

Magazine pictures of food
Scissors, glue

could tell God thank-you for our food. Let's pretend we are on a picnic today. Let's spread out our blanket and eat. When the children are ready pray, **Thank You, God, for our good food.**

God's Wonders Center

Unit 2—Talking to God

Items to Include:

Lesson 6
Loaf of bread
Peanut butter or finger gelatin
Knife
Cookie cutters
Paper plates

Purpose: The child will pray in many situations and activities.

Things to Do and Say

Lesson 6

If you use finger gelatin, prepare it before class. To make finger gelatin, boil 1 1/2 cups water. Add three packages of unflavored gelatin and dissolve. Add 12 oz. thawed frozen juice concentrate. Put in the refrigerator to set. Cut gelatin squares slightly larger than the largest cookie cutter. Place each square on a paper plate. Provide cookie cutters in shapes from nature, such as stars, flowers, animals, and so forth.

Show the children the cookie cutters. **Here are the shapes of some things from God's world. Let's name these things. Do you have a kitty at home? Thank You, God, for kitties. . . . Do you see the stars in the sky at night? Thank You, God, for the pretty stars. . . . Our Bible words say, "I pray to God." Let's say our Bible words together. "I pray to God." When we thank God for things in His world, we pray to God.**

Help children cut a shape from a piece of bread or from the gelatin. Help them spread peanut butter on the bread. As the children prepare the snack, talk about food. **God gives us our food. We can thank God for our food. Thank You, God, for food.** When the snacks are prepared, lead the children to pray, **Thank You, God, that we can talk to You. Thank You, God, for our food.**

Music/Drama Center

Unit 2—Talking to God

Items to Include:

Purpose: The child will know that God hears us when we pray.

Things to Do and Say

Lesson 6

Jesus liked to talk to God. The Bible says that Jesus prayed in the morning. The Bible says that Jesus prayed at nighttime. Lead children in singing this song to the first two lines of "Old MacDonald Had a Farm."

In the morning (*yawn and stretch*), Jesus prayed. He prayed. He prayed. He prayed.
(*Fold hands together when saying the word prayed.*)
Jesus prayed, "Thank You, God" (*Hold out hands.*). He prayed, He prayed, He prayed.
In the nighttime (*head on hands; close eyes*), Jesus prayed. He prayed. He prayed. He prayed.
Jesus prayed, "Thank You, God." He prayed. He prayed. He prayed. (*Fold hands.*)
God heard Jesus when He prayed. God heard. God heard. God heard.
(*Cup hands behind ears at the word heard.*)
Jesus prayed, "Thank You, God." God heard. God heard. God heard. God heard.

We can be like Jesus. We can pray to God. Our Bible words say, "I pray to God." Lets say our Bible words. "I pray to God." When can we pray to God? We can pray in the morning. We can pray at nighttime. We can pray anytime.

God's Wonders Center, continued

Lesson 7
Magnifying glass(es)
Dress-up clothes
Gold construction paper
Crown pattern (page 285)
Transparent tape

Lesson 7

Make one crown from gold construction paper for each child.

Solomon was a very wise king. He liked to talk to God. He was a very wise king because he prayed to God. Let's pretend we are King Solomon. Let's take a walk in our palace gardens. What kinds of things do kings wear? Yes, kings wear royal robes and crowns. I have a crown for each one of you. Adjust a crown to fit each child's head, and then tape it together. If dress-up clothes are available, have children put them on. Take the group on a walk outside the church building. Point out things in the yard such as the green grass and trees. Use the magnifying glass to take a closer look at them. Let each child look through the magnifying glass. Say, **Thank You, God, for the grass.** Do this for each item.

Music/Drama Center, continued

Sing the song several more times using a child's name in place of Jesus' name. Do this for each child. Point to, stand by, or put a hand on the child being named in the song.

Lesson 8
Black construction paper

Lesson 8

From black construction paper, prepare a paper chain with eight links for each child.

The Bible tells us that God hears us when we pray. God heard Peter's friends pray when Peter was in jail. God freed Peter from jail. Peter's chains fell off. An angel led Peter out of the jail.

Let's pretend to be Peter in jail. Have pupils sit against the wall with legs outstretched. Drape the paper chains across the children's feet. Ask, **Do you like being chained up in jail? No! How are we going to get out of jail? We will pray to God. Our friends will pray to God. What will we say? What might our friends say? Help me! Look, our chains are falling off!** Remove chains. **We can walk out of jail!** Lead children out of jail. **God hears us when we pray. Thank You, God, that we can talk to You. Thank You for hearing us when we pray.**

Lesson 9
Cube made from page 289

Lesson 9

Have children take turns rolling the cube. Hold up the cube with the picture that came on top showing. Ask, **Who is in this picture? This is King Solomon (Jesus, Peter, or a child). What is he doing? He is praying. Let's pretend we are King Solomon (Jesus, Peter, or us). How might King Solomon (Jesus, Peter, we) pray to God? What might we say to God? Did God hear King Solomon (Jesus, Peter, us) when he (we) prayed? Yes, God hears us when we pray.**

When the pictures of the praying hands come up on top, have the children say the Bible words, "I pray to God," followed by "God hears me when I pray."

 Instructions for making a puzzle are on the Book/Puzzle Learning Center Card.

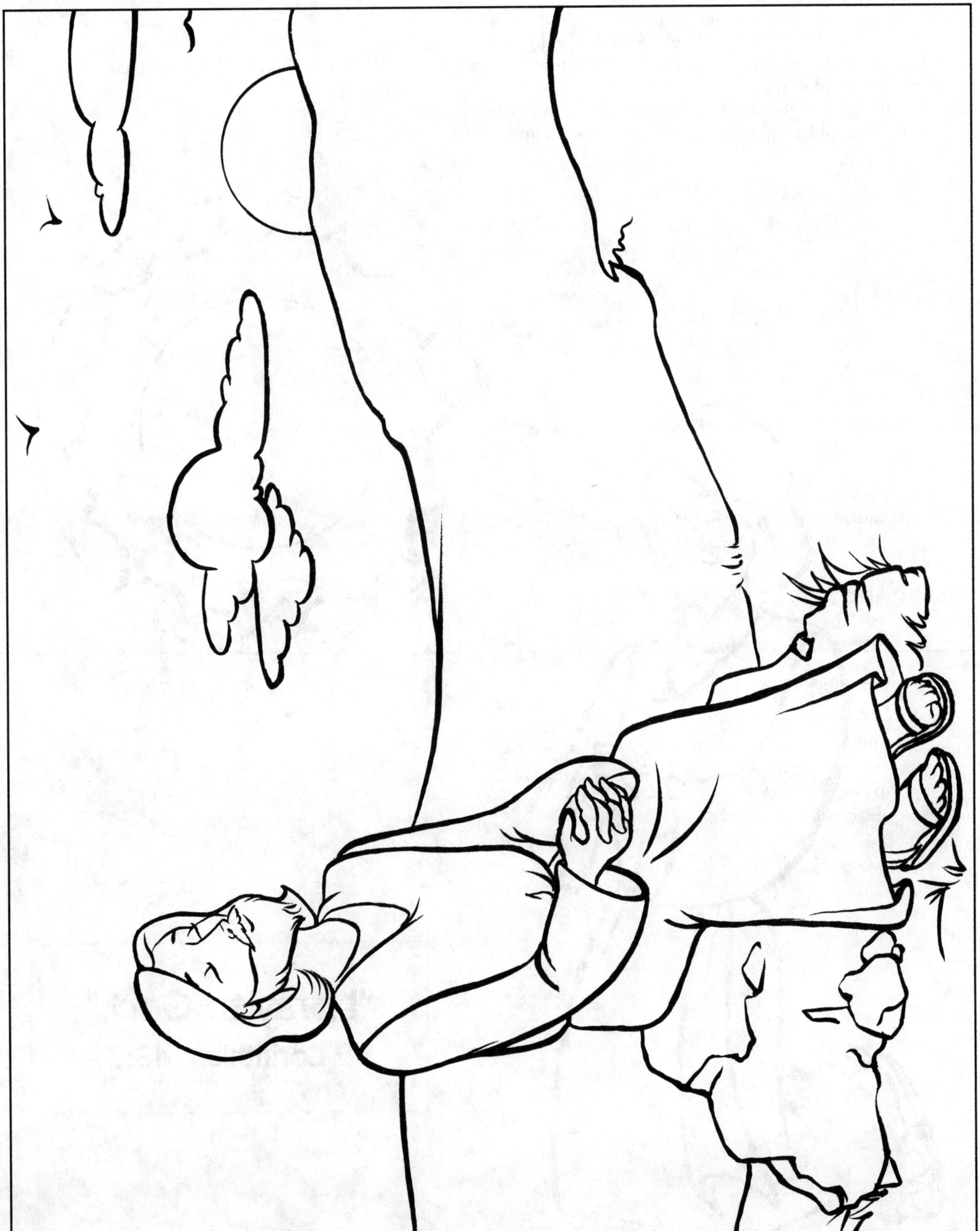

Summer, Unit 2

Instructions

1. Make a copy of this page for each child.
2. Paint a mixture of 2 parts white glue and 1 part vinegar on the backs of the papers. Let this dry.
3. In class, let the children color the stickers before you cut them out. If time is short, add color and cut out stickers ahead of time.
4. Use damp sponges to wet the backs of the stickers before applying.
5. Help the children place their stickers on their papers.

"I pray to God."

2 Corinthians 13:7

Place on fold

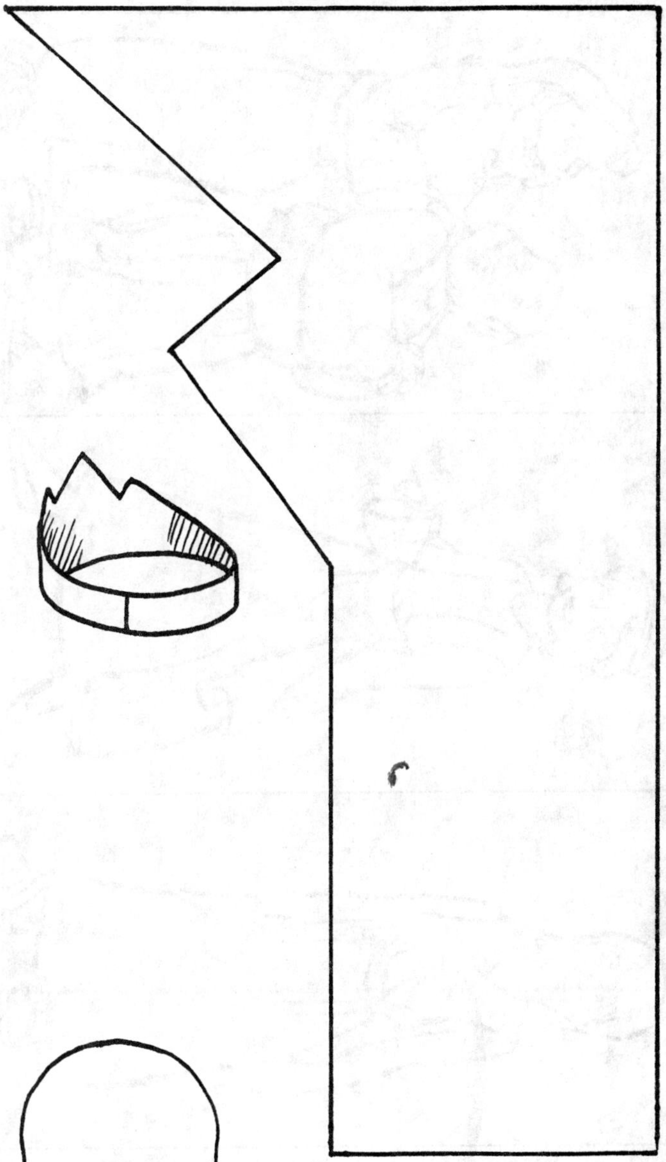

Summer, Unit 2

Instructions for making crowns:

1. Make a cardboard pattern of the crown.
2. Trace onto gold construction paper.
3. Add a 1 3/4" wide strip of the gold paper to make the crown large enough to fit a child's head.
4. Adjust each child's crown on the child's head.
5. To make a crown for Zach, reduce the size of the crown according to the puppet's head.

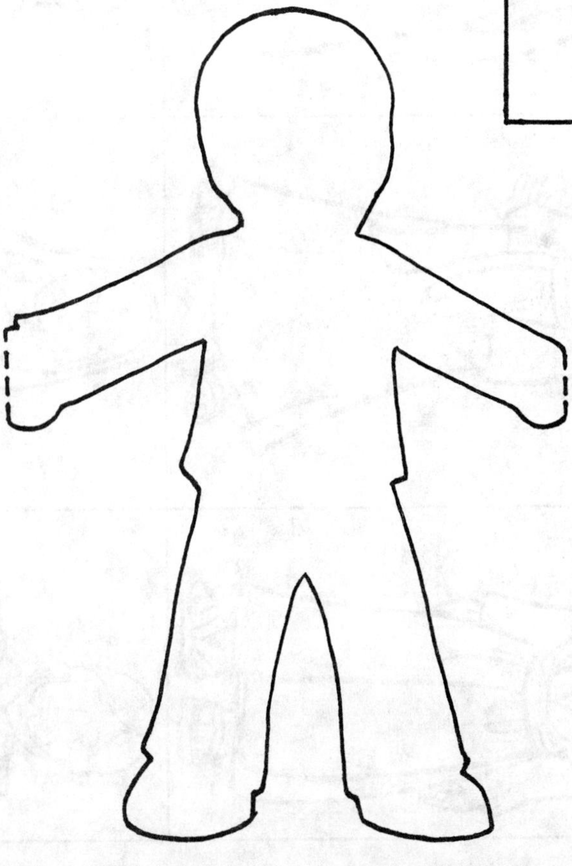

Directions for making paper dolls are on the Art Center Card, Lesson 8.

Directions for Friend Cards are on Game Center Card, Lesson 8.

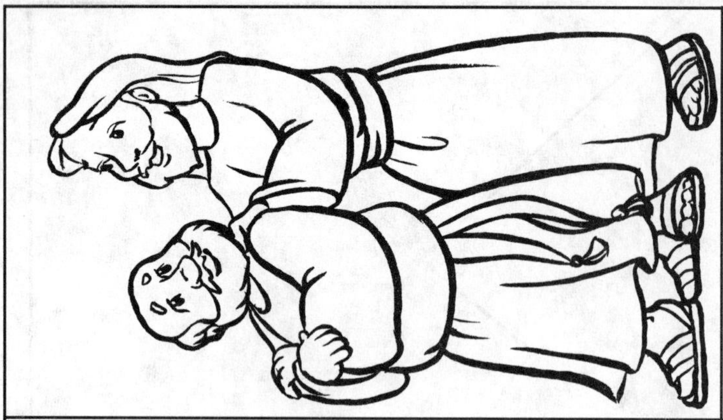
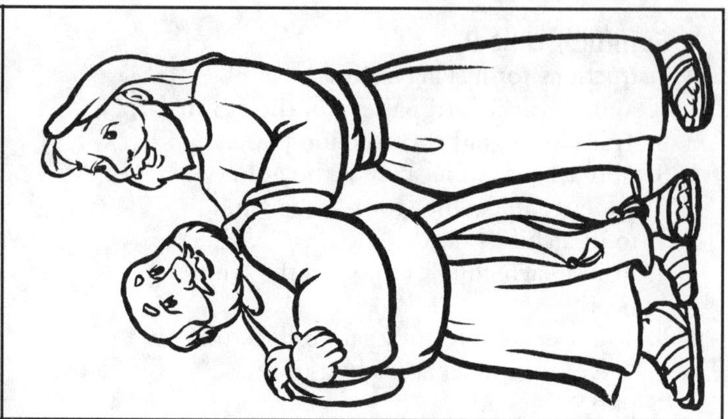
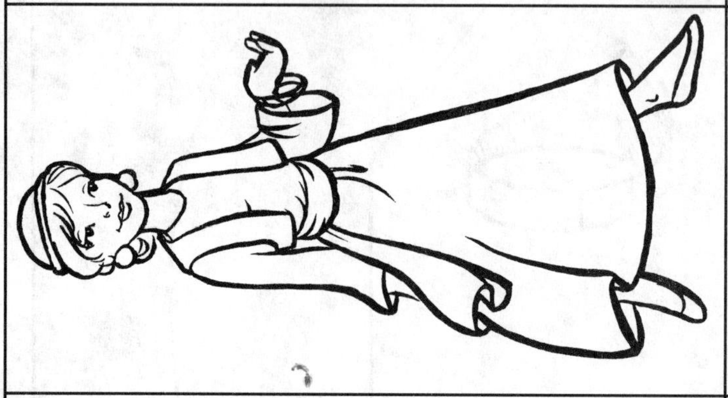
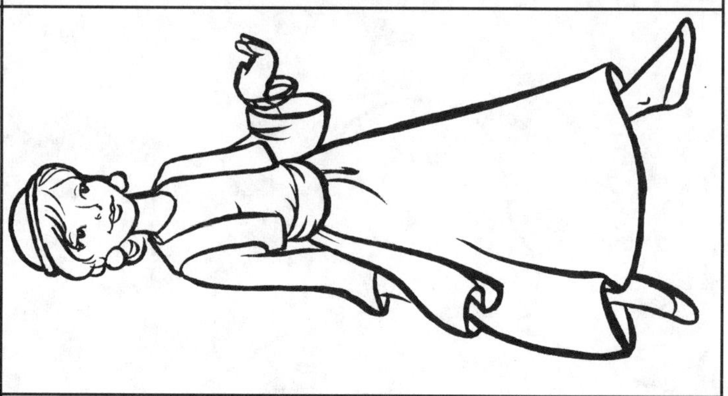
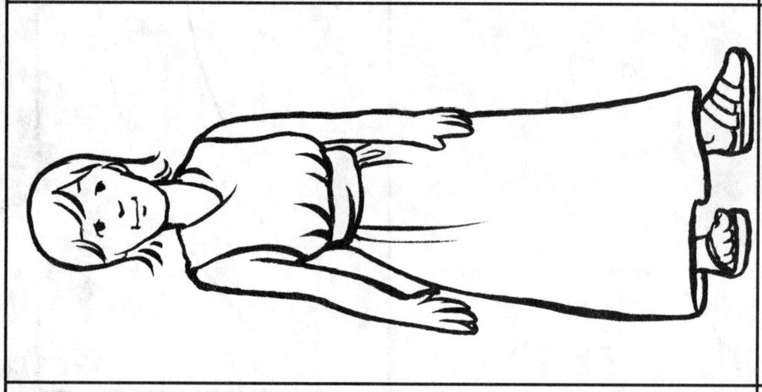
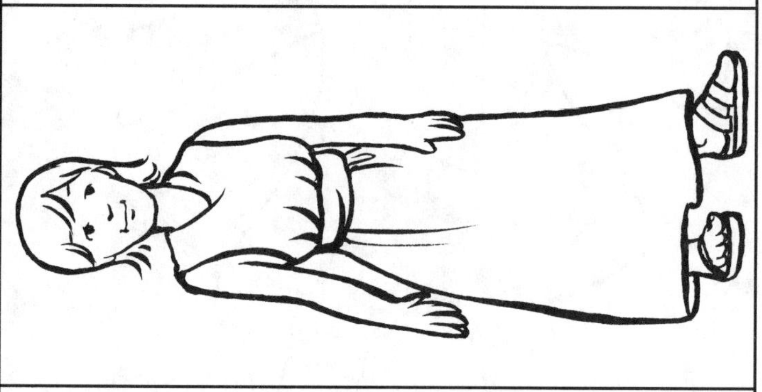
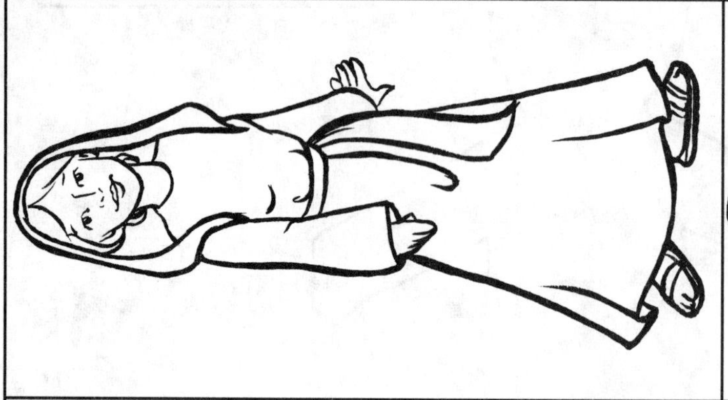

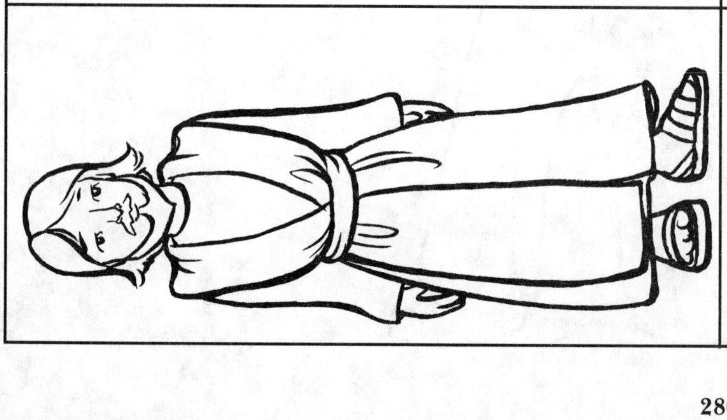
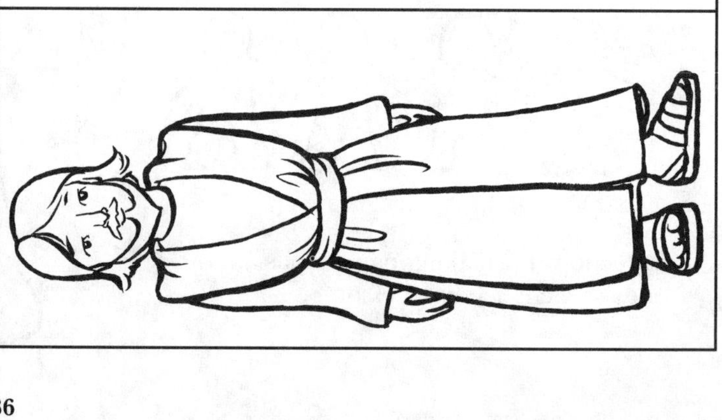

Summer, Unit 2

Mirror pattern for Art Center, Lesson 9

Instructions

1. Make a cardboard pattern of the mirror.
2. Use the pattern to make mirrors out of colored poster board.
3. Glue circles of aluminum foil on mirrors.
4. Children will glue tissue-paper balls to backs of mirrors.
5. Make Bible-words stickers from page 284.

Summer, Unit 2 Stick puppets for Lesson 9

Copy page onto construction paper. Cut on solid lines. Glue a craft stick on the back of each puppet.

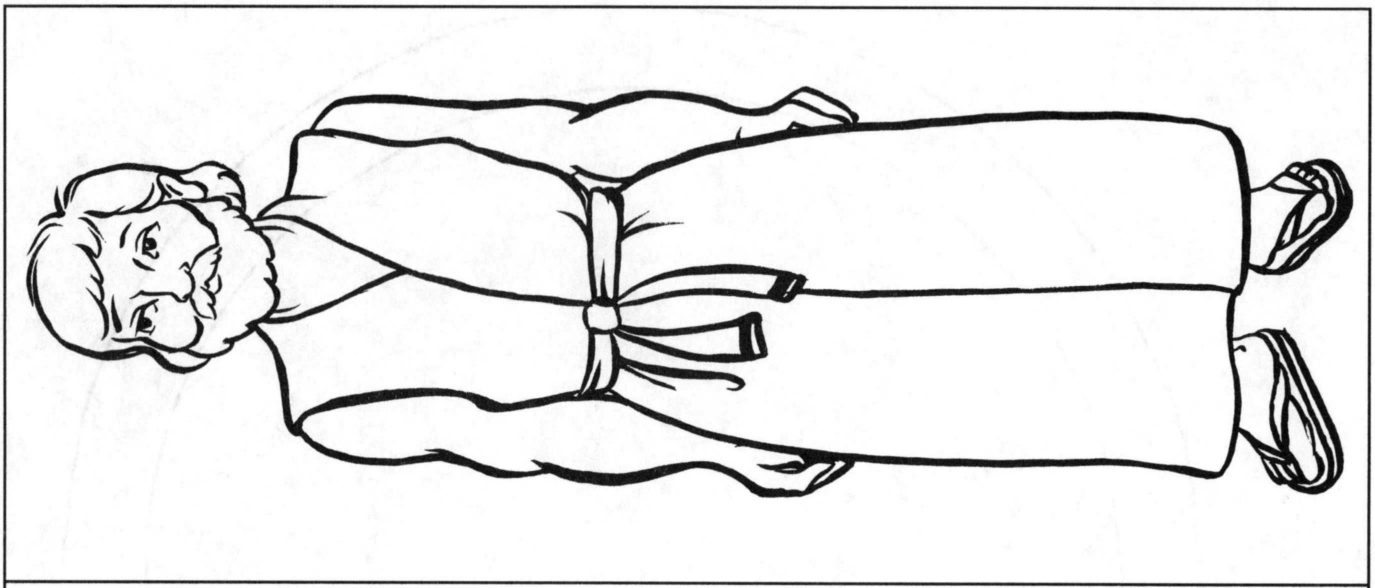

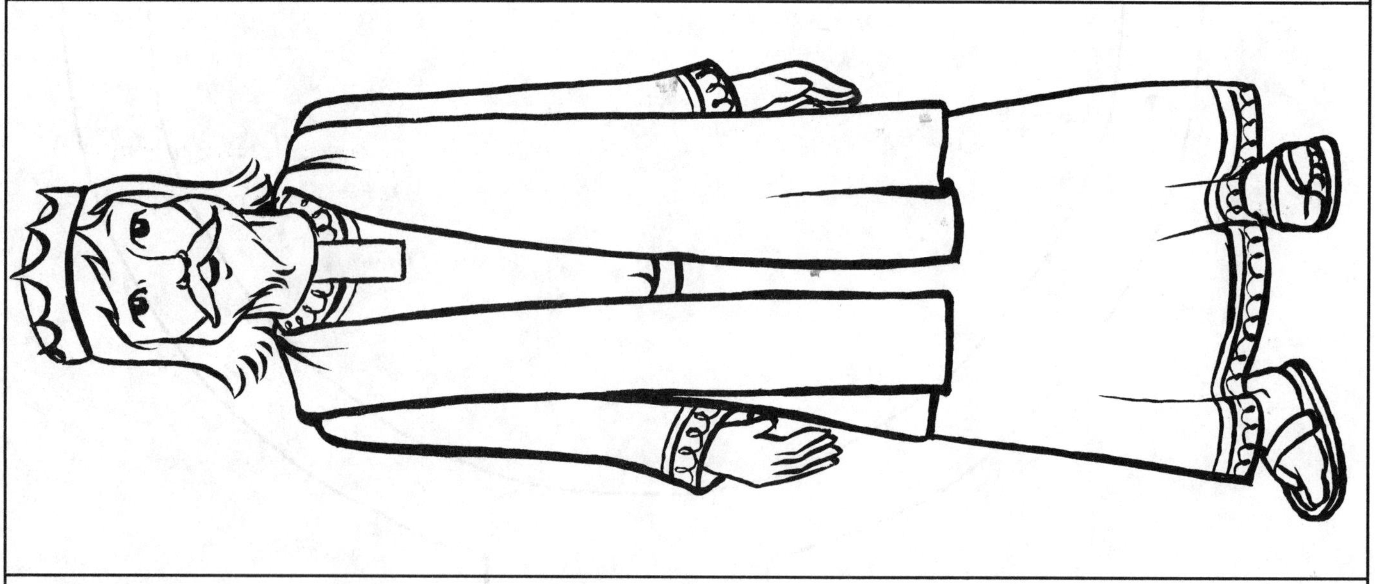

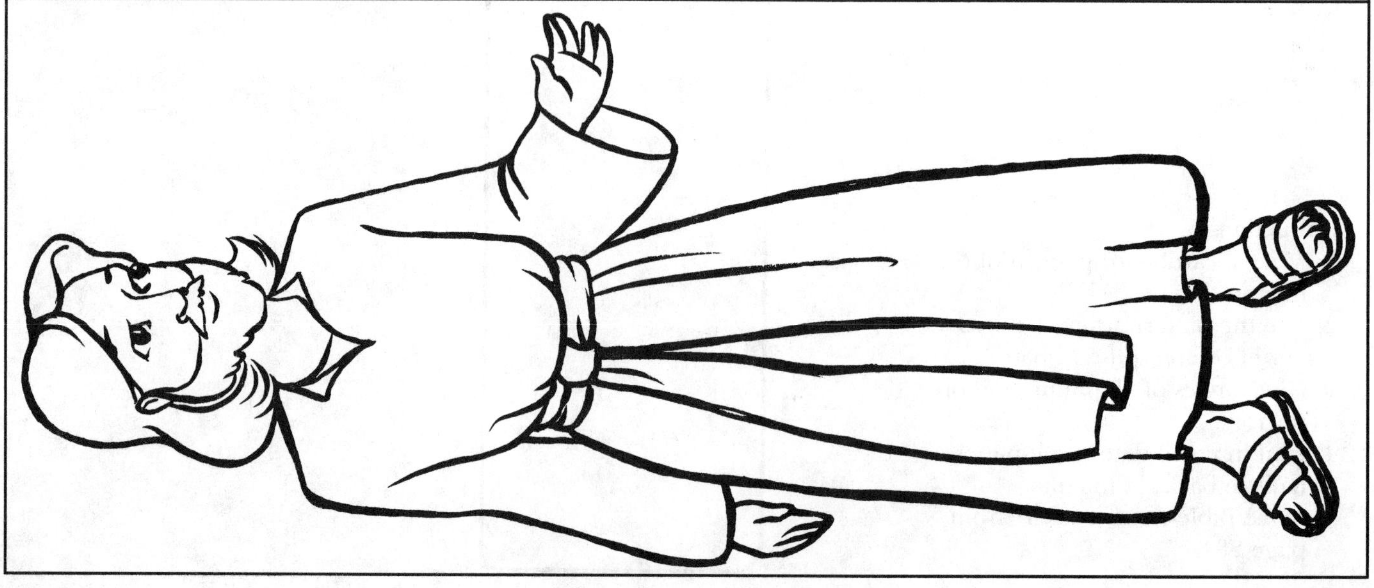

Summer, Unit 2

Instructions

1. Photocopy cube onto construction paper.
2. Fold on dotted lines.
3. Glue where indicated.
4. Use according to suggestions on the Music/Drama Card, Lesson 9.

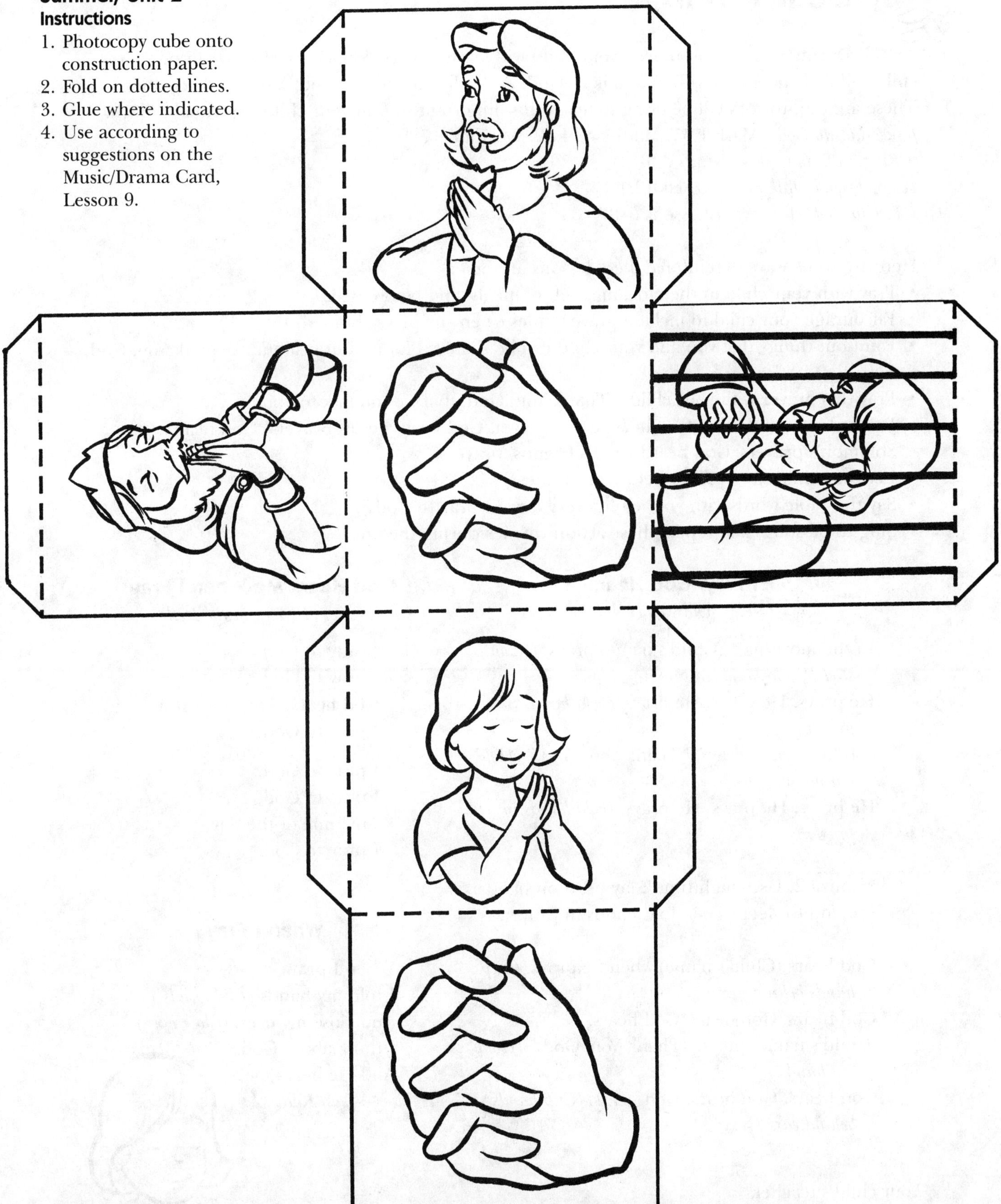

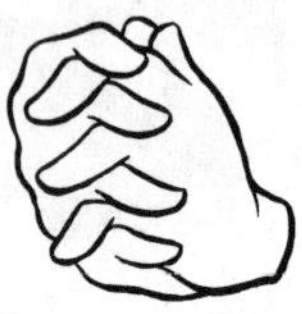

Dear Parent,

During this unit on prayer, your child will learn that God hears us when we pray. Your child will feel eager and willing to talk to God, and will pray in many situations and activities. These are the stories we'll be using to teach this important step in your child's spiritual growth.

Jesus Talks to God (Mark 1:35; Matthew 14:22, 23; John 17)
A King Talks to God (1 Kings 3:3-14)
Peter's Friends Talk to God (Acts 12:1-17)
I Talk to God (Review of Lessons 6–8)

Here are some ways to reinforce these lessons at home:

- Pray with your child in the morning, before meals, and before bed.
- Encourage your child to include prayer times when she plays "house."
- Point out things that you and your child can be thankful for and pray aloud, "Thank You, God, for ________."
- Pray this prayer with your child: "Thank You, God, that we can talk to You."
- Remind your child that God hears every prayer. God heard Jesus' prayers. God heard Solomon's prayers. God heard Peter's friends' prayers.
- Let your child say a prayer before mealtimes.
- Say the Bible words with your child every day: "I pray to God."
- Sing these songs and repeat these action rhymes during the unit.

I Pray, God Hears

(Tune: "Old MacDonald")

In the morning*, (Child's name) prays. *(Yawn, stretch; fold hands in prayer.)*
He prays. He prays. He prays. *(Fold hands in prayer.)*
(Child's name) prays, "Thank You, God." *(Hold out hands.)*
He prays. He prays. He prays. *(Fold hands in prayer.)*

*Stanza 2: Use "nighttime"; lay head on hands, pretend to sleep. Then fold hands in prayer.

God hears (Child's name) when he prays. *(Cup hands behind ears.)*
God hears. God hears. God hears.
(Child's name) prays, "Thank You, God." *(Hold out hands.)*
God hears. God hears. God hears. *(Cup hands behind ears.)*

God Hears Me When I Pray

(Tune: "Farmer in the Dell")

I pray to God.
I pray to God.
God hears me when I pray.
I pray to God.

I pray to God.
I pray to God.
Any time of the day.
I pray to God.

When I Pray

When I pray,
I fold my hands *(Fold hands.)*
And close my eyes. *(Close eyes.)*
I think about God,
And He hears me.
—*Jean Katt*

Your child's teacher,

Unit 3: Helping Others

Lessons 10–13

By the end of the unit, the children will

Know Bible people who were helpers; know that helping shows we love God.

Feel happy and eager to help others.

Help in a variety of situations.

Unit Bible Words

"Love one another." (John 15:17)

Books

from Standard Publishing

Sharing Makes Me Happy 24-03589

All About Hands 24-03593

Busy Feet 24-03594

Look, I'm Growing Up 24-04233

The Unit at a Glance

10 Jesus Helps a Boy — **John 4:46-54**

Jesus uses words to make a sick boy well.

11 A Lady Helps Others — **Acts 9:36, 39**

Dorcas made clothes for people who needed them.

12 Church Friends Give Money to Help — **2 Corinthians 8:1-5; Romans 15:25, 26**

The church in Macedonia sends money to the church in Jerusalem.

13 I Can Help — **Review of Lessons 10–12**

Why Teach This Unit?

At two and three years of age most of your pupils are used to receiving help—lots of help—sometimes too much help. In fact, many children in the United States are handicapped by having too much done for them instead of too little. They experience a great deal of freedom when they are taught how to do things for themselves and a great deal of satisfaction in discovering they can do things for other people.

During this unit the children will learn through the Bible stories about people who helped others. They will learn some practical skills. They will actually experience helping others!

Use your Bible words often as you talk with the children. Say such things as, **When we help others we show we "love one another." . . . When I see you helping I remember the Bible words, "Love one another."**

Highlight and mark the Bible words in your classroom Bible so you can turn to them and point to them whenever a child shows interest.

Things to Do for This Unit:

- Photocopy the Learning Center Cards (pages 301-306); cut pages apart on solid lines. Mount side 1 of a card on cardboard; then mount side 2 on the back of the cardboard. Do this for all cards. Laminate them for durability.

- Gather/prepare materials listed on the Learning Center Cards.
- For Lesson 10, make stick puppets of Jesus and the man, page 307.
- Make copies of the Parents' Letter, page 314.
- For Lesson 11, make visual aid from pages 308 and 309.
- For Lesson 12, make visual aid on page 310.
- For Lesson 13, make booklets from pages 311 and 312.

Use These Songs and Action Rhymes During Unit 3

I Can Help

(Tune: "Mary Had a Little Lamb")

God gave me feet to help,
Feet to help, feet to help.
God gave me feet to help.
I'll use them every day.

(As time and situations allow, substitute these words: hands, arms, a mouth, and legs.)

I Will Help

(Tune: "Row, Row, Row Your Boat")

I will help at home. I will help at home.
I am big enough to help.
I will help at home.
(Substitute "at church," or "my friends," to fit the lesson.)

I Can Talk to God

G. S. GERTRUDE SHANNON

Love One Another

S. T. SYLVIA TESTER

I Want to Help

I want to help in every way!
With ears, and eyes, and mouth, *(Point to each.)*
With feet, *(Bend down and touch feet.)*
And hands, *(Clap hands.)*
I want to help today. —*Dorothy Fay Richards*

My Bible

This is my Bible; *(Palms held together.)*
I'll open it wide *(Open hands; keep them touching.)*
And see (or say) what is written
On the inside! *(Say Bible words: "Love one another.")*
—*Jean Baxendale*

The Busy Fingers

Busy little finger people, *(Hold up closed hands.)*
Who will put the toys (blocks, etc.) away?
"I will," "I will," "I will," "I will," "I will,"
All the fingers say.
(Raise fingers one at a time, beginning with thumbs.) —*Louise M. Oglevee*

make him well? Children respond. **No! He just had to say the word and the boy was well!**

We can't make sick people well the way Jesus did, but we can do things to help sick people feel better. We named some of those things earlier. One of the most important things we can do is to pray for people who are sick. Can you think of someone who is sick right now? If the children can't come up with names, mention some you know. **Let's ask God to help these people get well.** Pray for people by name.

Our Bible words say, "Love one another." We show love for each other when we help each other and pray for each other. Have the children repeat the Bible words with you. If there is time, let the children take turns holding the Bible and "reading" the words aloud.

Learning Activities

(20 minutes)

Let's Play Awhile

Have the children stand and do the action rhyme, "I Want to Help."

In order to be a helper, we don't have to wait until we find someone who is sick. Any time we are around other people we can find someone or some way to help. If you have a baby in your home, you can help by bringing things for the baby. That helps Mommy too. Play the game suggested in the Game Center now.

Let's Go Home

When the game is finished, have Zach say, "We show that we 'love one another' by keeping our room neat so someone else does not have to work hard to clean up after us."

Make sure each child has his or her personal objects and a Parents' Letter to take home. Try to give each parent a positive word about his or her child.

Jesus Helps a Boy

John 4:46-54

Bible Words: "Love one another" (John 15:17).

Lesson Value: One of the most important things preschoolers, or all of us, need to learn is to follow the example of Jesus. When we begin to teach a new virtue, it is natural to begin with an example of Jesus exhibiting that virtue. The examples of Jesus as a helper are endless, but this one of Jesus helping a little boy should be especially meaningful to young children. Of course, we all must accept that our abilities to help anyone are slight when compared to Jesus' abilities, but we always need to hold up His willingness to help and compassion for those who needed help as a goal for which to strive.

Know: Know Bible people who were helpers; know that helping shows we love God.
Feel: Feel happy and eager to help others.
Do: Help in a variety of situations.

Children will accomplish the goals when they:

1. Say the Bible words, "Love one another."
2. Pray, "Dear God, help us be helpers for You."
3. Tell what Jesus did to help.
4. Help someone in the classroom.

Let's Get Ready

Make sure a box of tissues is available for the introduction. You will also need Zach. For the Bible Story you will need a Bible and the stick puppets from page 307.

Set up the Family Living Center, the Block Center, and the Book and Picture Center. If you are the only teacher, use just the Family Living Center. The Game Center will be used after the Bible story.

Learning Activities

(30 minutes, including 10 minutes presession)

Let's Get Started

Have Zach greet each child by saying, "I see Todd, who is a good helper. Good morning, Todd." After each child has added his or her attendance sticker, say, **Would you prefer to work in the Block Center or the Family Living Center first?** Allowing the child to make a choice is good as long as either choice is acceptable to you. Then make sure that the child sticks with his choice and becomes involved in the activity. A child who does not take part in an activity is not learning all he can, and may become a problem to you as well as to the other children.

Worship and Bible Story

(15 minutes)

Let's Worship God

About two minutes before you have Zach announce clean-up time, gently remind the children at each center that it is almost time to stop their playing. As the first child arrives in the story circle, begin singing the song, "I Can Help." As time allows, substitute hands, a mouth, legs, and arms. Talk about ways children can use those body parts to help others. Introduce the song, "I Will Help." Lead the children in the action rhyme, "I Want to Help." (All songs and action rhymes are on page 292.) Pray, **Dear God, help us to find ways to be helpers.**

Let's Learn From the Bible

Introduction: Have Zach pretend to sneeze. Say, **Oh dear, I believe Zach is getting a cold. What can we do for him?** Let the children suggest some things to help anyone get over a cold. Say, **Abby, will you please bring Zach a tissue? We cannot make someone who has a cold well, but there are many things we can do to help him.**

Our Bible story tells about someone who did make sick people well. I would like for each of you to take a tissue and hold it. When you hear me say the name of the person who could make people well, you hold up your tissue. Put Zach away now. Place your story notes and stick puppets inside your Bible, which should be on your lap.

The Bible Story: One day Jesus *(hold up Jesus stick puppet)* was in a town called Cana. A man *(hold up second stick puppet)*, whose little boy was very sick, went up to Jesus. The man begged Jesus, "Please, sir, come before my little boy dies!"

Jesus told the man, "Go. Your little boy will live." Jesus did not have to go to the man's home to make the boy well!

The man left Jesus and started home. *(Turn man around and move away from Jesus; then remove Jesus puppet.)* On his way home some men met the man and told him, "Your little boy is well!"

The man asked, "What time did my little boy begin to get well?"

When the men answered, the man knew his little boy had gotten well just when Jesus had spoken the words, "Your little boy will live." How happy the man was that Jesus had helped his little boy!

Let's Apply the Lesson

What did the man want Jesus to do? Let the children respond. **Did Jesus have to go to where the sick boy was to**

need clothes? (Giving money or giving away clothes they have outgrown.)

Our Bible words say, "Love one another." Dorcas did not have to tell people she loved them. She showed people she loved them by working hard to make them good clothes to wear. Please say our Bible words with me as you bring your piece of clothing to put back in the pillowcase.

Learning Activities

(20 minutes)

Let's Play Awhile

Today, some people help other people by making clothes for them. People who sew have many things to help them sew that Dorcas did not have. Play the game suggested on the Game Center Card for Lesson 11.

Let's Go Home

When the game is finished, have Zach remind the children to show love by putting the room back in order. When the children have finished, gather them together and sing a favorite song. Show them the covered container they all worked on in the Art Center and remind them that it will be taken to someone who cannot get out and come to church. Say, **I am sure this will help (name) feel better. I hope each of you finds a special way to help someone this week.**

A Lady Help Others

Acts 9:36, 39

Bible Words: "Love one another" (John 15:17).

Lesson Value: Dorcas is a Christian woman with whom preschoolers can identify. In fact, many of them may know someone a lot like Dorcas. Dorcas did practical things for people, such as providing clothes. Children know that people need clothes. The example of Dorcas can help preschoolers understand that they too can help others in practical ways. They can also learn from these lessons that Dorcas helped because she followed the example of Jesus.

Know: Know Bible people who were helpers; know that helping shows we love God.
Feel: Feel happy and eager to help others.
Do: Help in a variety of situations.

Children will accomplish the goals when they:

1. Say the Bible Words, "Love one another."
2. Pray, "Dear God, help us be helpers for You."
3. Tell what Dorcas did to help.
4. Help someone in the classroom.

Let's Get Ready

You will need Zach and a pillowcase of old clothes for the introduction. For the Bible story you will need the visuals made from pages 308 and 309 and a Bible. You may want to color in the quilt designs.

Prepare the Family Living Center, the Art Center, and God's Wonders Center for this period. If you are the only teacher, use just the Art Center. After the Bible story, have the Game Center ready.

Learning Activities

(30 minutes, including 10 minutes presession)

Let's Get Started

Have Zach greet each child by commenting on what he or she is wearing. Zach could say something like, "Good morning, Mark. I see you are wearing a nice blue shirt. Did someone give you your shirt?" Give the child a choice of learning activities. Say, **Would you like to wash clothes or glue a quilt first?**

Worship and Bible Story

(15 minutes)

Let's Worship God

Give the children a two-minute warning before clean-up time. Have Zach give the actual clean-up signal. As the first child arrives in the story circle again sing "I Can Help," using "hands" instead of "feet." If time allows also use the words *mouth, legs, feet,* and *arms.* Then sing "I Will Help," using "at home" and "my friends." Pray, **Dear God, help us find ways to be good helpers.**

Let's Learn From the Bible

Introduction: Fill a pillowcase with enough old clothes for each child to pull out one item. Have Zach ask each child in turn what piece of clothing he has and who might wear something like that. Have Zach say, "Dogs do not need clothing, but people do."

Respond by saying, **That's right, Zach, people do need clothing. Some people cannot get clothing by themselves. They need someone to make or buy clothing for them. Today we are going to learn about a lady who made clothes for people. Boys and girls, hold onto your clothing and pretend to sew while I tell you about her.** Demonstrate sewing actions for the children. Now put Zach away. Place your Bible, with story notes and visuals inside, in your lap as you begin.

The Bible Story: The Bible tells us about a woman everyone loved. Her name was Dorcas. Dorcas was like Jesus—she helped people. She couldn't make people well like Jesus could. But she did help people by sewing for them. The Bible does not tell us that Dorcas made quilts, but we are going to make a quilt about her. *(Place strips 1 and 2 on felt board side by side.)* Dorcas must have had a real talent for sewing. *(Place strip 3 on board under strip 1.)*

Many people who can sew make beautiful things for themselves. The Bible tells us that Dorcas used her sewing to help others. Dorcas made clothes for children. *(Place strip 4 on felt board beside strip 3.)* Dorcas made clothes for grown-ups. *(Place strip 5 under strip 3.)* Dorcas made clothes for people who did not have enough clothes. Everyone loved Dorcas because she helped others *(Place strip 6 beside strip 5.)*

Let's Apply the Lesson

How did Dorcas help other people? Let the children respond. **You have been pretending to sew while you listened to the Bible story today. Most of us can't sew well enough to make clothes for other people like Dorcas did. Can you think of ways that we can help other people who might**

Let's Apply the Lesson

Thank you for keeping your hands in the shape of a church building. The church-friends in Jerusalem and the church-friends in Macedonia didn't have a church building that looked like this. Can you open your building and look inside? *(Demonstrate how to do this.)* **Look, I see people. They are really the church.**

Our Bible words say, "Love one another." Do you think the church-friends in Macedonia *(show side B)* **loved the church-friends in Jerusalem?** *(Show side A.)* Let the children respond. **Yes, I think they did. Even though they never met each other, they loved the church-friends in Jerusalem.**

Let's say the Bible words together. Do so. **How can we help our church-friends?** Let the children suggest ways. Give them help only if it is necessary. **Could we help some church-friends far away? Yes, we could send some money to help them.**

Learning Activities

(20 minutes)

Let's Play Awhile

Let the children stand and stretch. Then do the action rhyme, "I Want to Help."

Now we are going to make a picture to remind us that church-friends are helpers. Help the children get started on their stenciling. Have the paint in shallow dishes with sponges in the paint. Ask one child to hold the stencil for you. Show how to press your sponge on the sponge in the paint, then on the plate inside the stencil.

Let's Go Home

If you have time, do the action rhyme, "The Busy Fingers." See that each child has his art activity ready to take home. If the plates are too wet, they may have to be left until next week.

Church Friends Give Money to Help

2 Corinthians 8:1-5; Romans 15:25, 26

Bible Words: "Love one another" (John 15:17).

Lesson Value: Many preschoolers view the church as a building rather than a gathering of loving believers. This lesson is a good place to *begin* to change that concept. They need to know that people who make up Jesus' church are people who will help because they follow the example of Jesus in loving and caring for others. Remember, however, the lesson you begin teaching today will be reinforced over and over again as your preschoolers grow up.

Know: Know Bible people who were helpers; know that helping shows we love God.
Feel: Feel happy and eager to help others.
Do: Help in a variety of situations.

Children will accomplish the goals when they:

1. Say the Bible Words, "Love one another."
2. Pray, "Dear God, help us be helpers for You."
3. Tell what the church-friends did to help.
4. Help someone in the classroom.

Let's Get Ready

For the Bible story, have a bank that Zach can "hold" and shake. Prepare the circle visual aid from page 310. You will also need your classroom Bible.

Prepare the activities in the Family Living Center, the God's Wonders Center, and the Block Center. If you are teaching alone, use just the Family Living Center. Be ready to do the Art Center project after the Bible story.

Learning Activities

(30 minutes, including 10 minutes presession)

Let's Get Started

Have Zach say something like, "I'm glad you could come to church today. We're going to find out today how everyone in the church can be a helper." Say, **Right now, some of you can go outside where we are going to help the people who take care of the churchyard. We are going to pull some weeds** (or whatever job you have found to do). **After that you can either bake a pie or build with the blocks.**

Worship and Bible Story

(15 minutes)

Let's Worship God

Go to each center and warn the children that Zach will be around soon to tell them to begin cleaning up. Have Zach follow in about two minutes. As the children gather in the worship area, begin singing songs from this unit. After everyone has gathered sing these words to the tune of "Mary Had a Little Lamb."

God wants the church to help,
Church to help, church to help.
The church has many hands and feet.
God wants the church to help.

Ask the children what the line, "The church has many hands and feet," means. If they cannot tell you, say, **The church is made up of people. Most people have two hands and two feet, so the church has many hands and feet.** Pray, **Dear God, thank You for the church. Help us to make this church a helping church.**

Let's Learn From the Bible

Introduction: Have Zach hold a bank and shake it. Say, **Raise your hand if you think you know what Zach has in his bank.** Let the children guess. Then say, **If you guessed money, you are right. We are going to find out how long ago some church-friends helped some other church-friends with money.**

Show the children how to make the classic church building by interweaving their middle, ring, and small fingers, and making a steeple with their index fingers and a door with their thumbs. Ask them to hold their hands like that while you tell the Bible story. If possible, have another adult lead in doing this. Put Zach away at this time. Have your story notes and visual aid in your Bible, on your lap or by your side.

The Bible Story: *(Show side A of your visual.)* The Bible tells us that the church in Jerusalem needed help. They had helped many people in the past. They had given money to help other people. Then there came a famine. That means that no food would grow. The people in the Jerusalem church were hungry!

(Turn circle around.) Far away in a place called Macedonia, some church-friends heard about the hungry people in Jerusalem. They wanted to help. Even though the people in Macedonia were poor, the Bible tells us that they gave a lot of money to help their hungry church-friends in Jerusalem. *(Show side A again, then turn back to B.)* The church-friends in Macedonia went without some of the things they needed to help another church. By helping the hungry church-friends, they showed they loved God. How pleased God must have been!

Dorcas helped with her hands. How can we help with our hands? Let the children respond. **One church helped with money. How can we help with money?** Let the children respond.

Our Bible Words say, "Love one another." We show love to others by helping them. We also show our love for God when we help others. We can help and show love by telling others our Bible words. Let's say them together. Do so. **Will you help someone this week by saying those words to them?**

Learning Activities

(20 minutes)

Let's Play Awhile

Today we are going to make something that you can use to let you be a helper at home. Do the activity suggested on the Art Center Learning Card. If you have time, you might repeat one of the activities in the Game Center.

Let's Go Home

As the children are working with their dusters, have Zach remind them to help by picking up any toys that have been left out. Make sure each child has her duster and mini-Bible storybook before her parents arrive.

I Can Help

Review of Lessons 10–12

Bible Words: "Love one another" (John 15:17).

Lesson Value: The children have seen the examples of Jesus, Dorcas, and church-friends helping others. The children need to know that there are ways for them to follow those examples even though they are very young. Being able to do things for themselves gives preschoolers a great deal of confidence. Being able to do things for others will give them a great deal of satisfaction and begin a habit of helping that should last a lifetime.

Know: Know Bible people who were helpers; know that helping shows we love God.
Feel: Feel happy and eager to help others.
Do: Help in a variety of situations.

Children will accomplish the goals when they:

1. Say the Bible Words, "Love one another."
2. Pray, "Dear God, help us be helpers for You."
3. Tell what Bible people did to help.
4. Help someone in the classroom.

Let's Get Ready

For the Bible story, use the patterns on pages 311 and 312 to make a mini-Bible storybook for each child and for yourself. Follow the directions on page 313 to make stick-on glue to put on the stickers for this lesson. You will also need your classroom Bible.

Prepare materials for the Family Living Center, God's Wonders Center, and the Book and Picture Center. If you are the only teacher, use just the Book and Picture Center. Have the materials ready to do the art project in the Art Center.

Learning Activities

(30 minutes, including 10 minutes presession)

Let's Get Started

Have Zach say, "Here is Anna. Anna, how have you been a helper this week?" Give each child two choices from the three learning centers suggested for this period. If you do not have enough staff to do all three at the same time, you could wait until the end of this period and do the God's Wonders Center as a group.

Worship and Bible Story

(15 minutes)

Let's Worship God

Warn the children that it is time to be finishing up their activities about two minutes before Zach announces clean-up. As the children gather together, have them sing favorite songs from this unit or from the entire quarter. Finish with the song, "I Can Help." As the children suggest the various "tools" (hands, feet) that God gave them to help with, ask them how they can help with these. Pray, **Dear God, thank You for making our bodies so they can be used to help others.**

Let's Learn From the Bible

Introduction: Say, **I'm thinking of someone who used words to make a sick boy well. Can you guess who I am talking about?** Let the children respond.

I'm thinking of a lady who used her hands to help others. Can you guess who I am talking about? Let the children respond.

I'm thinking of some people who gave money to help. Can you guess who they are? Let the children respond. **I have a small Bible storybook for each of you. I want you to turn your pages with me as I find the story in my big Bible.** Give the children the Bible storybooks you made before class.

The Bible Story: *(Open your mini-Bible and your big Bible to John 4:46-54.)* The Bible tells us about a time when Jesus said some words in one town and a boy who was very sick in another town was made well. Jesus used words to help. Our words are not as powerful as the words of Jesus, but we can use our words to help others.

(Open your mini-Bible and your big Bible to Acts 9:36, 39.) The Bible tells us about a woman who used her hands to sew clothes for many people. She helped people keep warm and feel better about themselves by sewing with her hands. Our hands may not be able to make clothes, but we can use our hands to help.

(Open your mini-Bible and your big Bible to 2 Corinthians 8:1-5.) The Bible tells us that church-friends in Macedonia sent money they really needed themselves to help the church-friends in Jerusalem who were hungry. We may not have a lot of money, but we can use the little bit of money we do have to help others.

Let's Apply the Lesson

Let the children lick and stick the appropriate stickers into their books as you talk about each story. **Jesus helped with words. How can we help with words?** Let the children respond. If the children have trouble, suggest things such as saying kind things or telling someone you love him or her.

Art Center

Unit 3—Helping Others

Items to Include:

Lesson 11
- 1" squares of fabrics
- Large plastic container
- Glue
- Flowers or candy

Lesson 12
- Stencil (page 313)
- Paint
- Sponges
- Paper plates

Purpose: The child will learn that helping others shows we love God.

Things to Do and Say

Lesson 11

If your group is large, have several containers for the children to work on. Let the children work together by placing squares of fabric over the glue you spread on the outside of the container(s). When the container is completely covered, let the children fill it with flowers or candy.

Say, **I liked the way you worked together to make this pretty gift. We will take it to Mrs. Smith who is sick. I am sure she will feel happy when she sees it. Helping others shows we love God. He wants us to "love one another."**

Lesson 12

Make stencils out of cardboard from the pattern on page 313, one for every two children in your class. Print "Church friends 'love one another.'" around the edges of the paper plates, one for each child. Let the children work in pairs. Have one child hold the stencil on the plate while the other child sponge paints over the stencil. Then have the children reverse roles.

Say, **I like to see church-friends help each other. Helping others shows we love God. What did the church-friends in our Bible story do to help other church-friends who needed food and clothing? Yes, they sent money to them.**

Game Center

Unit 3—Helping Others

Items to Include:

Lesson 10
- Non-breakable baby bottles
- Tape player
- Tape of children's music

Lesson 11
- Sewing equipment

Purpose: The child will know that helping shows we love God.

Things to Do and Say

Lesson 10

Some of your children may have younger brothers and sisters or may be expecting siblings. To help the children know there are ways they can help a younger sibling, have them play "Pass the Bottle."

Say, **Sometimes a mommy with a very little baby needs someone who can carefully hand her things for the baby. God is pleased when you help others. Helping others shows we love God. We're going to play a helping game. When you hear the music, please pass the bottle to the person next to you.** Demonstrate this. **When the music stops, hold on to the bottle. Let's play like we are helping our mommies now.**

Lesson 11

Before class hide some sewing equipment (tape measure, pin cushion without pins, a pattern, buttons on a card, some trimmings, etc.) around your classroom or, better still, outside. Let the children find the items and bring them to you. When you have them all, talk about how each can be used to make an item of clothing.

Our Bible story was about a lady who sewed lots of clothes. What was her name? That's right, Dorcas. She made clothes for poor people who needed them. She was a good helper. Dorcas showed she loved God when she helped others.

Art Center, continued

When the children have finished, help them "read" the words printed on their plates. Make sure you allow time for the children to wash their hands.

Lesson 13
18" squares of flannel
Ping Pong balls

Lesson 13

Before classtime, print "______ Can Help," along one edge of each flannel square. Fill in a child's name in the blank space of each square. To make a "Helper Doll," hold the Ping Pong ball and let the child place the square over it. Fasten a rubber band around the fabric enclosing the ball as a head. Help each child draw facial features on his or her "Helper Doll."

Show the children how to dust with a "Helper Doll." Say, **You can use your "Helper Doll" to help your mom dust furniture. When you have helped so much that your doll is dusty, your mom can put it in the washer. Helping others shows we love God. The Bible tells us to "love one another." You will be loving your mom when you help her.**

Book/Picture Center

Unit 3—Helping Others

Items to Include:

Books listed on page 291

Lesson 10
Books and pictures of children helping

Lesson 13
Books of Bible stories
Books of community helpers

Purpose: The child will know Bible people who were helpers; know that helping shows we love God.

Things to Do and Say

Lesson 10

Put out books and pictures suggested on page 291. Let the children look through them. Ask questions about pictures. Read at least one book.

Look at this girl. What is she doing? Yes, she is helping her mommy set the table. She looks like she is happy to help her mommy. Helping is fun! . . . What is this boy doing? I think he is helping the old man climb the stairs. Helping others pleases God. I like to help people, don't you? . . . What is this child doing? Do you think you could do that? I think you could. You are big enough to help!

Lesson 13

Let the children look at books and pictures. Say, **What is this police officer doing? Yes, he is helping that little girl cross the street. When you grow up, you may be able to help someone that way. You can help in other ways right now. God gave you hands. How can your hands help? God gave you feet. How can your feet help?** If the children have difficulty coming up with ways to help, give them hints or suggestions to get them started.

There were lots of people in the Bible who helped others. Look at this picture of

Block Center

Unit 3—Helping Others

Items to Include:

Large cardboard blocks
Cars and trucks

Purpose: The child will have opportunities to help in play situations.

Things to Do and Say

Lesson 10

Have the blocks and vehicles spread out so several children can play at the same time. Let the children build anything they want—buildings, roads, and so forth. Whenever you see a child help, comment on this. **I like the way Tony helped Jennifer by giving her some blocks. . . . When we share the blocks and cars we are helping each other. . . . Thank you for helping me pick up the blocks and cars.**

Encourage the older children to help the younger ones. Say, **Can you show me how you would teach another child how to use blocks carefully?** You may need to guide this activity. Say, **I'm sure God is pleased when we help someone learn to do something.**

Lesson 12

Encourage the children to build two church buildings with a road in between. Explain that the people in one church need help. Have everyone drive from one church to the church that needs help.

The Bible tells about some church-friends who helped other church-friends who needed money for food and clothing. Let's play like the people here (point to one building) **need help. We will drive from our church building** (point to the other

Block Center, continued

building) **to take the people some help. What do you think we should take them?** Let the children suggest things, or suggest some yourself if they aren't able to think of anything. **God is pleased when we help others. The Bible says to "love one another." When we help someone we "love one another."**

Book/Picture Center, continued

Jesus. He helped many people. Helping others shows you love God. Jesus certainly loved God! . . . I like to help others. And I love God! I know you do too.

Family Living Center

Unit 3—Helping Others

Items to Include:

Lesson 10
Baby bottles
Baby clothes
Baby toys
Dish washing detergent (non-phosphorus)

Lesson 11
Dolls
Doll clothes

Purpose: The child will help in a variety of play situations.

Things to Do and Say

Lesson 10

Demonstrate how baby bottles and toys need to be washed and baby clothes need to be folded. Let the children try the activities, using cool water. You may want to tie bath towels around the children to keep them dry. Say, **Babies need many things and all of those things need to be kept clean. You can help. I am sure God is pleased when you find ways to help.**

Lesson 11

Let the children work together to dress one or more dolls. Two's may be able only to wrap blankets around the dolls.

Say, **Your babies have nice clothes. You are doing a good job dressing your babies. Today we will learn about a Bible woman named Dorcas who made clothes to help dress many people. . . . The Bible tells us to "love one another." Dorcas showed she loved others by sewing for them. We can show we "love one another" by helping in many ways. . . . You could help Mommy dress your little sister, Bethany. You are big enough to help.**

God's Wonders Center

Unit 3—Helping Others

Items to Include:

Lesson 11
Basket

Lesson 12
Watering cans
Small brooms

Purpose: The child will feel happy and eager to help others.

Things to Do and Say

Lesson 11

Show the children how to pull weeds from an area around the church building. Say, **When you pull weeds from around flowers, you help the flowers grow and make them look pretty. Everyone can see the pretty flowers God made. I like to help this way, don't you? Helping others makes me feel good. Helping others shows we love God.**

If this activity is impractical for your situation, find a job the children can do inside the building, perhaps taking care of plants. Praise children for doing a good job. Be specific in your praise so the children will know what they did well. Indiscriminate praise is confusing and misleading to children.

Lesson 12

Let the children water plants and flowers around the church building. If it is a rainy day, make sure there are some inside plants for them to water, even if you have to bring some from home. Show the children how to sweep the floor with a broom.

Say, **Church-friends help around the church building to keep it looking nice so people will want to come to learn about Jesus. I like helping this way, don't you? Helping others is fun!**

God's Wonders Center, continued

Lesson 13

Go on a walk and look at the areas where the children have pulled weeds and watered plants. Say, **Look how nice these flower beds look. Look how healthy these plants are. We can use the hands and feet God gave us to help in many ways. I'm glad we could help in this way. Thank You, God, for letting us help.**

Family Living Center, continued

Lesson 12

Pie crust
Pie filling
Pie plate

Lesson 12

Say, **Sometimes church-friends help other church-friends by taking food to someone who is sick. Let's bake a pie to take to** (name family in need of food because of sickness). Have the children wash their hands, unfold pie crust, place it in the plate, and add filling. Let an adult helper take the pie to the church kitchen for baking.

If you cannot bake a pie, have ingredients for making instant pudding or some other non-cooked food. Pudding can be shaken in a container with a tight lid. Or, have several kinds of cookies and pretty containers to pack them in. Let the children arrange the cookies and cover them with foil or plastic wrap. Have someone in mind who will appreciate the cookies. Explain to the children who will be getting whatever food you prepare.

Lesson 13

Two dishpans
Plastic dishes
Dish washing detergent
Dish towels
Duster

Lesson 13

Say, Let me show you some ways you can be helpers at home. Demonstrate how to wash dishes in one pan, rinse in another, and dry. Demonstrate how to dust. You may also want to bring washcloths for folding. Say, **Even though you are little, you can find ways to help. God is pleased when we help others. . . . Helping is fun! I'm glad we can work together to help others.**

Summer, Unit 3

Instructions for stick puppets for Lesson 10 visual:

1. Photocopy page onto light tan construction paper or manila paper.
2. Add color with markers.
3. Cut around figures; glue onto cardboard to strengthen.
4. Glue craft sticks between fronts and backs.

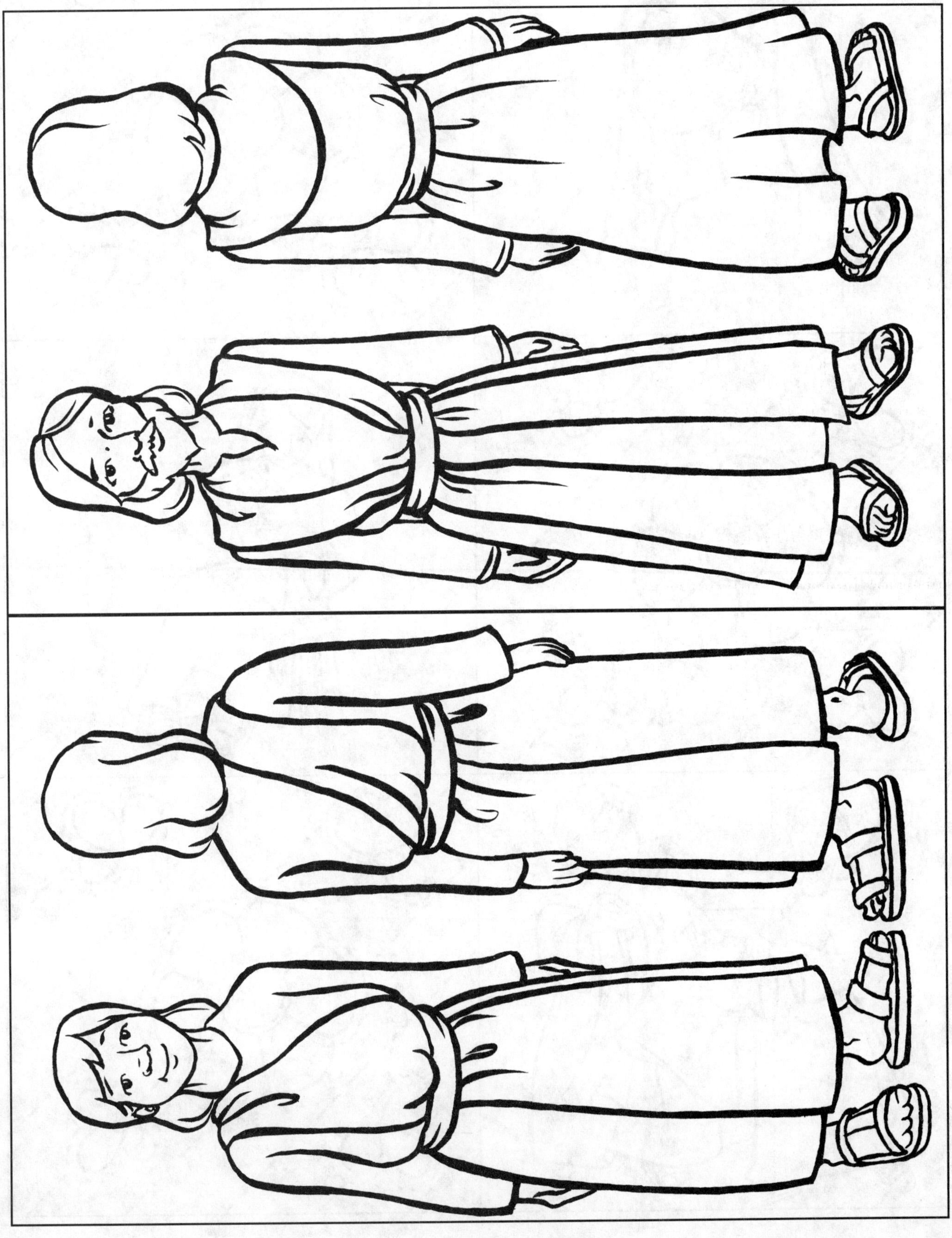

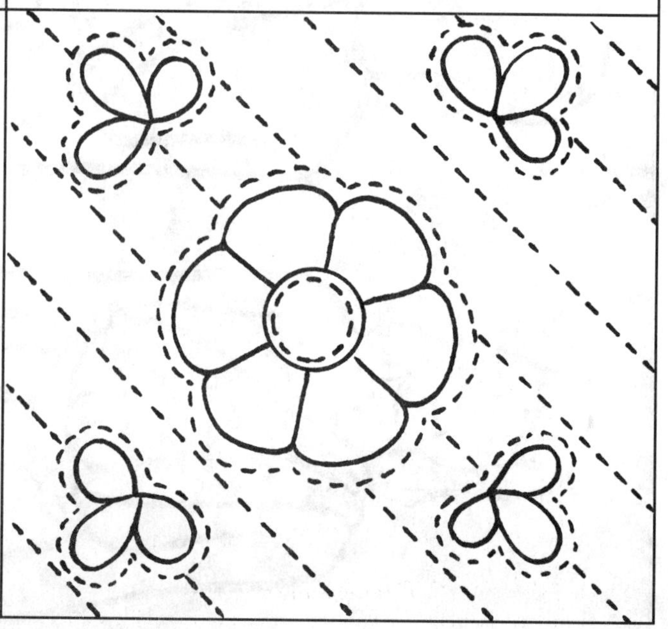

Summer, Unit 3

Visual for Lesson 12

Instructions

1. Photocopy page.
2. Add color; cut out circles.
3. Glue circles together, with a craft stick in between for a handle.

My Bible Storybook

FOLD

FOLD

Summer, Unit 3

Instructions

1. Photocopy both page 309 and 310, back-to-back if possible, one per child.
2. Cut on solid lines and fold on dotted line.
3. If you did not copy back-to-back, glue pages together, back-to-back.
4. Children will add stickers from page 311 at end of Bible-story Review, Lesson 13.

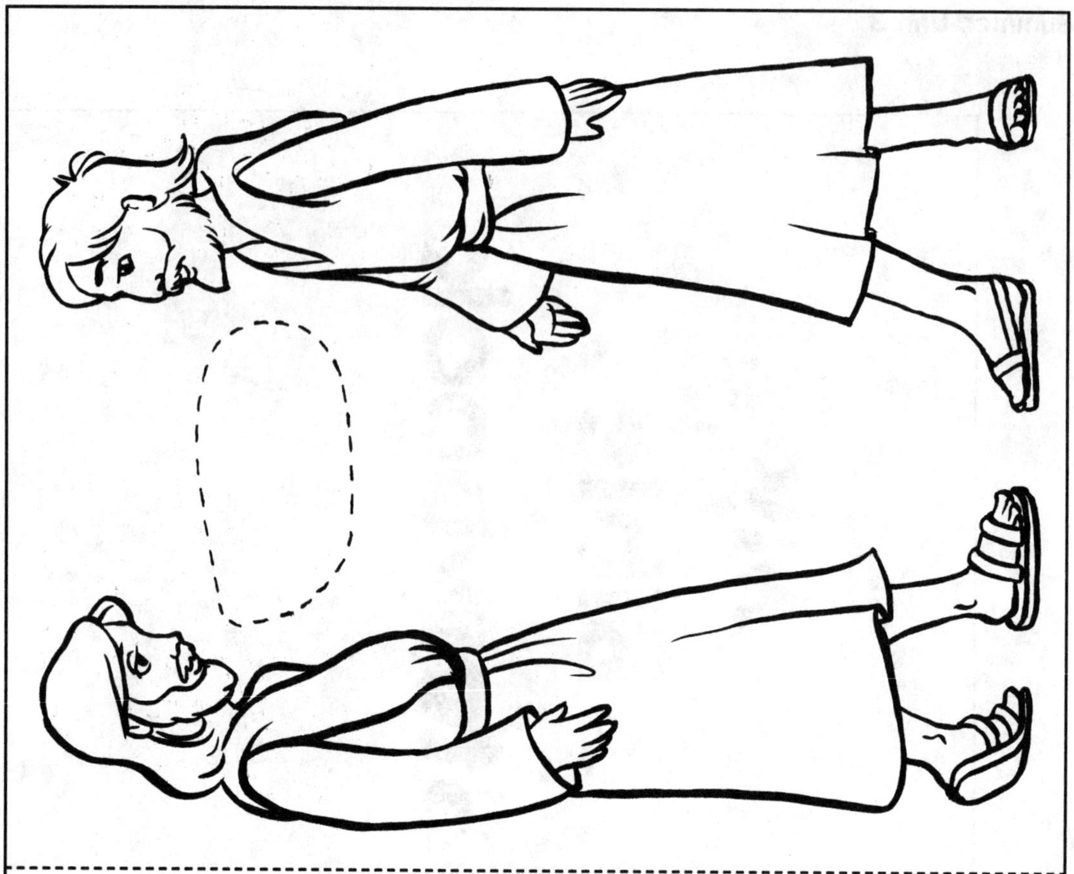

FOLD HERE

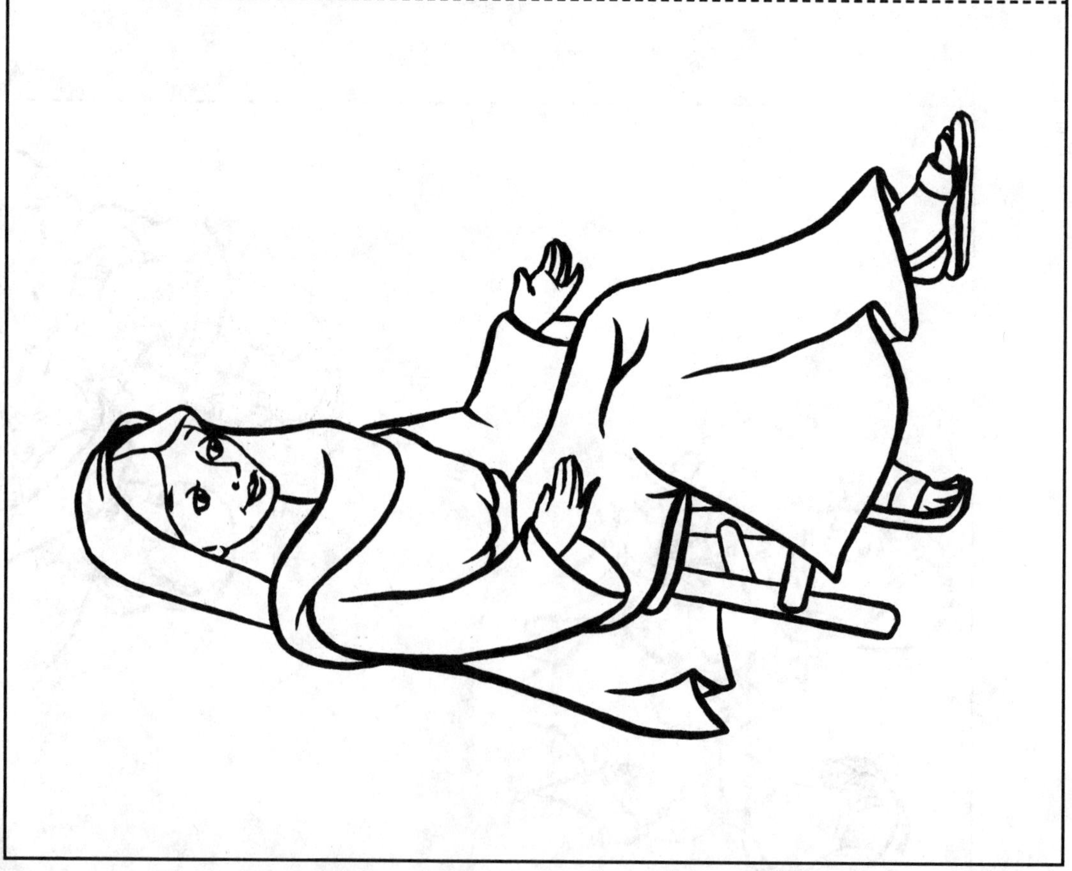

Summer, Unit 3

Instructions

1. Photocopy pictures. Use several colors of paper.
2. Paint backs of sheets with a mixture of 2 parts white glue and 1 part vinegar. Peppermint extract may be added.
3. When glue is dry, cut out stickers. Mix these so each child will have a variety of colors.

Summer, Unit 3

Stencil for Art Center, Lesson 12

Instructions

1. Make a cardboard stencil by photocopying or tracing the pattern.
2. Cut around church building carefully.
3. Draw around the cutout building on more sheets of cardboard. Make one for every two children in your class.
4. Cut out the church buildings, leaving just the frames.
5. Children will work in two's, one holding the stencil in place on a paper plate, while the other one sponge paints over the stencil.

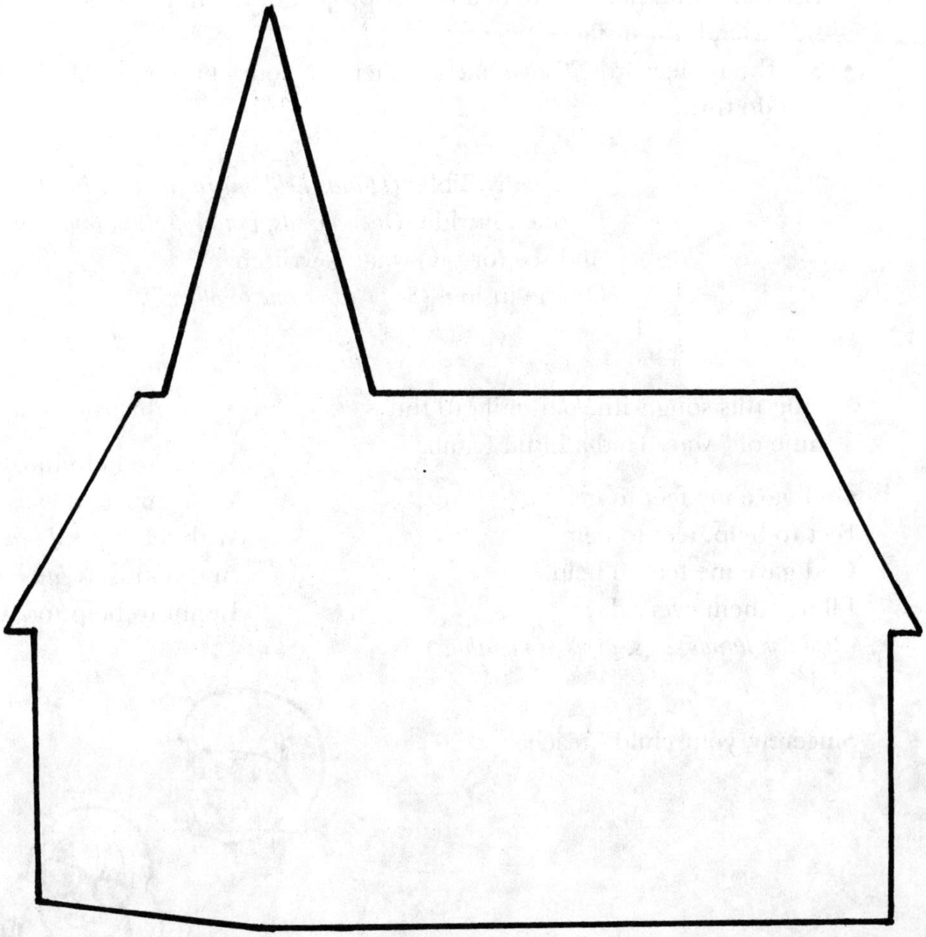

Dear Parent,

Learning to help is one of the most important lessons your child can learn in these early years. Up until now, your child has probably had most everything done for him. Now your child is ready to learn that he can help others. Learning this will give your child a sense of freedom to be able to do more for himself, and a great deal of satisfaction in discovering he can do things for others.

In class, your child will be learning about examples of helpers from God's Word. She will also be learning some basic helping skills and experience opportunities to help someone else.

These are the Bible stories your child will be hearing during this unit on helping.
Jesus Helps a Boy (John 4:46-54)
A Lady Helps Others (Acts 9:36, 39)
Church Friends Give Money to Help (1 Corinthians 8:1-5: Romans 15:25, 26)
A review of Lessons 10–12 will help to review facts and reinforce the important concept of helping others.

Here are some ways to reinforce these lessons at home:

- Take time to teach your child some helping skills.
- When your child asks, "Can I help?" find ways to let her, even though it would be easier to do the job yourself.
- When your child makes a genuine attempt to help, praise him for specific acts of helping. For example, "Thank you for folding the washcloths," or "I like the way you put the silverware on the table. Thank you for helping me."
- Let your child participate in a family project of helping someone else. (Delivering food to a sick friend, for instance.)
- Say the Bible words, "Love one another," to your child each day. Use this action rhyme to help you do this.

This is my Bible; *(Hands held out in front, palms together.)*
I'll open it wide *(Open hands, but keep them touching.)*
And see (or say) what is written
On the inside! *(Say, "Love one another.")*
—*Jean Baxendale*

- Sing this song with your child to the tune of "Mary Had a Little Lamb."

God gave me feet to help,
Feet to help, feet to help.
God gave me feet to help.
I'll use them every day
(Also use hands, legs, arms, a mouth/it.)

- Do this rhyme with your child too.

I want to help in every way!
With ears, and eyes, and mouth, *(Point to each.)*
With feet, *(Bend down and touch feet.)*
And hands. *(Clap hands.)*
I want to help today.
—*Dorothy Fay Richards*

Sincerely, your child's teacher

Zach, the Puppet

Zach, the puppet, is meant to be the class mascot—the children's friend. Two's and 3's love puppets, and are fascinated by one even though they can see you holding the puppet on your hand and talking for him. Having Zach give instructions, suggestions, or warnings can be more effective than your telling the children what to do.

Zach should not be used to tell the Bible story, however, because the Bible story should be real, not a tale told by an animal. Also, make sure that Zach is used only by adults. He will lose his effectiveness if the children are allowed to treat him like a toy.

If you already have a dog puppet, or you can find one ready-made, by all means use it. If you need to make one, however, here are several suggestions.

Materials to make puppet using these patterns:

Scissors
Cardboard
Felt—tan, off-white, or light brown (features won't show up on dark colors)
Markers
Fabric glue

Directions to make puppet using these patterns:

1. Photocopy patterns onto paper. Enlarge patterns when you copy.
2. Trace pieces onto felt.
3. Go over features with markers.
4. Cut out pieces.
5. Glue front and back head pieces around edges, leaving a small opening in which to stuff cotton. Let dry.
6. Stuff head with cotton; glue opening closed. Let dry.
7. Glue front and back body together around edges, leaving bottom open for operator's hand. Let dry.
8. Glue neck to back of head piece. Lower part of head should not be glued tight to body.
9. Glue ears to sides of head.

Note: The puppet can also be made from a soft fabric such as fake fur, velour, or velveteen. You may have to embroider features onto the fabric rather than use markers.

You can also make a puppet one of these ways:

1. Purchase or find a toy stuffed dog. Rip a seam at lower back of dog. Pull out some stuffing so you can insert your hand into toy, with fingers in the front legs. Make sure you can manipulate dog well. Push stuffing up far enough so it won't come out. If necessary, finish seam to keep it from raveling. (Whip edges with needle and thread, or use fabric glue on edges.) You may find the toy dog will work better if you cut off the lower part of the body so that you have a larger opening for your hand. (You don't need the back legs for the puppet.) Finish the bottom edges as suggested previously.

2. Obtain stuffed toy dog. Purchase or find a piece of fabric to match the dog as closely as possible. Cut out a pocket that will allow you sufficient room to put your hand into and manipulate the dog like a puppet. Turn under edges of pocket and sew around pocket by hand onto back of dog. Or, attach with fabric glue.

See page 266 for doghouse suggestion.

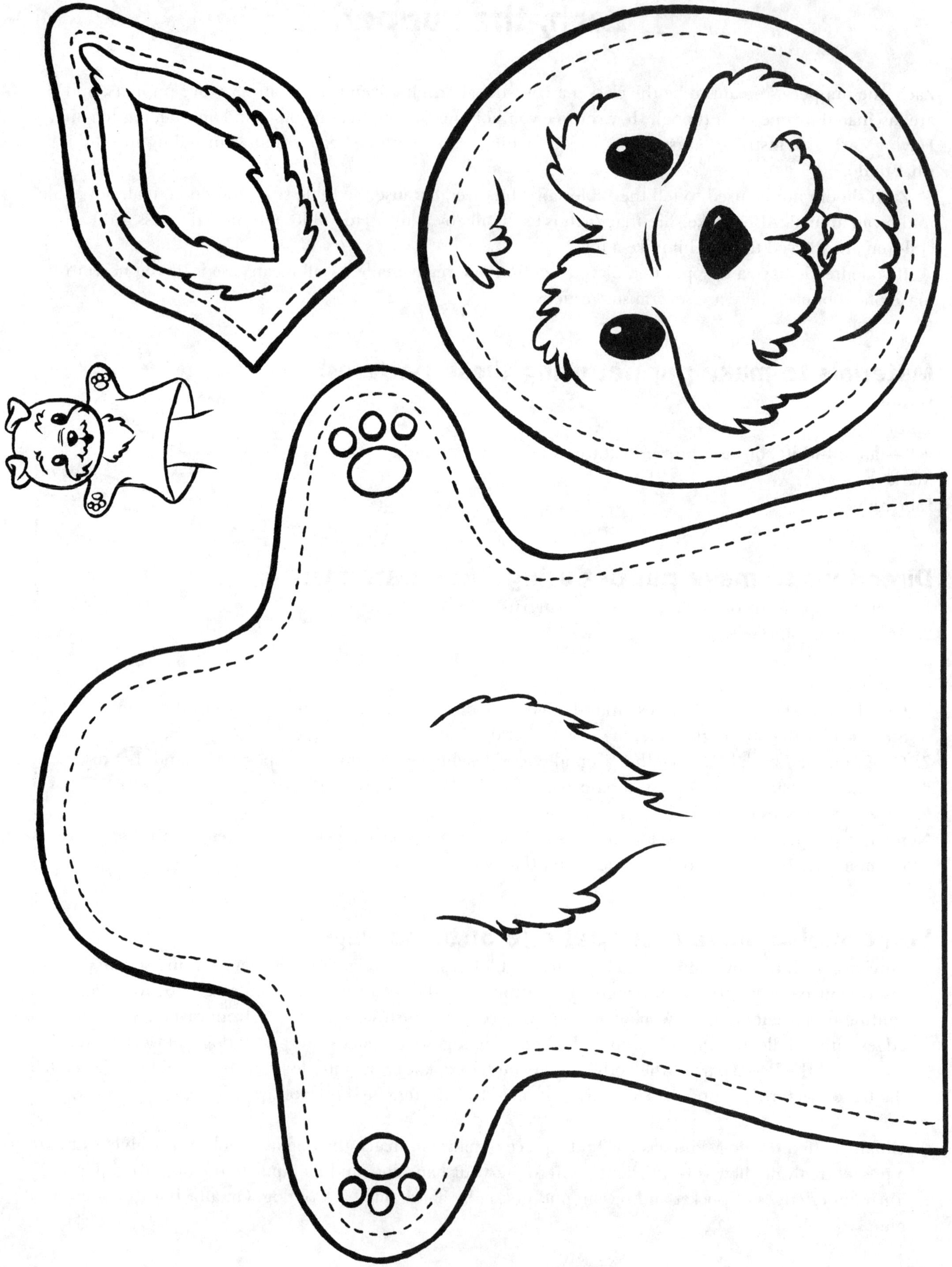

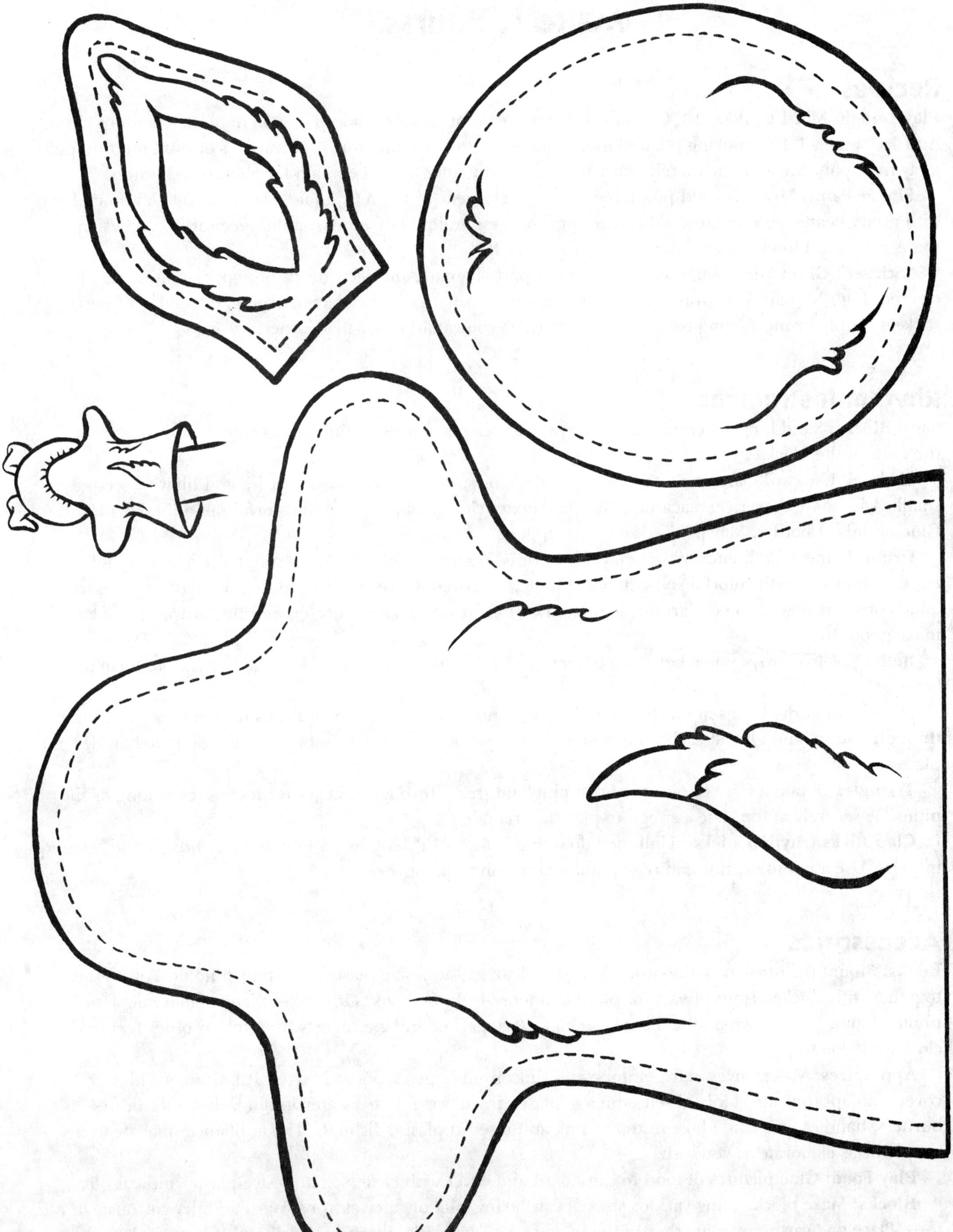

Make It Yourself

Recipes

Play Dough: Mix 1 C. flour, 1/2 C. salt, and 2 tsp. cream of tartar in saucepan. (Do not omit cream of tartar.) Add 1 C. water, 1 Tbs. cooking oil, and food coloring. Cook, stirring, for three minutes or until mixture pulls away from pan. Knead immediately. Store in airtight container. Makes enough for about six children.

Finger Paint: Mix 1 C. mild powdered soap or detergent with 1/3 C. liquid starch (or 1/4 C. water). Beat with rotary beater until mixture is like frosting. (Add more liquid or more soap if necessary. Starches and soaps vary.) Add food coloring last.

"Sticker" Glue: Mix 2 parts white glue and 1 part vinegar. Add a few drops of peppermint extract if desired. Lightly "paint" mixture onto backs of uncut stickers. Let dry. Color stickers if needed. Cut out stickers. Apply by moistening backs of stickers just as you would ready-made ones.

Rhythm Instruments

Sand Blocks: Sand lumber scraps (about 5" x 3"). Cover one side with fine sandpaper, tacked or glued to the ends of the blocks.

Shakers: Use cardboard or metal boxes (bandage or spice cans) or plastic bottles and fill with seeds, small rocks, dry beans, rice, macaroni, etc. Tape boxes closed and cover with colorful self-adhesive plastic. Glue on lids of bottles. May be used singly or in pairs.

Drum: Remove both ends of a one-, two-, or three-pound coffee can. Make sure there are no rough edges. Cover can with colorful self-adhesive plastic, if desired. Cover ends by gluing on plastic lids. Use hands or short dowels to beat drums. Ice cream cartons (round), large shortening cans, or waste baskets also make good drums.

Bells: Sew five or six jingle bells to a 6" length of 1/2" elastic. Sew ends of elastic together to form a bracelet.

Maracas: Put dry beans in salt boxes and tape spouts shut. Use 1/4" dowel rods for handles. Poke these through bottom and glue at each point where dowel and box touch. Cover boxes after you glue handles in place.

Triangle: Obtain a 6" to 8" piece of brass pipe and string through it heavy twine 3 times as long as the pipe. Tie securely at top. Use a spoon to play the triangle.

Clap sticks (rhythm sticks): Half-inch doweling cut into 12" lengths and sanded on ends should be used in pairs. Use a nontoxic, nonlead base paint if you wish to paint them.

Accessories

Books: Mount pictures on cardboard, cover with clear self-adhesive plastic, and punch holes. Put these together with chicken rings or yarn or place in a loose-leaf notebook. Or, mount pictures in a magnetic photo album. For a touch-and-feel book, stitch cloth together and cut objects from felt or other textured cloth and glue to pages.

Appliances: Make stoves, refrigerators, and sinks from large cardboard boxes. Paint the outsides or cover with appropriate colors of self-adhesive plastic if you wish. Use a waterproof marker to indicate burners, handles, etc. Cut a hole in top of sink and insert a plastic dishpan. The appliances may be as simple or as elaborate as you wish.

Play Food: Glue pictures of food to cardboard and cover with clear, self-adhesive plastic and cut out.

Blocks: Make blocks using various sizes of cardboard milk or juice cartons. Wash and dry cartons; cut off tops. Place one carton over another of the same size. Cover with colorful self-adhesive plastic if desired. Blocks can also be covered with appropriate pictures and then covered with clear plastic.

Unit Planning Sheet

Quarter:
Unit:

Bible Words:
Unit Aims:
KNOW

FEEL

DO

To Do Ahead

Lesson One:
Learning Activities:

1.
Materials needed:

2.
Materials needed:

3.
Materials needed:

4.
Materials needed:

Materials for the Bible story:

2.
Materials needed:

3.
Materials needed:

4.
Materials needed:

Materials for the Bible story:

Unit songs/action rhymes to learn and/or tape:

Special arrangements for unit:

Room/bulletin board decorations:

Materials for unit party:

Lesson Two: ______

Learning Activities:

1. ______

Materials needed: ______

2. ______

Materials needed: ______

3. ______

Materials needed: ______

4. ______

Materials needed: ______

Materials for the Bible story:

Lesson Three: ______

Learning Activities:

1. ______

Materials needed: ______

2. ______

Materials needed: ______

3. ______

Materials needed: ______

4. ______

Materials needed: ______

Materials for the Bible story:

Lesson Four: ______

Learning Activities:

1. ______

Materials needed: ______

2. ______

Materials needed: ______

3. ______

Materials needed: ______

4. ______

Materials needed: ______

Materials for the Bible story:

Lesson Five: ______

Learning Activities:

1. ______

Materials needed: ______